MW00790877

VALUES AND VIOLENCE

STUDIES IN GLOBAL JUSTICE

VOLUME 4

Aims and Scope

In today's world, national borders seem irrelevant when it comes to international crime and terrorism. Likewise, human rights, poverty, inequality, democracy, development, trade, bioethics, hunger, war and peace are all issues of global rather than national justice. The fact that mass demonstrations are organized whenever the world's governments and politicians gather to discuss such major international issues is testimony to a widespread appeal for justice around the world.

Discussions of global justice are not limited to the fields of political philosophy and political theory. In fact, research concerning global justice quite often requires an interdisciplinary approach. It involves aspects of ethics, law, human rights, international relations, sociology, economics, public health, and ecology. Springer's new series *Studies in Global Justice* up that interdisciplinary perspective. The series brings together outstanding monographs and anthologies that deal with both basic normative theorizing and its institutional applications. The volumes in the series discuss such aspects of global justice as the scope of social justice, the moral significance of borders, global inequality and poverty, the justification and content of human rights, the aims and methods of development, global environmental justice, global bioethics, the global institutional order and the justice of intervention and war.

Volumes in this series will prove of great relevance to researchers, educators and students, as well as politicians, policy-makers and government officials.

For other titles published in this series, go to
www.springer.com/series/6958

Values and Violence

Intangible Aspects of Terrorism

Editors

IBRAHIM A. KARAWAN
University of Utah, Salt Lake City, UT, U.S.A.

WAYNE McCORMACK
University of Utah, Salt Lake City, UT, U.S.A.

STEPHEN E. REYNOLDS
University of Utah, Salt Lake City, UT, U.S.A.

Editors
Prof. Ibrahim A. Karawan
University of Utah
260 So. Central Campus Dr.
#205
Salt Lake City UT 84112
USA
ibrahim.karawan@poli-sci.utah.edu

Prof. Wayne McCormack
University of Utah
332 So. 1400 E
Salt Lake City UT 84112
USA
mccormackw@law.utah.edu

Prof. Stephen E. Reynolds
University of Utah
260 So. Central Campus Dr.
#205
Salt Lake City UT 84112
USA
reynolds@csbs.utah.edu

ISBN: 978-1-4020-8659-5 e-ISBN: 978-1-4020-8660-1

Library of Congress Control Number: 2008931158

Printed on acid-free paper

9 8 7 6 5 4 3 2 1

springer.com

Contents

Contributors

Akeel Bilgrami
Columbia University, ab41@columbia.edu

M. Cherif Bassiouni
DePaul University, cbassiou@depaul.edu

Martha Crenshaw
Stanford University, crenshaw@stanford.edu

Tom Farer
University of Denver, tfarer@du.edu

Marilyn Friedman
Washington University St. Louis, friedman@artsci.wustl.edu

Amos N. Guiora
University of Utah, guioraa@law.utah.edu

George Hepner
University of Utah, george.hepner@geog.utah.edu

Bruce Hoffman
Georgetown University, brh6@georgetown.edu

Ken Jameson
University of Utah, jameson@economics.utah.edu

Benjamin N. Judkins
University of Utah, benjamin.judkins@poli-sci.utah.edu

Ibrahim Karawan
University of Utah, ibrahim.karawan@poli-sci.utah.edu

Wayne McCormack
University of Utah, mccormackw@law.utah.edu

Richard Medina
University of Utah, richard.medina@geog.utah.edu

Martha C. Nussbaum
S.J. Quinney Lecture at the University of Utah, University of Chicago, martha_nussbaum@law.uchicago.edu

Monisha Pasupathi
University of Utah, monisha.pasupathi@psych.utah.edu

Stephen E. Reynolds
University of Utah, stephen.reynolds@csbs.utah.edu

Frank Salter
Max Planck Research Group for Human Ethology, fssalter@aol.com

Amartya Sen
Harvard University, slrich@fas.harvard.edu

Cecilia Wainryb
University of Utah, cecilia.wainryb@psych.utah.edu

Polly Wiessner
University of Utah, wiessner@soft-link.com

Introduction

Wayne McCormack

The essays in this volume are products of a conference at the University of Utah that itself was the outgrowth of an in-house study group which began meeting in 2005. Early on, we realized that there was a substantial amount of talent and expertise in Utah regarding matters of international and global violence, but we also knew that there were many others in the world focusing their attention on such issues. So we asked ourselves what we brought to the table that could be unique, and we asked government officials what they saw to be needed. The answer in both instances came out the same: "Values and the Quest for Human Dignity in Confronting Political Violence."

When we learned that government professionals, particularly in the justice and military sectors, were thirsting for focused attention to bedrock principles, we thought we had a match with what academics could offer. The astounding response of the elite scholars represented here shows that our instinct was right.

The focus of our discussions was the role of values in forming terrorist activity, in assessing the impacts of that activity, and in forming policies for responses to it. These are values that should be timeless and universal, but the crises in which they are challenged always seem to be unique at the moment. Thus, these essays extend far beyond terrorism but have significance in the fears and concerns of the moment.

Society will no more eliminate terrorism than it will eliminate crime – the challenge for containment of both is to understand and provide ethical options for rational decision makers. These essays assess normative and policy questions involved in terrorism from a number of perspectives – the belief systems that lie behind the patterned use of violence in various cultures, normative issues in assessing risks of violence, and the implications of the internationalization of violence.

Policy makers need a formal framework of analysis to avoid making unguided ad hoc decisions, but there are limits to the accuracy of empirical predictions. These two boundaries set the parameters for the exercise of professional judgment – the making of informed decisions on the basis of a rigorous analysis with less-than-certain outcomes. Long-term, we need to take existing information, exercise normative judgments as well as assess historical experience, and construct a decision framework that takes all factors into account and provides a basis for professional and political judgments.

Internationalization has changed the face of terrorism dramatically. Patterned violence against civilians has been part of human history for at least 4000 years and is not likely to go away. But transportation and communication systems, along with destructive technology, allow violence to occur anywhere and for its effects to be felt immediately in remote locations.

Normative and ethical evaluations are part of every important decision. Most obviously, the consequences of policy choices cannot be assessed without attention to the culture of an affected region or group, but even assessing the likelihood of various threats requires attention to human norms. For example, weather forecasting is a "hard" science only in the sense that much of its data is observable. And as global warming shows, the choice of what data to collect is almost as normative as the questions of what to do with predictions of consequences.

Our principal message is that the pragmatic politician ignores normative values at great peril. Those values that have been crafted over long periods of time under a variety of conditions endure for good reason. Those long-held values lead to principles that do not need to be rethought in times of crisis when judgments can be skewed by fear and emotion. At the end of this Introduction, we will offer a dozen suggestions that flow from the essays, but we emphasize that these are our impressions from the collected wisdom here.

Structure of the Volume – Beginning, Middle, End

This collection of essays proceeds by examining some sources of political violence, moving to the impacts and scope of threats, and finishing with the policy choices available for response to political violence.

A number of analyses have addressed such factors as the motivations of individual terrorists, the "culture" of terrorist organizations, the political contribution of "failed states," the effect of economic oppression, and the cultural-ideological origins of fundamentalism. It should be possible to examine correlations among these factors. The essays in Part I of this collection examine a number of correlations to begin that process. Many questions remain to be explored more thoroughly. How do different cultures express the notions of fairness and recompense for harms? How do these cultural values interact with economics, geography, political and historical forces? What are the implications of international interdependence and information technology on the proliferation of terrorism? What is the significance of migration and the apparent decline of state control over borders? What can be done to enhance international cooperation and the role of regional or international organizations?

Part II of this collection begins exploration of risk assessment in a normative context. It is not possible to eliminate all threats of harm, particularly in an open society. A society with high levels of individual autonomy is vulnerable to clandestine violence from nonstate actors, while a tightly controlled society tends to foster state violence. Security planning is the art of making a reasonable allocation of resources to minimize various threats of harm while taking into account desired levels of individual autonomy. Policy analysis can bring a much higher level of sophistication to this effort by delineating the factors that should go into assessing the likelihood of a particular threat (how likely can a group acquire a nuclear weapon or small arms), comparing the potential impacts of each threat as carried out in different times and places (explosions in a crowded shopping mall or in a deserted mosque), and detailing what is given up to achieve a defined level of security. Today, there are ongoing efforts to encapsulate risk assessment in a computer program that rates various levels of impact weighted by the likelihood of each. It is important to realize, however, that the accuracy of the results will be only as good as the information put into the formula. Moreover, the weighting of outcomes contains important normative judgments as to what effects carry different values. There is a risk that producing a mechanical-appearing formula will eliminate or substitute for human experience and evaluative judgment. The expertise and judgments of both professionals and academics must be brought together to ensure that analytic tools do not become mechanical formulae.

Some consequence prediction is implicit in every policy choice, but prediction is more art than science. The consequences of military tactical choices, for example, can be predicted to some extent from models based on past experience. Likewise, the political-cultural consequences of strategic choices can be predicted based on knowledge of the politics and culture of a particular group. None of these predictions will be any more reliable than the combination of available experience data and the expertise of those making the normative assessments from that data. Policy makers and decision makers both need to appreciate the complex roles of cultural influences and history in the terrorism arena. Culture does not alone dictate any particular mode of behavior. Levels of violence tend to vary greatly within the same society. Nor is history an infallible guide to the future. But culture and history do matter. Grudges and glory from the past are infinitely retrievable, today's actions are tomorrow's history, and the norms and values we lay down today will set the course for future response.[1] Policy makers inevitably will exercise judgment about how and under what conditions violence may occur. Similarly, they need to exercise judgment about what effects different policies will have in different cultural settings.

Part I – Social Identity and Political Violence

The first part of our volume speaks to the question of who and why but not in the usual sense of trying to profile the terrorist. Some observers have come to the conclusion that no such profile can exist, while others have argued that certain elements could be included in or excluded from a profile. Our contributors looked at the question from the perspective of what lies behind the terrorist in a more general sense – social identities, indoctrination, gender-cultural roles, and religious-cultural issues are all considered as contributing factors in the terrorist mix.

---

[1] Thanks to one of our authors, Polly Wiessner, for contributing this insight.

Amartya Sen writes about *Violence in Identity*, drawing from his recent book IDENTITY AND VIOLENCE. He argues that there are two faces to identity: the first generates creativity and the second spurs hostility. Each individual has many identities: race, religion, socioeconomic status, political affiliations, family, and the like. Terrorist organizations, however, want to reduce an individual's character to a single identity, both in recruiting accomplices and in identifying their targets. For recruitment, they often exploit a particular grievance within that identity. For targeting, they identify people as "haves" and "have-nots," thus feeding the myth on which the recruitment was based. This strategy prevails even though leaders are seldom from the same socioeconomic class as the followers that they recruit. A large part of why an individual, or group, may resort to violence is how they identify themselves. While violence is often accompanied by poverty, to reduce the cause of violence to economic conditions is a grave mistake. Sen recommends that to resolve the negative effects of identity-based thinking, we must avoid identifying others and ourselves by a single identity. Inasmuch as we can, our bonds become broader than just belonging to a single identity that represents a part of our individual character. World peace demands an inclusive vision.

Akeel Bilgrami examines some misconceptions about religion and secular humanism in *Gandhi, Newton, and the Enlightenment*, exposing implications for how religious or ethnic identities can become precursors to violence. He starts with an observation that Gandhi was critical of scientific rationality on the ground that Newtonian science placed nature apart from humankind, making it seem that nature was inert and brute, something to be controlled and exploited by the rationality of humans. Similarly, the colonial era produced a tendency to think of "others" as standing apart from humanity, or at least from the civilized world, and thus needing to be controlled and exploited by rational beings. Bilgrami is sympathetic to the Gandhi critique but argues that it works better as a statement about rationality rather than an empirical observation about science itself. Drawing from Gandhi, his own critique of scientific rationality is directed to that part of rationality which would deny that the natural world is suffused with values or capable of making normative demands on us. If we realize that values are not apart from the world in which humans exist, then we have a better opportunity to appreciate the values of others as part of both their world and our own.

Ibrahim Karawan, *Militant Islamist Groups in Egypt*, starts by pointing out that ideas from Egypt have long had influence outside of the nation's borders. The Arab world is heavily influenced by activity in Egypt. The Muslim Brotherhood was one of those militant Islamist groups whose roots are in Egypt. Terrorist groups often emphasize urgency, an idea that is important for them to be able to create a desire for immediate action among their members. They also work in intimate groups to minimize the number of people that have access to information. In fighting terror, the worst kind of oppression is a mild one, because it stirs without undermining.

Marilyn Friedman considers the special case of *Female Terrorists* from the standpoint of whether martyrdom can contribute to social equality and whether a woman might be justified in committing a terrorist act for which a man would have no moral claim of right. Women are often more effective as terrorists because of cultural norms – people are less skeptical of women and allow them more access to potential strike sites. Women also garner more publicity for their actions. No strength or military expertise is required for suicide bombers, so in a male-dominant society suicide martyrdom is one of the few methods where women can reach an equal plane with men. If suicide itself is morally O.K. and if terrorism is justifiable at all, then the morality of suicide terrorism is dependent on the justifiability of the terrorist act itself. Assuming that the act can be justified, then the question would be whether the act promotes gender equity, and the answer is unlikely. If the suicide bomber is driven to that act by social reasons rather than independent choice, then there is no equity in the act.

Frank Salter looks at *Ethnicity and Indoctrination for Violence* to determine whether propaganda and persuasion can be effective in producing a terrorist. Obviously, terrorists are indoctrinated and trained, and the frequency of such events as suicide attacks points to an extraordinarily efficient processing of recruits. But research comparing methods of persuasion in various social settings indicates that the effectiveness of indoctrination is more dependent on perceptions of threats to the subject's ethnic, religious, or national group than on techniques of persuasion. Salter discusses a number of ethnic behaviors and concludes that it should be possible to identify interventions that would render the indoctrination of suicide terrorists inefficient. In particular, he suggests acting to remove those threats to the ethnic, religious, or national group that facilitate indoctrination to violence.

Martha Nussbaum asserts in *The Clash Within: The Hindu Right and Democratic Values* that democracy is under attack in India as a result of group hate-mongering by the Hindu right. By tracing the rise of the *Hindutva* movement and through an analysis of its religious extremism, she lays down the principal factors that contribute to the Indian democracy's ability to survive this attack. They include the rule of law, the independence of the press, and critical thinking in education, the last being gravely threatened in the present era. A major factor contributing to violence, by contrast, is a culture of victimhood that leaves Hindu males feeling required to assert their masculinity. The real "clash of civilizations" in India, she concludes, is not a clash between peaceful democratic values and aggressive Islamic values; it is a struggle within each citizen, as anxious fear and shame contend against compassion and concern.

Part II – Scope of the Terrorist Threat

The second stage of our inquiry asks questions about the way in which values affect the nature of terrorism and the scope of its threat. These essays carry us into the realm of group dynamics and global structures. Among the innovative approaches here are attempts to describe terrorist groups in the language of business enterprises and spatial arrangements. The theory of terrorist operations will help us understand ways to approach these groups with effective antidotes.

Bruce Hoffman focuses on *Assessing the State of al Qaeda and Current and Future Terrorist Threats*. He contests the claim that al Qaeda has been weakened in recent years. He points out that al Qaeda combines both a "bottom up" approach – encouraging independent thought and action from low (or lower-) level operatives – and a "top down" one – issuing orders and still coordinating a far-flung terrorist enterprise. He describes the al Qaeda movement as consisting of four distinct, though not mutually exclusive, dimensions – al Qaeda Central, affiliates and associates, and franchised local operations, and the larger network. New threats and new challenges require a new strategy and institutional behaviors. The threat posed by elusive and deadly irregular adversaries emphasizes the need to anchor changes that will more effectively close the gap between detecting irregular adversarial activity and rapidly defeating it. The effectiveness of U.S. strategy will be based on our capacity to think like a networked enemy, in anticipation of how they may act in a variety of situations, aided by different resources. In addition to traditional "hard" military skills of "kill or capture" and destruction and attrition; "soft" skills such as information operations, negotiation, psychology, social and cultural anthropology, foreign area studies, complexity theory, and systems management will become increasingly important in the ambiguous and dynamic environment in which irregular adversaries circulate.

Martha Crenshaw, in *The Debate Over "New" vs. "Old" Terrorism*, renews a dialogue that she has been conducting with those who believe that terrorism has taken on new characteristics in recent decades. She notes that academics have been considering the subject for years, and that much of what might be viewed as new today has been a part of terrorism for decades: women, religion, martyrdom, and structures. Although terrorism associated with religion has been particularly lethal in recent years, empirical evidence does suggest that it is usually religion and some other element and rarely just religion. In fact, people who know more about religion are actually less likely to be recruited into extremist organizations. Most scholars realize that there really is nothing new in terrorism, but merely, perhaps, a new spin on old ideas. As we look to end terrorism we must consider that religion and the media – two elements some see as central to the success of terrorism – may also be two significant tools for fighting terrorism in the future.

Ben Judkins and Steve Reynolds, in *Globalization, Social Capital, and Networked Violence: The Role of Values* point out that once a firm establishes a reputable brand name it generally spends large quantities of money protecting and extending that brand name. Among terrorist groups, this phenomenon has held true. For instance, al Qaeda has spread its brand through the media and through offshoot groups who now identify themselves as part of al Qaeda. Historically, anarchists and communists were no strangers to the notion that one could develop a reputation through violence and then allow others to take up the reigns. Likewise, al Qaeda has realized that its renown allows it to successfully recruit and subsequently expand the circle of its influence. Globalization has become a central and necessary element to a terrorist group's expansion success. Individuals who lie on the edge of communities constitute fertile recruiting ground for terrorist groups. It is not difficult for a terrorist organization to recruit from those less integrated community members; conversely, those that are entrenched in their communities are very difficult for a terrorist organization to reach. In fighting the growth of these terrorist networks, governments should look to build the sense of community in potentially vulnerable individuals. It is the lack of "bonding capital" (in religion, common social interest, etc.) in a society that allows terrorist organizations to extend their appeal to individuals who would not be otherwise susceptible to their recruiting efforts.

Richard Medina and George Hepner chart some previously unmapped terrain in *Terrorist Networks in Social and Geographic Space*. Geographers may illuminate terrorist networks by manipulating data to uncover patterns. Three network models are: (1) hierarchical, pyramidal networks typified by organizations such as the Irish Republican Army; (2) decentralized networks with no hierarchy and self-determinative nodes, with al Qaeda as an illustration; and (3) leaderless resistance networks with no structure but typically having an inspirational leader. Traditional social network analysis can uncover relationships that illuminate networks. Networks manifest in spatial patterns that can be analyzed to uncover behavioral and communications relationships. Future research is suggested to investigate further use of GIS to give important insights into network behavior.

Cecilia Wainryb and Monisha Pasupathi argue in *Developing Moral Agency in the Midst of Violence* that the impact that involvement in political violence has on children goes well beyond the distress symptoms typically captured by mental health outcomes (e.g., PTSD). Their research with children in displaced camps in Colombia, and their analyses of narrative accounts of child soldiers, point to the more long-lasting effects of such experiences on children's developing moral capacities. In particular, their data suggest that children growing up in the midst of political violence, who typically both endure and engage in victimization, have difficulties negotiating views of themselves as moral agents. While raising the alarm about the implications of political violence for children's long-term development and for the possibility of breaking cycles of violence, Wainryb and Pasupathi also point to areas in which there may be reservoirs to call on, for rehabilitating children's sense of moral agency.

Ken Jameson and Polly Wiessner take a look at *Violent and Non-Violent Responses to State Failure* by contrasting the effects of Ecuador and Papua New Guinea returns to tribalism. The central states in these cases failed because of the attack on the strength of the state by populism and globalism. In Ecuador, the tribes were given a formal role in the state. By the 1980s, the state had lost the ability to "buy in" new sections of the population and the tribes emerged as an alternative means of defense and identity. Culturally, the Ecuadorian tribes stressed family, consensus, and environmental protection. The tribal social movement became the kingmaker of the state through non-violent direct action. In contrast, Enga Province in Papua New Guinea is comprised of numerous tribes with mutually unintelligible languages and cultures stressing honor, property, and reputation. The Melanesian Way prefers clan voting over individual voting, clan representation, tribal land ownership, kinship preferences over obedience to law, collective wealth ownership, and preference for local over national agendas. National politics became a competition for the distribution rights to government largesse directed to the politicians' tribes and clans. Local politics are often resolved by warfare. Traditionally, such warfare has been regulated by a hierarchy of elders, minimizing the violence. Now competition for the largesse of the state, along with the introduction of firearms to traditional tribal warfare, results in destructive internecine warfare.

Part III – Values and Policy Choices

Part III carries us into the realm in which politicians and academics have clashed repeatedly – the arena of setting policy in the "real world." Here is where the role of values is least understood but perhaps most critical. The essays in this volume try to elaborate the reasons why policy makers must consider theoreticians and vice versa. As the essays demonstrate, without constant attention to values, policy can fly off in unknown and dangerous directions. Conversely, the role of theoreticians requires constant attention to the consequences of choices to update and improve our values.

Tom Farer, in *Terrorism, Islam and America: In Search of a Disarming Narrative*, contends that current national policy offers an unpalatable version of the West that is unable to counter the broad appeal of the jihadist movement. He argues that the neo-conservative approach to a new narrative tries to join a "God-fearing majority of Americans and the traditionalist majority in the Islamic community" against a common enemy of liberal secularism. This narrative he decries as both inaccurate and ineffective. Similarly, by support of autocratic regimes in the Middle East, the United States has already forfeited the prospect of casting itself as a benefactor and promoter of democratic principles in the region. A narrative with a better chance of success would build from a posture of contrition for the recent past and a spirit of mutual respect made concrete with a commitment of non-intervention in the Muslim world.

Cherif Bassiouni, in *"Terrorism:" Reflections on Legitimacy and Policy Considerations*, starts from the observation that there are three regimes of law that apply to violence: international criminal law, international humanitarian law, and international human rights law. Even though these three regimes are based on the same commonly-shared values, they contain gaps, overlaps and ambiguities that give rise to competing claims of legitimacy which are used by state and non-state actors to rationalize their acts of violence. Indeed, international legal systems often raise expectations but fail to fulfill them – prompting those with such expectations to believe that they have no recourse other than the use of force. Since the enforcement of all three regimes is essentially left to states, states' interests will play a role in the way in which enforcement is carried out. On the one hand, very few of the millions of post-World War II fatalities have been redressed by legal sanctions. In other situations, states will over-react, as has been the case in the U.S. after September 11th, so that the state loses the high moral ground and bolsters the claims of legitimacy by the other side. When those who are socially, politically, and economically oppressed see the double-standards applied in connection with violence, their hope for a more justice-oriented world diminishes. Dual standards employed by governments undermine international legitimacy and reinforce the legitimacy claims of those who argue that the ends justify the means. By contrast, democracy based on the rule of law and respect for human rights is one of the most effective ways of combating "terrorism." The asymmetry of power relations between states and nonstate actors, and the absence of effective mechanisms for conflict resolution, enhance noncompliance with international law and thus increase the likelihood of "terrorism." In tracking these issues of law, Bassiouni lays out the role that values play in shaping policy for enforcement of the rule of law in both response to violence and protection of human rights.

Amos Guiora, in *The Importance of Values in the Fight Against Terrorism*, makes a strong demand for government veracity on the most important issues of our day – Iraq and terrorism. He asserts that the Congressional resolution supporting the decision to invade Iraq reflects a fundamental lack of oversight and inquiry, while similar acquiescence has yielded to executive power in counterterrorism. Government effectiveness is predicated on an educated, moral public demanding that its elected leaders recognize not only the limits of power but the obligation to come forth with the truth. As the executive branch invariably seeks greater, unfettered power for itself, it is the role of the Courts, Congress and media to assume active roles of review, oversight and skepticism. Understanding terrorism and counterterrorism requires that we address two critical issues: how to balance the rights of the individual with the equally legitimate national security right of the state and how to resolve complex legal, moral and policy dilemma facing the public and decision makers alike. The individuals who comprise terror organizations have a clear sense of mission. To counter this, our leaders must be able to clearly articulate a mission and state the truth, however unpleasant it may be. To that end, it is the public's responsibility to make those demands on the leadership or else we fail both our leaders and ourselves.

Finally, Wayne McCormack attempts to specify the *Value Choices in the Struggle with Terrorism*. Why is terrorism terrorizing? In number of deaths, it pales in comparison to the devastation created by natural disasters, traffic accidents, individual violence, and even human trafficking. Acts of terrorism are designed to challenge societal values: terrorism is insulting, most acts are purposefully random (a fearful populace is a tense populace), they are carried out by a faceless organization, and they challenge the legitimacy of government itself. Is there something new about terrorism today? Communication, military and other technologies have advanced, but the purposes and basic strategies of terrorism have been the same for millennia. Protective services, law enforcement, and the military form a tripod of protection, and each carries its own set of values and limitations. Following 9/11, the U.S. precipitously switched from an emphasis on the law enforcement model to emphasize military and preventive strategies. Values such as protection of the rule of law, privacy concerns, respect for life and dignity, are represented in the specific rules that apply to each leg of the tripod. Government actions that ignore, or attempt to create exceptions from, those rules and underlying values threaten the very integrity and credibility of government in just the fashion that terrorists hope to achieve. Thus, the pragmatic politician needs to be cognizant of background societal values or risk flawed decisions and failure.

Suggestions

The dozen suggestions below are the impressions of the editors drawn from the essays in this volume. They are not the specific work of the contributors nor even a consensus among them. The conference at which these essays were presented produced numerous points of disagreement and contention. The suggestions here, however, are those that seemed to have enough support to justify listing them for convenience:[2]

1. Develop a coherent approach to understanding the cultural backgrounds of groups that resort to political violence.
2. Promote research into ideological, ethnic, and cultural influences in political violence.
3. Analyze how emerging or rebuilding nations can build institutions that address basic needs for human dignity.
4. Develop a proactive process and methodology for anticipating the timing and locations of future terrorist havens across the globe.
5. Employ a more refined risk assessment strategy to guide the allocation of resources to combat global terrorism.
6. Investigate the use of social capital to address the terrorist situation and the supporting communities across the globe.
7. Evaluate which nations and regions of the world are conducive to adopting democracy and capitalism to counter terrorism and which are not. Policy should reflect this evaluation.
8. Focus on policies to upgrade the education, awareness, and role of women in many areas of the world to combat underlying causes of societal disaffection leading to terrorism.
9. Emphasize implications of the language and rhetoric of terrorism and war.
10. Detail the essential ingredients necessary to have a global rule of law and supporting legal system to address non-state, global terrorism and terrorism support.
11. Seek a balance among preventive, criminal, and military approaches to combating terrorism.
12. Develop federalism models for global approaches to economic disparities and physical violence.

---

[2] Thanks to George Hepner for assembling this list from the contributions of our authors.

Part I
Social Identity and Political Violence

Violence in Identity

Amartya Sen

1

I am very grateful to the University of Utah not only for its kindness in inviting me, but also for arranging a conference here on the important – indeed urgent – subject of "Values and Violence: Intangible Aspects of Terrorism," a conference I am attending with much interest and benefit. Given the rampant presence of violence and persistent outbreaks of terrorism in the fiercely turbulent times in which we live, it is important to investigate *whether* and *how* these transgressions and brutalities connect with the values that are cherished – and cultivated – in the world.

The specific subject of this lecture is "violence in identity," but more generally I must also consider the broader connections between *values* and *violence*, the general subject matter of this conference. I can well imagine that some people here may take the skeptical view – plausible enough I suppose – that I must be quite unfit to talk about "values" since I am primarily an economist, and an economist, we have been told repeatedly in the form of a famous saying, "knows the price of everything and the value of nothing." That aphorism is sometimes backed up by Edmund Burke's eighteenth-century complaint that economists are partially responsible for extinguishing forever "the glory of Europe" – presumably because those whom Burke called "sophisters, economists, and calculators" know so little about the deeper values that make life worth living.

I must, however, say in my defence that I lack the sophistication needed to qualify as a genuine "sophister," and also know extremely little about prices of anything anywhere. I have been telling myself that this level of abysmal ignorance about prices cannot but be rewarded by generating some understanding of values in me, if the dissonance between prices and values emphasized in that often-repeated famous saying is right.

It would, actually, be very hard for anyone to miss the fact that there must be some obvious connections between values and violence. Wars and strifes have very often been fed by appeals to certain types of values that emphasize differences with

A. Sen
First Annual Lecture of the Barbara L. and Norman C. Tanner Center for Nonviolent Human Rights Advocacy
e-mail: slrich@fas.harvard.edu

I.A. Karawan et al. (eds.), *Values and Violence*,

others, while glorifying dedicated warfare in defence of what is seen as one's "own people" – the country, the nation, the community, or whatever. For example, appeals to country and nationality played a rousing role in the immensely bloody war in Europe between 1914–1918. Before the horrors of the First World War took the freshly recruited Wilfred Owen's life in the battlefield, he had the time to write his own protest about values that glorify violent combat for the cause of one's fatherland – this is in a poem called "Dulce et Decorum est":

> My friend, you will not tell with such high zest
> To children ardent for some desperate glory,
> The old lie: Dulce et Decorum est
> Pro Patria Mori.

Horace's ringing endorsement of the honour of death for (or *allegedly* for) one's country could be seen as catering to the violence of nationalism, and it was this invocation against which Wilfred Owen was emphatically protesting. The same kind of sectarian glorification translates easily into similar celebrations of the imagined honour of dying, while killing others, for many different types of collectivities, not just nation and citizenship, but also religion, race, community, or the newly popular but deeply befuddling category now called "civilization." The mesmerizing appeal of such sentiment is devastatingly used today, just as in the past, with newer areas of explosive application, to entrap the young in a magnification of the nasty ways of the old. The "children ardent for some desperate glory," as Owen called them, are often ready to blow themselves up to blow out others.

The tactics of suicide bombing and other techniques of super-violence may be new in today's world, but it is extremely important to remember that the exploitation of the violence in the use of identity-based reasoning has been in use for a very long time, in many different forms, particularly those based on appeals to nationalism. Even suicide attacks were in use during the Second World War, made famous by kamikaze pilots from Japan destroying naval vessels of the allied forces.

More generally, forms of belligerent identity with one's nation, pitted against "enemy countries," generated and sustained the violent sentiments that fed the warriors in many wars including the two world wars – Wilfred Owen, who was quoted earlier, was raising his voice against just this process. The Second World War, unlike the First, did have some other appeals to loyalty as well, since there were major ideological issues in addition to nationalism, such as fascism and Nazism as well as pluralist democracy and communism. And yet there was some role for national identities too, both in Europe (for example, in the cultivation of German nationalism in Nazi Germany which had a territory of its own that transcended the general philosophy of Nazism) and in Asia (for example in the Japanese hostilities in China).

It is useful to remember the co-existence of the two faces of nationalism in Japan – the positive face that gave encouragement to the Japanese to make spectacular economic and social advance to catch up with Europe and the negative face that allowed and even encouraged the atrocities perpetrated in the wars that were waged. It was that pervasive duality that disturbed Rabindranath Tagore, the Indian poet and writer, who saw in the Japanese experience a huge example of the real fragility of the creative aspects of nationalism. The Japanese military adventures graphically illustrated for him how the creative and elevating identity with one's own nation could deeply confound even a country – Japan – with such past accomplishments and also such rapidly growing further achievements – achievements that could be, as it happens, better fostered by peace rather than by war (as Japan's post-war experience shows).

Tagore went on writing about – and lecturing in – Japan on his criticisms of what he saw as a deflection from the creative side of national unity. Rabindranath Tagore's much publicized criticisms did not convince, at that time, many people in Japan and their main effect was that Tagore rapidly lost the huge following he earlier had in Japan. But there were also continued efforts from Japan to get Tagore's sympathetic ear, both because his views were influential in the world and because he had been so "pro-Japanese" earlier on. In 1938, Yone Noguchi, the distinguished poet and friend of Tagore (and of W.B. Yeats), wrote a pleading letter to make Rabindranath change his mind on the subject of Japan's relations with China and other countries.

Radindranath's reply was altogether unambiguous and stubborn. He wrote to Noguchi, on the 12th of September 1938:

> It seems to me that it is futile for either us to try to convince the other, since your faith in the infallible right of Japan to bully other Asiatic nations into line with your Government's policy is not shared by me....Believe me, it is sorrow and shame, not anger, that prompt me to write to you. I suffer intensely not only because the reports of Chinese suffering batter against my heart, but because I can no longer point out with pride the example of a great Japan....You know I have a genuine love for the Japanese people and it is sure to hurt me too painfully to go and watch crowds of them being transported by their rulers to neighbouring land to perpetrate acts of inhumanity which will brand their name with a lasting stain in the history of man.[1]

Rabindranath would have been much happier with the post-war emergence of Japan as a peaceful power, and by its reassessment of its role and responsibilities in the world. But he had died even before the second world war was finished. When I had the opportunity, many years later, to have some fairly long conversations with the Japanese novelist and writer Kenzaburo Oe (he and I did a joint tour of some Japanese cities, arranged by a leading Japanese newspaper), I was struck by the many different ways in which Oe's deeply humanistic and constructive vision fitted in with Tagore's own hopes about political priorities, not least in the Japan he used to love and admire so much. The violence in identity-based thinking can come as a tide but – and this is extremely important to remember in the dejected contemporary world – can recede rapidly as well. For that to happen, we have to think through and act on the real problems that need addressing, not imagined ones that befog the mind and confound policy options.

2

In what follows in this lecture, I want to pay particular attention to two distinctions that look like cases, in terms of appearance, of comprehensive dissonance, and yet which are, in fact, deeply interrelated and interdependent. The first distinction is that

[1] Republished in *Tagore for All* (Calcutta: Visva-Bharati, enlarged edition, 1984), pp. 134–137.

between the two faces of identity on which I have already said something. There is the face that generates warmth and the one that champions hostility. The relation between the two faces can, I think, be seen in terms of the contrast between identifying with one's so-called "own" group, that is, with other members of the group to which this person is persuaded he or she "actually belongs," and the other face that sustains – and sometimes feeds – hostility to *non*-members of that distinguished group. It is the symbiotic relation between the two contrary faces – with love for members and non-love for non-members – that makes identity such a potent force in the world with great creative powers as well as massively destructive potentials.

Rabindranath Tagore was commenting on the two faces of identity with one's nation, but the problem is much more general than that. The recent outbursts of violence have been linked with other chosen groups and other selected identities, such as religion (for example, the al Quaeda as a global terrorist movement) and *ethnicity* (for example, the Hutu violence against Tutsis in Rwanda a little over a decade ago).

The second dissonance that I want to talk about deals with thinking of the roots of violence, including terrorism, in two contrasting – and apparently unrelated – lines of explanation, one doing it in primarily economic and material terms and the other through cultural and political factors. The first line of explanation is well illustrated by seeing violence and terrorism as being, ultimately, the result of economic poverty and social deprivation, which generate the anger and disquiet that burst into violence. The second approach can be illustrated by attempts to explain violence through the influence of identity politics, cultural alienation, and the fostering of sectarian thinking, which can similarly lead to strife and turmoil. In trying to link them together, I will argue that each line of explanation has some explanatory power on its own, but also has some deep weaknesses when seen in isolation. There is a need for a fuller picture that demands a more integrated understanding. I would like to suggest some elementary ideas on how such an integration could be attempted. But first I must say more about each of these distinct elements, seen on their own.

3

How can the thesis linking poverty to violence be illustrated? That is not hard to do – at least in terms of immediacy, if not critical sustainability. Many countries have experienced – and continue to experience – the simultaneous presence of economic destitution, on the one hand, and political strife and violence, on the other. From Afghanistan and Sudan to Ethiopia and Somalia, there are plenty of examples of the dual adversities faced by people in different parts of the world.

It is not surprising that possible connections between the two great afflictions that characterize the contemporary world, viz. (1) violent and persistent conflicts, and (2) massive economic inequality and poverty, should attract attention. Even though definitive empirical work on the causal linkages between political turmoil and economic deprivations may be relatively rare, the basic presumption that the two phenomena have firm causal links has considerable plausibility and is very commonly taken to be true. Furthermore, it is not uncommon to presume that a basic characteristic of an enlightened attitude to war and peace must go beyond the immediately obvious into the "underlying" and "deeper" causes, including economic ones, of these phenomena, and that we must look for the roots of discontent and disorder in economic destitution. Sometimes this connection is given a ready-to-use shape in the form of what may be called "economic reductionism," whereby social and political strife is explained straightaway by what are taken to be their "hidden economic roots."

The empirical claim that poverty is responsible for group violence is, however, far too simple both because the linkage of poverty and violence is not at all universal, but also because a serious causal analysis is needed to identify the ways and means through which poverty can influence violence (in a fuller understanding of the causes of violence). Destitution can, of course, yield provocation enough to defy the established laws and rules, but it need not give people the initiative, courage and actual ability to do anything very violent. Indeed, destitution can be accompanied not only by economic debility, but also by political helplessness. A starving wretch can be too frail and too dejected to fight and battle, and even to protest and holler. It is, thus, not surprising that often enough intense suffering and inequity have been accompanied by peace and quiet.

Indeed, the economic connections between poverty and violence are quite complex and far from capturable in the simple form in which economic reductionism tends to proceed. For example, the violent history of Afghanistan cannot be unrelated to poverty and indigence that the population have experienced, and yet to reduce the causation of violence there entirely to this singular economic observation would be a great mistake. Much else is clearly involved, related to Afghanistan's particular history (including Soviet occupation, the emergence of militant Islam, American role in feeding the rebellion against the Soviets through assisting Islamic political groups, the part played by neighbouring countries including Pakistan and its links with the Taliban, and so on). We have to try to understand how these multi-factor processes work, and how the different causal influences work together – and often kill together.

The observed empirical connections between poverty and violence are quite contingent on many other circumstances. There is, to be sure, no dearth of evidence of conflicts and confrontations in economies with a good deal of poverty and much inequality. But, at the same time, there are also other economies with no less poverty or inequality that seem to stay sunk just in economic hardship, without necessarily generating serious political turbulence. Indeed, very severe poverty and even acute famines can co-exist with evident peace and apparent tranquillity. As it happens, many famines have occurred without there being much political rebellion or civil strife or inter-group warfare. For example, the famine years in the 1840s in Ireland were among the most peaceful, and there was little attempt by the hungry masses to intervene even as ship after ship sailed down the river Shannon laden with rich food, carrying it to well-fed England away from starving Ireland.

It would be amazing if such experiences of deprivation and malgovernance – the Irish famines of the 1840s would be hard to beat as spectacular examples of both – were to leave no impact on peace and quiet in the long run, but the influences did not work with the immediacy and simplicity that the deprivation-centred theory of causation of violence seems to seek. So what about the alternative line of explanation in terms of cultural and political alienation and the divisive effects of singular identities?

Identity is certainly a double-edged sword. We have to recognise the basic fact that identity-centred sentiments have many positive and socially constructive features. The new schools of communitarian thinking, which have flourished over several decades now, have done much to bring out the positive features of communal identities. The perception of identity over a broad group that crosses country borders has also done much to generate and sustain demands for fairness and justice across the world. This applies to anti-racist political agitations defending the rights of the racial underdogs in many different countries as well as to feminist and more generally to gender-egalitarian movements for equity between women and men. The world would be a more impoverished place without the social and political commitment directly inspired by the identity of disadvantaged people with other people who are similarly deprived. A sense of identity can be a source not merely of pride and joy, but also of strength and confidence, and it would be wrong to see identity only as a problem rather than also as an asset.

And yet identity can also kill – and decimate with abandon. A strong – and exclusive – sense of belonging to one group can go with the perception of distance and divergence from other groups and can contribute to fomenting conflicts organized around group categories. Within-group solidarity can go hand-in-hand with between-group discord, as I have tried to discuss in some detail in my book *Identity and Violence*.[2] We may be suddenly informed that we are not just Rwandans but specifically Hutus ("we hate Tutsis"), or we are not really mere Yugoslavs but actually Serbs ("we absolutely don't like Albanians"). From my own childhood memory of Hindu-Muslim riots in the 1940s, linked with the politics of partition, I recollect the speed with which the broad human beings of January were suddenly transformed into ruthless Hindus and fierce Muslims of July. The broader identities that got suppressed during those brutal moments would return again before long (as the storm passed), but meanwhile hundreds of thousands perished at the hands of people who, led by the captains of carnage, slayed others on behalf of their "own people."

Violence is fomented by the imposition of singular and belligerent identities on gullible people, championed by proficient artisans of terror. The currency of group love leaves room for an invitation to group hatred. The cordiality of identifying with others in an affiliative group seems to stand in some readiness to be extended to the scalding or burning of others excluded from – and seen as an enemy of – one's own affiliated group.

---

[2] *Identity and Violence: The Illusion of Destiny* (New York: Norton, and London and New Delhi: Penguin, 2006).

Our understanding of the role of identity has been very substantially enhanced by new explorations of social psychology and public action. Even though a good deal of traditional economic theory tended to rely exclusively on the assumption of purely self-interested conduct, there have been important recent developments – for example by Akerlof, Kranton, Davis, Kirman and others – in incorporating identity-based thinking in the characterization of economic behaviour and in investigating the far-reaching accomplishments of this motivational broadening. It has also been enriched by the discernment of the positive contribution of "social capital" – analyzed by Robert Putnam and others – in the form of people's propensity to help others in the same community with a spontaneity that would be hard to generate by narrowly self-centred behaviour of intellectually isolated human beings. Communitarian theorists, from Charles Taylor to Michael Sandel, have also shown the positive role played by the recognition of identity with one's own community in yielding impressive social achievements at a reflective as well as material level.

What must be added to the understanding generated by these investigations is the basic recognition that a sense of identity can totally exclude many people even as it warmly embraces others. The well integrated community in which residents instinctively do helpful things for each other with great immediacy and solidarity may also be the community in which bricks are thrown through the windows of immigrants who move into the region from elsewhere. It has been observed, for example, that anti-immigrant violence aimed at Turks trying to settle in Germany has sometimes been sharpest in precisely those regions of the country where the solidarity of the local old communities is strongest. The adversity of exclusion can go hand in hand with the gifts of inclusion. The so-called "social capital" may fail to be "capital" in the basic sense of being an all-purpose resource to promote desirable objectives in general, since the same social disposition may make the lives of some – the "outsiders" – much more barbed even as it helps the lives of "insiders" to flourish more fully and more easily.

To understand the brutal potentials of identity-based politics, we have to see that this operates through prioritizing some identities and downgrading the relevance of other identities, including our broadest identity of a shared humanity, but also identities linked to economic, political and other social commonalities. What makes the divisiveness of an imagined, unique identity potentially so brutal and relentless is not the mere presence of that divergence, but the overlooking of the other identities that human beings also have and which too can claim our attention.

Identity politics acquires its deadly potential by denying the claims of identities other than some *one* identification that is championed for use in fomenting a particular belligerence. A Hutu labourer from Kigali may be pressured to see himself only as a Hutu and incited to kill Tutsis, and yet he is not only a Hutu, but also a Kigalian, a Rwandan, an African, a labourer, and a human being. In resisting this invitation to violence, there is a need not only to recognise the plurality of our identities and their diverse demands, but also the important role of choice in determining the cogency and relevance of particular identities which are inescapably diverse. The use of identity-based thinking in generating conflict and violence is closely connected with the illusion that identity is just a matter of "discovery," rather than also of choice. Encouraging that illusion is a part of the martial art of the architects of sectarian violence. But it has also been much encouraged by cultural theories that try to classify the world into self-contained baskets of civilizations (a line of reasoning that *precedes* any thesis of a clash of civilizations but on which the clash thesis parasitically depends) and obsessive communitarian thinking that sees the world as a federation of communities, overlooking all the other identities that human beings simultaneously have.

4

So far so good, at least as far explanation goes, though we are dealing with the bad, not good, phenomenon of cultivated divisiveness. But is it adequate to see the phenomenon in wholly – or even mainly – isolated and endogenous forms? How do the manipulators of divisive identities end up being so successful? Why do they fail some times and succeed in other cases? To see the entire process in terms of the irresistible machinations of wily instigators would be to miss out a central feature in the causal process involved in the prevalence – and its contingencies – of identity-based violence.

A big difference can be made by the exploitability of potential grievance, discontent and disaffection, which can provide fertile ground for the alienating campaigns of identity politics. This is where the other causal factor, to wit, poverty and deprivation, can link up and magnify the force of identity divisions.

The sense that the world is divided between "haves" and "have-nots" greatly helps in the cultivation of harsh disaffection, opening up possibilities of recruitment in the cause of what is seen as retaliatory – or even remedial – violence. In order to understand how this works, it is necessary to distinguish between the leaders of violent insurrection and the much larger populations on whose support the leaders rely. Leaders like Osama bin Laden do not – to say the least – suffer from poverty and may have no economic reason to feel left out from sharing the fruits of global capitalism. And yet the movements that are led by leaders of violence rely greatly on a sense of injustice, iniquity and humiliation that the established world order is seen as having produced. A growing tolerance of terrorism by an otherwise peaceful population is another peculiar phenomenon in many parts of the contemporary world, particularly those that feel badly treated by the privileged people of the world, and have the sense of being left behind in global economic, social and political processes. A feeling of "unfairness" in the unequal sharing of the benefits of globalization has often been invoked to help both the recruitment of the cannon-fodders of terrorism, and the creation of a general climate where terrorism is tolerated (and sometimes even celebrated).

The years of the Irish famines in the 1840s might have been a time of peace and law and order (it was perhaps the peace of the grave, as some might be tempted to say), but that gigantic experience not only led to massive emigration to America, but it also left a lasting legacy of Irish anger against British dominance. Indeed, the violence of the Irish separatist movements, which has, happily, at last calmed down after nearly a century, could not be understood without reference to the history of malgovernance and deprivation in Ireland that preceded it.

Similarly, the memory of ill treatment of the Arab world by Western powers, including the redrawing of the boundaries as the colonial powers willed, still lingers in West Asia and contributes to the ability of terrorists to recruit volunteers for violence. What is seen as the violence of "Islamic extremism" has many components, but the anger of the ill-treated has a huge role in facilitating its appeal and reach. Since the recent events in the Middle East have done nothing to remove that memory – in fact quite the contrary – the grievances that are channelled into violent resolves remain totally untamed. And grievance-based thinking, which dominates so much of what is happening in the Middle East today, also encourages other complaints and other protests that are brought to the fore and made to generate new lines of violence.

5

The connections between identity-based alienation and deprivation-based conflicts can work in many different ways, of which the potential for violence through the exploitation of grievances against those who are seen as fostering – or even just tolerating – deprivation is only one. Cultural generalizations have great effectiveness in fixing our ways of thinking. The fact that such generalizations abound in popular discourse can be easily recognised. Not only are discriminatory convictions the frequent subject matters of racist jokes and ethnic slurs, they sometimes surface as grand theories. When there is an accidental correlation between cultural prejudice and actual economic and social contrast, a theory is born, and it may refuse to die even after the chance correlation has vanished altogether.

Consider the frequency of laboured jokes against the Irish (such crudities as "how many Irishmen do you need to change a light bulb"), which has had much currency in England for a long time, had the superficial appearance of fitting well with the depressing predicament of the fumbling Irish economy, when the Irish economy was doing quite badly. The economic deprivation of Ireland got merged with the cultural prejudice of the English society. Such prejudices have lives of their own, quite defiantly of the phenomenal world that can be actually observed. Even when the Irish economy started growing astonishingly rapidly – indeed in recent years faster than any other European economy (Ireland is now richer in per-capita income than nearly every country in Europe) – the cultural stereotyping and its allegedly profound economic and social relevance were not chucked into the dustbin of dead thoughts.

The close relation between deprivation and alienation can sometimes help to sustain each other in very powerful ways. I have discussed elsewhere – in my book *Identity and Violence* – how the cultural contrasts and the associated identities fed by pre-existing deprivation can, in turn, help to generate further deprivation, when the ruling powers use their economic and cultural differentiation as justification for their unhelpful policies. Indeed, the deep English scepticism of the Irish played a major part in allowing amazing malgovernance, including terrible mismanagement of the famines of the 1840s. Charles Edward Trevelyan, the Head of the Treasury during the famines, expressed his belief that Britain had done what it could for Ireland, even as the famine killed rampantly (in fact, the percentage of mortality was larger in the Irish famines than in any other recorded famine anywhere). Trevelyan also pointed to some remarkable cultural explanations of the manifest hunger, including: "There is scarcely a woman of the peasant class in the West of Ireland whose culinary art exceeds the boiling of a potato."[3] It is not surprising that, armed with such deep understanding of the causation of the Irish famine, public policy made in London achieved remarkably little to stop the famine or to alleviate the suffering of the Irish.

6

Time to end. I will not try to summarize the different but interconnected points I have tried to make in this lecture, but I will separate out a couple of major concerns that I have and which I would argue deserve more attention than they tend to get.

First, the cultivation of a singular identity as a basis of thinking about human beings carries the ever-present possibility of easy translation into violence and brutality. This does not, of course, deny the fact that a singular identification has often played a very beneficial role. But the two faces of identity – the creative and the destructive – are closely linked together, and the cultivation of the former always carries the potential, of which we have to be aware, of fostering – wilfully or inadvertently – groundwork for identity-based violence.

A singular concentration on nationality has been a part of the martial art used in sustaining the battles of many past wars, and a similar role can be – and often is – played today by a singular concentration on religion or community or ethnicity or culture. What is perhaps more disturbing is the recognition that what the artisans of terror do by design (that *is* their weapon), the befuddled fighters against terrorism, on the other side, end up doing through lazy and unclear thinking, by falling for the simple temptation to define people – mainly or even only – by one identity only. For example, when a person is defined just as a British or an American Muslim, not only is the richness of that person's plentiful life, with language, literature, profession, artistic and scientific taste, or membership of other institutions and associations, ignored, the person is invited or pushed to see himself in terms of the demands of that one identity only.

Second, in the linkage between the two faces – constructive and destructive – of identity, the contrasts in economic and social circumstances can play a powerfully effective role. That connection may work not only through the easy cultivability of the anger of the deprived, but also through feeding the prejudices of the affluent and the rulers of the world – in the past and even today. I would argue that we cannot begin to understand the conflicts that we see around us, and also those that

[3] See Cecil Woodham-Smith, *The Great Hunger: Ireland 1845–9* (London: Hamish Hamilton, 1962), p. 76.

have visited us over the last couple of hundred of years, without seeing the role of economically, socially and politically divided fortunes in feeding the hold and violence of identity-based thinking.

The violence of identity can draw on other sources of division that characterize the world in which we live. It is not only that both identity and deprivation have roles to play in the generation of violence, but also that they cannot be seen as additive factors that cumulatively make up the whole – one added to the other. Our attempts to help cultivate peace in the world have to come to terms with the interactive and dynamic relations between these different but interlinked sources of tension and stress. World peace cannot, of course, be brought about by some magic bullet, but it does demand something of an inclusive vision that incorporates a fuller understanding of the interdependence between apparently disparate and dissonant factors that influence human life. This can, in fact, be quite important for the violence-ridden world in which we live.

Gandhi, Newton, and the Enlightenment

Akeel Bilgrami

Salman Rushdie once said, no doubt under duress, that secular humanism was itself a religion, thereby selling short both religion and secular humanism in one breath. I reckon (this is a conjecture) that he made that equation so that he could repudiate the charge of apostasy. One cannot, after all, be committing apostasy if one is only opposing one religion with another. Under the threat of execution, one may be allowed a confused thought, but with a clear mind no one with even a vestigial understanding of the mentalities and the realities of religion *or* the aspirations of secular humanism would be tempted by Rushdie's equation.

Though his equation itself may be quite wrong, I do now want to briefly pursue with some variation, a theme it opens up.

What I want to ask is really a familiar question, and trace some of the philosophical attitudes and intellectual history that makes it familiar, the question whether there can be in the secular a form of continuity with something in the religious, in my view a continuity which actually stood for a particular form of humane radical politics that was very early on thwarted by a very specific notion of scientific rationality, which in this lecture I will call a "thick" notion of scientific rationality. By constantly appealing to this notion of scientific rationality, a dominant orthodox strand in thinking about the Enlightenment has consistently tarnished a certain kind of radical questioning of this orthodoxy with charges of irrationalism. It is worth exposing a sleight of hand in all this.

A good place to begin is with Gandhi, a humanist and secularist yet by open declaration opposed to the Enlightenment and also avowedly a Hindu, even if by the lights of high Hinduism, a highly heterodox one. I will be focusing (and focusing selectively) only on Gandhi's thought and writing and not his political interventions during the long freedom movement.[1] What Gandhi says about the

A. Bilgrami
Columbia University
e-mail: ab41@columbia.edu

[1] There is something particularly thankless about writing an interpretative essay on someone as intellectually and politically creative, perverse, and prolific, as Gandhi. I have hardly ever spoken on him in public (or indeed in private) without someone offering a refutation by citing either some action or proposal of his during the freedom movement, or by mentioning some action or attitude

I.A. Karawan et al. (eds.), *Values and Violence*,

Enlightenment as well as, what he often omnibusly called, "the West," relates closely to his view of science.

In careless moments, Gandhi often said that it was a *predisposition* of science from its earliest days that it would lead to a way of thinking that was disastrous for politics and culture in ways that he outlined in great detail. This notion of a predisposition is obscure because general claims about the predispositions of something like science (something that is at once a theoretical pursuit as well as a practice, something that is defined in terms that are at once conceptual, methodological, and institutional) are hard to pin down and study, leave alone confirm or refute, if they are intended to be empirical hypotheses. So, in this essay, I will instead sympathetically read his hunch about such a predisposition by situating it in a certain intellectual history. At the end of this exercise, it will emerge that a far better way to put his point would be in terms, not of an empirical hypothesis about "science" as a self-standing human cognitive enterprise, but rather to see it as a critique of a certain very specific notion of scientific "rationality."

The notion of rationality as it governed our thought about history and politics and culture has in the past – famously – taken an idealized form, with a progressivist or developmental, conception of these subjects; and for a few decades now that has been under a thoroughly critical scrutiny, as is the notion of modernity with which it is so often coupled. Much more often than not the *telos* that defines the progressivist trajectory is in terms of an envisaged ideal or *end-point* and the dialectic by which the end is (or is to be) realized is the large subject of the relevant historiography. Yet it is sometimes more fruitful to focus on the *beginnings* of such a sequence, since it may give a more truthful sense of the notions of rationality that are at stake than those defined by an idealized statement of the normative end. So I will argue.

In general, a sequence, especially when it is consecutively narrativized and dialectically and cumulatively conceived, as progressive ideals are bound to conceive it, cannot have started from the beginning of thought and culture itself. If a sequence is to aspire to conceptual and cultural significance (as the very idea of progress suggests) it cannot have *its* beginnings at the very beginning of conceptual and cultural life. That would trivialize things – evacuate the notion of sequence of any of the substance and significance that progressivist narrative aspires to. It cannot be that we have been converging on this significant end from the random inceptions of

---

of his towards his wife or children or ashram companions, or, more soberly, reminding me of some passage in his writing that is in tension with what I have just said. So, let me repeat right at the outset that I will be doing *merely* what I say: focusing *selectively* on some of his *writing* with a view to offering a partial (but I hope interesting) interpretation of it that frees us of some of the standard, clichetic ways of thinking of him: a saint on the one hand or a shrewd politician rather than a thinker or philosopher, on the other ... a nostalgist and traditionalist, or more specifically, a reactionary holding back the progressive, modernist tendencies in the nationalist movement ... and so on. The idea is not – not by any means – to write anything even approximating a definitive interpretative essay, as if that could be any sensible person's idea. The fact is that Gandhi, remarkable philosopher though he was, was not a systematic thinker, not a philosopher in the sense that the academic subject of philosophy circumscribes. So it is tiresome to keep demanding of him that he be entirely consistent in all his writing. Not only would he have had to be a much less interesting thinker than he was to have that rightly demanded of him, he would have had to be born all over again.

our intellectual and cultural existence. One assumes rather that there were many strands at the outset, endless false leads, but then at some point (what I am calling the *beginning* of the progressivist trajectory) we got *set* on a path, which we think of as the *right* path, from which point on the idea of *cumulative* steps towards a broadly specifiable end began to make sense, a path of *convergence* towards that end. Accumulation and convergence, then, don't start at the beginning of thought, but rather they start at some juncture that we think of as the *start* onto a *right* path.

This has many implications for historiography, some of them highly critical. Just to give you one example, I think, it implies a real difficulty for philosophers such as Hilary Putnam when they say that scientific realism is true because it is the only explanation of the fact that there is a *convergence* in scientific theories – that is to say, the posits of science must be real because it is only their reality which would explain the *cumulative* nature of the claims of scientific theories over time. What is the difficulty with this that I have in mind? It is this. Here too, the fact is that these converging and cumulative trends have not existed since the beginning of theorizing about nature. In fact, Putnam would be the first to say that it is only sometime in the seventeenth century that we were set on the right path in science and from then on there has been a convergence that is best explained by the corresponding reality of what the converging scientific theories posit. But now a question arises. *What* makes it the case that *that* is when we were set on the *right* path? What is the notion of *rightness*, here? If we have an answer to this last question (about what makes the path the *right* path at *that* starting point), then that notion of rightness would *already* have established scientific realism and we don't need to wheel in scientific realism to explain the subsequent convergence.

Well, my subject is not the merits of such well known arguments nor even scientific realism but the point I am making is generalizable to efforts that characterize modernity in progressivist terms, indeed it is even generalizable to interesting recent efforts to characterize modernity in sequential terms that are *not* progressivist.[2] These too cannot avoid the hard question of the sequence's starting point, which may have the greater power to illuminate than the sequence itself.

So let me explore these beginnings briefly by recording the detailed affinities between Gandhi's ideas about science and the metaphysical and political and cultural anxieties that first surfaced at the very site and time of the new science as it first began to be formulated in the seventeenth century in the West. There are many passages in Gandhi's dispatches to *Young India* and also in some passages in his book *Hind Swaraj*[3] that suggest a line of argument something like this.

Sometime in the seventeenth century we were set on a path in which we were given the intellectual sanction to see nature as – to use a Weberian notion – "disenchanted." This coincided with the period of the great revolutionary changes in scientific theory, so Gandhi crudely equated it with science itself and its newly and self-consciously formulated experimental methods. And he saw in it a conception of

---

[2] For a very interesting such effort see Sudipta Kaviraj's "An Outline of a Revisionist Theory of Modernity", *European Journal of Philosophy*, 2006.

[3] M.K. Gandhi, *Hind Swaraj and Other Writings* (Cambridge: Cambridge University Press, 1997).

nature whose pursuit left us disengaged from nature as a habitus, and which instead engendered a zeal to control it rather than merely live in it. And my claim is that these criticisms by Gandhi have extraordinarily close and striking antecedents in a tradition of thought that goes all the way back to the second half of the seventeenth century in England and then elsewhere in Europe, *simultaneous* with the great scientific achievements of that time. It goes back, that is, to just the time and the place when the outlook of scientific "rationality" that many place at the defining centre of what they call the "West," was being formed, and it is that very outlook with its threatening cultural and political consequences that is the target of that early critique.

It should be said emphatically right at the outset that the achievements of the "new science" of the seventeenth century were neither denied nor opposed by the critique I have in mind, and so the critique *cannot* be dismissed as Luddite reaction to the new science, as Gandhi's critique is bound to seem, coming centuries later, when the science is no longer "new" and its effects on our lives, which the earlier critique was warning against, seem like a *fait accompli*. What the critique opposed was a development in *outlook* that emerged in the *philosophical surround* of the scientific achievements. In other words, what it opposed was just the notion of what I am calling a "thick" rationality that is often described in glowing terms today as "scientific rationality." What do I have in mind by calling it a "thick" notion (a term I am recognizably borrowing from Clifford Geertz)?

To put a range of complex, interweaving themes in the crudest summary, the dispute was about the very nature of nature and matter and, relatedly therefore, about the role of the deity, and of the broad cultural and political implications of the different views on these metaphysical and religious concerns. The metaphysical picture that was promoted by Newton (the official Newton of the Royal Society, not the neo-Platonist of his private study) and Boyle, among others, viewed matter and nature as *brute and inert*. On this view, since the material universe was brute, God was *externally* conceived with all the familiar metaphors of the "clock winder" giving the universe a push from the *outside* to get it in motion. In the dissenting tradition – which was a *scientific* tradition, for there was in fact no disagreement between it and Newton/Boyle on any serious detail of the scientific laws, and all the fundamental notions such as gravity, for instance, were perfectly in place, though given a quite different metaphysical interpretation – matter was *not* brute and inert, but rather was shot through with an *inner* source of dynamism responsible for motion, that was itself divine. God and nature were not separable as in the official metaphysical picture that was growing around the new science, and John Toland, for instance, to take just one example among the active dissenting voices, openly wrote in terms he proclaimed to be "pantheistic."[4]

---

[4] In a series of works, starting with *Christianity Not Mysterious* in 1696, more explicitly pantheistic in statement in the discussion of Spinoza in *Letters to Serena* (1704) and then in the late work *Pantheisticon* (1724). These writings are extensively discussed in Margaret Jacob's extremely useful treatment *The Radical Enlightenment* (George Allen and Unwin, 1981). In case it is a source of confusion, I should make clear that the metaphysical and scientific debate about the nature of

The link with Gandhi in all this is vivid. One absolutely central claim of the free-thinkers of this period was about the political and cultural significance of their disagreements with the fast developing metaphysical orthodoxy of the "Newtonians." Just as Gandhi did, they argued that it is only because one takes matter to be "brute" and "stupid," to use Newton's own terms, that one would find it appropriate to conquer it with nothing but profit and material wealth as ends, and thereby destroy it both as a natural and a human environment for one's habitation. In today's terms, one might think that this point was a seventeenth century predecessor to our ecological concerns but though there certainly was an early instinct of that kind, it was embedded in a much more general point (as it was with Gandhi too), a point really about how nature in an ancient and spiritually flourishing sense was being threatened and how therefore this was in turn threatening to our moral psychology of engagement with it, including the relations and engagement among ourselves as its inhabitants.

Today, the most thoroughly and self-consciously secular sensibilities may recoil from the term "spiritually," as I have just deployed it, though I must confess to finding myself feeling no such self-consciousness despite being a secularist, indeed an atheist. The real point has nothing to do with these rhetorical niceties. If one had no use for the word, if one insisted on having the point made with words that we today can summon with confidence and accept without qualm, it would do no great violence to the core of their thinking to say this: the dissenters thought of the *world* not as brute but as *suffused with value*. That they happened to think the source of such value was divine ought not to be the deepest point of interest for us. The point rather is that if it were laden with *value*, it would make *normative* (ethical and social) demands on one, whether one was religious or not, normative demands therefore that did not come merely from our own instrumentalities and subjective utilities. And it is this sense of forming commitments by taking in, *in our perceptions*, an evaluatively "enchanted" world which – being enchanted in this way – therefore *moved* us to normatively constrained *engagement* with it, that the dissenters contrasted with the outlook that was being offered by the ideologues of the new science.[5] A brute and disenchanted world could not move us to any such engagement since any perception of it, given the sort of thing it was, would necessarily

matter and nature, whose centrality I am insisting on, should not be confused with another debate of that time, perhaps a more widely discussed one, regarding the "general concourse," which had to do with whether or not the deity was needed after the first formation of the universe, to keep it from falling apart. In that debate, Boyle, in fact, wrote against the Deists, arguing in favour of the "general concourse," of a continually active God. But *both* sides of that dispute take God to be external to a brute nature, which was mechanically conceived, unlike Toland and his "Socratic Brotherhood" and the dissenting tradition I am focusing on, who denied it was brute and denied that God stood apart from nature, making only external interventions. The dispute about "general concourse" was only about whether, the interventions from the outside of an *externally* conceived God were or were not needed after the original creative intervention.

[5] I have written at greater length about this conception of the world as providing normative constraints upon us and the essential links that such a conception of the world has with our capacities for free agency and self-knowledge, thereby making both freedom and self-knowledge thoroughly normative notions, in my book *Self-Knowledge and Resentment*, Chapters 4 and 5, (in press, Cambridge, Mass: Harvard University Press). For the idea that values are perceptible

be a *detached* form of observation; and if one ever came out of this detachment, if there was ever any engagement with a world so distantly conceived, so external to our own sensibility, it could only take the form of mastery and control of something alien, with a view to satisfying the only source of value allowed by this outlook – our own utilities and gain.

We are much used to the lament that we have long been living in a world governed by overwhelmingly commercial motives. What I have been trying to do is to trace this (just as Gandhi did) to its deepest *conceptual* sources and that is why the seventeenth century is so central to a proper understanding of this world. Familiarly drawn connections and slogans, like "Religion and the Rise of Capitalism", are only the beginning of such a tracing.

In his probing book, *A Grammar of Motives*, Kenneth Burke says that "the experience of an impersonal outlook was empirically intensified in proportion as the rationale of the monetary motive gained greater authority. . . ."[6] This gives us a glimpse of the sources. As he says, one had to have an impersonal angle on the world to see it as the source of profit and gain, and vice versa. But I have claimed that the sources go deeper. It is only when we see the world as Boyle and Newton did, as against the freethinkers and dissenters, that we understand further why there was no option but this impersonality in our angle on the world. A desacralized world, to put it in the dissenting terms of that period, left us no other angle from which to view it, but an impersonal one. There could be no normative constraint coming upon us from a world that was brute. It could not move us to engagement with it on *its* terms. All the term-making came from us. We could bring whatever terms we wished to such a world; and since we could only regard it impersonally, it being brute, the terms we brought in our actions upon it were just the terms that Burke describes as accompanying such impersonality, the terms of "the monetary" motives for our actions. Thus it is, that the metaphysical issues regarding the world and nature, as they were debated around the new science, provide the deepest conceptual sources.

The conceptual sources that we have traced are various but they were *not* miscellaneous. The diverse conceptual elements of religion, capital, nature, metaphysics, rationality, science, were *tied together* in a highly *deliberate* integration, that is to say in deliberately accruing worldly *alliances*. Newton's and Boyle's metaphysical view of the new science won out over the freethinkers' and became official only because it was sold to the Anglican establishment and, in an alliance with that establishment, to the powerful mercantile and incipient industrial interests of the period in thoroughly predatory terms. Terms which stressed that how we conceive nature may now be transformed into something, into the *kind* of thing, that is indefinitely available for our economic gain by processes of extraction, processes such as mining, deforestation, plantation agriculture intended essentially as what we today would call "agrobusiness." None of these processes could have taken on the *unthinking* and yet *systematic* prevalence that they first began to get in this period unless one

external qualities, see John McDowell's pioneering essay, "Values and Secondary Qualities" in Ted Honderich (ed.), *Morality and Objectivity*,(London: Routledge and Kegan Paul, 1985).

[6] (Berkeley and Los Angeles: University of California Press, 1969).

had ruthlessly revised existing ideas of a world animated by a divine presence. From an anima mundi, one could not simply proceed to take at whim and will. Not that one could not or did not, till then, take at all. But in the past in a wide range of social worlds, such taking as one did had to be accompanied by ritual offerings of reciprocation which were intended to show respect towards as well to restore the balance in nature, offerings made both before and after cycles of planting, and even hunting.

The point is that, in general, the revision of such an age-old conception of nature was achieved in tandem with a range of seemingly miscellaneous elements that were brought together in terms that stressed a future of endlessly profitable consequences that would accrue if one embraced this particular metaphysics of the new science and build, in the name of a notion of rationality around it, the institutions of an increasingly centralized political oligarchy (an incipient state) and an established religious orthodoxy of Anglicanism that had penetrated the universities as well, to promote these very specific interests. These were the very terms that the freethinkers found alarming for politics and culture, alarming for the local and egalitarian ways of life which some decades earlier the radical elements in the English Revolution such as the Levellers, Diggers, Quakers, Ranters, and other groups had articulated and fought for. Gandhi, much later, spoke in political terms that were poignantly reminiscent of these radical sectaries and, in *Hind Swaraj* and other writings, he wrote about science and its relations to these political terms in ways that echoed the alarm of the somewhat later scientific dissenters.

These scientific dissenters themselves often openly avowed that they had inherited the political attitudes of these radical sectaries in England of about fifty years earlier and appealed to their instinctive, hermetic, neo-Platonist, and sacralized views of nature, defending them against the conceptual assaults of the official Newton/Boyle view of matter. In fact, the natural philosophies of Anthony Collins and John Toland and his Socratic Brotherhood (and their counterparts in the Netherlands drawing inspiration from Spinoza's pantheism, and spreading to France and elsewhere in Europe, and then, when strongly opposed, going into secretive Masonic Lodges and other underground movements) were in many details anticipated by the key figures of the radical groups in that most dynamic period of English history, the 1640s, which had enjoyed hitherto unparalleled freedom of publication for about a decade or more to air their subversive and egalitarian views based on a quite different conception of nature. Gerard Winstanley, the most well known among them, declared that "God is in all motion" and "the truth is hid in every *body*" (my italics).[7] This way of thinking about the corporeal realm had for Winstanley, as he puts it, a great "leveling purpose." It allowed one to lay the ground, first of all, for a democratization of religion. If God was everywhere, then anyone may perceive the divine or find the divine within him or her, and therefore may be just as able to preach as a university-trained divine. But the opposition to the monopoly of so-called experts was intended to be more general than in just the religious sphere. Through their

[7] Cited by Christopher Hill, *The World Turned Upside Down* (London: Penguin, 1975) p. 293, from G. H. Sabine (ed.), *The Works of Gerard Winstanley* (Ithaca: Cornell University Press, 1941).

myriad polemical and instructional pamphlets, figures such as Winstanley, John Lilburne, Richard Overton, and others reached out and created a radical rank and file population which began to demand a variety of other things, including an elimination of tithes, a leveling of the legal sphere by a decentralizing of the courts and the elimination of feed lawyers, as well as the democratization of medicine by drastically reducing, if not eliminating, the costs of medicine, and disallowing canonical and monopoly status to the College of Physicians. The later scientific dissenters were very clear too that these were the very monopolies and undemocratic practices and institutions which would get entrenched if science, conceived in terms of the Newtonianism of the Royal Society, had its ideological victory.

Equally, that is to say, conversely, the Newtonian ideologues of the Royal Society around the Boyle lectures started by Samuel Clarke saw themselves – without remorse – in just these conservative terms that the dissenters portrayed them in. They explicitly called Toland and a range of other dissenters, "enthusiasts" (a term of opprobrium at the time) and feared that their alternative picture of matter was an intellectual ground for the social unrest of the pre-Restoration period when the radical sectaries had such great, if brief and aborted, popular reach. They were effective in creating with the Anglican establishment a general conviction that the entire polity would require orderly rule by a state apparatus around a monarch serving the propertied classes and that this was just a mundane reflection, indeed a mundane *version*, of an *externally* imposed divine authority which kept a universe of brute matter in orderly motion, rather than an *immanently* present God in all matter and in all persons, inspiring them with the enthusiasms to turn the "world upside down," in Christopher Hill's memorable, eponymous phrase. To see God in every body and piece of matter, they anxiously argued, was to lay oneself open to a polity and a set of civic and religious institutions that were beholden to popular rather than scriptural and learned judgement and opinion. They were just as effective in forging with the commercial interests over the next century, the idea that a respect for a sacralized universe would be an obstacle to taking with impunity what one could from nature's bounty. By their lights, the only obstacles that now needed to be acknowledged and addressed had to do with the difficulties of mobilizing towards an economy geared to profit. No other factors of a more metaphysical and ideological kind should be allowed to interfere with these pursuits once *nature* had been transformed in our consciousness to a set of impersonally perceived "*natural resources*."[8]

---

[8] The conceptual links between (1) the democratization of religion that is possible when one has a sacralized view of nature and body and (2) the resistance to the cast of mind that rationalizes the commercial plunder of the bounties of nature by the very same sacralized conception of nature, is essential to the reading I am giving of Gandhi through the affinities he has with the seventeenth century dissenters. As Utsa Patnaik acutely pointed out in a discussion after my verbal presentation of this lecture at Jawaharlal Nehru University, if (1) were emphasized without (2), other movements such as Bhakti, which are commonly cited in the Indian context could also be assimilated with the critique of thick scientific rationality being presented here. Thus (2), or more accurately, (1)'s *necessary and conceptual links* with (2), are indispensable to the argument being made here.

It was this scientific rationality, seized upon by just these established religious and economic alliances, that was later central to the colonizing mentality that justified the rapacious conquest of distant lands. The justification was merely an extension of the connections that I have outline to colonized lands, which too were to be viewed as brute nature that was available for conquest and control – but only *so long as one was able to portray the inhabitants of the colonized lands in infantilized terms*, as a people who were as yet unprepared – by precisely a *mental lack* of such a notion of *scientific rationality* – to have the right attitudes towards nature and commerce and the statecraft that allows nature to be pursued for commercial gain. It is this integral linking of the new science through its metaphysics with these attitudes that I am calling the "thick" notion of scientific rationality.

There is a fair amount of historical literature by now on the intellectual rationalizations of colonialism, but I have introduced the salient points of an *earlier pre*-colonial period's critique here in order to point out that Gandhi's criticisms had a very long and recognizable tradition going back to the seventeenth century *in the heart of the West* which anticipated in detail and with thoroughly honourable intent, those lamentable developments around the thick notion of scientific rationality. What he called, perhaps confusedly, a "predisposition" of science itself, is exactly what was being expressed in these prescient anxieties that these early freethinkers were voicing about how these alliances around a certain outlook generated by the new science was "thickening" what should otherwise have been an innocuous (and "thin") conception of science and rationality.

Once that point is brought on to centre stage, a standard strategy of the orthodox Enlightenment against fundamental criticisms raised against it, is exposed as defensive posturing. It would be quite wrong and anachronistic to dismiss this initial and early intellectual and perfectly *scientific* source of critique, from which later critiques of the Enlightenment derived, as being irrational, unless one is committed to a very specific orthodox understanding of the Enlightenment, of the sort I am inveighing against. It is essential to the argument of this paper that far from being anti-Enlightenment, Gandhi's early antecedents in the West, going back to the seventeenth century and in recurring heterodox traditions in the West since then, constitute what is, and rightly has been, called "the Radical *Enlightenment*."[9] To dismiss its pantheistic tendencies that I cited, as being unscientific and in violation of norms of rationality, would be to run together in a blatant slippage the general and "thin" use of terms like "scientific" and "rational" with just this "thick" notion of scientific rationality that we have identified above, which had the kind of politically and culturally disastrous consequences that the early dissenters were so jittery about. The appeal to scientific rationality as a defining feature of our modernity trades constantly on just such a slippage, subliminally appealing to the hurrah element of the general and "thin" terms "rational" and "scientific," which we all applaud, to tarnish critics of the Enlightenment such as Gandhi, while ignoring the fact that in

---

[9] See Margaret Jacob, *The Radical Enlightenment: Pantheists, Freemasons, and Republicans*, (Lafayette, LA: Cornerstone Book Publishers, 1981).

their critique the opposition is to the thicker notion of scientific rationality, that was defined in terms of very specific scientific, religious, and commercial alliances.

Were we to apply the *thin* conception of "scientific" and "rationality" (the one that I imagine most of us embrace), the plain fact is that *nobody* in that period was, in any case, getting prizes for leaving God out of the world-view of science. That one should think of God as voluntaristically affecting nature from the outside (as the Newtonians did) rather than sacralizing it from within (as the freethinkers insisted), was not in any way to improve on the *science* involved. Both views were therefore just as "unscientific," just as much in violation of scientific rationality, in the "thin" sense of that term that we would now take for granted. What was in dispute had nothing to do with science or rationality in that attenuated sense at all. What the early dissenting tradition as well as Gandhi were opposed to is the *metaphysical* orthodoxy that grew around Newtonian science and its implications for broader issues of *culture and politics*. This orthodoxy with all of its implications is what has now come to be called "scientific rationality" in the "thick" sense of that term and in the pervasive cheerleading about "the West" and about the "Enlightenment," it has been elevated into a defining ideal, dismissing all opposition as irrationalist, with the hope that accusations of irrationality, because of the *general* stigma that the term imparts in its "*thin*" usage, will disguise the very specific and "thick" sense of rationality and irrationality that are actually being deployed by the opposition. Such (thick) irrationalism is precisely what the dissenters yearned for; and hindsight shows just how admirable a yearning it was.

So the dismissals of Gandhi's critique of the Enlightenment ideals as a kind of irrationalism and nostalgia have blinded us to making explicit the interpretative possibilities for some of his thinking that are opened up by noting his affinities with a longstanding, dissenting tradition in the most radical period in English history. I am not suggesting for a moment that what was radical then could be retained without remainder as being radical today or even at the time when Gandhi was articulating his critique But I *am* saying that it opens up liberating interpretative options for how to read Gandhi as being continuous with a tradition that was clear-eyed about what was implied by the "disenchantment" of the world, to stay with the Weberian term. It is a tradition consisting not just of Gandhi and the early seventeenth century freethinkers, but any number of remarkable literary and philosophical voices in between such as Blake, Shelley, not all of Marx, but one strand in Marx, William Morris, Whitman and Dewey in this country, and countless voices of the non-traditional Left, from the freemasons in the early eighteenth century down to the heterodox Left in our own time, voices such as those of E.P. Thompson and Noam Chomsky, and the vast army of heroic but anonymous organizers of popular grass roots movements – in a word, the West as conceived by the "radical" Enlightenment which has refused to be complacent about the orthodox Enlightenment's legacy of scientific rationality that the early dissenters in England had warned against well over three centuries ago.

To move away now from the specific sacralized formulations of Gandhi and his antecedents in intellectual history, we should be asking in a much more general way, what their view amounts to, once we acknowledge that we have our own intellectual demands for more secular formulations. This is a tractable, historically situated, version of the question I began with: is there something interesting in the secular that is continuous with something in the religious? Even so situated, it is a very large question which requires a far more detailed inquiry than I can give in the little while I have left of what is already quite a long lecture, but I do want to say something now to give at least a very general and preliminary philosophical sense of what I think is the right direction for its answer.

I had said earlier that our own secular ways of re-enchanting a world made brute by the rampant adoption of the ideologies around the thick notion of scientific rationality, turns on seeing the world as "suffused with value," without any compulsion to see this as having its source in the pantheistic terms of a divinity.

Here, then, is how I've allowed myself to think towards that idea. Spinoza, in a profound insight, pointed out that one cannot both intend to do something and predict that one will do it, *at the same time*. Predicting what one will do is done from a detached point of view, when one as it were steps outside of oneself and looks at oneself as others would, from a *third* person point of view. But intending is done from the *first* person point of view of agency itself. And we cannot occupy both points of view on ourselves at once. *Now*, I want to claim that there ought to be *an exactly similar distinction*, not on the points of view that we have *on ourselves* which was Spinoza's concern, but the points of view we have *on the world*. The world *too* can be seen from a detached, third person or an engaged, first person point of view. And it is the availability of the world to us through its value properties (which move us to our first personal engagement with it) that provides the minimal continuity with the sacralized picture – the rest of which we cannot find palatable any longer.

Thus putting it in the most abjectly simple terms, one might for instance find, from a certain perspective of the study of populations and disease and so on, that this or that segment of a population has a certain average daily caloric intake and that they, as a result, die of old age at an average in their late forties, a metaphor for their malnutrition. But that is only one perspective that I could take on the matter, one of detached, roughly scientific, study. I could then switch perspectives and see those very people as being in *need*. And the crucial point is that need is a *value* notion quite unlike the notions of caloric counts and, therefore, it makes *normative* demands on me. To view the world from this quite other perspective is, as I said earlier, to view it from the point of view of engagement rather than detachment. To be able to perceive the evaluative aspects of the world, one therefore has to possess agency, one has to have the capacity to respond to its normative force. In fact, we *experience* ourselves as agents partly *in* the perceptions of such a value-laden world.

Our agency and the evaluative enchantment of the world, then, are inseparably linked. That is why Spinoza's insight about ourselves can be extended outwards onto the world. In a long and unsatisfactory philosophical tradition of moral psychology (deriving from philosophers such as Hume and Adam Smith), values are said to be given to us in our desires and moral sentiments. This is precisely the tradition that leaves out the evaluative properties from being in the world to which our agency responds. So here, then, is the absolutely crucial point. If my extension of Spinoza's point is right, the *objects* of our desires must be *given to us* as desi*rable*, that is, *as* desi*rabilities* or value elements in the world itself. If they were not, if their givenness to us was not as "desirable" but as "desired" (as Hume and Adam Smith's moral psychology claims) then they could only be given to us when we step outside of ourselves and perceive what our desires are from the third person point of view. But that is precisely to abdicate our agency, our *first* person point of view. Agency is possible only if we take the desirabilities or evaluative properties in the world itself as *given* to us *in* the *experience* of our desires.

I have said that these evaluative properties are contained in the world and can be perceived or apprehended as such. But I have also said that this evaluative aspect of the world is nothing, it is darkness, to subjects that do not possess agency, a capacity for normative engagement. One reductive confusion to watch out for here is to think that because subjects capable of agency and engagement alone are capable of perceiving values in the world external to them, that values must therefore *not* be external after all and ultimately come from us. Another – related – confusion is to think that because some people may see some values in the world and others may not (you may see someone as being in need and be moved normatively by it, I may not), it is wrong to think that values are in the world at all and that we respond to them normatively – rather the world is indeed brute and value-free as Newton and Boyle claimed, and it is *we* who through our moral sentiments *make up* values and project them differentially onto the world. This is as confused as saying that because observation of things, of objects in the world, is theory-laden, i.e., because  when we hold different physical theories we will perceive different objects in the world, we must therefore in some sense be making up objects. These confusions may be natural, but they are elementary and are easy to identify and resist.

A more ideological confusion that all this amounts to something unscientific is no less elementary, but being ideological it may be harder to resist. I've said that even irreligious people committed to scientific rationality in the *thin* sense of the term[10] can embrace this way of thinking of the enchantment of the world because I insist that there is nothing unscientific about it. To view nature and the world not as brute but as containing value that makes normative demands on our agency is not by any means to be unscientific. It only means that natural science does not have full coverage of nature. In general, it is not unscientific to say that not all themes about nature are scientific themes. It is only unscientific to give unscientific responses to science's themes – as hypotheses about creationism or intelligent design do (being, as they are, responses to scientific questions about the origins of the universe).

The point here is not the point often made by so many that we do not know very much scientifically. One can say that science knows only a very little bit of what might be known without in any way upsetting the scientistic naturalist picture that I think a re-enchantment of nature would and should upset. The point is not just to be humble about how little we have managed to come to know and may ever come

[10] By rationality in the "thin" sense I mean just the standard codifications of deductive rationality and inductive rationality or confirmation theory, and decision theory.

to know, but to say that nature consists of more than science can know because it is not the *business* of science to cover all that is *in nature*.

Nor is the point the same as the perfectly good point many have made before which is that science has told us how to study nature but not how to study the human subject. The point is rather that there is no studying what is special about human subjectivity *unless we see nature and the world itself* as often describable in terms that are not susceptible to the kind of inquiry that natural science or even social *science* provides. There is a revealing point here about someone like Weber and his legacy. He, among others, is seen as having directed us to what is now fairly widely accepted as an undeniable truth, viz., that what makes the study of *human beings* stand apart from the natural sciences is that such study is "value-laden." But – bizarrely – he never linked this now familiar point explicitly with his own lament about the disenchantment of nature. The fact is that there is no understanding what makes the study of human society stand apart by its value ladenness unless we see that fact as being *of a piece* with an equally fundamental insight about a value laden natural and human environment, in virtue of which our agential engagements with it are prompted. Without that further link the insight that the study of human society stands apart from scientific study in its value-ladenness is incomplete, and the claim to the naturalistic irreducibility of the human subject is shallow.

I don't want to give the slightly misleading impression that *all* I am concerned to deny, in order to gain an enchantment of the world that is continuous with something in the religious, is to deny the scientistic picture which has it that *natural* science has total coverage of the world and nature. In fact that will not suffice and that is not all that I am concerned to say. This is because the scientistic picture accommodates much more than *natural* science.

Under the influence of a familiar orientation in the social sciences, one might aspire to a certain picture of the world that concedes that one does not have to view it as brute. In other words, one can allow that it may contain more than what *natural* science studies, it contains *opportunities* for us to satisfy our desires. Thus, one might say, if I were to take a purely impersonal and scientific perspective on the world, I would see the water in the glass in front of me as H_2O, but with the social scientific broadening of this perspective to include a certain expanded notion of scientific rationality, one could also see that very glass of water as an *opportunity* to satisfy a desire of mine, to quench my thirst. This loosens things up a bit to allow the world to contain such strange things as opportunities, something the physicist or chemist or biologist would never allow nor could study, since opportunities, whatever they are, are not the subject-matter of these sciences. Rather they are the subject matter of Economics and more broadly the social and behavioural sciences which could now be seen to be, among other things, the science of desire-satisfaction in the light of (probabilistic) apprehension of the desire-satisfying properties in the world, i.e., opportunities that the world provides to satisfy our wants and preferences.

But this is not the loosening up of the world that is needed for a secular *enchantment* of the world that is continuous with the religious. Though it grants that the world is not entirely brute and it grants that the world contains something (opportunities) that escapes the purview of the natural sciences, it doesn't grant enough. It may be a first step but to stop there is merely to extend the reach of scientific rationality in the thick sense, it is not to show its limitations in its conception of nature and the world. Nothing short of seeing the world as containing *values* (an older Aristotelian idea, if recent writers such as McDowell read him rightly) does that limitation get revealed, for it is values not opportunities that put *moral* demands on us. Thus even if we respond to others with a view to gratifying our moral sentiments of sympathy towards them, we are not quite yet on board with the depth of the demand that a perception of others needs is the perception of something that puts normative *demands* on our individual and collective agency. It is in this deep respect that Marx's talk of needs in his slogan "From each according to his abilities, to each according to his needs" went beyond the moral psychology of Hume and Adam Smith.

Perceiving opportunities in the world merely tells us that the world is there for satisfying our desires and preferences, however filled with sympathy for others those desires are, but it doesn't conceive of the desires themselves as responding to what I have described as "desirab*ilities*" in the world. This has impoverishing implications for how can may think of more specific questions relevant to politics and political theory, implications I can do no more than hint at here by merely saying that I believe that it is why, for example, the endless bickering within the orthodox enlightenment's framework about the extent to which one may or may not emphasize equality over liberty (or autonomy) cannot *have* an end within that framework precisely because the framework doesn't have the conceptual ingredients to allow even those who favour the emphasis on equality to claim that values like equality are not separable from a fully meaningful *autonomy*, that they are an essential part of one's own *self*-realization (as a result of being moved by an evaluatively enchanted world which our agency collectively inhabits and to whose normative demands our agency responds). In short, equality when it is in concert with a range of other values that the world constrains us with and to which we respond is a value that then becomes an essential part of an *unalienated life*. Nothing short of perceiving in the world values that move our agency to respond in ethical terms, then, will re-enchant it and help to arrest our alienation from it,[11] providing the initial steps to a *secular* version of what Gandhi and the freethinkers of the seventeenth century were struggling to find.

That the deliverances of their struggles yielded sacralized and pantheistic conceptions of the world with which we have little sympathy today, does not at all imply that those struggles were not honourable. But to say that their struggles are honourable is to say that they must be the antecedents to our own philosophical struggles to re-characterize the world and nature, and in doing so to reorient our entire range

[11] Actually the relation between opportunities in the world and values in the world is a close, complicated and interesting one. It is arguable that values in the world cannot be acted on unless we also see the world as containing opportunities. All that I am opposing is that it is *sufficient* to repudiate the picture of a brute nature and world by pointing out that the world contains opportunities. I am not denying that seeing the world as containing opportunities is *necessary* for that repudiation.

of social scientific and historiographic interests away from the obsessively causal explanatory methods that dominate them. This disciplinary reorientation based on such a re-view of nature may have some chance of laying the ground of resistance to the ubiquitously narrowing effects of the orthodox Enlightenment's legacies not just in the universities but in our moral and political lives generally.

In a previous essay of mine called "What is a Muslim?,"[12] I had tried explicitly to locate the forms of political pacification that come from a loss of agency owing to a picture of things in which a third person, rather than a first person, point of view dominates our conception of *ourselves* and our cultural and political identity. In the present lecture, I have tried to integrate those ideas with the politics that grew around the new science for the first time some centuries ago as a result of an increasingly third person conception not of ourselves, but of the *world and nature*. Many more deep connections between metaphysics, moral psychology and politics and culture still need to be drawn which I could not possibly have drawn here and likely don't have the intellectual powers ever to do, before anything of genuinely theoretical ambition is constructed on the subjects of identity, democratic politics, and disenchantment. But even without them it is possible at least to state the issues and aspirations at stake.

What Gandhi's and the early freethinkers' intellectual efforts made *thinkable*, and what I am trying to consolidate in secular terms in my last many remarks, is something that goes measurably beyond what recent scholars have started saying is our best and only bet: the placing of *constraints* on an *essentially utilitarian* framework so as to provide for a social democratic safety net for the worst off. Salutary though the idea of such a safety net is (how could it fail to be given the wretched conditions of the worst off?), it is a project of limited ambition, in which Adam Smith and Hume remain the heroes and Condorcet (among others) is wheeled in as the radical who proposed the sort of requisite constraints we need. In a recent book, Gareth Stedman Jones,[13] chastened by the failures to put into practice more ambitious intellectual frameworks, comes to just these modest conclusions about our world as we have inherited it from these more ambitious theories and their failures. By contrast, the heroes of this essay, Gandhi and the key dissenting figures of the seventeenth century, through whose lens I have been reading him, wanted it to be at least thinkable that that world could be "turned upside down."[14]

---

[12] See "What is a Muslim," *Critical Inquiry*, Summer 1992.

[13] Gareth Stedman Jones, *An End to Poverty? A Historical Debate* (New York: Columbia University Press, 2005).

[14] This paper is a very highly summarized version of a much longer chapter of my forthcoming book "Gandhi's Integrity," attempting to rescue Gandhi from the reputation of being some sort of diehard 'anti-modernist' and situating his anti-Enlightenment ideas instead in a tradition of the 'radical enlightenment' going back to mid-seventeenth century radicals in England and the somewhat later scientific dissenters that are discussed above.

Ideas as Weapons: Militant Islamist Groups in Egypt

Ibrahim Karawan

It is important at the outset to make two sets of distinctions. The first is between Islamic groups which tend to focus on individual redemption, as well as social and cultural reform, and Islamist groups which focus primarily on gaining state power. The second distinction is between political Islamist groups that use peaceful and gradual means to obtain power and militant Islamist groups, or MIGs, who strive primarily to seize state power through violent means.[1] Failing to disaggregate these types is highly problematic for any analysis.

Much has been written during the last quarter century about what some called "the root causes" behind the resort to large-scale violence and terrorism in the Muslim world. Many identified factors which if addressed effectively the threat of terrorism will either cease to exist or will get drastically reduced till it withers away. Among these are the following: economic deprivation and class differences which are conditions that get aggravated further by globalization, and a growing asymmetry of power along ethnic and national lines in an interdependent world linked by the new media.

These features are significant since they can provide causes, triggers, or facilitating conditions for the spread or perpetuation of terrorism. Whether each of them is always or often decisive, is a proposition that should be assessed by comparing its relative explanatory power or relative potency in specific cases. In other words, we should not adopt an explanation because it may make sense, but because we argue it makes more sense than others. This has to be substantiated, and not merely assumed.[2]

I. Karawan
University of Utah
e-mail: ibrahim.karawan@poli-sci.utah.edu

[1] Ibrahim Karawan, The Islamist Impasse (New York: Oxford University Press, 1971), Chapter 1. Regarding militant groups see Saad Eddin Ibrahim, "Egypt's Islamic Militants," MERIP Reports (February 1982), pp. 5–14.

[2] One of the best works that made the case for the primacy of the realm of ideas and belief systems in shaping the activities of militant groups is Mary Habeck, Knowing the Enemy: Jihadist Ideology and the War on Terror (New Haven: Yale University Press, 2006). With regard to the impact on the MIGs of an Islamic thinker such as Ibn Taymiyya see Johannes J.G. Jansen, The Neglected Duty:

I.A. Karawan et al. (eds.), *Values and Violence*,

This paper examines the role of the ideas of a strategic minority of militants in the case of Egypt in justifying a jihadist struggle, maintaining control over rank and file, legitimizing taking grave risks and making huge sacrifices, competing with other militant Islamist groups on the ideological level, and providing programmatic guide or "road maps" for action, not only on the national level but also on the transnational level. In other words, Ideas of Islamist theoreticians play important roles, roles that are not often linked to class structures or international systems. Rather than being marginal as some argue, such ideas play a role in conditioning and guiding the MIG's actions, and not only unexplained variance in their actions. This paper will not dwell on examining the impact of ideas in socio-political life in broad terms, which specialists in history, philosophy, and politics have wrestled with for long.[3] Paraphrasing Judith Goldstein and Robert Keohane, the issue is not whether ideas matter, but how they matter, under what conditions, and the best ways to study their impact.[4]

It has been argued that waves of Islamist militancy in Egypt had significant impact beyond Egypt's borders into the Arab world. The Muslim Brotherhood was started by Hassan al-Banna in Egypt in 1928 and gradually its branches and ideology have spread all over the Arab World. Its resort to violence in the late 1940s via its secret apparatus or al-jihaz al-Khas had inspired other Arabs and Muslims beyond Egypt's borders. What has come to be known as *al-tanzim al-'Alami lil Ikhwan* or the International Organization of the Brothers was largely controlled by Egyptian Ikhwan leaders. It is the Egyptian graduate of Cairo University, Ayman al-Zawahiri, who has been acting for years as the one-man think tank of al Qaeda and its satellite and in recruiting and indoctrinating the young for waves of violence after their training.

At one point or another, the tapes and books of the Egyptian Sheikh Omar Abdel Rahman, were passed from hand to hand from Kuwait to Casablanca, providing the young with radical Islamist views that advocate violence in the name of Islam. More importantly, it was the Egyptian Sayyid Qutb and, to a lesser extent later, his brother Mohammed Qutb, who provided Islamists with their equivalent of V.I. Lenin's "What is to be Done?" In the words of Gilles Kepel, "The Egyptian example . . . stands as a kind of paradigm" against which other manifestations of Islamism can be measured.[5]

The Creed of Sadat's Assassins and Islamic Resurgence in the Middle East (New York: MacMillan, 1986), pp. 161–182. See also Ahmad al-Moussalli, Radical Islamic Fundamentalism: The Ideological and Political Discourse of Sayyid Qutb (Beirut: the American University of Beirut, 1992), Chapters 1 and 2; Bassam Tibi, The Challenge of Fundamentalism: Political Islam and the New World Disorder (Berkeley: University of California Press, 2002), Chapter 1; Reuven Firestone, Jihad: the Origins of Holy War in Islam (New York: Oxford University Press, 1999), Chapters 1 and 2.

[3] Judith Goldstein and Robert Keohane, eds., Ideas and Foreign Policy (Ithaca, New York: Cornell University Press, 1993), pp. 3–4.

[4] Goldstein and Keohane, Ideas and Foreign Policy, pp. 4–6.

[5] Gilles Kepel, Muslim Extremism in Egypt: The Prophet and the Pharaoh (Berkeley: California University Press, 1984), pp. 22–23.

Egypt had a recent experience with violence in the name of Islamism. During the period between 1992 and 1997, the country has suffered from a wave of insurgency launched by militant Islamist groups (MIGs), such as the Islamic Group and the Jihad Organization.[6] In their resort to violence, these Groups did not distinguish between combatants and non-combatants, the military and civilian. Their main objective was to destabilize the regime, seize power, and create an Islamic state. Different from the case of Sadat's assassination, their exercise of violence was based on the notion of a sustained campaign to eradicate what their leaders deemed to be a non-Islamic or anti-Islamic regime.

The fatwas that had characterized the regime as such were crucial for legitimizing the wave of violence that followed. Gunning down a leader was no longer sufficient for them. In other words, the ideas of the top leaders of the MIGs provided a programmatic guide for action. For them, the main task is not pursuing individual redemption or gradual reform. Islamists who go along that incrementalist path suffer from false consciousness. When it comes to correct Islamist action, there is no alternative to a confrontational and combative approach.[7]

Looking for constant and unchanging features of Islam as determining factors behind violence is an exercise in futility. It clearly ignores the difference between the sufi orders for instance and political as well as militant groups. Many Muslims and non-Muslims resent the U.S. policies in the post-Cold War era without ever contemplating the resort to acts of terrorism as militants do along radical ideological lines advocated by few leaders. The failure to differentiate Islamic schools of thought and practice is bound to be misleading and it can contribute to the creation of exaggerated fear and produce serious overextension, outcomes which militants themselves wish if they were to materialize.

The real choice that analysts have with regard to militancy is not between compelling socio-economic and international structures on the one hand and the realm of ideas on the other. Structures and systemic forces do not after all reduce the choices available to activists for any cause, let alone that of militancy, to just one option. Ideological and political leaders in fact often rebel against the notion of the tyranny of structural factors in light of vast asymmetry of power. For Sayed Qutb and Ayman al-Zawahiri such asymmetry is a strong indication of the correctness of their cause and of their commitment to the Islamist struggle.

That is why many of those ideologues start their writings with a comparative and critical review of other Islamist ideas and approaches to the struggle with the objective of demonstrating their futility as well as the superiority of the ideas and the approaches which they advocate. We can see all that in the writings of Sayed Qutb, Salih Sariyyah, Shukri Ahmed Mustapha, Mohamed Abdel Salam Farag, Omar Abdel-Rahman, and Ayman al-Zawahiri. Despite differences in their approaches of moving from what they deemed un-Islamic present to an ideal Islamic future,

---

[6] Ibrahim Karawan, "Egypt: The State and Islamist Militancy," in Dick Clark, ed., Political Islam: Challenges for U.S. Policy (Washington, D.C.: Aspen Institute, 2005), p. 7.

[7] Yvonne Haddad, "Sayyid Qutb: Ideologue of Islamic Revival," in John Esposito (ed.), Voices of Resurgent Islam (New York: Oxford University Press, 1983), p. 85.

they saw their roles in mapping this transition along the path of correct ideas as a major obligation that sets them apart from other Islamists activists. In other words, those leaders come up with ideas that not only challenge existing systems and their prevailing corruption but also confront the views of other Islamist groups in a way that makes them the vanguard to be followed.[8]

It is important to examine some of these battles over the justifications of violence. For the theoreticians of Islamist militancy, gaining the support of the masses was not ranked as a top priority. They stressed rather confronting ideologically the Muslim Brothers (MB) who had been much more influential. Since many MBs were released from prison by Sadat, they have opted to abandon violence as an instrument to establish an Islamic state, to act within existing dimensions of political legitimacy, and to adopt gradual approach to spreading Islamic value in society. For militants, a successful confrontation with the very ideology of the Muslim Brothers was almost more necessary than their own confrontation with what they considered to be the secular state. For the leaders of the MIGs, Muslim Brothers deviated from the correct path of Islam when they bestowed legitimacy on a state that does claim that 70% or 80% of its laws are in accordance with the Islamic law. According to them, Islamic laws represent an indivisible package that must be actually implemented in its entirety.

MIG leaders launched a campaign of condemnation against the willingness of the Muslim Brotherhood to compromise with "the infidel holders of state power," as a betrayal of the legacy of the "great Islamist martyr, Sayyid Qutb." Leaders of these groups argued that according to Qutb "Jahiliya is not a period in time, but a condition is repeated every time society veers from the Islamic way, whether in the past, the present, or the future." To de-legitimize the peaceful approach of the Muslim Brothers further, militant leaders argued that this approach has lent credence to Western notions of popular sovereignty instead of Quranic sovereignty and government of humans instead of the government of God.[9]

According to one of the leaders of the Jihad Organization, 'Aboud al-Zumur, one of the top theoreticians of violence who is still imprisoned in Egypt, the Egyptian state would never respond to moral appeals, religious sermons, party practices, legal arguments, or peaceful marches. The current regimes must be eradicated through an insurrectional approach. This uncompromising approach must be planned and

---

[8] Aboud al-Zumur, "Manhaj Jama'at al-Jihad al-Islami," unpublished paper written in the Turah Prison, 1986. See also an interview with Omar Abdel Rahman, in al-Arab (London), June 26, 27, 1987, al-Watan (Kuwait), February 23, 1989, and al-Anbaa (Kuwait), October 10, 1984 and June 16, 1989, an interview with Karam Zuhdi, one of the top leaders of the Islamic Group in the Kuwaiti newspaper al-Anbaa, August 19, 1989, pp. 14–15. See also Emmanuel Sivan, Radical Islam (New Haven: Yale University Press, 1985) and Yahya Sadowski, "Egypt's Islamic Movement," Middle East Insight, no. 5 (1987), pp. 37–45.

[9] On that clash between the MIGs and the Muslim Brothers, see Nabil Omar in Roz al-Youssef, no. 3141, August 22, 1988, pp. 12–15.

pursued by a believing minority, a vanguard of an Islamic generation of a new type, or a select few who know what nobody else in the Muslim world knows.[10]

According to this road map, three dimensions are necessary. First, the militant Islamist action has to shake and undermine one key foundation of the state, namely its *hybah* or sense of invincibility, which the state is keen on cultivating and perpetuating in society. That is why Sadat was assassinated while reviewing a televised military parade in a restricted area and protected by many Egyptian security agencies. The speaker of the Parliament was gunned down in downtown Cairo and in the middle of the day. A well-protected Prime Minister, Interior Ministers, and a chief-editor of a leading publication who was close to Mubarak were targeted for assassination in the middle of Cairo. In upper Egypt, MIGs attacked police stations and police officers as symbols of the state. Behind these acts was the interest of the MIG leaders in sending a message to the society at large, the essence of which was that the state was a paper tiger and that the symbols of the state were vulnerable to the long arms of these groups. If the Egyptian state could not protect its top officials and its strategically located institutions, the society at large should not fear their power or hybah based on the state's perceived coercive power.

Second, the state is not only *hybah*, but it is also *mawarid* (resources) through which it can buy societal support. Violence by MIGs must be aimed at undermining the extractive and resource generating power of the state. The strikes by the MIGs against tourism, given its significance to the Egyptian economy, does illustrate that notion. They did not have to launch many large-scale operations. The spillover effects of a few well-publicized operations such as that of Luxor had a very negative impact on tourism and the economy. Militant leaders also argued that state owned banks should be attacked to make depositors withdraw their funds in a hurry with the damaging repercussions of that on the financial system at large.

---

[10] For the ideas of the Muslim Brothers in response see Salim al-Bahnassawi, Shubuhat Hawla al-Fikr al-Islami al-Mu'asir [Doubts about the Contemporary Islamic Thought], (al-Mansurah: Dar al-Wafaa, 1989), pp. 321–323. See also by Salim al-Bahnassawi, Adwaa'alla Ma'alim fi al-Tariq [Shedding Light on Signposts] (Kuwait: Dar al-Buhuth, 1985), pp. 234–235 and Sayyid Qutb Bayna al-'atifah wa al-Mawdou'iya [Sayyid Qutb] Between Emotionalism and Objectivity (Alexandria: Dar al-Da'wa, 1986), pp. 19–22, 50–55. In response to the attacks of the MIG leaders, the leader of the Muslim Brotherhood, Mustafa Mashhour wrote under the title, "Moderates and Will Remain Moderates, God Willing," in al-Shaab, February 2, 1989. For more on the ideas of the MIG leaders see Gilles Kepel, Muslim Extremism in Egypt: The Prophet and the Pharoah (London: al-Saqi Books, 1985), and also by Gilles Keper see Jihad: The Trail of Political Islam (Cambridge: Harvard University Press, 2002). For more see Rudolph Peters, Jihad in Classical and Modern Islam (Princeton: Markus Weiner Publishers, 1996). Given that many militants have joined al Qaeda and influenced its ideas, see Michael Doran, "The Pragmatic Fanaticism of al Qaeda: An anatomy of Extremism," Political Science Quarterly, 117, no. 2 (2002); Nimrod Raphaeli, "Ayman Muhammad Rabi' al-Zawahiri: The Making of an arch Terrorist," Terrorism and Political Violence, 14, no. 4 (Winter 2002), pp. 1–22; Quintan Wiktorowicz and John Kaltner, "Killing in the name of Islam: al Qaeda's Justification for September 11," Middle East Policy, 10, no. 2 (Summer 2003) and by someone who knew al-Zawahiri and the evolution of his ideas quite well see Montasser al-Zayat, The Road to al-Qa'eda: The Story of Osama bin Laden's Right-Hand Man (London: Pluto, 2003).

Third, in addition to targeting the coercive and the extractive arms of the state, the MIG leaders identified the importance of provoking state leaders to strike back massively and indiscriminately through emergency laws, wide-spread arrests, restricting movements of citizens, and thus creating deeper grievances and resentment in society. In other words, the reaction of the state to their provocative acts, may deepen the dilemma of the state and make it ripe for failure.

Any strategy of confronting the MIGs requires understanding their mindset, their defining characteristics, and their programmatic guides for action pursued by them. The fact that they claim to act in the name of religion does not mean that analysis of their actions should look primarily for clues in religious texts. Such search for the so-called essence of Islam will not go far. "Islamic arguments" may be used to justify and critique diametrically opposed positions. Islam has generated over many centuries a vast body of texts, scholarship, and judgments through which rival actors can search and find support for contradictory positions on matters of war and peace, or tolerance and intolerance. Militants use parts from the Qur'an to legitimize their actions. However, their positions were considered misguided and distorted by many Islamic thinkers.

Rather than looking at certain religious texts for explanations of militant actions, one should examine the ideas and beliefs of militant leaders regarding notions of time, reliance on small numbers, modalities of recruitment, funding sources, fronts of action, and provoking adversaries to overreact to violence. It is important to recall that MIGs are highly centralized and personalized. Understanding the mindset or the operational code of the few at the top of their pyramids of power can have significant explanatory power with regard to their strategies. Let me look briefly at six fundamental arguments.

First: Shrinking Time

Even though the MIGs share with the political Islamists the declared objective of gaining power and building Islamic regimes, they use violent means in ways that reflect their sense of the emergency and urgency of direct confrontational action. They have a particular sense of time (to be found in statements of Sayyid Qutb, Ayman al-Zawahiri, among others) that sees Islam as facing a cluster of grave dangers from within and also from without. The rulers within are collaborators with forces of international domination and the grave threats include cultural, political and economic marginalization, identity distortion, as well as subservience to Western forces. Under these conditions, the threat is not only that of continued inequality vis-à-vis the West, but also growing subjugation to it and the loss of Islamic values, identity, and authenticity.

According to these perspectives, if such trends continue, the menace they pose to Islamic beliefs will become enormous and the repercussions for the umma as a whole can become catastrophic. It is similar to the image of five minutes to midnight, an image that requires not an incremental action to face and overcome it, but an uncompromising rage for God. From such perspective, the option of doing nothing is similar to working within existing systems of domination: namely a non-starter. Even if militant actions did not produce the intended results, their success in creating a powerful climate of both fear and unpredictability in the hearts and minds of the enemies of the militants is desirable according to their thinkers.

This is a distinct militant perspective and not just an Islamist one in general. Political Islamists like the Muslim Brothers, for instance, have a different assessment of the time dimension as it relates to their reading of the current situation. In fact, they believe that time has worked in their own favor and that Islamist reliance on violent means is both unwarranted and counter productive. Nasser in Egypt, Bourgiba in Tunisia, Atatourk in Turkey, and the Shah of Iran, the Muslim Brothers argued, tried to weaken the social and political influence of the Islamic movements and ideas in their societies, but they failed drastically. Why should Islamists resort to violence and then provoke massive repression by the state unnecessarily at a time when the moderate Islamists are winning the game or gaining greater support in society whenever they have the opportunity to engage in competitive politics in syndicates, parliaments, associations, and student governments?

Leaders of the Muslim Brothers also stressed not only that they opted for the path of moderation as the most prudent or most calculated course of action, but that in doing so they were actually following the example of the Prophet. The Supreme Guide of the Muslim Brothers, Mostafa Mashhour, published a series of articles that stressed that the Prophet, who should obviously be a model for all Muslims, did not venture to start his struggle by using force to destroy the idols of the Jahiliya and to defeat his enemies. Rather, he began his confrontational campaign only after eight years had passed since he migrated from Mecca to Medina and after the Islamic movement gained enough power to conquer Mecca. According to Mashhour, while commanding power is truly an Islamic duty, power should not be automatically or impulsively equated with the rush to violence. His critique of MIG leaders whom he described as "misguided enthusiasts" has almost approached the notion of what may be described as an infantile disorder in Islamism. The first level of power is doctrinal which is manifested in the strength of religious faith and conviction. The second level is organizational power, as illustrated in group cohesion and effectiveness. Finally, there is the material power as reflected in military strength as well as military preparedness.

For leaders of militant groups to start their action by military confrontation is to rush to a course of action which is doomed to fail, according to the leaders of the Muslim Brothers, because such approach disregards "the example of the Prophet Mohammed." However, the leaders of the MIGs insist that the key criteria of success for them is not to have more bearded men going to newly built mosques, or to see more women wearing veils in public places, or to have six of every ten books published in this Arab country or the other deal with Islamic topics. For them, the real and central task is to seize state power and establish Islamic systems because without that, the passing of time will pose grave threats to Islamic beliefs and interests. This is why they believe in what is known as *hatmiyat al-muwajahah* or inevitability of confrontation according to a member of the Jihad group and former colonel in Egyptian Military Intelligence, Abboud al-Zumur. Combative action is unavoidable for MIGs. Compromising strategies such as those adopted by Muslim Brothers by working within existing systems or competing with non-Islamist forces through elections are both misleading and deviationist.

Second: The Superiority of Small Numbers

Most of the MIGs are composed of a small number of cadres relatives to the military and security institutions they have to confront. Clearly, one has to take into account that while the cadres that implement their strategy of violence are tiny minority, others are involved in the process in planning, funding, intelligence, and training, among the activities necessary for the functioning of these groups. Even with taking that into account, memoirs of militant leaders and estimates by security agencies agree that their numbers have been small. In most cases, these groups were not willing to trust much more potential recruits whom they might suspected as possible infiltrators working for the enemy, namely state or foreign security agencies.

Militant groups find in their small numbers an evidence of the ideological correctness of their cause as a "believing minority" or a "Quranic generation of a new type" in the image of the early Muslims during the foundation period of Islam. This vanguard, as described by Sayyed Qutb, a leading ideologue of Islamist militancy, has to be composed of the select few who know what nobody else knows. They have to be small because the society at large and not only the leadership of the regime is corrupt. It is based on an image of a dedicated vanguard that directs the struggle, not according to what the masses may want at a given moment in time, but in pursuit of what they ought to have wanted, but did not. Here the analogy with V. I. Lenin's conceptualization of the distinctiveness of the communist party is rather striking, though important details are decidedly different. I am referring here to the central and directing role played by an elite that monopolizes knowledge of the direction of change and commands the strategy necessary to attain it through disciplined hierarchical organization. If left to itself, the society is not likely to rise in favor of revolution or to for taking grave risks. No wonder that many writers have compared Qutb's book Signposts on the Road to Lenin's What is to be Done. Such Islamic vanguard is a minority that can be trusted as the true Muslims who act as fighters at a critical stage when loyalty is more important than large numbers.

Small numbers are not only ideologically correct, but they also provide certain strategic and tactical advantages. They can hide in a sea of millions and tens of millions. It may be difficult for state authorities to strike at these small numbers with a high degree of precision and when they do miss, they can pay a heavy political price. Small numbers of militant cadres and their handlers can inflict heavy human and economic losses, as the events of September 11 and the cases of Algeria and Egypt have demonstrated already. In the case of Egypt in 1997, just six militants were able to inflict considerable harm on the economy by striking and killing 58 foreign tourists which was followed by massive cancellation of tourist reservations.

A lower number of militants launched painful strikes in Taba and Sharm al-Sheikh. Such small numbers have proven to be hard to identify and difficult to trace similar to what has happened in the underground trains in London and in trains in Spain and India.[11]

Third: The Logic of Recruitment

Most of the leaders of the MIGs have been recipients of modern, not religious education. After all Salih Sariyah has received a Ph.D degree in educational science, Ayman al-Zawahiri is an MD, Magdi al-Safti the leader of Those Who Have Been Saved From Hell was an MD too, Osama bin Laden studied public administration, Mohamed Atta, who played an important role in the September 11 operation had studied computer sciences. Very few philosophy, sociology, or political science majors have managed to join the MIGs or to be among their top leaders!

Their familiarity with modern sciences and their ideological commitment give them a sense of not being intimidated by the West. For them the overall package offered by the West is divisible, not indivisible. They can deal with the Western systems in a selective way. Recent recruitment of members in militant groups seems to value those with scientific background, use computers, and know foreign languages. These skills may be necessary to do research on the internet, fly airplanes, or know which airport has a low security record. They were sent to their ultimate targets after exposure to more or less similar environments, such as sending cadres with no known record of involvement in violence to European countries first before forwarding them to the U.S. in the case of the September 11 operation.

MIGs are centered around an individual at the top of the hierarchy but with separate "one man think tanks" who report directly to the leader to maximize operational secrecy, without significant institutionalization of decision making. The case of Ali Mohammed provides an example. Many of them are often upper-middle-class types who engage in these activities because they want to, not because they have to do it from a socio-economic vantage point. The case of Ayman al-Zawahiri with his quite affluent family background illustrates another example in that regard.[12]

The mechanisms of member recruitment are kinship, friendship and worship plus regional and tribal affiliations. They are marked by the politicization of religiosity over a period of time. The operational principle of the MIGs is that they are looking for a select few. Obviously, one does not apply to join these MIGs, but when one arrives, he is approached and tested more than once before joining the group. There is recruitment of individuals and cooptation of whole groups. It started with the war in Afghanistan when militant groups from Egypt and Algeria were recruited by Usama Bin Laden. His group provided the funding and the zeal. The leaders of the

---

[11] See Jessica Stern, Terror in the Name of God: Why Religious Militants Kill (New York: Harper Collins, 2003), pp. 261–277.

[12] See Lawrence Wright, "The Man Behind Bin Laden," The New Yorker, September 16, 2002.

Egyptian MIGs have provided the strategic thinking and training. The outcome was a cartel of sorts. Each side had what the other exactly lacked. It could be argued that as the Saudi state hires Egyptian experts in development, the MIGs hire experts in violence to plan attacks and fight way beyond the borders of their country.

Fourth: Privatization of Funding

At the beginning of the Islamist resurgence, particularly after the oil boom, militant groups relied on state funding from one Muslim country or another. They learned quickly that it was a risky enterprise to depend on such aid. More prudent from their perspective was to rely on remittances from their members and sympathizers working in the oil-producing countries in the Middle East. Remittances were not subjected to restrictions. The amount of resources involved was huge. If those sending money sent back only 10% of their incomes, the revenues generated would have been significant in funding Jihad, buying weapons, supporting families of imprisoned members, and so on.

Donations for the Muslim fighters in Chechnya, Bosnia, Kosovo, Kashmir, or Palestine in response to a wave of publicity and agitation about the religious duty to give in order to end the suffering of innocent Muslims in one of these places can produce good results in terms of revenues. Of course, there is no way to verify that the money would not be used for other purposes. This constant state of fundraising has been going on in supermarkets, sports clubs, banks and business institutions. It is important to remember that contributing or tabarau' is one of the ways of deleting sins in preparation for the Day of Judgment. Another possible way is fasting. Perhaps, for some, financial contribution to Islamic charity organizations is often seen as easier than the alternative!

Fifth: Shifting Fronts

The MIGs move from national to international contexts based on expediency or an assessment of the strategic situation they face. Here is one example from the Middle East: During the period of 1979–1982, the hopes of the leaders of the MIGs got high as the acts of Islamist militancy escalated in Saudi Arabia, Egypt, and Syria. Other cases of militancy have materialized in Jordan, Iraq, Yemen, and Algeria over the following two decades. However, the dominos expected to fall into the hands of the MIGs did not do that. The states targeted by their campaigns proved to be more resilient, more cunning, and more repressive than many anticipated. The regimes expected to collapse "in the short run" are still with us; and if they actually happen to disintegrate, there is no reason to conclude that the MIGs will be their inheritors. Militant roads to power through assassination, military coups, and insurrection had a vast record of failures in achieving their objectives.

When the MIGs found their paths to power blocked, they began to develop alternative strategies. Some sought to reach ceasefires with their regimes in order to deal with their political and organizational losses and internal divisions (e.g., the Jihad group).

The attacks by the MIGs against American targets starting in 1996 reflect that shift which culminated in attacks on major symbols of American economic and military power in New York and Washington, D.C. The groups behind these attacks hoped to return to their home countries with two messages. To their masses, they had this message: "Why are you afraid of America? America is basically a paper tiger! We are not humiliated anymore after these strikes." To the regimes in their home countries that had a high level of dependence on the U.S., they had this message: "If America could not protect its most secure military institutions from our long arm, why should you or anyone else think that it would protect you?" In short, they were asserting through a series of dramatic deeds that they really have a global reach powerful enough to strike at their enemies everywhere.

Sixth: Cumulative Provocation

The last component of the ideas of the MIGs is what may be described as the logic of cumulative provocation." The leaders of the MIGs tell us and tell their followers that their primary objective is to shake what they deem to be the state's basic foundation, namely its *hybah* or the sense of awe it engenders among the masses. This *hybah* is to be undone by demonstrating the state's failure to protect its leaders and its own interests.

In response, states are not expected to simply do nothing. Doing nothing under such conditions can amount to committing political suicide. MIGs aim to provoke the state machinery to strike back indiscriminately that the societal resentment of emergency laws, mass searches and mass arrests, restrictions on movement, and heavy repression could weaken the legitimacy of the state in the eyes of its society and/or the credibility of its policies on the international level. They hoped this would have happened in the case of September 11. Imagine if, in response to these events, U.S. authorities were so provoked to intern tens of thousands of Muslims living in the U.S. and the political repercussions in the Muslim world of such acts.

Concluding Remarks

In the battle for dominance over the "Islamic street" in Egypt, the approach of the Muslim Brothers (which adhered to non-violence) seems to have gained the upper hand. The MIGs became less effective and they have clearly stalemated. Clearly, they did not reach the masses and state repression and the stand of the Muslim Brothers on the ideological front have largely isolated and weakened them. The Ministry of Religious Endowment organized religious consciousness caravans particularly in localities where the MIGs had significant influence, though the militants, with there elitist posture, did not rate the support of the masses as a particularly a high priority in their action.[13] By 2002, the imprisoned militant leaders characterized their earlier strategy as a great sin that cost many innocent people their lives without valid religious reasons. Leaders of the groups, such as Karam Zuhdy, Najih Ibrahim, Safwat Abdel-Ghani, Ali al-Sharif, and the rest of the members of the Shura Council, produced at least four monographs that denounced militancy. The group remains committed to refraining from violence even though many of its members were already released from prisons. Their ideas turned into weapons and programs for action, but their failures triggered years later an interest in reassessing their policy as well as ideology.

Among the reasons behind the failure, there are factors pertaining to their own divisions and fragmentation. In fact, conflicts between the MIGs have been so acute that each group refused to recognize the legitimacy of the others. Each tended to be centered around one individual leader who commanded total loyalty, a personality cult of sorts, that discouraged cooperation across group lines. No single group could seize power by itself or was willing to build an alliance with others. The centrality of the group leader nourished dreams of despotism among MIG leaders. Obviously this is not the case of political Islamist groups such as the Muslim Brotherhood.

---

[13] See Gilles Kepel, "God Strikes Back: Reislamization Movements in Contemporary History," in Contention, ed. Nikki Keddie, 2, no. 1 (Fall 1992), pp. 151–160; Ibrahim Karawan, "Reislamization Movements According to Kepel: On Striking Back and Striking Out," in Contention, ed. Nikki Keddie, 2, no.1 (Fall 1992), pp. 161–179.

Female Terrorists: Martyrdom and Gender Equality

Marilyn Friedman

Women's Suicide Terrorism: Some Background

Suicide terrorism is especially deadly. In the period from 1980 through 2003, just 3% of the terrorist attacks around the world were suicide attacks. Yet, according to Robert Pape, who collected comprehensive data on those attacks, they caused 48% of all the deaths due to terrorism during that time. And this figure ignores the huge losses of September 11th.[1]

This chapter is about female suicide terrorists. Female gender can be advantageous to terrorism generally. Women can sometimes be more *effective* as terrorists than men.[2] Gender stereotypes lead authorities to monitor suspicious young men for signs of terrorist activity and to ignore women. Also, cultural norms of modesty sometimes protect female terrorists from body searches by male authorities. Female terrorists often find it easier than men to gain access to target sites wearing explosives under their clothing. As well, women's terrorist acts may also attract more of the desired publicity than men's terrorist acts; public audiences are both repelled and fascinated by women who kill.[3]

In addition to their general advantages for terrorism, women can become *suicide* terrorists relatively easily. For one thing, suicide explosive belts are easily hidden under many types of women's clothing. Also, there is no need to plan an escape for a suicide terrorist, thus making it more effective and cheaper than other forms of terrorism, something that is true whether the terrorist is female or male. In addition, if successful, the suicide terrorist dies in the act so her terrorist group does not

M. Friedman
Washington University St. Louis
e-mail: friedman@artsci.wustl.edu

[1] Robert A. Pape, *Dying to Win: The Strategic Logic of Suicide Terrorism* (New York: Random House, 2005), p. 6.

[2] Karla Cunningham, "Cross-Regional Trends in Female Terrorism," *Studies in Conflict & Terrorism*, 26 (2003), pp. 171–195; Karla Cunningham, "Countering Female Terrorism," *Studies in Conflict & Terrorism*, 30 (2007), pp. 113–129.

[3] Debra D. Zedalis, "Female Suicide Bombers" [electronic resource] (Carlisle, PA: U.S. Army War College, Strategic Studies Institute, 2004), p. 7.

I.A. Karawan et al. (eds.), *Values and Violence*,

have to worry that she might become an informant, perhaps under torture. As well, detonating an explosive belt does not require a lot of training, combat strength, endurance, stealth, or knowledge of how to handle weapons. Ordinary women, who lack special military training and have usually not been socialized for physical aggression, can be suicide terrorists. This ready availability of female recruits effectively doubles the number of potential actors for a terrorist cause.

Four hundred sixty-two people committed acts of suicide terrorism from 1980–2003. Robert Pape was able to get information about the sex of 381 of them. Fifty-nine of those, or 15% of the total of 462, are known to have been female.[4] The first known suicide bombing by a female occurred in 1985. Khyadali Sana, a 16 year old girl who worked with the Syrian Socialist National Party killed two Israeli soldiers who were part of the Israeli occupation of Lebanon, by driving a truck into their military convoy.[5]

Since 1985, women have carried out suicide missions in Lebanon, Israel, Turkey, Sri Lanka, Russia, and Chechnya. They have worked with Al Aqsa Martyr's Brigade, Palestinian Islamic Jihad, Hamas, the Chechen rebels, the Kurdistan Workers Party, and the Liberation Tigers of Tamil Eelam.[6] The percentages have varied greatly from group to group. Al Qaeda had used no females up to 2003, whereas over 50% of the suicide terrorists for both the Chechens and the Kurdistan Workers' Party had been women.

The Liberation Tigers of Tamil Eelam (who are fighting to secede from Sri Lanka) had committed about 200 suicide attacks in the period from 1980 through 2003 and had used women in 30–40% of those missions. The female suicide bomber unit of the Tamil Tigers is called the Black Tigresses. These women have been particularly effective. The female suicide terrorist with the highest-ranking victim ever was a Black Tigress named Thenmuli Rajaratnam, and known as Dhanu. According to some accounts, Dhanu had been raped and had had four brothers killed by Indian soldiers who were part of a so-called Indian Peacekeeping Force that had entered Sri Lanka to quell the Tamil Tigers' insurgency.[7] (Other women with the Tamil Tigers are also believed to have been the victims of rape, either by Indian soldiers or the soldiers of the majority ethnic group of Sri Lanka, the Sinhalese.) The Tamil community stigmatizes a woman whom they believe to have been raped and she has no chance of getting married or having children in the community.

Rajiv Gandhi was the Prime Minister of India who had ordered the military intervention into Sri Lanka in which Dhanu is supposed to have been raped. In 1991, Gandhi was out of office but was campaigning to be re-elected Prime Minister. Dhanu attended one of Gandhi's political rallies. She got close to him, put a garland of flowers around his neck, bowed at his feet, detonated the explosive belt she was wearing, and blew the two of them up, killing sixteen other people in the blast.[8]

---

[4] Pape, *Dying to Win*, p. 208.

[5] Zedalis, "Female Suicide Bombers," p. 2.

[6] Zedalis, "Female Suicide Bombers," p. 2.

[7] Pape, *Dying to Win*, p. 226.

[8] Pape, *Dying to Win*, p. 230; Zedalis, "Female Suicide Bombers," p. 2; *Wikipedia*, http://en.wikipedia.org/wiki/Thenmuli_Rajaratnam, accessed 8 Feb 07.

In this essay, I shall focus on the recent suicide terrorism by Palestinian women. In Part II, I shall sketch my views on whether terrorism in general can ever be justified and briefly consider the additional moral issues that are raised by *suicide* terrorism. In Part III, I shall briefly explore the cultural conditions that surround Palestinian women's acts of suicide terrorism on behalf of the Palestinian cause. In Palestinian society, it appears that women, who are otherwise widely subordinated to men, can attain a heroic sort of gender equality by participating in suicide terrorism on behalf of the people in their fight against the Israeli occupation. The story of Wafa Idris, the first female suicide terrorist for the Palestinians, will center this discussion in Part IV. Finally, in Part V, I shall ask what is added to the general moral equation when the terrorist is a female from a female-subordinated culture. I shall explore whether a culture of women's subordination makes any difference to the moral meaning suicidal terrorist acts. Does the moral significance of terrorism change when the terrorist is a woman whose culture subordinates her to men and denies her any other political role?

The Morality of Suicide Terrorism

Terrorism, these days, is typically defined in part in terms of the intended killing of innocent persons and/or noncombatants. If terrorism by definition involves the aim to kill persons who are either innocent or noncombatants,[9] then terrorist acts are aimed to kill people who do not deserve to be the intended targets of military force. From a deontological perspective, the death of a person who does not deserve to be killed cannot be justified merely in terms of a greater social good of any old sort. It could only be justified, if at all, for the sake of preventing a greater evil of at least the same degree of moral magnitude as the killing of the innocent, for example, to prevent an even greater number of killings of innocent persons. Other conditions may also apply. The bar is thus set very high for justifying an act of terrorism.

One way of trying to justify an act of terrorism is to see whether it meets a variety of requirements that are like those of Just War Theory. Under the rules of Just War Theory, unprovoked aggression against a state by another state is a legitimate cause for which the attacked state may use military force in self-defense. Suppose we widen the concept of aggression so that it includes forms of oppression such as military occupation or forceful colonization by another state. An occupation may involve conditions that are brutal and humiliating to the occupied people. Conditions may have already gone on for a generation or more with no end in sight. Peaceful means of ending the occupation may, for all practical purposes, have been exhausted to no avail. The only means of resisting such an occupation may include violent actions that risk innocent or noncombatant lives among the people of the occupying

---

[9] The distinction between "innocent persons" and "noncombatants" is not relevant to this discussion so I leave unspecified the exact wording for those persons who ought not to be intended targets of violent military or terrorist action.

nation. Such violent resistance is, in effect, terrorism. Under some circumstances terrorist self-defense could conceivably constitute the "least of all evils" for the occupied people. The point is that when a people's homeland is occupied or colonized and they are oppressed, humiliated, impoverished, violated, or brutalized by another state, then terrorism by the occupied people and on their behalf might be justified.

Just War Theory prescribes that a war be fought in such a way that innocent persons or noncombatants are not to be intentionally targeted with lethal force except as the side-effect of violent action aimed at some other, legitimate military purpose. However, terrorism by definition involves the moral wrong of aiming to kill people who do not deserve to be targeted with lethal force. In order for terrorism to be justified in a manner analogous to the rules of Just War Theory, the targeting of innocents and/or noncombatants must not be the direct aim of the terrorist act. It is hard to see how the argument would go because targeting innocent civilians is essential to the way in which terrorist acts *terrorize* the enemy people. Perhaps the terrorist killing of innocent people could be regarded as the necessary means by which to terrorize an enemy population, itself a necessary means for pressuring the enemy state into ending its occupation or oppression of the terrorist's own people. For the sake of this discussion, I leave that possibility open. Even with this possibility left open, the bar for justifying terrorism is very high.[10]

I will proceed by assuming without further argument both that acts of terrorism can be justified and that the justification would be a very demanding one. My *question* is this: what does *suicide* add to the morality of a terrorist act? Does anything about the nature or justification of a terrorist act change when the terrorist carries out the act by means that involve her deliberate, self-inflicted death?

We know that suicide can increase the *effectiveness* of terrorism by a huge magnitude. If terrorists are willing to die in their actions, they can get closer to highly populated target sites and cause a large number of casualties using few resources of their own. September 11th taught that lesson tragically. My question, however, is not about the practical effectiveness of the suicidal dimension of some terrorist acts, but rather about its *moral significance*. Imagine an act of terrorism that leads to the death of, say, ten people. Would the act be morally better, worse, or merely different on moral grounds if the same ten people were killed by a terrorist who also killed herself intentionally in the process?

Some people believe that suicide is always morally wrong. For them, the moral wrongness of suicide terrorism would be the simple sum of the wrongness of the terrorist's suicide added to the wrongness of the terrorist's killing of other people. However, my concern is not with the morality of suicide in its own right. I am asking how the morality of the terrorist killing of other persons is affected by the fact that the terrorist kills herself in the *process* of killing others. This is a question about whether the self-inflicted death of a terrorist changes the moral significance of her killing of innocent others, something she does for an independent political cause.

---

[10] Other Just War requirements, such as necessity and proportionality, must also be met.

Perhaps someone who kills others, a wrongful act on the fact of it, might be adding a mitigating factor by giving up her own life in the process. Is there something possibly *redemptive* about the sacrifice this involves? Or does the terrorist's self-inflicted death make her act of killing others morally worse than it would be if she remained alive? Does her suicide aggravate or does it mitigate the wrongness of what she does?

Here is how Christoph Reuter summarizes some of the moral significance that suicide terrorism had for the target population. He writes that terrorists:

> remind us that there are people who consider their struggle – whatever the cause – to be more important than their own lives. They stir up fear in us.... For there is no way to retaliate against attackers who strike, not merely in order to kill people, but to die at the same stroke. They annihilate the entire logic of power, since no credible threat can be made against someone who has no desire to survive.... Deterrence, punishment, and retaliation all become meaningless.[11]

Reuter captures much of the moral meaning and impact that makes suicide terrorism so riveting and fearful. Even the citizens of powerful nations must cringe in the face of threats that they may not be able to thwart despite all their technological "superiority."

Terrorism has been described as part politics and part theatre. One aim of terrorist violence is to gain publicity and win sympathy for the cause. Suicide terrorism can aid in this effort by the dramatic manner in which the terrorist shows the strength of her commitment to the cause. This display of dedication has a powerful impact on the various public audiences of the terrorist act. The commitment that suicide fighters display may win sympathizers for her cause even among the people who are her enemies, her targets. When witnessing someone's extreme, self-sacrificing devotion to a cause, even some people in the population attacked by a suicide terrorist may give some thought to whether the terrorist was fighting for a worthwhile cause. And for those who continue to oppose the suicide terrorist's cause, the rhetorical power of her display of commitment is so forceful that it must be publicly discredited. She must be portrayed as a fanatic or an extremist, or perhaps as the brain-washed dupe of her manipulative "handlers." In order to make it seem legitimate to fight against a group whose members are willing to die when fighting back, one has to represent their suicidal dedication as completely irrational and pathological.

This portrait, however, is not persuasive to all audiences. Some cultures bolster the rhetorical effectiveness of suicidal terrorism by providing a powerful concept in terms of which it can be understood and supported. The relevant concept is that of the "martyr." A terrorist who sacrifices her life to carry out an act of terrorism for a just cause is a *martyr* for the cause. Martyrdom has an exalted history in various religions. A martyr who defends what a religious tradition holds to be of highest value – either the god worshiped by the faithful, the community of the faithful on earth,

[11] Christoph Reuter, *My Life is a Weapon: A Modern History of Suicide Bombing* (Princeton: Princeton University Press, 2002), pp. 2–3.

or the martyr's own public expression of faithfulness to that god – is glorified as a hero or a saint, or both. For receptive audiences, the religious reverence for martyrs has a powerful meaning and rhetorical impact. Today, it is sometimes invoked to celebrate acts of suicide terrorism and to revere the memories of those who carry it out.

Robert Pape argues that suicide terrorism, in the period from 1980–2003 that he studied, was based primarily not on religious motives but on nationalist concerns. He argues that recent suicide terrorism has been aimed at resisting what the terrorists regarded as an unjust occupation by a foreign power of the terrorists' homeland. Even when religious reasons were invoked, Pape believes that recent suicide terrorism has been based primarily on *nationalistic* aims.[12]

A nationalistic aim does not render the concept of martyrdom irrelevant. If the idea of religious martyrdom is prominent in a culture, this can predispose the people of that culture toward revering anyone who makes a supreme personal sacrifice for any earthly cause. As well, the concept of martyrdom can be defined in secular as well as religious terms. Dying for one's religion does seem to be part of the primary definition of "martyr." However, dying for one's principles or a worthy cause is a secondary definition of the concept.[13] The Tamil Tigers and the Kurdistan Workers' Party are both secular terrorist groups that recruit and train people for suicide missions for the political wellbeing of their respective people. If a military occupation brutalizes and humiliates a people, leaving them with no realistic options for peaceful resistance, then sacrificing oneself for the sake of liberating one's people from an oppressive occupation could well be a noble cause that elevates one's act of suicide to the status of secular martyrdom.[14]

Thus both secular and religious terrorist groups can offer the individual terrorist a mode of behavior that has transcendent value and that will be understood that way by her people. The religious martyr sacrifices herself for her god; the secular nationalist martyr sacrifices herself for her people. Either sort of martyr sacrifices herself for the sake of something she regards as more elevated and worthy than her own individual life. A suicide terrorist who acts on a motivation that combines both religious and secular aims, by understanding the good of her people as *embodying* the glory of her god has, so to speak, the best of both worlds.

So martyrdom, whether religious or secular, has transcendent moral meaning and value for those who believe in the martyr's cause. However, one morally important feature that must not be ignored when calculating the morality of suicide terrorism is the fact that such an act is never *merely* martyrdom, never *merely* the self-inflicted death of the agent for the sake of her people. Suicide terrorism is always also aimed at killing others. Suicide terrorism is martyrdom that kills. Its

---

12 Pape, *Dying to Win*, p. 21.

13 *Funk & Wagnalls Standard Dictionary of the English Language*, International Edition (Chicago: Encyclopedia Britannica, 1965), p. 782.

14 As noted earlier, the additional requirements of Just War Theory must also be met, for example, that the innocent persons targeted for attack were somehow not ultimately the intended targets of the terrorist cause.

immediate victims are typically the random mix of people who happen to be at a particular location at the wrong time.[15] Sometimes they are children or babies. The killing of innocents or noncombatants is a necessary feature of an act of terrorism according to contemporary definitions of terrorism[16] because this killing is the means by which terrorism *terrorizes* a larger population, making them fear for their own safety. Any moral assessment of suicide terrorism as martyrdom must not fail to take account of its aim to kill other people *besides* the agent, people who are innocent in a morally relevant sense. The death of innocent persons or noncombatants is always a *prima facie* moral wrong. As I suggested earlier, it can be justified only to prevent a still greater moral wrong of at least the same high degree of moral importance.

My suggestion about the morality of the suicidal aspect of suicide terrorism is this: Suppose that we do not consider suicide to be necessarily wrong in its own right. Suppose also that we allow that terrorism might be justified as self-defense by a people against aggression or oppression. On the basis of these two assumptions, the added moral weight of suicide is going to depend on the independent moral value of the terrorist act. If terrorism is unjustified under the circumstances, then it is a tragic additional waste for a terrorist to sacrifice herself for the cause. On the other hand, if the terrorist act is justified, then the terrorist's suicide adds to it the moral value of supreme self-sacrifice for an oppressed people. Like any act of supreme self-sacrifice for a greater good, the act would be both noble and tragic at the same time.

Everything depends, however, on the independent moral value of the terrorist act under the circumstances, and in particular, on whether the intentional killing of innocents or noncombatants is justifiable at all in that case. The suicidal dimension, I claim, does not have an independent moral significance of its own. Its moral value is derivative from that of the act of killing others in that context. If terrorism is justified on a particular occasion, the suicide of the terrorist is tragically heroic and noble. If the terrorism is unjustified, the suicide of the terrorist is merely a wasteful added tragedy.

The main question of this essay is this: what else enters the moral equation when a suicide terrorist is *female*? How does the gender of the terrorist affect the moral assessment of suicide terrorism? I shall try to answer this question by considering one society that has recently given rise to female suicide terrorists, the Palestinian society in its struggle against the Israeli occupation of the West Bank and Gaza.

---

[15] If a violent act is aimed solely at killing a politically or militarily important official, then I call it "assassination" rather than terrorism. However, if precautions are not taken to prevent the (reasonably expected) collateral deaths of innocent bystanders, then the act is more complex and moves into the category of terrorism once again.

[16] See, for example, Saul Smilansky, "Terrorism, Justification, and Illusion," *Ethics*, 114 (July 2004), pp. 790–791.

Palestinian Terrorism

The first Palestinian intifada, or uprising, began in 1987. According to journalist Barbara Victor, during that time, women found themselves engaged in active support of the uprising and in handling many daily tasks and routines normally carried out by men, such as running the family business, in the way that has happened to women in many societies during wartime. Many people in Palestinian society regarded women's participation in the First Intifada as a positive step toward eliminating women's second-class status in their community. This development did not progress evenly. A year after the uprising began, radical Islamic Palestinian groups such as Hamas and Islamic Jihad had become powerful and they opposed women's participation in public and violent demonstrations. The moderate Palestinian leadership did not want to divide the Palestinian struggle, so women's equality took a back seat to the national movement.[17]

Suicide bombings were not prominent in the First Intifada. They gained greater prominence in the Second Intifida, which started in 2000. Hamas and Islamic Jihad seemed to have no problem finding men who would carry out such missions. However, Yassir Arafat, who was at that time fighting to retain political power among Palestinians, did have trouble finding men to carry out suicide bombings for his faction, Fatah, and its militant wing, the al-Aqsa Martyr's Brigade.[18] That is, until he came up with a new strategy.

On January 27, 2002, Arafat gave a speech at his compound in Ramallah intended specifically for Palestinian women. Over a thousand women came to hear him speak. Here is how journalist Barbara Victor describes the occasion:

> "To thunderous applause and cheers, Arafat stressed the importance of the woman's role in the Intifada.... [H]e made it clear that women were not only welcome but expected to participate in armed resistance against Israeli occupation. "Women and men are equal," he proclaimed...." You are my army of roses that will crush Israeli tanks."[19]

In his speech, Arafat used the word, *shahida*, a feminine form of *shahide,* the Arabic word for martyr. He was calling upon Palestinian women to become *shahidas* to help end the Israeli oppression of the Palestinian people.

That afternoon, Wafa Idris became the first *shahida* to commit suicide bombing for the Palestinian cause. Al-Aqsa Martyr's Brigade claimed her as their own. A new trend had begun for Palestinians. Wafa Idris blew herself up in a shopping district in Jerusalem, killing an 81 year old man and injuring a hundred other people.[20] After her suicide, Wafa Idris became a hero to her own people; her photograph was displayed on buildings all over the West Bank. All did not go well for her family; the Israeli military partially destroyed the family home. However, this response did

---

[17] Barbara Victor, *Army of Roses: Inside the World of Palestinian Women Suicide Bombers* (Rodale: U.S.A., 2003), pp. 9–12.

[18] Victor, *Army of Roses*, pp. 16–18.

[19] Victor, *Army of Roses*, p. 19.

[20] Zedalis, "Female Suicide Bombers," p. 2.

not discourage many Palestinian girls and women from seeking to follow in Wafa Idris's footsteps.[21]

Victor writes that despite Arafat's "army of roses" speech, Fatah and the al-Aqsa Martyr's Brigade at first resisted claiming responsibility for Wafa Idris's attack because they still felt uncomfortable about the use of women as suicide terrorists. Only after the reaction "in the street" was "unanimously positive" did they claim responsibility for her attack. According to Victor, "a burst of spontaneous praise" arose "throughout the Arab world." Halim Qandil, acting editor of *Al-Arabi*, the Nasserities weekly magazine, wrote in an editorial that "She is Joan of Arc, Jesus Christ, and the Mona Lisa . . . ."[22]

Unlike Al-Aqsa Martyr's Brigade which is a secular group, Islamic Jihad and Hamas are fundamentalist Islamic. They had been avoiding the use of women as terrorists for a variety of religious reasons.[23] However, the positive response by Palestinian society to female terrorist acts obviously influenced the fundamentalist groups to modify their doctrines. After Wafa Idris, subsequent female suicide terrorists came from the fundamentalist Muslim as well as the secular Palestinian groups. In May 2003, Heiba Daragmeh became the first woman to commit suicide bombing for Palestinian Islamic Jihad. In January 2004, Reem Riashi became the first woman to commit suicide bombing for Hamas.[24] The religious concerns have apparently been put in abeyance.

For any female suicide terrorist, there are both general conditions that might explain why they committed suicide terrorism and special circumstances unique to their own particular biographies. It is probable that, as with any suicide terrorist, the full explanation in each case combines a number of factors, some that are general and some that are unique to the case at hand. I am particularly interested to see how female suicide terrorists might be affected by coming from a society that casts women in a severely subordinated or constrained social role. Let us consider the story of Wafa Idris to see how the relevant factors combined in her case.

The Story of Wafa Idris

Iyad Sarraj, a Palestinian psychiatrist from Gaza who has studied the Palestinian societal influences that produce *shahides* and *shahidas* believes that the First Intifada produced the more recent suicide bombers. The children who saw "their fathers and other male relatives being beaten and humiliated by Israeli forces" have become "the martyrs of today." Barbara Victor thinks Wafa Idris went through this experience. Wafa was 12 years old during the start of the First Intifada in 1987 when a friend lost

---

[21] Victor, *Army of Roses*, pp. 5–6, 182–191.

[22] Victor, *Army of Roses*, pp. 25–27.

[23] See David Cook, "Women Fighting in Jihad?," *Studies in Conflict & Terrorism*, 28 (2005), pp. 375–384.

[24] Mia Bloom, *Dying to Kill: The Allure of Suicide Terror* (New York: Columbia University Press, 2005), pp. 150, 152.

an eye due to Israeli military action. Wafa's mother, Mabrook Idris, says that Wafa was affected "very deeply" by this event. In general, according to Wafa's mother, Wafa had a great deal of nationalist fervor, more so than religious fervor. Wafa's childhood friend claimed that Wafa loved her homeland and often said that "she wished she could sacrifice herself for the country."[25] However, her personal life, which may have been a crucial determinant of her ultimate motivation to become a *shahida*, tells us more about Palestinian society's treatment of women than it does about the Israeli occupation.

Wafa had gotten married in 1991 at the age of about sixteen. She did not became pregnant until 1998. Unfortunately, the pregnancy ended in a premature delivery of a stillborn daughter. The family was devastated by this event. The husband, Ahmed, was accused by his own family of being weak and unable to create an infant that could survive. After this trauma, a "local" doctor told Wafa and her husband, in front of their families, that she was unable to carry a pregnancy to term. She would never have children, the doctor said. Her husband says that after losing the baby, Wafa stopped doing household chores, stopped eating and talking, and stayed in bed all the time. A close friend, Itimad Abu Lidbeh, says that when Wafa lost her baby, "she lost the will to live." Her husband was utterly distraught. He simply did not know how to change Wafa's behavior. So in 1998, he divorced her. She was about twenty-four years old. Two weeks later, Ahmed married another woman.[26]

Wafa Idris' mother, Mabrook Idris, said, "My daughter's husband divorced her because she couldn't have children.... Wafa knew she could never marry again because a divorced woman is tainted... She was young, intelligent, and beautiful and had nothing to live for." Wafa's friends later said to Victor that "Wafa was never quite the same since her husband divorced her several years before." Although she had an "independent mind" and a "profound feeling of resentment against the occupation," she also was prone to "bouts of melancholy and depression."[27]

Wafa's husband sent her back to her childhood home. However, her father had died years earlier and her brothers, who were therefore responsible for her support, were not wealthy and had their own families to support. Because of her divorce and believed sterility, she could never marry again. As well, Wafa had no cultural options for becoming self-sufficient. According to Dr. Mira Tzoreff, a professor at Ben Gurion University who specializes in women's history in the Middle East, Wafa could not leave the situation to make a better life for herself elsewhere. It is even more disgraceful to run away from family and friends in Palestinian society under such circumstances than to stay. As Tzoreff said to Victor, "she [Wafa] had no future" and was "the ultimate *shahida*": "a talented young woman, married and divorced because she was sterile, desperate because she knew perfectly well there was no future for her in any aspect of the Palestinian society. She knew better than anyone else that the only way for her to come out against this miserable situation was

---

[25] Victor, *Army of Roses*, pp. 27, 40.
[26] Victor, *Army of Roses*, pp. 42–49.
[27] Victor, *Army of Roses*, p. 41.

to kill herself." Islam provided an option. As Tzoreff told Victor, "In our religion, martyrs don't die. They simply move to Paradise and live a better life with dignity." Wafa Idris blew herself up in an act of martyrdom on January 28, 2002 at the age of twenty-eight.[28]

After Wafa's death, her mother had a memorial ceremony for her. A genuine funeral was not possible. The Israeli government does not release the bodies of terrorists to their families but instead buries them in unmarked graves. So Wafa's mother had a ceremony with an empty pine box. At least 2000 mourners marched behind it through the streets of Ramallah, where the family lived. There were ceremonies all over Gaza and the West Bank for Wafa. Fatah held a symbolic funeral in which she was eulogized in these words, "Wafa's martyrdom restored honor to the national role of the Palestinian woman, sketched the most wonderful pictures of heroism in the long battle for national liberation."[29]

Wafa's influence spread quickly. In 2002, Victor visited a school in the Jabaliya refugee camp in Gaza that was run by the U.N. She visited a class of 6 year old girls and asked the class how many wanted to be martyrs, *shahidas*. "All the hands went up." Then she visited a class of 12 year olds. Several girls in this group as well asserted that they wanted to be *shahidas*. One said, "To follow my brother. And, in honor of Wafa Idris, who proved that women can do as much as men." Other girls did not mention Wafa Idris by name but had clearly succumbed to the allure of becoming female martyr-heroes for the Palestinian people. Another girl said to Victor, "I want to give back to my country everything I can, in gratitude to God. It is only normal that I give the most I can, which is my life, to free my people from occupation." Still another girl said, "My reasons are obvious: the massacre in Jenin, in Jabaliya, in Nablus, Gaza, and Ramallah. There is no hope for peace because the Jews have no heart. They destroy everything and every Palestinian knows there is no chance to make peace with them." She said her parents were "proud" of her plans "because they know it is the only way to conquer the Jews and have a homeland." According to Victor, there is now a Women for Wafa Idris Martyr's Brigade that females can join as early as age 15, and "commit their acts of *shahida* in their idol's name."[30]

The Meaning and Morality of Women's Suicide Terrorism[31]

A suicide bomber's action can have a symbolic meaning for a community, but the meaning will differ depending on which community, which audience, is in question.[32] There are at least three target audiences for terrorists. First there is the

---

[28] Victor, *Army of Roses*, pp. 47–48.

[29] Victor, *Army of Roses*, pp. 53–54.

[30] Victor, *Army of Roses*, pp. 182–191; Bloom, *Dying to Kill*, p. 148.

[31] The analysis in this chapter depends heavily on Barbara Victor's account of Palestinian society. If that account is inaccurate, the analysis may still apply to any societies that happen to be like the portrait Victor paints of Palestinian society.

[32] This paragraph was influenced by discussion with Eric Schliesser.

terrorist's own community on behalf of which she acts. Her terrorist action may promote their support for a violent uprising and may encourage new recruits to volunteer for the cause. Second, there is the community of those who are attacked, the community that the terrorist hopes to *terrorize*. The terrorist usually wants to scare and coerce this community into doing something that will end the oppression of her people. She may also be motivated by sheer revenge, in which case, no further good needs to come of her action since it achieves its end simply by its own destructiveness. Third, there is a larger regional or world community from which the terrorist may want to promote support for her cause or at least sympathy, an absence of resistance, and an absence of support for the nation that oppresses her people. How a terrorist's act is understood by its various audiences is a crucial part of its effectiveness.

For the acts of female terrorists, there may be at least two narratives of understanding that differ from those in terms of which the actions of male terrorists can be understood. First, there is the widespread stereotype of the female gender. Women are widely considered to be much less violent than men, so women's violence is unexpected and may reflect differently on her cause than does the violence of men. Expectations of women's less violent nature can often enhance the symbolic meaning of a female terrorist's act from the standpoint of various publics. By being performed by a non-violent sort of person, a woman's terrorist act makes a testimonial claim that the oppression of her people is so bad that even women are desperate enough to resist it with violence.

Of special interest in this paper is a second sort of symbolic meaning that sometimes attaches to women's terrorist acts, especially to acts of suicidal terrorism. As Barbara Victor asks, what about "the idea that women who die as martyrs will finally achieve *equality to men*"?[33] Suppose the society from which a female terrorist comes is characterized by severe gender inequality that constrains the life prospects of the terrorist herself. And suppose that, in addition, that society glorifies martyrdom on behalf of supremely worthy causes, such as defending the faith or defending the people against threatening forces. Against these two background conditions, a woman's act of suicide terrorism takes on a special meaning that is unavailable to male terrorists. Male terrorists may be able to become martyrs for their people's faith or survival as a community. However only women's martyrdom for the same cause can acquire the added meaning of promoting an unusual sort of gender equality for members of the society in question. In case daily conditions in the society do not afford equality to women in all contexts or relationships, women's martyrdom would contrast with daily life in virtue of realizing that end.

In Palestinian society, according to Barbara Victor, women are otherwise subordinated to men, sometimes in very severe ways. However, martyrdom offers the prospect of realizing gender "equality" when women commit the ultimate sacrifice for the community. Women can martyr themselves as part of the resistance against

---

[33] Victor, *Army of Roses*, p. 46 (italics mine).

the Israeli occupation. As martyrs, they can attain a public recognition of equality that may be unavailable through ordinary daily living.

How should we understand that aspect of Palestinian women's suicide terrorism? Under normal conditions, that is, conditions devoid of terrorist violence, anything that promotes social recognition of gender equality is, on the face of it (I am assuming), a good thing. Any act that elevates women's social standing and cultural esteem would be, in that respect, worthwhile. An act that is otherwise morally neutral or mixed, but not seriously wrong, would gain moral value if it brought women's social standing closer to that of men.

However, it seems tragically ludicrous to suggest that an act of killing innocent people could gain moral value by promoting women's equality. Do we want women's equality to be achieved at the cost of blood? Even a staunch defender of women's rights would not be tempted by this thought. Or would they? Before we consider this option, let's clear away some other issues.

There are obvious reasons to wonder whether Palestinian women are choosing voluntarily to become suicide terrorists. Some of these women are motivated by traumatic personal experiences that seem to compromise the voluntariness of their choices. These experiences may include the death of a relative or friend due to Israeli military power. Experiences of that sort, to be sure, may not differ from the experiences of many male suicide terrorists.[34] However, at least some of the women have also suffered personally in ways that directly reflected their subordinate status as women within Palestinian society. Some, like Wafa Idris, have been marginalized or stigmatized and their options severely curtailed because they became somehow "unsuitable" for marriage or motherhood. Others may have suffered dishonor, and dishonored their families, because they engaged in some sexual transgression or were the mere victims of sexual transgression that was perpetrated against them.

Victor claims that Palestinian women live under "stringent... social and religious rules." A Palestinian woman can get into trouble for looking at a man or refusing to marry. If she sleeps with a man or, worse yet, gets pregnant, she "disgraces the family and risks death at the hands of her male relatives." Women face "punishment and prohibition" in their society in addition to the hopelessness of the occupation. So, "if they are offered equality and respect only by becoming martyrs, it is not surprising that there is an increasing number of Palestinian women who are opting for the latter alternative."[35] Barbara Victor writes that Palestinian women

> understand from the beginning that men do not accept them as equals or look upon them as warriors within their ranks until they achieve Paradise and are accepted as such at Allah's table. But by then they are dead. And there are no women who can testify to having had those promises fulfilled in another life.[36]

---

[34] Some commentators believe that personal factors are emphasized more in the explanations given for women's terrorist acts than they are in the explanations given for men's terrorist acts.

[35] Victor, *Army of Roses*, pp. 193–194.

[36] Victor, *Army of Roses*, p. 235.

The conditions of being marginalized, stigmatized, or dishonored, with no other options available, are hardly conducive to a genuinely voluntary choice of whether or not to end it all in a blaze of redemptive martyrdom glory. Whether their choices to sacrifice their lives are voluntary choices thus seems to be an open question, no matter how legitimate the nationalist cause on behalf of which they sacrifice themselves.

One way to think about the voluntariness of choices to become martyrs is to consider whether such choices are *rational* for women to make. A completely irrational choice seems more likely to have been the product of pressure or coercion rather than the product of the woman's careful consideration of the context. Martyrdom's primary meaning is as a religious ideal. If martyrdom is done for religious reasons, we would have to consider whether it really constitutes a religious good and is rewarded in Paradise, as the Islamic account promises. Whether one takes religious martyrdom seriously or not has a great deal to do with one's own religious commitments.

If martyrdom is done for *nationalistic* reasons, the situation is more widely open to speculation. I have suggested that suicide terrorism undertaken to free a people from occupation or oppression derives its value from the value of the nationalist cause and whether or not this cause has sufficient moral weight to overcome the burden of justifying the killing of innocent persons. This takes us back to the conditions that might or might not justify terrorism. If terrorism is not justified for the Palestinian cause, then martyrdom adds only more tragedy to the act of terrorism. If terrorism *is* justified for the Palestinian cause, then terrorism carried out by means of suicide or martyrdom would seem to add additional moral value to the act. Indeed, from the standpoint of Palestinian people, the suicide terrorist is probably regarded as a hero. This applies to both female and male suicide terrorists. Women have just as much (or as little) genuine reason to choose martyrdom as do men. Since the choice may have reason on its side, the concerns of nationalism provide no basis for suspecting that Palestinian women are being irrational or nonvoluntary when choosing to sacrifice themselves for their people.

Is women's self-sacrifice different from that of men? Does it matter that self-sacrifice is often women's lot in life? Is women's martyrdom for the Palestinian people tainted by the fact that women around the world are often called upon to sacrifice their identities, their interests, and their individual well-being for the greater good of others? Is the call of terrorist martyrdom merely a tragic extension of this same old demand on women's lives? Women's martyrdom seems not to be a liberating opportunity for them but a sad extension of the sacrifices they have always been called upon to make.

Yet nationalist martyrdom may involve a self-sacrifice that differs in kind from the sort of self-sacrifice that is part of women's typical social role. In a society in which women are largely excluded from political or public life, women are not routinely called upon to make sacrifices at a level of high public heroism. This sort of role is left to men who are held responsible for the crucially important defense of the nation or people and who are usually the only ones to share in the glory and public adulation that most societies confer on those who achieve political or military heroism. If women are allowed or encouraged to contribute to the military defense of a nation, it is important that the self-sacrifice this involves is not limited to women only. Nationalistic self-sacrifice brings a level of cultural honor and esteem that is beyond anything normally available to women in severely female-subordinated societies.

To be sure, some of the terrorist's personal motivation to become a martyr may come from the earthly "rewards" she believes that martyrdom will bring her or her family. According to Dr. Abdul Aziz al-Rantisi, a spokesperson for Hamas (quoted by Victor), whichever group takes credit for a suicide bombing, whether Hamas, Islamic Jihad, or the Palestinian Authory, gives a "lifetime stipend" of $400 per month to the families of men who commit suicide bombing. However, a distinct gender *in*equality appears in this practice. It seems that the militant groups give only *$200* per month to the families of *female* suicide terrorists.[37] This is not exactly gender equality in the economics of martyrdom.

Does this unequal posthumous treatment of the *shahides* and *shahidas* affect the meaning of martyrdom for female suicide terrorists? It certainly limits what the female suicide terrorists accomplish here on earth by their martyrdom. Yet it does not eliminate the equality entirely. A smaller stipend may still represent more money than a woman could otherwise bring into a family's life. And the degree of honor that has been bestowed on the memories of the female suicide terrorists and on their families seems, by all accounts, genuine and widespread throughout Palestinian society. In the public understanding of those women, they are true national heroes.

However, women's voluntariness may be compromised in other ways. Women are also pressured by the brutalities and humiliations of the occupation itself. These constraints were well expressed by a Palestinian woman whom Victor encountered during the Lebanese war in the 1980s. Victor had entered the Sabra and Shatilla refugee camps in Beirut in 1982, after the massacres that occurred there. She approached a Palestinian woman who was sitting on the ground amidst the "stench of death," holding a lifeless child. The woman realized that Victor was an American after Victor asked a few questions. The woman replied in good English, "You American women talk constantly of equality. Well, you can take a lesson from us Palestinian women. We *die* in equal numbers to the men."[38] If the suffering caused by the occupation is a reason for a Palestinian man to seek to martyr himself in resistance to it, then it would seem to be equally so for a Palestinian woman. Given these conditions, there is no reason to think Palestinian women are making nonvoluntary choices when they become martyrs.

However, there is still one more reason to wonder about the voluntariness of women's choices to become suicide terrorists. There is some evidence that terrorist recruiters have pressured women to become terrorists. Based on research into the lives of Idris and three other women who followed in her footsteps, Victor claims that the women were never recruited to be suicide bombers by other women. All

---

[37] Victor, *Army of Roses*, p. 35.

[38] Victor, *Army of Roses*, p. 2 (italics mine).

their recruiters and trainers had been men. Victor also claims that the four women she studied, along with other women she interviewed who had tried and failed to become martyrs, "had personal problems that made their lives untenable within their own culture and society."[39] Victor questioned some of the male recruiters and claims that all of them had managed to convince the women that only their martyrdom would redeem them and their families for some dishonor resulting either from the women's transgressions or wrongs committed by their male family members.[40] Thus there are reasons for thinking that the men who recruited Wafa Idris and some of the other female terrorists were either using pressure tactics or exploiting the women's constrained social positions – or both – in order to convince the women to become suicide terrorists. This evidence provides a different reason for doubting the voluntariness of the women's choices.

As Jon Elster points out, the leaders of terrorist organizations that recruit suicide terrorists may have reasons and motivations that differ from those of the individual terrorists themselves.[41] For example, the terrorist leaders may try to recruit would-be martyrs by using religious ideas to which they, the leaders, are not committed. More importantly for this discussion, terrorist leaders may recruit would-be *female* martyrs by using the lure of gender equality to which the leaders are not themselves committed. Women might become easier to recruit if they are made to believe they can realize gender equality only by engaging in terrorist suicide for their people. In that case, the leaders would be exploiting the facts of women's subordination in combination with the prevailing rhetorical narrative that declares women's suicide terrorism to be a victory for women's liberation. Victor claims that male Palestinian leaders "package the notions of equality, respect, and reverence so artfully that it becomes impossible for the vulnerable, fragile, and naïve girl or distraught young woman not to buy into them."[42]

Because of these social pressures on women, Victor argues that the balance of responsibility for women's terrorism shifts toward the male society leaders who create or perpetuate women's inequality and then convince women that the only way to achieve equality is to kill themselves and others. Victor argues that the most immoral act is committed by the male terrorist leaders who recruit, train, and direct women to kill themselves and others "under the guise of equality," the saving of their reputations, or the promise of "a better life in Paradise."[43] The suggestion seems to

---

[39] Victor, *Army of Roses*, p. 7. Elsewhere, I have raised concerns about these sorts of explanations of the terrorist acts of women; see my "Female Terrorists: What Difference Does Gender Make?," unpublished paper, presented at North American Society for Social Philosophy, University of Victoria, Victoria, Canada, August 2006. There may be a general tendency to explain women's violent actions in personal terms, rather than in terms of political or nationalist commitments. In the present context, I leave these issues aside.

[40] Victor, *Army of Roses*, pp. 7–8.

[41] Jon Elster, "Motivations and Beliefs in Suicide Missions," in Diego Gambetta (ed.), *Making Sense of Suicide Missions* (Oxford: Oxford University Press, 2005), pp. 246–258.

[42] Victor, *Army of Roses*, p. 235.

[43] In Victor's view, men have a greater variety of "attractive" opportunities for their lives, so their choices to become suicide bombers are made more freely; *Army of Roses*, p. 288.

be in part that the female terrorists are *less* responsible for what they do than their male handlers because the women are not choosing their acts voluntarily; instead they are dupes of their handlers.

If the promise of gender equality were an illusion cooked up by terrorist leaders to lure women to suicidal terrorist acts, would a woman's choice to become a suicide terrorist therefore be nonvoluntary? According to Victor, some female Palestinian political activists agree with her reservations about the gender equality of Palestinian martyrdom. Leila Khalid is a famous female Palestinian terrorist from the 1970s who engaged in airplane hijackings but never suicide terrorism.[44] Still alive in 2002, and a political activist at the time, she told Barbara Victor that "men and women should struggle for our homeland equally because all of us suffer equally under occupation." However, she rejected the idea that women should seek equality as *suicide* bombers. "Everyone is equal in death – rich, poor, Arab, Jew, Christian, we are all equal. I would rather see women equal to men in life."[45]

Yet against this background of reasons for thinking Palestinian women's suicide terrorism does not realize genuine gender equality and is not chosen voluntarily, there are considerations on the other side. As noted earlier, Palestinians do seem to regard acts that Westerners call "suicide terrorism" as having the nobility of martyrdom – martyrdom undertaken for the good cause of ending the Israeli occupation and bringing freedom and dignity to the Palestinian people. Children declare that they want to die for their people as Wafa Idris did, and her picture is reputedly posted on public buildings all over the West Bank, as are the pictures of other martyrs for the Palestinians, both male and female. The *shahidas* as well as the *shahides* are praised, honored, and revered in death.

Even some Palestinian feminists seem to tolerate the *shahidas*, if not to honor them. Alice Chalvi founded the Women's Network, a group advocating women's rights in the Middle East. She had previously been a professor at Hebrew University in Jerusalem and had worked together with Israeli and Palestinian feminists. She said to Victor, "If a society prizes above all else the readiness to fight for your country, if that is such a criterion for excellence, then you cannot exclude women just because they are women. It doesn't seem right that women should be excluded from attaining that kind of glory, and one can argue in a perverted way that everything has to be open to women, and if everything includes dying or killing oneself in battle, then that has to be acceptable as well."[46]

Women's suicide terrorism could further the cause of women's equality by undermining the stereotype of women as non-violent, a trait often associated with weakness and culturally scorned. Women's suicide terrorism might promote future respect for women of the sort that men get for contributing to national defense. Female suicide terrorists could be promoting equality of societal esteem and standing

---

[44] Her group was the Popular Front for the Liberation of Palestine, a Marxist and communist group. In 1970, after a failed airplane hijacking attempt, she was apprehended and then released later in a trade of prisoners for captures hostages; Victor, *Army of Roses*, p. 61.

[45] Victor, *Army of Roses.*, pp. 63–64.

[46] Victor, *Army of Roses*, p. 236.

for women in the future by their public acts of unusual, non-stereotypical self-sacrifice on behalf of their people. The women's actions might cause some real change in cultural attitudes that leads to future gains in women's social stature and a lessening of the strictures that constrain them.

Women's terrorist activism might promote women's equality despite the fact that terrorist leaders had no such aim in mind when recruiting or training those women. Women would be "equal" in that they were undertaking difficult missions of national self-defense along with men; their very acts of suicide terrorism would constitute the playing of an equal role in the serious business of defending their people against the occupation. If Palestinian society is currently justified in resisting the Israeli occupation by the use of terrorist force, then there seems to be no reason why women should refrain from undertaking those risky or self-destructive actions on behalf of their people. This would not be violence for the sake of the glorification of violence. It would be violence only as a means of legitimate self-defense against an illegitimate occupation, and a means to seek freedom, dignity, and self-government for Palestinian society.

As well, even if the families of female martyrs are not paid as much for the loss of their daughters as they would be for the loss of their sons, still there is some payment and a good deal of publicized reverence for the women. Because there have been fewer female suicide terrorists than male suicide terrorists among the Palestinians, and because women's terrorist actions are still a novelty, the individual women gain a great deal more publicity and, it seems, a great deal more honor among the Palestinians than the individual men.

It is crucial to emphasize that the aim to achieve gender equality does not, *in itself*, justify or excuse the terrorist killing of innocent persons or noncombatants. Women's subordination within Palestinian society certainly does not justify terrorism against Israel. Israeli citizens are not the ones who perpetrate women's subordination in Palestinian society. Considerations of gender equality are tangential to the reasons that might do the work of justifying the terrorism. The justification of terrorism by Palestinians has to do with whether the Israeli occupation of the West Bank and Gaza constitutes illegitimate aggression against, or oppression of, the Palestinian people. Women's subordination in Palestinian society does not justify Palestinian women in killing Israeli citizens who happen randomly and by terrible bad luck to be in the wrong shopping mall at the wrong time.

However, if terrorism on behalf of the Palestinian people is independently justified, then it becomes relevant to consider the possibility that a suicidal terrorist act by a woman might have its own valuable consequences over and above what would be true of suicide terrorism by a Palestinian man. Her act but not his would constitute or promote an unusual sort of gender equality in her culture. The (presumably) justified aim of resisting the oppression of her society would converge with the (presumably) justified impact of elevating the status of women in her society.

Jon Elster distinguishes two sorts of values that suicide terrorism can promote for the terrorist and her group.[47] First, there is the instrumental value of efficiently

[47] Elster, "Motivations and Beliefs in Suicide Missions," p. 255.

killing the largest number of enemy deaths for the smallest number of terrorist deaths. However, more important in this context, there is the symbolic value of a self-inflicted death carried out for political ends. Suicide terrorism symbolizes extreme commitment to the cause on the parts of the terrorists. Elster suggests that this symbolic value is greater if the terrorist is a "healthy person" with a great deal to lose by dying.

My argument has been that acts of suicide terrorism by *women* who are from, and acting on behalf of, a female-subordinated society can realize symbolic values beyond what men can realize by their suicide terrorism. This higher symbolic value is realized in part because women are regarded as non-violent. It is also realized when a few women make the ultimate sacrifice for their people that men also make and that is highly revered when men make it. Women's martyrdom for their people can display to the world that women as well as men can show the highest level of nationalistic virtue a community can demand of its members for the sake of its survival and well-being. In martyrdom, women can give as much to their communities as can men in a way that is as fully public and political as any act men can perform. People in the nation that is *targeted* for terrorism may not be able to empathize with this aspect of women's suicide terrorism for it is targeted against them. Nevertheless, for the sake of understanding the appeal of suicide terrorism to Palestinian women, this meaning of their actions should not be ignored.

To conclude: there are at least three components that should be part of the assessment of acts of suicide terrorism by Palestinian women. First, any act of terrorism involves the killing of innocent persons or noncombatants and, in this respect, such acts are clearly immoral on the face of it. However, second, Just War Theory can provide a model for trying to justify terrorist acts as forms of legitimate violent action against military aggression or oppression by another nation or state. The terrorist killing of innocents would have to be a necessary part of resistance to aggression or oppression and must not be a direct aim in its own right; rather, it must be in some genuine sense an unintended but necessary means of actions aimed at resisting the aggression or oppression. And the terrorist resistance movement must meet all the other sorts of requirements that are part of Just War Theory.

Third, the subordination of women in Palestinian society generally must be taken into account. This subordination creates a background against which, *if* Palestinian terrorism is permissible on independent grounds, then *women's* acts of suicidal terrorism against the occupation of the Palestinian people take on an additional meaning and moral significance as the acts of women. Even if they were not attempting to gain gender equality by their actions, female Palestinian terrorists may unwittingly contribute to that end by their terrorist acts. Promoting gender equality does not, in itself, eliminate the immorality of an act of unjustified killing. However, if suicide terrorism is independently justified as terrorism on grounds similar to those of Just War Theory, then the promotion of gender equality adds to the moral value, although tragically so, of women's suicide terrorist acts.

Ethnicity and Indoctrination for Violence: The Efficiency of Producing Terrorists

Frank Salter

Definitional Problem

There is no authoritative definition of terrorism, but a good starting point is one offered in the U.S. Code of Federal Regulations: "[T]he unlawful use of force and violence against persons or property to intimidate or coerce a government, the civilian population, or any segment thereof, in furtherance of political or social objectives."[1] This definition identifies the key aspect of intimidation. A behavioral focus requires that we broaden the definition by including legal acts (terror has been used by governments) and acts whose goals are unclear (surely an act can constitute terrorism as a means when its end is unknown). Terrorism also needs to be distinguished from warfare if the study of its motivation is not to expand to the study of the soldier. A behaviorally-oriented definition is: "The use of force and violence against persons or property to intimidate or coerce a government, the civilian population, or any segment thereof."

Typically terrorism is the killing of noncombatants aimed at inducing fear among a civilian population or government. This is different to warfare, which is combat between armies. When Bin Laden's forces downed Soviet military helicopters over Afghanistan that was warfare. When his forces downed civilian airplanes that was terrorism. The distinction between primary and double effect originating with Aquinas helps isolate the essence of terrorism in the following manner. The killing of civilians constitutes terrorism if it is a means of causing terror, not if it is a side effect of destroying legitimate military targets. So Iraqi civilians caught in the crossfire between the U.S. military and insurgents are not the victims of terrorism. That is only true when the combatants do not target civilians or accept the harm done to them partly because of desired psychological impact. But civilians targeted by car bombs or any other weapon are the victims of terrorism. This distinction has dirty

F. Salter
Max Planck Research Group for Human Ethology
e-mail: fssalter@aol.com

[1] 28 C.F.R. § 0.85 (2007).

I.A. Karawan et al. (eds.), *Values and Violence*,

hands because is has been used to excuse unnecessary harm. But analytically it is indispensable when trying to understand what motivates terrorists.

Introduction and Framework

It is often assumed that indoctrination is a necessary and sufficient condition for the terrorism afflicting many countries. It is assumed that without systematic education away from spontaneous human values terrorism would be reduced, especially the type involving suicide by the attacker. This approach is evident in analyses that focus predominantly on types of beliefs such as religious faith and by implication indoctrination in the etiology of terrorism.[2] One version of this view was expressed by Richard Dawkins shortly after the 9/11 attacks, that suicide bombing would be much less likely if people were not deceived into believing in an afterlife. Dawkins did not mention other motives except to indicate that Islamic violence is due to religion. The important causal factor, he contended, was the removal of restraint by religious indoctrination. "[T]estosterone-sodden young men too unattractive to get a woman in this world might be desperate enough to go for 72 private virgins in the next. . . . [I]s it any wonder that naive and frustrated young men are clamoring to be selected for suicide missions?"[3] The implication by omission is that indoctrination alone can produce terrorists including the self-sacrificial kind.

But indoctrination is costly when the subject does not seek it. It is even more costly when the subject resists. Brainwashing is the most powerful form of indoctrination. It has been used to some success in changing the allegiance of captured professionals and soldiers. As set out by Robert Jay Lifton, the process begins with imprisonment and strict control of the information received by the subject – "milieu control."[4] It then requires the full-time ministrations of trained interrogators and collaborators among the prisoners, with about a one-to-one ratio of indoctrinators to subjects.

Brainwashing is too inefficient to indoctrinate an indifferent population to the point where it produces a steady flow of volunteers for terrorism. Yet clearly indoctrination is involved. The routinization of terrorism, including that which relies on suicide bombers, depends on an administrative apparatus that includes systematic preparation of volunteers. In this paper, I argue that indoctrination is too inefficient to be a sufficient cause of routine terrorism yet is still a necessary condition for it. That argument needs to be situated within a general causal framework of terrorism, one that includes evolutionary causes.

---

[2] Mark Juergensmeyer, *Terror in the Mind of God: The Global Rise of Religious Violence* (Berkeley: University of California Press, 2000).

[3] Religion's Misguided Missiles," *Guardian Unlimited*, September 15, 2001, (http://www.guardian.co.uk/Archive/Article/0,4273,4257777,00.html).

[4] "Thought Reform of Western Civilians in Chinese Communist Prisons," *Psychiatry* 19 (1956), pp. 173–195; *Thought Reform and the Psychology of Totalism: A Study of 'Brainwashing' in China* (Chapel Hill: University of North Carolina Press, 1989).

Charlesworth provides a comprehensive taxonomy or framework of causes, including evolved predispositions, that might contribute to terrorist acts.[5] "Taxonomy" indicates lack of commitment to any particular causal model, though this strikes me as too modest because the data reviewed by Charlesworth favor ethological mechanisms. Indeed Charlesworth adopts a broad ethological approach that treats terrorist acts as a single dependent variable and focuses on the category of individuals that commits them.

The starting point is recognition of terrorism as a type of aggression. In ethological theory aggression is an evolved behavior that is universal to the species and serves adaptive functions in regulating relationships between individuals and between groups. Genetically-based learning dispositions direct the individual to acquire adaptive behaviors such as aggressive and affiliative motivations from observing the family during development, from parental training, and from the wider cultural and social system. Terrorism probably derives from the repertoire evolved to manage inter-group relations.

Evidence of the deep evolutionary roots of aggression includes its universality and the documentation of systematic lethal aggression shown by chimpanzees towards neighboring communities, especially on the borders separating community territories. This leads Charlesworth to include evolutionary causes ("ultimate" causes) in his framework, which he terms *predisposing factors*. His taxonomy allows for other evolved predispositions related to aggression, such as ethnocentrism and the capacity for self-sacrificial altruism in defense of the tribe.

Charlesworth then defines three other types of causes: facilitating, sustaining, and situational.

Facilitating causes operate from birth to about puberty. These include expression of the child's unique genome and parental treatment. There is evidence of aggression-inducing effects of weak parental attachment even in the first two years of life. Early experience of neglect and humiliation is held by some researchers to lead to heightened fear reactions and callousness in the child. These effects can also be produced directly or indirectly by occupying powers, either by rendering the environment stressful for families through threat or resource deprivation, by mistreating children, or by presenting violence and repression in a legitimate light.

Charlesworth qualifies this review by noting the near absence of research on the genetics of early socialization, whether from the perspective of parental or child behavior. Neither do studies report the number of children that suffer abuse in the various societies studied, nor account for children who develop normally despite deprived early environments. He concludes that early environment does not produce aggressive behavior but rather dampens or magnifies a genetically-given base level. Base levels vary between individuals.

As discussed further with regard to behavioral mechanisms, normal social development entails group identification, beginning with the family. By age five children

---

[5] "Profiling Terrorists," pp. 241–264.

begin to learn the social categories that include them – ingroups – and those that do not – outgroups.

Sustaining causal factors operate from puberty through to early adulthood. This is the age range where individuals begin to take an interest in ideological/religious ideas and begin to be recruited into institutions that, even if not malign at first, can act to prepare them for revolutionary or paramilitary causes. Nine-year-old children are sometimes enlisted into military bodies as combatants, porters, sentries and spies. But typically indoctrination into combat groups and combative ideas takes place from puberty to early adulthood. This process develops aggression already latent from earlier development, including the effects of deprived and abusive conditions. Its expression is elicited and directed against particular enemies. "Such preparation is made easier if the children are brought to perceive themselves as victims of historically unjust systems."[6] Indoctrination is most effective when the process is framed as a simulacrum of the evolutionary environment, typically as preparation to defend the ethnic group or nation. The effect is enhanced by portraying ingroup and outgroup as victim and aggressor respectively.

Because he is presenting a framework of possible causes, not a particular hypothesis, the mechanisms suggested by Charlesworth are not always consistent. For example, he states that indoctrination necessary to prepare juveniles to kill enemies must be "vigorous and prolonged." On the other hand, he points to evidence of the normality of inter-group hostility at this age. Juvenile boys in all cultures direct homicidal fantasies against threatening outgroups, indicating a phylogenetic origin in group defence.[7]

Charlesworth surmises that the task of indoctrination for conducting suicide attacks is eased by adolescent boys' proclivity for heroism in battle. Cultures and religions such as Christianity and Islam celebrate martyrs and some rehearse martyrdom in ritualistic form despite condemning murder. Roger Masters hypothesizes that poor societies with large families and low parental investment might be more willing to sacrifice juvenile boys in battle than societies with small families and high parental investment.[8] Charlesworth also refers to the higher rate of suicide among depressive individuals. He notes that depression is often caused by inability to achieve personal goals, and draws a hypothetical parallel with societies undergoing stress. Feelings of worthlessness and consequent self-destructive behavior can result from poor environments and health, emotionally inadequate relationships, lack of prospects for heterosexual relationships, marriage and children, and the sense of being a burden on loved ones. Martyrdom could provide an outlet for such feelings when it is perceived as likely to raise the family's status and reduce its economic burden.

---

[6] Charlesworth, "Profiling terrorists," p. 255.

[7] Charlesworth cites D. T. Kenrick and V. Sheets, "Homicidal fantasies," *Ethology and Sociobiology* 14 (1993), pp. 231–246.

[8] Masters, "Explaining and responding to terrorism: Inclusive fitness theory and suicide bombers," paper presented to the Association for Politics and the Life Sciences, Montreal, August 2002.

Situational causes are the immediate conditions that give rise to terrorist acts. Charlesworth dates the beginning of this phase as the time the subject receives the order to attack, and he deals only with suicide attacks. This brief period is poorly researched and Charlesworth can only speculate about psychological and behavioral states of the terrorist leading up the act. The scant data offered include the fact that an order and approbation are received. There is sometimes a martyr ceremony. According to the kin of Gaza suicide bombers, the terrorist sometimes visits a religious center or shrine or a place that holds special memories. The terrorist is rehearsed in the attack plan, is armed and dressed.

Charlesworth then uses his framework to contrast alternate hypotheses and show that they emphasize different parts of the causal chain. Gene-based models place great weight on predisposing factors, early-experiential models emphasize facilitating causes, and indoctrination models place much weight on sustaining causes. All three models might be valid if each applies to one type of individual or another. For example, analysts should be alert for predisposing (idiosyncratic genetic) and sustaining causes (intense indoctrination) in the case of a terrorist who is the product of a comfortable middle class family belonging to a secure ethnic group. But facilitating causes are likely to be more influential in the case of terrorists who come from an economically depressed family and a neighborhood that has been under enemy occupation for decades and who has had friends or relatives killed or humiliated by those forces. Charlesworth notes the need for further research to increase the predictive value of such profiles.

Comments on Charlesworth's Framework

Recall that Charlesworth is not offering a particular causal model so much as a taxonomy of possible causes. By carving at the joints of individual social development this framework seems general enough to allow for a range of hypotheses. A taxonomy, however, is not a hypothesis. Indeed it allows for the compilation of inconsistent causes, as noted earlier. Charlesworth's framework can be whittled down at least part way towards a causal model by adding information that favors one model over another, as I shall do concerning facilitating causes, at least with regard to suicide terrorists.

My starting point is the observation that self-sacrifice for one's community is generally not the result of defective development and impaired cognition, though it might be related to elevated indoctrinability. Charlesworth's own data on Palestinian suicide bombers indicate the opposite. He found that suicide bombers were slightly more religious and came from slightly larger families compared to controls; none had psychological or social problems, apart from being caught up in the Intifada. Charlesworth cites interview data on Palestinian suicide bombers as well as the Basque terrorist group ETA.[9] The anger and feelings of desperation experienced

9 Charlesworth, "Profiling terrorists," p. 250.

by these terrorists appear not to have been the result of anti-social personalities but to have been the proximate result of economic deprivation and harassment by occupying authorities.

Wiessner's field study of cyclical revenge in contemporary Highlands Papua New Guinea also identifies prosocial motivation, though magnified in effect to a maladaptive level by the availability of assault rifles and the breakdown of traditional society. Young revenge fighters are partly motivated by loyalty to their clans and distribute income to their communities, who honor them for their service.[10]

I also want to look more closely at the excellent points made by Charlesworth regarding threats to resources as a spur to inter-group violence. He states that in addition to immediate environmental stressors, "aggressive behavior is associated with population density, territory and boundary disputes, all related to lack of resources necessary for survival."[11] He goes on to argue that territory "is the pre-eminent resource" providing ready access to vital resources and "the time and opportunity to engage in peaceful . . . creative life activities without threat and interruption from the outside." This conclusion is argued from the perspective of behavioral ecology, both anthropological and zoological. In humans, coalitions of relatively poor young males recur as agents of violence with other similar coalitions and better-off groups.

Based on this ecological perspective Charlesworth then criticizes theories of human conflict that emphasize what he sees as non-ecological causes, namely nationalism, ethnic enmity, and religious/ideological fanaticism. Surely, he argues, these ideological factors are "complementary" such that they "causally interlock" with ecological variables. He refers to the evidence of the territorial component of terrorist motivation, including Bin Laden's justification of al Quaida on the grounds of the infidel presence in or occupation of Islamic countries and their exploitation of local resources undermining the Islamic religion and culture.[12]

It is here that Charlesworth's framework can be expanded and linked with contemporary research on ethnicity and nationalism. The theories that omit genetic and territorial factors belong to the modernist school of nationalism studies that has been dominant in Western universities since the Second World War. Modernist theories of ethnicity and nationalism see both phenomena as constructed, whether by elites or by the state.[13] One modernist conception of the nation is that it constitutes a power container essentially synonymous with the state.[14] The nation is typically dated by

---

[10] Wiessner, "From Spears to M-16s: Testing the imbalance of power hypothesis among the Enga," *Journal of Anthropological Research* 62 (2006), pp. 165–191.

[11] Charlesworth, "Profiling terrorists," p. 247.

[12] Charlesworth, "Profiling terrorists," p. 248, citing Usama bin Laden, "Declaration of war against the Americans occupying the Land of the Two Holy Places," in Y. Alexander and M. S. Swetnam (eds.), *Usama bin Laden's al-Quaida: Profile of a terrorist network* (Ardsley, New York: Transnational Publishers, 1996), pp. 1–22.

[13] See, e.g., John Breuilly, *Nationalism and the State* (Manchester: Manchester University Press, 1993).

[14] Anthony Giddens, *The Nation-State and Violence* (Cambridge: Cambridge University Press, 1996).

modernists from the French Revolution of 1789 on the basis that the revolutionary state invented the French nation.[15] National sentiment serves purely economic, practical purposes such as finding employment for a new literate clerical class.[16] Ethnic identities are likewise held to be constructed by self-interested elites, typically the capitalist class. Nations are "imagined communities" that emerged from print capitalism and rising popular literacy spreading ideas of national identity, fraternity, and freedom.[17]

Modernism's view of ethnicity and nationalism as constructed, top-down phenomena fits a rational choice approach to motivation.[18] People choose to belong to ethnic groups and nations because they believe that doing so serves their personal interests. Mainstream modernist theory has had no place for ethnic or national interests; indeed it has generally sought to deconstruct what it sees as an outdated destructive form of false consciousness.

Clearly modernist theories of this stamp, whatever their sophistication in treating economic and political aspects, will not fully engage a theory of terrorism that includes genetic and developmental-biological variables. Nor do they explain the passion and altruism of ethnic and national conflict.[19] There are alternative schools of nationalism theory that provide or at least allow such engagement and such explanation. These are primordialism,[20] ethnic nepotism theory,[21] and perennialism,[22] the latter a modernist theory that incorporates primordialist ideas and is compatible with behavioral and evolutionary mechanisms.[23]

Instead of describing these schools of nationalism theory I shall limit myself to describing some core definitions that they share, that are becoming widely accepted

---

[15] Eric Hobsbawm and Terrence Ranger (eds.), *The Invention of Tradition* (Cambridge: Cambridge University Press, 1992).

[16] Ernest Gellner, *Nations and Nationalism* (London: Cornell University Press, 1983).

[17] Benedict Richard O'Gorman Anderson, *Imagined Communities: Reflections on the Origin and Spread of Nationalism* (London: Verso Editions, 1983).

[18] Michael Hechter, "A Rational Choice Approach to Race and Ethnic Relations," in J. Rex and D. Mason (eds.), *Theories of Race and Ethnic Relations* (Cambridge: Cambridge University Press, 1986), pp. 268–277.

[19] Paul C. Stern, "Why do People Sacrifice for their Nations?" in Paul C. Comaroff and Paul C. Stern (eds.), *Perspectives on Nationalism and War* 7 (Amsterdam: Gordon and Breach, 1995), pp. 99–121.

[20] Clifford Geertz, *The Interpretation of Cultures* (New York: Basic Books, 1973); Steven Grosby, "Territoriality: The transcendental, primordial feature of modern societies," *Nations and Nationalism* 1, 2 (1995), pp. 143–162.

[21] Pierre L. Van den Berghe, *The Ethnic Phenomenon* (New York: Elsevier, 1981); Tatu Vanhanen, *Ethnic Conflicts Explained by Ethnic Neoptism* (Stamford, CT: JAI Press, 1999).

[22] Walker Connor, "The Timelessness of Nations," in Maria Montserrat Guibernau and John Hutchinson (eds.), *History and National Destiny: Ethnosymbolism and its Critics* (Oxford: Blackwell, 2004), pp. 35–47; Anthony D. Smith, *The Ethnic Origins of Nations* (Oxford: Basil Blackwell, 1986).

[23] Walker Connor, "Beyond Reason: The Nature of the Ethnonational Bond," *Ethnic and Racial Studies* 16, 3 (1993), pp. 373–389; J. Phillipe Rushton, "Ethnic Nationalism, Evolutionary Psychology, and Genetic Similarity Theory," *Nations and Nationalism* 11 (2005), pp. 489–507.

within anthropology, sociology, and political science and that help link ideas of evolutionary causation and territoriality to recent findings on behavior incident to ethnic and national identity. I shall conclude that there are well-established behavioral mechanisms that respond against threats to deeply held group identities, especially ethnicity, religion, and nationality. It is these mechanisms that give identity politics its heat. Such threats release innate motivations for aiding fellow ethnics and nationals and defending territory that forms part of ethnic or national identity.

Four Bridging Concepts

An *ethnic group* is a "named human population with myths of common ancestry, shared historical memories, one or more elements of common culture, a link with a homeland and a sense of solidarity among at least some of its members."[24] Members believe that they are descended from common ancestors. They might not occupy their ancestral homeland but their memory of that homeland forms part of their collective identity. Typically a substantial fraction of the ethny feels loyalty to fellow ethnics. Religious symbols can form part of ethnic identity and in some circumstances they constitute the core of that identity. Such has been the case with Orthodoxy and Islam and Medieval "Christendom." More often religion contributes to shared memories and culture due to a shared liturgy and beliefs and in the form of religious motifs in art and literature. Religion has often been the only institution able to reproduce historical memories across multiple generations.

A *nation* shares some aspects of ethnicity but is more of a political association. Nationals identify themselves by a collective proper name, occupy the historic territory that forms part of their national identity, have common political myths and memories, often have shared religious symbols, share a mass public culture, and share an integrated territorial economy and communications infrastructure. Nations can consist of a single ethnic group, and nations typically grow around an original ethnic group that provided the founding language, core culture and origin myths.[25] Nations such as Switzerland can be formed by more than one ethnic group sharing similar or the same religions that have lived together long enough to have formed a common culture and historic memories, for example of defeats and victories and other corporate achievements.

Nationalism has particularistic and universalist variants. The former motivates those seeking to throw off foreign rule. It is usually a social and political movement of the weak for securing their identity, unity and autonomy on behalf of an actual or potential nation. Religious symbols often form part of the set of national symbols. Universalist nationalism is typically evinced by those not immediately threatened, who see some positive-sum material advantage or the realization of a universal ideal.

---

[24] John Hutchinson and A.D. Smith, "Introduction," in John Hutchinson and Anthony D. Smith (eds.), *Ethnicity* (Oxford & New York: Oxford University Press, 1996), p. 6.

[25] A.D. Smith, *The Ethnic Origins of Nations* (Oxford: Basil Blackwell, 1986).

Although it takes different forms a common formula is a world posited as being divided into nations, each with a distinctive character. The ideal includes national sovereignty. Universal nationalists believe that a just world order should defend the freedom of nations.

Particularistic nationalism but not the universalistic type has repeatedly proved capable of generating self-sacrificial commitment. This is the kind needed for weak powers to conduct asymmetric conflict, because it requires fighters willing to risk their lives.

Notice that neither an ethnic group nor a nation is synonymous with a *state*. Max Weber's description is still definitive: a state is a compulsory association that monopolize the deployment of legitimate force within a territory.[26] A nation-state is a nation that controls its own state apparatus.[27] There are few ethnically homogeneous nation states but that term still applies as long as there is a leading ethny. Typically the leading ethny is the majority but it need not be. In principle a minority population can control the state apparatus, typically also exerting economic and cultural hegemony.[28] A recent example is Apartheid South Africa. An example of minority cultural leadership is Anglo influence in the United States until the 1960s or 1970s.[29]

These definitions suggest how important putative kinship is to ethnic identity and shared historical memories and culture are to national identity. Territory is also important for both ethnic and national identity, an association not yet fully explained. Psychological theories of ethnic and national behavior also point to the importance of these features. There is no generally accepted unified theory in this field of study. Making behavioral connections will necessitate drawing knowledge from a range of social sciences.

Ethnic and National Behavior

Several ethnic behaviors are described and compared by MacDonald.[30] *Affiliation by similarity* is strong along the dimension of ethnicity, influencing choice of friends and mates. Assortment by similar characteristics is well confirmed by numerous

---

26 Max Weber, "The Nation," in H. H. Gerth and C. W. Mills (eds.), *From Max Weber: Essays in Sociology* (New York: Oxford University Press, 1946), pp. 82–83.

27 Walker Connor, "A Nation is a Nation, is a State, is an Ethnic Group, is . . .," *Ethnic and Racial Studies* 1, 4 (1978), pp. 378–400.

28 Donald Baker, "Race and Power: Comparative Approaches to the Analysis of Race Relations," *Ethnic and Racial Studies* 1, 3 (1978), pp. 316–335; H.M. Blalock, Jr., *Toward a Theory of Minority-Group Relations* (New York: Wiley, 1967); Eric P. Kaufmann (ed.), *Rethinking Ethnicity: Majority Groups and Dominant Minorities* (London and New York: Routledge, 2004).

29 E.D. Baltzell, *The Protestant Establishment: Aristocracy and Caste in America* (New York: Random House 1964); S. Huntington, *Who Are We: The Challenges to America's National Identity* (New York: Simon and Schuster 2005).

30 Kevin MacDonald, "An integrative evolutionary perspective on ethnicity," *Politics and the Life Sciences*, 20, 1 (2001), pp. 67–79.

studies.[31] *Social identity mechanisms* begin to appear by age five. Individuals are drawn to identify with various groups which they then evaluate positively while evaluating other groups negatively, even in the absence of group competition. Competition between groups magnifies the effect.[32] *Collectivism-individualism* is a dimension along which individuals and cultures are distributed. Collectively-minded individuals predicate personal decisions more on how outcomes will affect their families and communities than do the individually-minded.[33] *Human kinds* processing is the categorization of individuals and groups according to the imputed essential characteristic of shared biological descent. By age four children grasp that races are descent groups while other types of categories such as occupations and dress styles are not.[34] Two other behaviors not directly treated by MacDonald are territoriality and altruism.

Territoriality appears to be a cross-cultural universal in humans. Contemporary hunter-gatherer bands usually separate themselves spatially. Territory is sometimes shared with other groups as a means of sharing resources, but permission is given first. Unauthorized hunting on another band's territory leads to altercations and often conflict.[35] The innateness of territoriality is indicated by its presence in chimpanzees, who patrol their community territory and attack trespassers.[36] Themes of attachment to territory and its jealous defense are evident in patriotic discourse and are held by some scholars of ethnicity to be a core feature.[37]

Altruism is discussed by Charlesworth with reference to evolutionary theory. The hypothesis is not as important as the fact that heroic behavior on behalf of a community, whether ethnic, religious or national, is characteristic of contemporary terrorism. This is especially true in the case of individuals who give their lives in order to kill the enemy. Heroism is understood to be a type of altruism. Awards

---

[31] Miller McPherson, Lynn Smith-Lovin and James M. Cook, "Birds of a Feather: Homophily in Social Networks," in K. S. Cook and J. Hagan (eds.), *Annual Review of Sociology* 27 (Palo Alto: Annual Review, 2001), pp. 415–444; D. Theissen and B. Gregg, "Human assortative mating and genetic equilibrium: An evolutionary perspective," *Ethology and Sociobiology* 1 (1980), pp. 111–140.

[32] Dominic Abrams and Michael A. Hogg, *Social Identity Theory: Constructive and Critical Advances* (New York: Springer-Verlag, 1990).

[33] H. C. Triandis, "Cross-Cultural Differences in Assertiveness/Competition vs. Group Loyalty/Cooperation," in Robert A. Hinde and Jo Groebel (Cambridge: Cambridge University Press, 1991).

[34] Lawrence A. Hirschfeld, *Race in the Making: Cognition, Culture, and the Child's Construction of Human Kinds* (Cambridge, MA: MIT Press, 1996).

[35] E. Cashdan, "Territoriality among human foragers: Ecological models and an application to four Bushman groups," *Current Anthropology* 24, 1(1983), pp. 47–66; Irenaus Eibl-Eibesfeldt, *Human Ethology* (New York: Aldine de Gruyter, 1989), pp. 321–339.

[36] Christopher Boehm, "Segmentary 'warfare' and the management of conflict: Comparison of East African chimpanzees and patrilineal-patrilocal humans," in A. H. Harcourt and F. B. M. De Waal (eds.), *Coalitions and Alliances in Humans and Other Animals* (New York: Oxford University Press, 1992), pp. 137–173.

[37] Grosby, "Territoriality: The Transcendental, Primordial Feature of Modern Societies," *Nations and Nationalism* 1, 2 (1995), pp. 143–162.

for valor go to individuals who risk their lives for their comrades, and there is no higher form of valor than the deliberate, calm sacrifice of one's life, as demonstrated by suicide bombers. The passion and self-sacrifice shown in ethnic politics and conflict fit the psychological definition of altruism as unreciprocated giving and the biological definition as assistance that reduces the individual fitness of the giver.

Charlesworth summarizes an evolutionary hypothesis of suicide bombers proposed by Masters,[38] according to which juvenile (typically male) heroism, even when self-sacrificial, can pay off genetically when it promotes the reproduction of the hero's genes. This is a special case of a broader hypothesis of ethnic altruism developed originally by Hamilton [39] and Shaw and Wong.[40] Undoubtedly the threshold for such altruism can be lowered by religious doctrines, for example concerning an afterlife, as Dawkins argues. An evolutionary theory of suicide terrorism that analyses religion and young male coalitional raiding is presented by Thomson.[41] A full evolutionary account of warfare as male coalitional reproductive strategy must encompass raiding behavior common to humans and chimpanzees.[42] These analyses are sophisticated versions of Dawkins' approach. The present discussion does not contradict these analyses, but adds the premise that defensive ethnic behaviors release fighting motivation in the first place as well as lowering the threshold for altruism, mainly for kin groups (family, clan and ethny), religious community, and nation.

Dawkins also misses a critical element of religious motivation for terrorism, that it embues the cause with a sense of moral certitude. "God is on our side" is a common refrain in ethnic and national wars. Righteous punishment is delivered with considerable prejudice in defence of the tribe, as indicated by recent findings on altruistic punishment. Individuals playing bargaining games are eager to pay real money to punish free-riders – players who harm the "public good" by acting selfishly.[43] Ethnic competition magnifies the effect. In a recent experiment conducted in Papua New Guinea, players sacrificed a large part of a day's wage to

---

38 R. Masters, *op cit.*

39 W.D. Hamilton, "Selection of Selfish and Altruistic Behaviour in Some Extreme Models," *Narrow Roads of Gene Land, Vol. 1: Evolution of Social Behaviour* (Oxford: W. H. Freeman 1996), pp. 198–227; "Innate Social Aptitudes of Man: An Approach from Evolutionary Genetics," *ibid.* pp. 329–51.

40 R.P. Shaw and Y. Wong, *Genetic Seeds of Warfare: Evolution, Nationalism, and Patriotism* (London: Unwin Hyman 1989), Appendix 1: A cost-benefit framework applicable to ethnic conflict, pp. 211–31.

41 J.A. Thomson, "We Few, We Happy Few, We Band of Brothers (And Occasional Sister): The Dynamics of Suicide Terrorism" (Paper presented at the Biennial Congress of the International Society for Human Ethology, Detroit 2006).

42 J.M.G. van der Dennen, *The Origin of War. The Evolution of a Male-Coalitional Reproductive Strategy*. (Groningen, Netherlands: Origin 1995).

43 Ersnt Fehr and Simon Gachter, "Altruistic Punishment in Humans," *Nature* 415 (2002), pp. 137–140.

punish free-riders from a different ethnic group who harmed ingroup members.[44] Less was sacrificed to punish free-riders when all players came from the same tribe.

Ethnic Behavior and Charlesworth's Causal Framework

Knowledge of ethnic behavior allows a finer-grained analysis of the predisposing causes identified by Charlesworth. The ethnic behaviors described above are: affiliation by similarity, social identity, collectivism, human kinds processing, territoriality, and altruism. Some of these promote ethnic formation before conflict begins. Afterwards they facilitate attack against perceived enemies. The various behaviors seem to fit into Charlesworth's framework thus.

Predisposing causes. All of the behaviors qualify as predisposing causes because all appear to be evolved learning dispositions. They appear early, have a degree of automaticity, and are cross-cultural universals except for human-kinds research which has not yet been replicated cross-culturally.

Facilitating causes. These operate from birth through to puberty. I am not aware of research on early environmental-developmental effects on ethnic behaviors, but it is possible that social identity processes or territoriality, to take two examples, might be enhanced or reduced in salience by parental behavior or experiences with peers.

Sustaining causes. These causes operate from puberty through to early adulthood. In the case of terrorism they operate up to the point at which the individual decides to attack or is ordered to do so. One behavior likely to be involved in this stage is social identity mechanisms. Identification of different ethnic or national groups alone will prime the young adult to accept positive evaluations of the ingroup and negative evaluations of the outgroup. Plausible reports of attacks on the ingroup will release aggression toward the attacker. Categorizing the enemy as a different descent group will reduce sympathy for them. Collectivism is strongly influenced by culture. Any society under attack over a prolonged period can be expected to increase in collectivism as a defensive reaction. In addition, individual variation will mean that those who are more collectivist-minded will show higher levels of social responsibility by rallying to their community's defense. Invasion or occupation of the ethnic territory will release territorial-defensive motivation to expel the invader from "our" country, and injury to the ingroup will release altruism, including the wrath of altruistic punishment.

It is possible that some of these sustaining causes begin to operate in this early period. Discussion of the enemy, their misdeeds, and observation of the drama of conflict might be impressed on the young mind. This is made more likely by the fact that social identity mechanisms and human kinds processing begin by age five.

---

[44] Helen Bernhard, Urs Fischbacher and Ernst Fehr, "Parochial Altruism in Humans," *Nature* 442 (2006), pp. 912–915.

Situational causes are not much informed by ethnic behaviors, except to the extent that they maintain the terrorist's commitment to his goal in the final hours.

Efficient Indoctrination

It is well known that threats against the ethny or nation prime a population for war. Behavioral science explains some of the psychological and group processes. Leaders of societies at all stages of development have held up the "bloody shirt" of a slain group member as a means of uniting the group behind them.[45] Diaspora ethnic groups that have managed to avoid assimilation for centuries have "oppositional symbols" embedded in their religious rituals commemorating great victories and defeats.[46] Historical oppositional symbols are also important in mobilizing nations. For Serbians it is the defeat at Kosovo in 1389, for Americans it has been the War of Independence, the Alamo and Pearl Harbor, for Jewish Israelis the Holocaust, for African-Americans slavery. Oppositional symbols are the historical, long-range version of the "bad blood."

I began by noting the inefficiency of indoctrination directed at unwilling subjects. This can be put in context by comparing the techniques used in different types of persuasion. Table 1 set out some of those techniques across many different persuasion strategies. The point is that it is costly to change strongly held values. This was achieved by Communist Chinese brainwashing during the Korean War but is not achieved by the other types of persuasion. For example, cult persuasion works on volunteers, individuals who are at least partly motivated to join the group.[47]

Indoctrination is easy when limited to articulating and actuating an existing intent. This is all nations need do to train raw recruits in a popular defensive war. Boot camp is intense but brief. Indoctrination in such circumstances can be performed without lengthy imprisonment, without controlling all information available to the subject, without inducing mental and physical breakdown, and thus with a much lower ratio of instructors to subjects. That is why threats to group identity and autonomy make the work of preparing terrorists, and soldiers, so much easier than indoctrination from a cold start. Indeed when the homeland is in peril people, especially young men, *seek* indoctrination into fighting units.[48]

That is the basis of the hypothesis I seek to present: that in the absence of real threats to the ethny, religious community or nation, indoctrinating people to commit

---

45 H. P. Caton, *Descriptive Political Ethology* (Griffith University, 1994).

46 Edward H. Spicer, "Persistent Cultural Systems," *Science* 174 (November, 1971), pp. 795–800.

47 Frank Salter, "Indoctrination as Institutionalized Persuasion: Its Limited Variability and Cross-Cultural Evolution," in Irenaus Eibl-Eibesfeldt and Frank Salter (eds.), *Indoctrinability, Ideology, and Warfare: Evolutionary Perspectives* (Oxford and New York: Berghahn, 2001), pp. 421–452.

48 H. P. Caton, "Reinvent yourself: Labile psychosocial identity and the lifestyle marketplace," in Irenaus Eibl-Eibesfeldt and Frank Salter (eds.), *Ethnic conflict and indoctrination: Altruism and identity in evolutionary perspective* (Oxford and New York: Berghahn, 2001), pp. 325–343.

Table 1 Behavioural techniques of indoctrination [Approaches ranked in order of effectiveness – from Salter 2001/1998, p. 444]

Behavioural tactic	Full brain-washing	Deprog-ramming	Traditional initiation	Moonies: from first workshop	Leninist Bolshevism	Religious education	Moonies: at first contact	Advertising
PHYSICAL COERCION and restraint	●	●	●					
ROUTINE OBEDIENCE	●	?			●	●		
MILIEU CONTROL	●	●	●	●	●			
ISOLATION from information	●	●	●	●	●			
SEVERANCE of interpersonal bonds	●	●	●	●	●			
INTENSE PEER PRESSURE	●	●	●	●	●			
INTERROGATION	●							
THREAT	●	●	●		●			
RITUAL ATTACK ON OUTGROUP	●	●	?	?	●			
SLEEP DEPRIVATION	●	?	●	●				
PHYSICAL DEBILITATION	●		●	?	?			
SHACKLES – made highly dependent	●		●					
REPETITION of message	●	●	●	?	●	●		●
REHEARSE PETTY COMPLIANCE	●		●					
ACCUSATION	●	●				●		
MILD DEGRADATION – self-revelation	●			●	?	●		
INTENSE DEGRADATION – confession/apology	●					●		
PUNISHMENT AND REWARD	●					●		
ARGUMENTATION/statement of doctrine	●	●	●	●	●	●	●	●
PRESTIGE TESTIMONIALS	●	●	●	●	●	●		●
INTENSE AFFILIATION				●				
CONSIDERATION and concern at point of collapse	●		●					
EFFECTIVENESS	HIGH	HIGH	HIGH?	MID	MID	MID?	LOW	LOW

Key: ● = tactic used; ? = uncertain)

terrorism, let alone kill themselves in the process, is likely to be so inefficient that for practical purposes it will not work.

A Rationale for Conflict Resolution

Several strategies help reduce the incidence of terrorism, including military and police operations and regulating international money flows. In the long run the most effective strategies will work with human values. Motivations of defense, hostility, and self-sacrifice need to be replaced by cooperative values. The intermediate effect of doing so would be to render the cost of indoctrinating terrorists prohibitive.

Two strategies for reducing the efficiency of indoctrination suggest themselves. The first is to counteract the nationalist and religious ideologies that prime individuals to resist threats to their communities. The second is to remove those threats. Though both approaches are difficult, they are not necessarily mutually exclusive.

Suppressing and subverting nationalist ideology is recommended by the modernist theory discussed earlier. To be activated the behavioral tendencies described above require the release of national or ethno-religious culture. The first is a well-studied phenomenon. Modern nationalist ideology was invented by pre-Revolutionary French intellectuals in emulation of English national consciousness that had arisen by the 16th century.[49] That ideology then spread during the 19th century borne by Napoleonic invasion and facilitated by growing levels of education and the development of economic and communications infrastructure. The result is a nationalized conception of "us" and "them" that is culturally constructed from innate motivations. The process can also revolve around religious identity.

This account of the spread of nationalist ideology indicates that one means of counteracting or redirecting ethnocentric ideology might be to engineer a country's culture by controlling the mass media and education systems that disseminate ideology. Thus pressure has been put on Gulf states to reduce their funding for madrasa Islamic schools. The United States is directing substantial funds to Islamic countries in efforts to improve secular education and subsidize students wishing to leave the madrasa system. These efforts are currently directed to Egypt, Bangladesh, Afghanistan, Indonesia, Morocco, Pakistan, Yemen, and the West Bank and Gaza.[50] A related measure would be to induce terrorist-producing states to open their markets to allow foreign take-over of media assets. The wealth of the West would do the rest. Globalization has not yet extended this far and is likely to be resisted by local elites and middle classes.

The least effective intervention would be an attempt to destroy the infrastructure of indoctrination – schools, teachers, recruiters – because this infrastructure is

---

[49] L. Greenfeld, *Nationalism: Five roads to modernity* (Cambridge, Mass.: Harvard University Press, 1992).

[50] C.M. Blanchard, *Islamic Religious Schools, Madrasas: Background,* (Congressional Research Service, 2006), available at http://fpc.state.gov/documents/organization/61473.pdf.

large and distributed as well as portable and easily replaced. There are over 10,000 madrasas in Pakistan alone.[51]

The strategy of culture change directed at another country is likely to be fraught if it is perceived as a threat to national autonomy. Arguably this would be an accurate perception and thus difficult to avoid. Perceived threat to the nation or state would exacerbate defensive motivation. Thus subtlety of execution is necessary, yet errors are made in foreign policy as in all human enterprises.

The other approach would be to remove overt threats from states and communities that produce terrorists. This is recommended by the behavioral theory outlined above. The most effective interventions would be ones that eliminated or reduced those threats that release defensive behavior and increase the efficiency of indoctrination for terror. Communities should be able to secure the resources needed for sustenance and dignity. Material inequalities should be minimized. They should be allowed to develop their own political institutions. Occupation forces should be removed or made to keep a low profile. Political solutions should be found whereby both sides assent to borders. Where territory is contested a process of compromise should be set in train. If this fails, the more powerful side will be able to set the border where it wills, but it should do so in as fair a manner as consistent with its vital interests. Insults and incursions on holy sites need to be prevented. In an interdependent world of instant communications fairness is in the interests of the dominant power as well as the subordinate, since peace benefits all.

Calls for tolerance made without reference to group interests, without reference to what stands to be lost or gained by conflict, are literally unprincipled. Much more constructive is Michael Walzer's eloquent acknowledgment of parochial attachments:

> Tribalism names the commitment of individuals and groups to their own history, culture, and identity, and this commitment (though not any particular version of it) is a permanent feature of human social life. The parochialism that it breeds is similarly permanent. It cannot be overcome; it has to be accommodated, and therefore the crucial universal principle is that it must always be accommodated; not only my parochialism but yours as well, and his and hers in their turn.[52]

A successful strategy for long-term peace will not attempt to institute universal brotherhood since kinship attachment occurs only within restricted spheres, the largest of which is the nation. A workable formula would be a tradeoff between particular and general interests maintained by multi-lateral institutions and a shared analysis of where those interests lie. That tradeoff might be a universal nationalism in the tradition of Otto von Bismarck and President Woodrow Wilson, a graded parochialism.[53] That would involve liberal nationalism, which seeks to gain the

---

[51] Ibid.

[52] Michael Walzer, "Notes on the New Tribalism," in Chris Brown (ed.), *Political Restructuring in Europe* (London: Routlegde, 1994), pp. 187–200.

[53] Frank Salter, *On Genetic Interests: Family, Ethnicity, and Humanity in an Age of Mass Migration* (New York: Transaction, 2006).

public altruism of communities without the costs of chauvinistic conflict.[54] The right to national self determination within an international institutional framework will be a practical as well as an ideal goal if it undercuts terrorism.

I am not sanguine about the chances for such a strategy because the commitment needed to maintain it is not always apparent. I suspect that terrorism is perceived by some as a tolerable cost of global or regional inequalities or aggression. From this perspective the problem is limited to killing terrorists and reassuring targeted publics. Analysts who adopt this perspective show little interest in the motivations of terrorists except for tactical purposes. I suspect that drawing attention to legitimate aspirations of terrorist-producing communities is annoying to some because it tends to implicate their own interests.

Still the above argument is relevant because it indicates that the cost of continuing threats to ethno-religious communities and nations will likely be chronic. Also analysis of ethnic and national defensive behavior might allow some threats selectively to be withdrawn without much affecting vital interests.

---

[54] Eric P. Kaufmann, "Liberal Ethnicity: Beyond Liberal Nationalism and Minority Rights," *Ethnic and Racial Studies* 23, 6 (2000), pp. 1086–1119; Yael Tamir, *Liberal Nationalism* (Princeton: Princeton University Press, 1993).

The Clash Within: Democracy and the Hindu Right

Martha C. Nussbaum

Democracy Under Siege

On February 27, 2002, the Sabarmati express train arrived in the station of Godhra, in the state of Gujarat, bearing a large group of Hindu pilgrims who were returning from a pilgrimage to the alleged birthplace of the god Rama at Ayodhya (where some years earlier, angry Hindu mobs had destroyed the Babri mosque, which they claim is on top of the remains of Rama's birthplace). The pilgrimage, like many others in recent times, aimed at forcibly constructing a temple over the disputed site, and the mood of the returning passengers, frustrated in their aims by the government and the courts, was angrily emotional. When the train stopped at the station, passengers got into arguments with Muslim vendors and passengers. At least one Muslim vendor was beaten up when he refused to say "Jai Sri Ram" ("Hail Ram"), and a young Muslim girl narrowly escaped forcible abduction. As the train left the station, stones were thrown at it, apparently by Muslims.

Fifteen minutes later, one car of the train erupted in flames. Fifty-eight men, women, and children died in the fire. Most of the dead were Hindus. Because the area adjacent to the tracks was an area of Muslim dwellings, and because a Muslim mob had gathered in the region to protest the treatment of Muslims on the train platform, blame was immediately put on Muslims. Many people were arrested, and some of these are still in detention without charge – despite the fact that two independent inquiries into the event have established through careful sifting of the forensic evidence that the fire was most probably a tragic accident, caused by combustion from cook stoves carried on by the passengers and stored under the seats of the train.

In the days that followed, wave upon wave of violence swept through the state. The attackers were Hindus, many of them highly politicized, shouting Hindu-right slogans, such as "Hail Ram" (a religious invocation wrenched from its original devotional and peaceful meaning) and "Hail Hanuman" (a monkey god portrayed by the right as aggressive), along with "Kill, Destroy!" "Slaughter!" There is copious

M.C. Nussbaum
S.J. Quinney Lecture at the University of Utah, University of Chicago
e-mail: martha_nussbaum@law.uchicago.edu

I.A. Karawan et al. (eds.), *Values and Violence*,

evidence that the violent retaliation was planned by Hindu extremist organizations before the precipitating event. No one was spared: young children were burned along with their families. Particularly striking was the number of women who were raped, mutilated, in some cases tortured with large metal objects, and then set on fire. Over the course of several weeks, approximately two thousand Muslims were killed. Approximately half of the dead were women, many of whom were raped and tortured before being killed and burned. Children were killed with their parents; fetuses were ripped from the bellies of pregnant women to be tossed into the fire.

Most alarming was the total breakdown in the rule of law – not only at the local level but also at that of state and national government. Police were ordered not to stop the violence. Some egged it on. Gujarat's Chief Minister, Narendra Modi, rationalized and even encouraged the murders. He was later reelected on a platform that focused on religious hatred. (Because evidence of his criminal activity is so overwhelming, he has been denied a visa to enter the United States.) Meanwhile, the national government showed a culpable indifference. Prime Minister Vajpayee suggested that religious riots were inevitable wherever Muslims live alongside Hindus, and that troublemaking Muslims must have been to blame. Leading politicians conveyed the message that government would treat the nation's citizens unequally: some would receive the full protection of the law, and others would not. Prosecutions resulting from the riots have faced related problems: the bias of local judges, the intimidation and bribery of witnesses.

While Americans have focused on the war on terror, Iraq, and the Middle East, democracy has been under siege in another part of the world. India – the most populous of all democracies, and a country whose Constitution protects human rights even more comprehensively than our own – has been in crisis. Until the spring of 2004, its parliamentary government was increasingly controlled by right-wing Hindu extremists who condone and in some cases actively support violence against minorities, especially the Muslim minority. Many seek fundamental changes in India's pluralistic democracy. Despite their electoral loss, these political groups and the social organizations allied with them remain extremely powerful. Democracy and the rule of law have shown impressive strength and resilience, but the future is unclear.

What has been happening in India is a serious threat to the future of democracy in the world. The fact that it has yet to make it onto the radar screen of most Americans is evidence of the way in which terrorism and the war on Iraq have distracted Americans from events and issues of fundamental significance. If we really want to understand the impact of religious nationalism on democratic values, India currently provides a deeply troubling example, and one without which any understanding of the more general phenomenon is dangerously incomplete. It also provides an example of how democracy can survive the assault of religious extremism, from which all modern democracies can learn. In May 2004, the voters of India went to the polls in large numbers. Contrary to all predictions, they gave the Hindu right a resounding defeat. Because even exit polls, taken in cities and towns, did not predict the result, it is clear that impoverished rural voters played a major role in giving India a new government.

In this lecture, I shall use the case of Gujarat as a lens through which to conduct a critical examination of the influential thesis of the "clash of civilizations," made famous by Samuel Huntington. Huntington's picture of the world as riven between democratic Western values and an aggressive Muslim monolith does nothing to help us understand today's India, where the violent values of the Hindu right are imports from European fascism of the 1930s, and where the third-largest Muslim population in the world lives in peace, despite severe poverty and other inequalities. Through a study of this case, I shall argue that the real "clash of civilizations" is not the clash *between* "Islam" and "the West," but, instead a clash *within* virtually all modern nations – between people who are prepared to live with others who are different, on terms of equal respect, and those who seek the protection of homogeneity, and the domination of a single "pure" religious and ethnic tradition. At a deeper level, this book's thesis is the Gandhian claim that the real "clash of civilizations" is a clash within the individual self, between the urge to dominate and defile the other and a willingness to live respectfully on terms of compassion and equality, with all the vulnerability that such a life entails.

This argument about India will also suggest a way to see America, which is also torn between two different pictures of itself. One picture shows America and Americans as good and pure, its enemies as an external "axis of evil." The other picture, the fruit of internal self-criticism, shows America to itself as complex and flawed, torn between forces bent on control and hierarchy and forces that promote democratic equality. At a deeper level, what I've called the Gandhian level, my "internal-clash" picture shows Americans to themselves as people each of whom is capable of both respect and aggression, of both democratic mutuality and anxious domination. As George Kennan wrote:

> I wish I could believe that the human impulses which give rise to the nightmares of totalitarianism were ones which Providence had allocated only to other peoples and to which the American people had been graciously left immune. Unfortunately, I know this is not true... The fact of the matter is that there is a little bit of the totalitarian buried somewhere, way down deep, in each and every one of us.[1]

My argument, then, is focused on India, but it is also pertinent to other countries: for, as Nehru said on the eve of India's independence, "all the nations and peoples are too closely knit together today for any one of them to imagine that it can live apart."

[1] George Kennan, "Comments on the National Security Problem," in Giles D. Harlow and George C. Maerz (eds.), *Measures Short of War: The George F. Kennan Lectures at the National War College*, (Washington: National Defense University Press, 1990), p. 168. I am grateful to Peter Beinart's "The Rehabilitation of the Cold-War Liberal," *New York Times Magazine*, Sunday, April 30, 2006, pp. 40–45, which quotes a smaller piece of this passage, for sending me to the source.

The Ideology of the Hindu Right

According to the Huntington thesis, each "civilization" has its own rather unitary distinctive view of life, and Hinduism counts as a distinct "civilization." If we investigate the history of the Hindu right, however, we will see a very different story: traditional Hinduism was decentralized, plural, and highly tolerant, so much so that the vision of a unitary "pure" Hinduism that could provide the new nation with an aggressive ideology of homogeneity could not be found in India at all: the founders of the Hindu right had to import it from Europe. Today, European fascism is seated right at the heart of what parades, in some quarters at least, as Hindu civilization.

The Hindu Right's view of history is a simple one; like all simple tales, it is largely a fabrication, but its importance to the movement may be seen by the intensity with which its members go after scholars who present a more nuanced and accurate view: not only by strident public critiques, but by organized campaigns of threat and intimidation, culminating in some cases in physical violence. Here's how the story goes:

Once there lived in the Indus valley a pure and peaceful people. They spoke Vedic Sanskrit, a language revealed as that of the gods when the immortal Vedas were given to humanity. They had a rich material culture, well suited to sustain their prosperous life. Despite their peaceful temper, they were also well prepared for war: they had chariots, and even horses. Their realm was vast, stretching from Kashmir in the North to Sri Lanka (Ceylon) in the South. And yet they saw unity and solidarity in their shared ways of life, calling themselves Hindus and their land Hindustan. No class divisions troubled them; nor was caste a painful source of division. The condition of women was excellent.

This peaceful condition went on for centuries. Although from time to time marauders made their appearance at this people's doorstep (for example the Huns), they were quickly dispatched, because this people was aggressive when it needed to be, and its warlike strength was feared far and wide. Suddenly, rudely, unprovoked, invading Muslims put an end to all that. The early medieval period saw brief incursions by Muslims bent on the destruction of Hindu temples; these, however, proved short-lived. Disaster struck with a heavier hand, however, when Babur swept through the North of Hindustan early in the sixteenth century, vandalizing Hindu temples, stealing sacred objects, building mosques over temple ruins. For two hundred years, Hindus lived at the mercy of the marauders, until the Maharashtrian hero Shivaji rose up against the aliens and drove them back, restoring the Hindu kingdom. His success, however, was all too brief. Soon the British East India company and then the British themselves took up where Babur and his progeny had left off, imposing a tyranny upon Hindustan and her people. In short, despite the flawless excellence of indigenous Hindu culture, the men of Hindustan have lived for centuries in a humiliated condition. They can recover pride in themselves only by concerted aggression against alien elements in their midst. If they rise to the occasion, they can restore the original bliss, the time when Rama ruled the world with his blessings.

What is wrong with this picture? Well, for a start, the people who spoke Sanskrit almost certainly migrated into the subcontinent from outside, finding indigenous people there, probably the ancestors of the Dravidian peoples of South India. Hindus are no more indigenous than Muslims. Second, it leaves out problems in Hindu society: the problem of caste, which both Gandhi and Tagore took to be the central social problem facing India, and obvious problems of class and gender inequality. (When historians point to evidence of these things, they call them Marxists, as if that by itself invalidated the arguments.) Third, it leaves out the tremendous regional differences within Hinduism, and hostilities and aggressions sometimes associated with those. Fourth, it omits the evidence of peaceful coexistence and syncretism between Hindus and Muslims for a good deal of the Moghul Empire, including Akbar's well-known policies of religious pluralism. Muslims are nothing but bad, aggressive.

In the Hindu right version of history, a persistent theme is that of humiliated masculinity. According to the received story, Hindus have been subordinate for centuries, and their masculinity insulted, in part because they have not been aggressive and violent enough. Even while the violence of the conquerors is decried, Hindu males are encouraged to emulate that aggressive and warlike demeanor. Rabindranath Tagore, deeply perceptive here as always, represents his Hindu nationalist anti-hero, in *The Home and the World*, as wishing he could seize the woman he desires by force, but finds himself unable to do so. He blames this inability on his Hindu heritage, and wishes for a different nature. He says that there are two different sorts of music, the sound of the Hindu flute and the sound of the British military band. He wishes that he could hear in his blood the sound of the military band, rather than that disturbingly non-aggressive flute.

The two leading ideologues of the Hindu Right, who in different ways responded to this call for a warlike Hindu mascuilinity, are V. D. Savarkar, a freedom fighter who spent years in a British prison in the Andaman Islands, and who may have been a co-conspirator in the assassination of Mahatma Gandhi, and M. S. Golwalkar, a gurulike figure who was not involved in the independence struggle and who quietly, behind the scenes, built up the organization called the RSS (National Corps of Volunteers) that is now the leading social organization of the Hindu right. Savarkar's *Hindutva: Who is a Hindu*, first published in 1923, undertakes to define the essence of Hinduness for the new nation; his definition is exclusionary, emphasizing cultural homogeneity and the need to use force to ensure the supremacy of Hindus. For reasons of time, however, I shall focus on Golwalkar's *We, or Our Nationhood Defined*, published in 1939. Some of the remarks that I am about to quote are embarrassing to Hindus today, and members of the Hindu right hasten to assure one that Golwalkar knew nothing about the Holocaust and withdrew the offending statements in editions of the book published after the war. But 1939 was still after the Nuremberg laws (1935) and Kristallnacht (1938); moreover, my own copy of the fourth edition, published in 1947, still contains the statements, as quoted here.

Writing during the Independence struggle, Golwalkar sees his task as describing the unity of the new nation. He announces that most Indians' ideas about nationhood are mistaken. "They are not in conformity with those of the Western Political

Scientists. . . . It is but proper, therefore, at this stage to understand what the Western Scholars state as the Universal Nation-idea and correct ourselves. With this end in view, we shall now proceed with stating and analyzing the World's accepted Nation-concept."[2] Notice the unselfconscious deference to European scholarship as what "the World" thinks.

Golwalkar now turns to English dictionaries and to British and German political science. The five elements that he finds repeated as hallmarks of national unity are: geography, race, religion, culture, and language. Golwalkar examines each of these in turn and then analyzes several nations to see to what extent they embody the desired unities. Germany impresses him especially for the way in which it has managed to bring "under one sway the whole of the territory" that was originally held by the *Germani* but that was parceled out under different regimes.[3] Turning to race, he observes:

> German race pride has now become the topic of the day. To keep up the purity of the Race and its culture, Germany shocked the world by her purging the country of the semitic Races – the Jews. Race pride at its highest has been manifested here. Germany has also shown how well nigh impossible it is for Races and cultures, having differences going to the root, to be assimilated into one united whole, a good lesson for us in Hindusthan to learn and profit by.[4]

In the end, Golwalkar's vision of national unity is not exactly that of Nazi Germany. He is not very concerned with purity of blood, and far more concerned with a group's desire to merge into the dominant whole. Groups who fall outside the five-fold definition of nationhood, he concludes, can "have no place in the national life... unless they abandon their differences, and completely merge themselves in the National Race. So long, however, as they maintain their racial, religious and culture differences, they cannot but be only foreigners, who may be either friendly or inimical to the Nation."[5] Unlike Hitler, Golwalkar would probably be happy with the conduct of the many German Jews who converted to Christianity and assimilated their lifestyle to the dominant German lifestyle. Nonetheless, he is firmly against the civic equality of any people who retain their religious and ethnic distinctiveness, refusing to merge into the dominant Hindu whole. He speaks approvingly of the idea that people who refuse to assimilate will lose their civil rights, living "at the sufferance of the Nation and deserving of no special protection, far less any privilege or rights." Here is the way in which Golwalkar applies his ruminations about the "old nations" of Europe to the case of India:

> There are only two courses open to the foreign elements: either to merge themselves in the national race and adopt its culture, or to live at the sweet will of the national race. That is the only logical and correct solution. That alone keeps the national life healthy and undisturbed. That alone keeps the Nation safe from the danger of a cancer developing into its body politics [*sic*] of the creation of a state within the state. From this standpoint, sanctioned by

---

[2] Golwalkar, *We, or Our Nationhood Defined* (Nagpur: Bahrat Prakashan, 1939), p. 21.

[3] Golwalkar, *We, or Our Nationhood Defined*, p. 42.

[4] Golwalkar, *We, or Our Nationhood Defined*, p. 43.

[5] Golwalkar, *We, or Our Nationhood Defined*, p. 53.

> the experiences of shrewd old nations, the non-Hindu peoples in Hindusthan must either adopt the Hindu culture and language, must learn to respect and hold in reverence Hindu religion, must entertain no idea but those of glorification of the Hindu race and culture i.e. they must not only give up their attitude of intolerance and ungratefulness towards this land and its agelong traditions but must also cultivate the positive attitude of love and devotion instead – in one word they must cease to be foreigners, or may stay in the country, wholly subordinated to the Hindu nation, claiming nothing, deserving no privileges, far less any preferential treatment – not even citizen's rights. There is, at least should be, no other course for them to adopt.[6]

At this time, the RSS was a cultural movement without a distinct political arm. It disavowed connection with the more political Hindu Mahasabha, which later did propose that Muslims and Christians would lose all civil rights in the new nation. Clearly, however, this is his program, and we should not doubt that such aims lie underneath the modern political arm of the RSS, the political party known as the BJP.

At the time of independence, such ideas of Hindu supremacy did not prevail. Nehru and Gandhi insisted not only on equal rights for all citizens but on the most stringent protections for religious freedom of expression in the new Constitution. Gandhi always pointedly included Muslims at the very heart of his movement, and a devout Muslim, Maulana Azad, was not only one of his and Nehru's most trusted advisors, he was the person to whom Gandhi turned to accept food when he broke his fast unto death, a very pointed assault on sectarian ideas of purity and pollution. Such ideas never went uncontested.

On January 30, 1948, Mahatma Gandhi was shot at point-blank range by Nathuram Godse, member of the Hindu Mahasabha and former member of the RSS. Godse, who edited a newspaper called *Hindu Rashtra* (*Hindu Nation*) had left RSS because it seemed to him not political enough; the Mahasabha, a political party, was more congenial. As was shown by a letter written by Godse to Savarkar in 1938 and submitted to the trial court, Godse had long had a close relationship with Savarkar, whom he revered. "Since the time you were released from your internment at Ratnagiri," he wrote, "a divine fire has kindled in the minds of those groups who profess that Hindustan is for the Hindus."[7] He speaks of using the Hindu Mahasabha (of which Savarkar was then President) to build a National Volunteer Army, drawing on the resources of the RSS, where Godse was then a leading local organizer.

At his sentencing on November 8, 1949,[8] Godse read a long (book-length) statement of self-explanation, justifying his assassination for posterity. Although the statement was not permitted publication at the time, it gradually leaked out into the public. Translations into Indian languages began appearing, and in 1977 the English original was published by Godse's brother Gopal under the polite title, *May it Please Your Honour*. A new edition, with a long epilogue by Gopal, was published

---

6 Golwalkar, *We, or Our Nationhood Defined,* pp. 55–56.

7 Quoted in Rajesh Ramachandran, "The Mastermind?" *Outlook Magazine*, September 6, 2004.

8 Koenraad Elst, *Gandhi and Godse*, (2001), p. 3.

in 1993 under the more precise title *Why I Assassinated Mahatma Gandhi.*[9] Today the statement is also widely available on the Internet, where Godse is something of a hero on Hindu right websites, revered as a hero, and, on one website entirely devoted to his career,[10] known as "The True Patriot and the True Indian." (This website also contains the text of a recent Marathi-language play glorifying Godse that has been banned in India.)

Godse's self-justification, like the historical accounts of both Savarkar and Golwalkar, sees recent events against the backdrop of centuries of "Muslim tyranny" in India, punctuated by the heroic resistance of Shivaji, the eighteenth century Hindu leader who led a briefly successful rebellion against Moghul rule. Like Savarkar, he describes his goal as that of creating a strong, proud, India that can throw off the centuries of domination. Godse is appalled by Gandhi's rejection of the warlike heroes of classical Hindu epics: "It is my firm belief that in dubbing Rama, Krishna and Arjuna as guilty of violence, the Mahatma betrayed a total ignorance of the springs of human action." Indeed, he argues, it is Gandhi who is the more guilty of violence, since he exposes Indians to subordination and humiliation: "He was, paradoxical as it may appear, a violent pacifist who brought untold calamities on the country in the name of truth and non-violence, while Shivaji [and other resistance fighters] will remain enshrined in the hearts of their countrymen for ever for the freedom they brought to them." (So deep was Godse's objection to non-violence that he earlier refused the offer to commute his sentence to life imprisonment, saying, "Please, see to it that mercy is not imposed on me. I want to show that through me, Gandiji's non-violence is being hanged.")

Godse's second major objection to Gandhi is to his "pro-Muslim policy," which he sees in many aspects of Gandhi's politics, for example his support for Urdu alongside Hindi as national languages,[11] and his willingness to placate Jinnah and the Muslim League. Gandhi, he argues, has betrayed his role as father of the Indian nation and has become the father of Pakistan.

Godse tells us that he gradually came to the conclusion that Gandhi's (to him) disastrous policies could only be brought to an end by ending Gandhi's life. Such was Gandhi's personal charisma that so long as he lived, the Congress Party would have to "be content with playing second fiddle to all his eccentricity, whimsicality, metaphysics and primitive vision." Gandhi's "childish insanities and obstinacies, coupled with a most severe austerity of life, ceaseless work and lofty character made Gandhi formidable and irresistible." So, he planned in secret, he says, telling nobody about his plans, and fired the fatal shots.

Toward the end of Godse's statement appears a passage that heads the Hindu-right website devoted to his memory:

---

[9] See Elst, *Gandhi and Godse*, pp. 5–6.

[10] www.nathuramgodse.com.

[11] Hindi and Urdu are not very different as languages; they are slightly different dialects at most. The major difference between them is the script in which they are written: Persian script, in the case of Urdu, Devanagari (the Sanskrit script) in the case of Hindi. Thus it is odd to apply the ideas of linguistic nationalism to this question.

> If devotion to one's country amounts to a sin, I admit I have committed that sin. If it is meritorious, I humbly claim the merit thereof. I fully and confidently believe that if there be any other court of justice beyond the one founded by the mortals, my act will not be taken as unjust. If after the death there be no such place to reach or to go, there is nothing to be said. I have resorted to the action I did purely for the benefit of the humanity. I do say that my shots were fired at the person whose policy and action had brought rack and ruin and destruction to lakhs [tens of thousands] of Hindus.

Nehru believed that the murder of Gandhi was part of a "fairly widespread conspiracy"[12] on the part of the Hindu right to seize power; he saw the situation as analogous to that in Europe on the eve of the fascist takeovers. And he believed that the RSS was the power behind this conspiracy. In December 1947, he had already written to the provincial governors:

> We have a great deal of evidence to show that the RSS is an organization which is in the nature of a private army and which is definitely proceeding on the strictest Nazi lines, even following the technique of organization.... I have some knowledge of the way the Nazi movement developed in Germany. It attracted by its superficial trappings and strict discipline considerable numbers of lower middle class young men and women who are normally not too intelligent and for whom life appears to offer little to attract them.[13]

For reasons of time, we must now fast-forward to recent years. Although illegal for a time, the RSS eventually reemerged, and quietly went to work building a vast social network, consisting largely of groups for young boys, called "branches" or *shakas*, which, through clever use of games and songs, indoctrinate the young into the confrontational and Hindu-supremacist ideology of the organization. The idea of total obedience and the abnegation of the critical faculties is at the core of this solidaristic movement. Each day, as members raise the saffron flag of the warlike hero Shivaji, which the movement prefers to the tricolor flag of the Indian nation, with its Buddhist wheel of law reminding citizens of the emperor Ashoka's devotion to religious toleration, they recite the following pledge: "I take the oath that I will always protect the purity of Hindu religion, and the purity of Hindu culture, for the supreme progress of the Hindu nation. I have become a component of the RSS. I will do the work of the RSS with utmost sincerity and unselfishness and with all my body, soul, and resources. And I will keep this vow for as long as I live. Victory to Mother India." The organization also makes clever use of modern media: a nationally televised serial version of the classic epic *Ramayana*, in the late 1980s, fascinated viewers all over India with its concocted tale of a unitary Hinduism dedicated to the single-minded worship of the god Rama and to his birthplace at Ayodhya in north India. As a result of the propaganda stirred up in this and other ways, in 1992 Hindu mobs, with the evident connivance of the modern political wing of the RSS, the party known as the BJP, or Bharatiya Janata Party (National People's Party) destroyed a mosque in the city of Ayodhya that they say covers the remains of a Hindu temple marking Rama's birthplace.

---

[12] Letter to Ministers, February 5, 1948, *quoted in* Christophe Jaffrelot, *The Hindu National Movement in India* (New York: Columbia University Press, 1996), p. 87.

[13] Ibid.

Meanwhile, politically, the BJP began to gather strength in the late 1980s, drawing on widespread public dissatisfaction with the economic policies of the post-Nehru Congress party (although it was actually Congress, under Rajiv Gandhi, that began economic reforms), and playing, always, the cards of hatred and fear. It was during their ascendancy, in a coalition government that prevented them from carrying out all of their goals, that the destruction of the Ayodyha mosque took place. The violence in Gujarat was the culmination of a series of increasingly angry pilgrimages to the Ayodyha site, where the Hindu right has attempted to construct a Hindu temple over the ruins, but has been frustrated by the courts. Although the elections of 2004 gave a negative verdict on the BJP government, they remain the major opposition party and control state governments in some key states, including, today, Gujarat.

Lessons of Gujarat

For several years I have studied the Gujarat violence, its basis and its aftermath, looking for its implications for the ways in which we should view religious violence around the world. One obvious conclusion to draw is that each case must be studied on its own merits, with close attention to specific historical and regional factors. The idea that all conflict are explained by a simple hypothesis of the "clash of civilizations" proves utterly inadequate in the fact of Gujarat, where European ideas, borrowed to address a perceived humiliation, were used to create an ideology that has ultimately led to a great deal of violence against peaceful Muslims, and to the threat of more violence to come. Indeed, the clash of civilizations thesis is the best friend of the perpetrators, because it shields them and their ideology from scrutiny. Repeatedly in interviews with leading members of this group, I was informed that no doubt, as an American, I was already on their side, knowing that Muslims cause trouble wherever they are, and that there is nothing for it but to be prepared to take reactive, and even preemptive, measures against them. What we see in Gujarat is not that simplistic comforting thesis, it is something more disturbing: the fact that in a thriving democracy many individuals are unable to live with others who are different, on terms of mutual respect and amity. They seek total domination as the only road to security and pride. This is a phenomenon that is well known in democracies around the world, and it has nothing to do with an alleged Muslim monolith, and, really, very little to do with religion as such. (I've noted that the Hindu right are bent on recasting Hinduism into a newly violent and monolithic form.)

This case, then, informs us that we must look within, asking whether in our own society similar forces are at work, and, if so, what we might do to counteract them. Beyond that general insight, my study of the riots has suggested four very specific lessons.

1. The Rule of Law

One of the most appalling aspects of Gujarat was the complicity of officers of the law. Police sat on their hands, and indeed were ordered to do so, on penalty of demotion or transfer. The highest officials of state government, prominently including Chief Minister Narendra Modi, egged on the killing. The national government gave aid and comfort to the state government. The worst aspect of the unequal status of Muslims in Gujarat was this inequality before the law: Muslims at present are not equal citizens.

The institutions of government broke down at the local level, and to some extent at the national level. However, the institutional and legal structure of the Indian democracy ultimately proved robust, playing a key role in securing justice for the victims. The Supreme Court and the National Electoral Commission played very constructive roles in postponing new elections while Muslims were encouraged to return home, and in ordering change of venue in key trials arising out of the violence. Above all, there were free national elections in 2004, and these elections, in which the participation of poor rural voters was decisive, delivered a strongly negative verdict on the policies fear and hate, as well as the BJP's economic policies. The current government, headed by Manmohan Singh, India's first minority Prime Minister, has announced a firm commitment to end sectarian violence and has done a great deal to focus attention on the unequal economic and political situation of Muslims in the nation, as well as appointing Muslims to key offices. On balance, then, the pluralistic democracy envisaged by Gandhi and Nehru seems to be winning, in part because the framers had bequeathed to India a wise institutional and constitutional structure and traditions of commitment to the key political values this structure embodies.

It should be mentioned that one of the key aspects of the founders' commitments, which so far has survived the Hindu-right challenge, is the general conception of the nation and its unity as a unity around political ideals and values, particularly the value of equal entitlement, rather than around ethnic or religious or linguistic identity. India, like the United States, but unlike most of the nations of Europe, has rejected such exclusionary ways of characterizing the nation, adopting, in the Constitution, in public ceremonies, and in key public symbols, the political conception of its unity. India's national anthem, words and music composed by Rabindranath Tagore, is a paean to pluralism: it mentions the diverse ethno-geographical origins of Indians, and praises the fact that all alike show reverence to the moral law. This public commitment to pluralism is continually contested by the Hindu right, who prefer another anthem, warlike and exclusionary. So far, however, the founders' strategy has held firm. Political structure is not everything, but it can supply a great deal in times of stress.

2. The Press and the role of Intellectuals

One of the heartening aspects of Gujarat was the performance of the national media and of the community of intellectuals. Both print media and television kept up unceasing pressure to document and investigate the riots, and the role of key government officials was documented beyond doubt. At the same time, because the local police were not doing their job, many scholars, lawyers, and NGO leaders converged on Gujarat to take down the testimony of witnesses, help them file complaints, and prepare a public record that would stand up in court. The intellectual community has easier access to the national press in India than in the U.S., in part thanks to the somewhat greater financial independence of the national media, and these intellectuals seized the opportunity, producing a wonderful outpouring of trenchant and high-quality analysis. The only reason I felt the need to write about these events further myself is that these analyses have by and large not reached the U. S. audience. We can see here documentation of something long ago observed by Amartya Sen in the context of famines: the crucial role of a free press in supporting democratic institutions. And we can study here what freedom really means: I would argue that it requires a certain absence of top-down corporate control and an easy access to the major media of intellectual voices from a wide range of backgrounds. We in the U.S. should take note.

3. Education: the importance of critical thinking and imagination

So far I have mentioned factors that have helped the Indian democracy survive the threat of quasi-fascist takeover. Now we move to warning signs for the future, areas in which the democracy is currently weak and vulnerable. The public schools of the state of Gujarat are famous for their complete lack of critical thinking, their exclusive emphasis on rote learning and the uncritical learning of marketable skills, and for the elements of fascist propaganda that easily creep in when critical thinking is not cultivated. It is well known that Hitler is presented as a hero in history textbooks in this state, and nationwide public protest has not yet led to any change in this regard. To some extent the rest of the nation is better off than Gujarat: national-level textbooks have been rewritten to take out the false ideological view of history loved by the Hindu right and to substitute a much more nuanced view of history. Nonetheless, the emphasis on rote learning and on regurgitation for national examinations is distressing everywhere, and things are only becoming worse with the immense pressure to produce economically productive graduates. The educational culture of India used to contain progressive voices, such as the great Tagore, who emphasized that all the skills in the world were useless, even baneful, if not wielded by a cultivated imagination and refined critical faculties. Currently, these voices have been silenced by the sheer demand for profitability in the global market. Parents want their children to learn marketable skills, and their great pride is the admission of a child to the Indian Institutes of Technology and Management. They have contempt for the humanities and the arts. I fear for democracy down the road, when it is run, as it increasingly will be, by docile engineers in the Gujarat mold, unable to criticize the propaganda of politicians and unable to imagine the pain of another human being.

This is no humorous topic, but it can be illustrated by an odd story from my own experience investigating the Gujarati community in the United States, where fully 40% of Indian-Americans hail from that state. A large proportion of Gujarati Hindus belong to the Swaminarayan sect of Hinduism, which at present is distinctive for its emphasis on uncritical obedience to the utterances of the current head of the sect, whose title is Pramukh Swami. On a visit to the elaborate multi-million dollar Swaminarayan temple in Bartlett Illinois, I was given a tour by a young man recently arrived from Gujarat, who delighted in telling me the simplistic Hindu-right story of India's history, and who emphatically told me that whenever Pramukh Swami speaks one is to regard it as the direct voice of God and obey without question. At this point, with a beatific smile, this young man pointed up to the elaborate marble ceiling of the temple and asked me "Do you know why this ceiling glows the way it does?" I said I didn't know, and I confidently expected an explanation invoking the spiritual powers of Pramukh Swami. My guide smiled even more broadly. "Fiber-optic cables," he told me. "We are the first ones to put this technology into a temple." Here you see what can easily wreck democracy: a combination of technological sophistication with utter docility. I fear that many democracies around the world, including our own, are going down this road, through a lack of emphasis on the humanities and arts and an unbalanced emphasis on profitable skills.

4. The Creation of a Liberal Public Culture

How did fascism take such a hold in India? Hindu traditions emphasize tolerance and pluralism, and daily life in India, as in New York, tend to emphasize the ferment and vigor of difference, as people from so many different ethnic, linguistic, and regional backgrounds encounter one another. But the traditions contain a wound, a locus of vulnerability, and I would locate this wound in the area of humiliated masculinity. For centuries, some Hindu males think, they have been subordinated, laughed at, treated as weak, by a sequence of conquerors. The fact that the British really did despise Hinduism as what Winston Churchill called a "beastly religion" surely made matters worse, and Hindus came to identify the sexual playfulness and sensuousness of their traditions, scorned by the masters of the Raj, with their own weakness and subjection. So, a repudiation of the sensuous and the cultivation of the masculinity typified by Tagore's image of the British military band came to seem the best way out of subjection. One reason why the RSS attracts such a following is this widespread sense of masculine failure, a key aspect of the rhetoric of both Savarkar and Golwalkar, and of RSS shakhas in every part of India today.

At the same time, the RSS filled a void, organizing at the grass-roots level with great discipline and selflessness. The RSS is not just about fascist organization: it also provides needed social services, and it provides fun, luring boys in with the promise of a group life that has both more solidarity and more imagination than the tedious world of government schools. Golwalkar said that if he saw a beautiful peacock in his garden and wanted the peacock to become his pet, he would feed it little bits of opium until it became addicted, and that way it would come to his garden every day. He said that this was how the shakas work: by the lure of fun and games, they make boys obedient members of the organization.

So what is needed is some counter-force, which would supply a public culture of pluralism with equally efficient grass-roots organization, and a public culture of masculinity that would contend against the appeal of the warlike and rapacious masculinity purveyed by the Hindu Right. The "clash within" is not so much a clash between two groups in a nation who are different from birth, it is, at bottom, a clash within each person, in which the ability to life with others on terms of mutual respect and equality contends anxiously against anxiety and the sense of being humiliated. Gandhi understood this. During his lifetime, his powerful movement did purvey a counter-image to the images of domineering masculinity. He taught his followers that life's real struggle was a struggle within the self, against one's own need to dominate and one's fear of being vulnerable. He deliberately focused attention on sexuality as an arena in which domination plays itself out with pernicious effect, and he deliberately cultivated an androgynous maternal persona. I think that in some respects he went off the tracks, in his suggestion that sexual relations are inherently scenes of domination and in his recommendation of asceticism as the only route to non-domination. Nonetheless, he saw the problem at its root, and he proposed a public culture that, while he lived, was sufficient to address it. His followers understood that being a real man does not mean emulating British aggressiveness and learning to bash others. It meant having the courage not to bash, to stand up to aggression with nothing but one's naked human dignity around one. In the process, he won the respect of the entire world for India's men and their traditions (conceived as he conceived them). In a quite different way, Rabindranath Tagore also created a counter-image of the Indian self, an image that was more sensuous, more joyful than that of Gandhi, but equally bent on renouncing the domination that Tagore saw as inherent in European traditions.

After Gandhi, however, this part of the pluralist program has languished. Much though he loved and admired both Gandhi and Tagore, Nehru had contempt for religion, and out of his contempt he neglected the cultivation of that which the radical religions of both men had supplied: images of who we are as citizens, symbolic connections to the roots of human vulnerability and openness, and the creation of a grassroots public culture around these symbols. Nehru was a great institution-builder, but in thinking about the public culture of the new nation his focus was always on economic issues, not so much on cultural issues. Because he firmly expected that raising the economic level of the poor would cause them to lose the need for religion and in general for emotional sources of nourishment, he saw no need to provide a counterforce to the powerful emotional propaganda of the Hindu right. Today's young people in India, therefore, tend to think of religion, and symbolic culture-creation in general, as forces that are in their very nature fascist and reactionary, because that is what they have seen in their experience. When one tells them the story of the U. S. civil rights movement, and the role of both liberal religion and powerful pluralist rhetoric in forging an anti-racist civic culture in that movement, they are quite surprised. Meanwhile, the RSS, which understands human psychology rather well, goes to work unopposed in every state and region, skillfully plucking the strings of hate and fear. By now pluralists generally realize that a mistake was made in leaving grassroots organization to the right, but it is very difficult to jump-start a public pluralist movement. The salient exception has been, for some years, the women's movement, which has built at the grass-roots very skillfully, with the regional knowledge, the mixture of economic and cultural incentives, and the respect for the arts and the imagination, that the creation of such a movement requires.

It is comforting for Americans to talk about a clash of civilizations. This thesis tells us that evil is outside, distant, other, and that we are perfectly all right as we are. All we need do is to remain ourselves and fight the good fight. But the case of Gujarat shows us that the world is very different from the world as depicted in that comforting fable. The forces that assail democracy are internal to many if not most democratic nations, and they are not foreign: they are our own ideas and voices, meaning the voices of aggressive European nationalism, refracted back against the original aggressor with the extra bile of resentment born of a long experience of domination and humiliation. The implication of this idea is that all nations, Western and non-Western, need to examine themselves with the most fearless exercise of the critical capacities, looking for the roots of domination within and devising effective institutional and educational counter-measures. At a deeper level, the case of Gujarat shows us what Gandhi and Tagore in their different ways knew very well: that the real root of domination lies deep in the human personality, in the narcissistic desire to dominate others and to efface the inconvenient challenge posed by the other; in wounded masculinity that cannot rest until it has destroyed the source of its own perceived wound. It would be so convenient if Americans were pure and free from flaw: but we can now see that very fantasy of purity for what it is: as yet another form that the resourceful narcissism of the human personality takes on the way to bad behavior.

Looking at the clash in my way, as an internal clash, we will naturally focus on four strategies for the preservation and enhancement of democracy around the world: first, on getting institutional structures that can remain firm against fascist challenges; second, on bolstering the independence, including economic independence of the press and the free speech of intellectuals; third, on creating educational institutions that teach the skills of critical thinking and imagining that are so crucial for the health of democracy. And finally – what Martin Luther King. Jr. learned from Gandhi – creating a public culture of non-domination and equality that can inspire fearful human beings, for all of us are fearful, with the idea that comfort is to be found in mutual aid and reciprocity, rather than the quick and dirty victory over an enemy onto whom we have all too conveniently projected the negative aspects of our own history and our own anxious thinking.

Part II
Scope of the Terrorist Threat

Assessing the State of Al Qaeda and Current and Future Terrorist Threats

Bruce Hoffman

Six-and-a-half years ago, 19 terrorists hijacked four airplanes and changed the course of history. Just as we underestimated al Qaeda then, we risk repeating the same mistake now. Al Qaeda today is frequently spoken of as if it is in retreat: a broken and beaten organization, incapable of mounting further attacks on its own and instead having devolved operational authority either to its various affiliates and associates or to entirely organically-produced, homegrown, terrorist entities. Listening to President Bush and various pundits you would think al Qaeda is broken. Its leadership is living in caves, cut off somewhere in remotest Waziristan. Isolated and demoralized, it has been reduced to a purely symbolic role, inspiring copycat terrorist groups, perhaps, but lacking any operational capability of its own – a toothless tiger. "Al Qaeda," the President declared in October 2006, "is on the run."[1] That's the conventional wisdom. Al Qaeda in fact is on the march. It has re-grouped and re-organized from the setbacks meted out to it by the United States and our coalition partners and allies during the initial phases of the global war on terrorism (GWOT)[2] and is marshalling its forces to continue the epic struggle begun more than ten years ago.

Al Qaeda Today: Evolution, Adaption and Adjustment

Al Qaeda's obituary has been written often since 9/11. "Al-Qa'ida's Top Primed To Collapse, U.S. Says," trumpeted a *Washington Post* headline two weeks after Khalid Sheikh Mohammed, the mastermind behind the 9/11 attacks, was arrested

---

B. Hoffman
Georgetown University
e-mail: brh6@georgetown.edu

[1] Quoted in Peter Baker, "Bush Is Reassuring on Iraq But Says He's 'Not Satisfied'," *Washington Post*, 26 October 2006.

[2] The most stunning and consequential of these was achieved during "Operation Enduring Freedom," that toppled the Taliban regime ruling Afghanistan and destroyed al Qaeda's infrastructure in that country.

I.A. Karawan et al. (eds.), *Values and Violence*,

in March 2003. "I believe the tide has turned in terms of al-Qa'ida," Congressmen Porter J. Goss, then-chairman of the U.S. House of Representatives Intelligence Committee and himself a former CIA case officer who became its director a year later, was quoted. "We've got them nailed," an unidentified intelligence expert was quoted, who still more expansively declared, "we're close to dismantling them."[3] These up-beat assessments continued the following month with the nearly bloodless capture of Baghdad and the failure of al Qaeda to make good on threats of renewed attacks in retaliation for invasion.[4] Citing Administration sources, an article in the *Washington Times* on 24 April 2003 reported the prevailing view in official Washington that al Qaeda's "failure to carry out a successful strike during the U.S.-led military campaign to topple Saddam Hussein has raised questions about their ability to carry out major new attacks."[5] Despite major terrorist attacks in Jakarta and Istanbul during the latter half of that same year and the escalating insurgency in Iraq, this optimism carried into 2004. "The Al Qaida of the 9/11 period is under catastrophic stress," Ambassador Cofer Black, at the time the U.S. State Department's Counter-Terrorism Coordinator, declared. "They are being hunted down, their days are numbered."[6] Then came the Madrid bombings six weeks later and the deaths of 191 persons. The most accurate assessment, perhaps, was therefore the one offered by al Qaeda itself. "The Americans," Thabet bin Qais, a spokesperson for the movement said in May 2003, "only have predications and old intelligence left. It will take them a long time to understand the new form of al-Qaida."[7] Four years later we are indeed still struggling to understand the changing character and nature of al Qaeda and the shifting dimensions of the terrorist threat as it has evolved since 9/11.

Al Qaeda in fact is now functioning exactly as its founder and leader, Usama bin Laden envisioned it. On the one hand, true to the meaning of the Arabic word for the "base of operation"[8] or "foundation" – meaning the base or foundation from which a worldwide Islamic revolution can be waged (or, as other translations have it, the "precept" or "method")[9] – and thus simultaneously inspiring, motivating and

---

[3] Dana Priest and Susan Schmidt, "Al-Qa'ida's Top Primed To Collapse, U.S. Says," *Washington Post*, 16 March 2003.

[4] See, for example, CNN, "Alleged bin Laden tape a call to arms," at http://cnn.com/2003/WORLD/meast/02/11/sprj.irq.wrap and bin Laden's statement, "We want to let you know and confirm to you that this war of the infidels that the U.S. is leading with its allies . . . we are with you and we will fight in the name of God."

[5] David R. Sands, "Al-Qa'ida's credibility 'on the line' as war in Iraq winds down," *Washington Times*, 24 April 2003. See also, Dennis Pluchinsky, "Al-Qa'ida Identity Crisis," *Washington Times*, 28 April 2003.

[6] "U.S.: Al Qaida is 70 percent gone, their 'days are numbered'," *World Tribune.Com*, 23 January 2004.

[7] Sarah el Deeb, "Al-Qaida Reportedly Plans Big New Attack," *Associated Press*, 8 May 2003.

[8] Peter Bergen, *Holy War, Inc.: Inside the Secret World of Osama bin Laden* (New York: The Free Press, 2001), p. 29.

[9] As Jason Burke notes "'Al-Qaeda' is a messy and rough designation . . . . The word itself is critical. 'al-Qaeda' comes from the Arabic root *qaf-ayn-dal*. It can mean a base, as in a camp or a home, or a foundation, such as what is under a house. It can mean a pedestal that supports a column. It can also mean a precept, rule, principle, maxim, formula, method, model or pattern."

animating, radicalized Muslims to join the movement's fight. While, on the other, continuing to exercise its core operational and command and control capabilities: directing the implementing terrorist attacks.

The al Qaeda of today combines, as it always has, both a "bottom up" approach – encouraging independent thought and action from low (or lower-) level operatives – and a "top down" one – issuing orders and still coordinating a far-flung terrorist enterprise with both highly synchronized and autonomous moving parts. Mixing and matching organizational and operational styles whether dictated by particular missions or imposed by circumstances, the al Qaeda movement, accordingly, can perhaps most usefully be conceptualized as comprising four distinct, though not mutually exclusive, dimensions. In descending order of sophistication, they are:

1. Al Qaeda Central. This category comprises the remnants of the pre-9/11 al Qaeda organization. Although its core leadership includes some of the familiar, established commanders of the past, there are a number of new players who have advanced through the ranks as a result of the death or capture of key al Qaeda senior-level managers such as Abu Atef, KSM, and Hambali, and more recently, Abu Faraj al-Libi and Hamza al-Rabia.[10] It is believed that this hardcore remains centered in or around the Afghanistan and Pakistan borders and continues to exert actual coordination, if not some direct command and control capability, in terms of commissioning attacks, directing surveillance and collating reconnaissance, planning operations, and approving their execution.

This category comes closest to the al Qaeda operational template or model evident in the 1998 East Africa embassy bombings and 9/11 attacks. Such high value, "spectacular" attacks are entrusted only to al Qaeda's professional cadre: the most dedicated, committed and absolutely reliable element of the movement. Previous patterns suggest that these "professional" terrorists are deployed in pre-determined and carefully selected teams. They will also have been provided with very specific targeting instructions. In some cases, such as the East Africa bombings, they may establish contact with, and enlist the assistance of, local sympathizers and supporters. This will be solely for logistical and other attack-support purposes or to enlist these locals to actually execute the attack(s). The operation, however, will be planned and directed by the "professional" element with the locals clearly subordinate and playing strictly a supporting role (albeit a critical one).

2. Al Qaeda Affiliates and Associates. This category embraces formally established insurgent or terrorist groups that over the years have benefited from bin Laden's largesse and/or spiritual guidance and/or have received training, arms, money and other assistance from al Qaeda. Among the recipients of this assistance have been terrorist groups and insurgent forces in Uzbekistan and Indonesia,

---

Jason Burke, *Al-Qaeda: Casting A Shadow Of Terror* (London & New York: I.B. Tauris, 2003), p. 7. See also, idem., "Think Again: Al Qaeda," *Foreign Policy* (May/June 2004), accessed at http://www.foreign policy.com.

[10] A search on google.com for "al Qaeda Number 3's" illuminates how this movement has a deeper bench than is often thought and something akin to an institutionalized process of leadership succession.

Morocco and the Philippines, Bosnia and Kashmir, among other places. By supporting these groups, bin Laden's intentions were three-fold. First, he sought to co-opt these movements' mostly local agendas and channel their efforts towards the cause of global jihad. Second, he hoped to create a jihadi "critical mass" from these geographically scattered, disparate movements that would one day coalesce into a single, unstoppable force. And, third, he wanted to foster a dependent relationship whereby as a quid pro quo for prior al Qaeda support, these movements would either undertake attacks at al Qaeda's behest or provide essential local, logistical and other support to facilitate strikes by the al Qaeda "professional" cadre noted above.

This category includes groups such as: al-Ittihad al-Islami (AIAI), the late Abu Musab Zarqawi's al Qaeda in Mesopotamia (formerly *Jamaat al Tawhid wa'l Jihad*), Asbat al-Ansar, Ansar al Islam, Islamic Army of Aden, Islamic Movement of Uzbekistan (IMU), Jemaah Islamiya (JI), Libyan Islamic Fighting Group (LIFG), Moro Islamic Liberation Front (MILF), Salafist Group for Call and Combat (GSPC), and the various Kashmiri Islamic groups based in Pakistan – e.g., Harakat ul Mujahidin (HuM), Jaish-e-Mohammed (JeM), Laskar-e-Tayyiba (LeT), and Laskar i Jhangvi (LiJ). Both the number and geographical diversity of these entities is proof of al Qaeda's continued influence and vitality.

3. Al Qaeda Locals. These are dispersed cells of al Qaeda adherents who have or have had some direct connection with al Qaeda – no matter how tenuous or evanescent. They appear to fall into two sub-categories.

One category comprises persons who have had some prior terrorism experience – having been blooded in battle as part of some previous jihadi campaign in Algeria, the Balkans, Chechnya, and perhaps more recently in Iraq, and may have trained in some al Qaeda facility whether in Afghanistan or Yemen or the Sudan before 9/11. Specific examples of this adversary include Ahmed Ressam, who was arrested in December 1999 at Port Angeles, Washington State, shortly after he had entered the U.S. from Canada. Ressam, for instance, had a prior background in terrorism, having belonged to Algeria's Armed Islamic Group (GIA). After being recruited to al Qaeda, he was provided with a modicum of basic terrorist training in Afghanistan. In contrast to the professional cadre detailed above, however, Ressam was given very non-specific, virtually open-ended targeting instructions before being dispatched to North America. Also, unlike the well-funded professional cadre, Ressam was given only $12,000 in "seed money" and instructed to raise the rest of his operational funds from petty thievery. He was also told by KSM to recruit members for his terrorist cell from among the expatriate Muslim communities in Canada and the U.S.[11] The al Qaeda operative, Andrew Rowe, a British national and Muslim convert, convicted for his involvement in the 2003 al Qaeda plot to attack London's Heathrow Airport is another example of this category.

The other category, as is described in the detailed discussion of the 7/7 London attacks below, conforms to the profile of the four British Muslims responsible for the

[11] See 1734HA01, United States District Court, Southern District of New York, United States of America v. Mokhtar Haouri, S4 00 Cr. 15 (JFK), 3 June 2001, pp. 538, 548, 589, 622, 658, & 697.

2005 bombings of mass transit targets in London. In contrast to Ressam and Rowe, none of the four London bombers had previously fought in any of the contemporary, iconic Muslim conflicts (e.g., Algeria, Chechnya, Kashmir, Bosnia, Afghanistan, etc.) nor is there *conclusive* evidence of their having received any training in an al Qaeda camp in Afghanistan, Yemen, or the Sudan *prior* to 9/11.[12] Rather, the ringleader of the London cell – Mohammed Siddique Khan, and an accomplice, Shahzad Tanweer, were brought to Pakistan for training and then returned to their homeland with both an attack plan and the knowledge to implement it. They then recruited others locally as needed into the cell and undertook a relatively simple, but nonetheless sophisticated and highly consequential attack.[13]

In both the above categories, however, the terrorists will have some link with al Qaeda. Their current relationship, and communication, with a central al Qaeda command and control apparatus may be either active or dormant and similarly their targeting choices may either be specifically directed or else entirely left to the cell to decide. The distinguishing characteristic of this category, however, is that there is some direct connection of some kind with al Qaeda.

4. Al Qaeda Network. These are home-grown Islamic radicals – from North Africa, the Middle East, and South and Southeast Asia – as well as local converts to Islam mostly living in Europe, Africa and perhaps Latin America and North America as well, who have no direct connection with al Qaeda (or any other identifiable terrorist group), but nonetheless are prepared to carry out attacks in solidarity with or support of al Qaeda's radical jihadi agenda. Like the "al Qaeda Locals" they too are motivated by a shared sense of enmity and grievance felt towards the United States and West in general and their host-nations in particular. In this specific instance, however, the relationship with al Qaeda is more inspirational than actual, abetted by profound rage over the U.S. invasion and occupation of Iraq and the oppression of Muslims in Palestine, Kashmir, Chechnya, and elsewhere. Critically, these persons are neither directly members of a known, organized terrorist group nor necessarily even a very cohesive entity unto themselves.

Examples of this category, which comprises small collections of like-minded locals who gravitate towards one to plan and mount terrorist attacks completely independent of any direction provided by al Qaeda, include the so-called Hofstad Group in the Netherlands, a member of whom (Mohammed Bouyeri) murdered the Dutch filmmaker Theo Van Gogh in Amsterdam in November 2004, and the so called "trolley bombers" (the two Lebanese nationals who placed bombs, that failed

---

[12] A confidential informant of the British Security Service (MI-5) claims to have traveled to Afghanistan in the late 1990s/early 2000s with another man named "Imran," who he later identified as the ringleader of the 7/7 London attacks, Mohammed Siddique Khan. That "Imram" was in fact Khan has not been confirmed. See Intelligence and Security Committee, *Report into the London Terrorist Attacks on 7 July 2005*, p. 16.

[13] See Honourable House of Commons, *Report of the Official Account of the Bombings in London on 7 July 2005* (London: The Stationary Office, HC 1087), 11 May 2006, titled "Were They Directed From Abroad?" pp. 24–27, accessed at http://www.official-documents.co.uk/document/hc0506/hc10/1087/1087.asp.

to explode, on two German commuter trains near Dortmund and Koblenz in July 2006).[14]

The most salient threat posed by the above categories, however, continues to come from al Qaeda Central and from its affiliates and associates. However, an additional and equally challenging threat is now posed by less discernible and more unpredictable entities drawn from the vast Muslim Diaspora in Europe. As far back as 2001, the Netherlands' intelligence and security service had detected increased terrorist recruitment efforts among Muslim youth living in the Netherlands whom it was previously assumed had been completely assimilated into Dutch society and culture.[15] Thus, representatives of Muslim extremist organizations – including, presumably, al Qaeda – had already succeeded in embedding themselves in, and drawing new sources of support from, receptive elements within established Diaspora communities. In this way, new recruits could be drawn into the movement who likely had not previously come under the scrutiny of local or national law enforcement agencies. Indeed, according to a BBC News documentary report broadcast in July 2006, Khan, the London bombing cell's ringleader, may have acted precisely as such an al Qaeda "talent spotter": trawling Britain's Muslim communities during the summer of 2001 – literally weeks before 9/11 – trying to attract new recruits to the movement.[16]

This new category of terrorist adversary, moreover, also has proven more difficult for the authorities in these countries to track, predict and anticipate. The Director of GCHQ (Government Communications Headquarters), Britain's equivalent of our NSA (National Security Agency) admitted this in testimony before a Parliamentary committee investigating the 7/7 attacks. "We had said before July [2005]," Sir David Pepper noted,

> there are probably groups out there that we do not know anything about, and because we do not know anything about them we do not know how many there are. What happened in July [the 2005 London bombings] was a demonstration that there were [material redacted for security reasons] conspiracies going on about which we essentially knew nothing, and that rather sharpens the perception of how big, if I can use [Secretary of Defense Donald] Rumfeld's term, the unknown unknown was.[17]

This adversary, comprising hitherto unknown cells, is difficult, if not impossible, to effectively profile. Indeed, this was precisely the conclusion reached by

---

[14] See "Lebanon holds train bomb suspect," *BBC News (Internatinoal Version)*, 24 August 2006 accessed at http://news.bbc.co.uk/2/hi/europe/5281208.stm.

[15] See General Intelligence and Security Service, *Recruitment for the jihad in the Netherlands: from incident to trend* (The Hague: Ministry of the Interior and Kingdom Relations, December 2002).

[16] A UK Muslim community leader interviewed in the documentary said that he approached by maintains Khan, who was accompanied by two other British Muslims named Asif Hanif and Omar Khan Sharif, who in 2003 would stage a suicide attack on a seaside pub in Tel Aviv, Israel. See BBC News Media Exchange, "Britain's First Suicide Bombers," broadcast on BBC2 on 11 July 2006, 2000 GMT.

[17] Quoted in Intelligence and Security Committee, *Report into the London Terrorist Attacks on 7 July 2005*, pp. 30–31.

the above-mentioned Parliamentary committee in their report on the London bombings.[18] Although the members of these terrorist cells may be marginalized individuals working in menial jobs from the lower socio-economic strata of society, some with long criminal records or histories of juvenile delinquency; others may well come from solidly middle and upper-middle class backgrounds with university and perhaps even graduate degrees and prior passions for cars, sports, rock music and other completely secular, material interests. For example, in the case of radicalized British Muslims, since 9/11 we have seen terrorists of South Asian and North African descent as well as those hailing both from the Middle East and Caribbean. They have included life-long devout Muslims as well as recent converts. Persons from the margins of society who made a living as thieves or from drug dealing and students at the London School Economics, one of the UK's premiere universities.[19] What they will have in common is a combination of a deep commitment to their faith – often recently re-discovered; admiration of bin Laden for the cathartic blow struck against America on 9/11; hatred of the U.S. and the West; and, a profoundly shared sense of alienation from their host countries. "There appear to be a number of common features to this grooming," the report of the Intelligence and Security Committee of the UK House of Commons concluded.

> In the early stages, group conversation may be around being a good Muslim and staying away from drugs and crime, with no hint of an extremist agenda. Gradually individuals may be exposed to propaganda about perceived injustices to Muslims across the world with international conflict involving Muslims interpreted as examples of widespread war against Islam; leaders of the Muslim world perceived as corrupt and non-Islamic; with some domestic policies added as "evidence" of a persecuted Islam; and conspiracy theories abounding. They will then move on to what the extremists claim is religious justification for violent jihad in the Quran and the Hadith. . . . and – if suicide attacks are the intention – the importance of martyrdom in demonstrating commitment to Islam and the rewards in Paradise for martyrs; before directly inviting an individual to engage in terrorism. *There is little evidence of over compulsion. The extremists appear rather to rely on the development of individual commitment and group bonding and solidarity* [my emphasis].[20]

These new recruits are the anonymous cogs in the world-wide al Qaeda enterprise and include both long-standing residents and new immigrants found across in Europe, but specifically in countries with large expatriate Muslim populations such as Britain, Spain, France, Germany, Italy, the Netherlands, and Belgium.

---

18 The report concluded that "The July attacks emphasized that there was no clear profile of a British Islamist terrorist." See Intelligence and Security Committee, *Report into the London Terrorist Attacks on 7 July 2005*, p. 29.

19 For instance, in the criminal category are Richard Reid (the so-called "shoe bomber," who attempted to blow up an American Airlines flight en route from Paris to Miami in December 2001) and Jermaine Lindsay (one of the 7/7 London bombers); while the two LSE students include Omar Saed Shiekh (who orchestrated the kidnapping and murder of the *Wall Street Journal* reporter, Daniel Pearl, in 2002) and Omar Sharif Khan (one of the two British Muslims who carried out a suicide bombing attack against a sea-side pub in Tel Aviv, Israel in April 2003).

20 Honourable House of Commons, *Report of the Official Account of the Bombings in London on 7th July 2005*, pp. 31–32.

The Perils of Wishful Thinking: Al Qaeda and The 7/7 London Bombings

The United Kingdom of course rightly prides itself on decades-long experience and detailed knowledge of effectively countering a variety of terrorist threats. Over the past dozen years the UK homeland itself has been subject to attack from a diversity of adversaries including: the Provisional Irish Republican Army,[21] renegade Palestinian factions[22] and both before and since 9/11 by al Qaeda as well.[23] Yet, despite Britain's formidable counterterrorist capabilities and unrivaled expertise, only a month before the 7 July 2005 London bombings, the Joint Terrorism Assessment Center (JTAC), the British counterpart of our own NCTC (National Counterterrorism Center) concluded that, "at present there is not a group with both the current intent and the capability to attack in the UK" and consequently downgraded the overall threat level for the UK.[24]

More astonishing perhaps was the dismissal of the prospect of suicide terrorist attacks occurring in the United Kingdom, despite the emerging global pattern of terrorism in this respect and the involvement of several British nationals in both attempted and successful suicide attacks elsewhere.[25] Seventy-eight percent of all the suicide terrorist incidents perpetrated between 1968 and 2004, for instance, have occurred in the years following 9/11. And, the dominant force behind this trend is religion – specifically groups and individuals identifying themselves as Islamic.[26] Indeed, of the 35 terrorist organizations currently employing

---

[21] During the 1990s alone, major terrorist bombings rocked the City, London's financial center and the equivalent of New York City's Wall Street, on at least three separate occasions, with massive explosions occurring at St Mary's Axe, the Baltic Exchange building, and Canary Wharf.

[22] For instance, the 1982 assassination attempt on Israel's ambassador to the UK by the Abu Nidal Organization and the 1994 bombing of the Israeli embassy in London.

[23] For instance, the intended massive truck bomb attack planned for downtown Birmingham in 2000 and the plans in 2003 to simultaneously hijack a plane from Eastern Europe and crash it into a terminal at London's Heathrow Airport and then launch a secondary attack with remote-control mortars (see David Leppard, "Al-Qaeda's Heathrow Jet Plot Revealed," *Sunday Times* (London), 9 October 2005 at http://www.timesonline.co.uk/article/0,2087-1817244,00.html.).

[24] Quoted in Intelligence and Security Committee, *Report into the London Terrorist Attacks on 7 July 2005*, p. 23. Note should be taken, however, that although the threat level was reduced to "Substantial," this designation still "indicates a continued high level of threat and that an attack might well be mounted without warning." See David Leppard, "Al-Waeda's Heathrow Jet Plot Revealed."

[25] For example, Richard Reid, the so-called "shoe bomber," who attempted to blow up an American Airlines flight en route from Paris to Miami in December 2001; the involvement of another Briton, Sajid Badat, in an identical inflight aircraft suicide bombing plot that same month; and the two British Muslims, Asif Hanif and Omar Khan Sharif, who carried out the suicide bombing of Mike's Place, a seafront pub in Tel Aviv, Israel in April 2003.

[26] That there has been a significant rise in the incidence of suicide terrorism since 9/11 is not disputed by scholars. See, for instance, Robert A. Pape, "The Strategic Logic of Suicide Terrorism," *American Political Science Review*, vol. 97, no. 3 (August 2003), pp. 343–361 and idem., *Dying To Win: The Strategic Logic Of Suicide Terrorism* (New York: Random House, 2005) p. 1; as well as Mia A. Bloom, *Dying To Kill: The Allure of Suicide Terror* (New York: Columbia

suicide tactics, 86 percent (31 of 35) are Islamic. These movements, moreover, have been responsible for 81 percent of all suicide attacks since 9/11.[27] Indeed, to date, suicide attacks have taken place in at least two dozen countries – including, the United Kingdom, Israel, Sri Lanka, Russia, Lebanon, Turkey, Italy, Indonesia, Pakistan, Colombia, Argentina, Kenya, Tanzania, Croatia, Morocco, Singapore, the Philippines, Saudi Arabia, Kuwait, and Iraq.[28] By comparison, at the dawn of the modern era of religious terrorism some twenty years ago, this was a phenomenon confined exclusively to two countries: Lebanon and Kuwait and employed by fewer than a half dozen groups.[29] Yet, only four months before the 7/7 bombings, the Joint Intelligence Committee (JIC), Britain's most senior intelligence assessment and evaluation body (one roughly similar to the American intelligence community's NIC, or National Intelligence Center), judged that "such attacks would not become the norm within Europe." This judgment, coupled with the testimony of Dame Eliza Manningham-Buller, the Director-General of the Security Service (MI-5), prompted the aforementioned Parliamentary committee to conclude that "The fact that there were suicide attacks in the UK on 7 July was clearly unexpected: the Director

---

University Press, 2005). The role of religion behind this increase, however, is debated. Pape argues in his seminal article that, "Religious fanaticism does not explain why the world leader in suicide terrorism is the Tamil Tigers in Sri Lanka . . ."; while conceding that "although religious motives may matter, modern suicide terrorism is not limited to Islamic Fundamentalism" ("The Strategic Logic of Suicide Terrorism," p. 343). In his book, however, Pape is more explicit, writing that the "presumed connection between suicide terrorism and Islamic fundamentalism is misleading . . . . there is little connection between suicidal terrorism and Islamic fundamentalism, or any of the world's religions. In fact, the leading instigators of suicide attacks are the Tamil Tigers . . . ." (*Dying To Win*, pp. 1–2). While I fully agree with Pape on this point that the Tigers are responsible for the largest number of suicide terrorist attacks between 1968 and 2001, they are *not*, however, the driving force behind the increasing use of this tactic *since* 9/11. In fact, since 2002 an uneasy truce between the Tigers and the Sri Lankan government has meant that the Tigers have largely abjured from engaging in any terrorist operations, much less suicide attacks. Moreover, Pape is not accurate in categorizing the Tamil Tigers as a "Marxist Leninist" group. It is more appropriately described as an ethno-nationalist/separatist movement. Further, while the Tigers are not a religious terrorist organization, they nonetheless share some characteristics more common with a religious cult than with their secular ethno-nationalist/separatists counterparts. For a particularly incisive critique of Pape's fundamental arguments about suicide terrorism see Bloom, *Dying To Kill*, pp. 83–84.

27 The RAND Terrorism Incident Database. As Mia Bloom also concludes in her exhaustive study of suicide terrorism, "There is an increasing an disturbing trend towards Islamic suicide terrorism." Bloom, *Dying To Kill*, p. 2.

28 Bloom, *Dying to Kill*, p. 2. See also, Israeli Security Agency, "Security Seminar on Combating The Threat of Suicide Bombers," Israeli Embassy, Washington, D.C., 16 September 2003.

29 Towards the end of the 1980s, however, suicide terrorism began to spread beyond the Middle East: first to Sri Lanka but then as the 1990s unfolded to India, Argentina, Israel, Saudi Arabia, Kenya, and Tanzania. It was also initially embraced by a couple of terrorist groups only: al Dawa, an Iraqi Shi'a group, and the Lebanese Shi'a organization Hezbollah (mostly using its cover name, Islamic Jihad). Hezbollah's example of successfully driving the U.S. from Lebanon with suicide attacks (as discussed below) subsequently inspired other groups to adopt this tactic, specifically: the Liberation Tigers of Tamil Eelam (LTTE or the Tamil Tigers), Hamas, Palestine Islamic Jihad, and al Qa'ida.

General of the Security Service said it was a surprise that the first big attack in the UK for ten years was a suicide attack."[30]

The point of this discussion is most certainly not to criticize our principal ally in the war on terrorism but rather to highlight the immense difficulties and vast uncertainties concerning countering terrorism today that have confounded even the enormously professional and experienced British intelligence and security services. Moreover, the danger of similarly cloaking ourselves in a false sense of security based on faulty assumptions or wishful thinking is omnipresent in so fluid and dynamic a terrorism environment as exists today. Indeed, the testimony presented to the Parliamentary committee investigating the 7/7 bombings by two persons at the apex of the United Kingdom's counterterrorism effort, encapsulate the central challenge today facing the United States in our own counterterrorism effort. "We were working off a script which actually has been completely discounted from what we know as reality," Andy Hayman, then Assistant Commissioner of Specialist Operations at Scotland Yard – arguably Britain's top counterterrorist cop – admitted.[31] Similarly, Tom Dowse, Chief of the Assessments Staff, testified that, "I think the more we learned over this period of several years, the more we began to realize the limits of what we knew . . ."[32]

Our appreciation and understanding of the current al Qaeda threat further underscores these perils. Both at the time of the London bombing attacks and since a misconception has frequently been perpetuated that this was entirely an organic or homegrown phenomenon of self-radicalized, self-selected terrorists. Such arguments often were cited in support of the argument that entirely homegrown threats had superseded those posed of al Qaeda; that al Qaeda itself was no longer a consequential, active terrorist force; and accordingly that the threat had both changed and perhaps even receded. The evidence that has come to light since the London attacks 18 months ago, however, points to the opposite conclusion: that al Qaeda is not only alive and kicking, but that it is still actively planning, supporting through the provision of training and perhaps even directing terrorist attacks on a global canvas. This was precisely the focus of a speech given in November 2006 in London by Dame Eliza Manningham-Buller, then Director of Britain's Security Service (MI-5). She warned of the scale of the threat to the UK as evidenced by the 30 plots that the Security Service was aware of. "These plots," she said, "often have links back to al-Qaeda in Pakistan and through those links, al-Qaeda gives guidance and training to its largely British foot soldiers here on an extensive and growing scale.... And

[30] Quoted in Intelligence and Security Committee, *Report into the London Terrorist Attacks on 7 July 2005*, p. 28.

[31] Quoted in Intelligence and Security Committee, *Report into the London Terrorist Attacks on 7 July 2005: Presented to Parliament by the Prime Minister by Command of Her Majesty*, Cmd 6785, May 2006, p. 30, accessed at http://www.cabinetoffice.gov.uk/publications/reports/intelligence/isc_7july_report.pdf.

[32] Quoted in Intelligence and Security Committee, *Report into the London Terrorist Attacks on 7 July 2005: Presented to Parliament by the Prime Minister by Command of Her Majesty*, Cmd 6785, May 2006, p. 10, accessed at http://www.cabinetoffice.gov.uk/publications/reports/intelligence/isc_7july_report.pdf.

it is not just the UK of course. Other countries also face a new terrorist threat, from Spain to France to Canada and Germany." Manningham-Buller also described he Herculean dimension of the security challenges confronting both the Security Service and the police. "My officers and the police are working to contend with some 200 groupings or networks, totalling over 1,600 identified individuals (and there will be many we don't know)," she explained, "who are actively engaged in plotting, or facilitating, terrorist acts here and overseas."[33]

Issues of classification and sensitive collection, as well as the British government's gathering of evidence for a number of criminal cases that remain *sub judice* have prevented further, full, public disclosure of al Qaeda's active involvement in the London attacks – and virtually every other major terrorist plot unmasked in the UK since 2003.[34] However, suffice it to say that what is publicly known and has been reported in unclassified sources, clearly points to such involvement. For instance, the aforementioned report by the Parliament's Intelligence and Security Committee, noted among its other conclusions, that

- "Investigations since July have shown that the group [the four London bombers] was in contact with others involved in extremism in the UK . . . "
- "Siddique Khan [the group's ringleader] is now known to have visited Pakistan in 2003 and to have spent several months there with Shazad Tanweer [another bomber] between November 2004 and February 2005. It has not yet been established who they met in Pakistan, but it is assessed as likely that they had some contact with Al Qaida figures."
- "The extent to which the 7 July attacks were externally planned, directed or controlled by contacts in Pakistan or elsewhere remains unclear. The [British intelligence and security] Agencies believe that some form of operational training is likely to have taken place while Khan and Tanweer were in Pakistan. Contacts in the run-up to the attacks suggest they may have had advice or direction from individuals there." [35]

---

[33] Quoted in BBC News "Extracts from MI5 chief's speech," 10 November 2006 accessed at http://newsvote.bbc.co.uk/mpapps/pagetools/print/news.bbc.co.uk/2/hl/news/6135000.stm.

[34] These include the so called "ricin plot" in January 2003 involving an Algerian al Qaeda operative named Kamal Bourgass and what British authorities refer to as "Operation Crevice" and "Operation Rhyme" as well as this past summer's abortive plot to crash ten U.S. airliners into American cities. See Elaine Sciolino and Don Van Natta, Jr., "2004 British Raid Sounded Alert on Pakistani Militants," *New York Times*, 14 July 2005; and idem., "Europe Confronts Changing Face of Terrorism," *New York Times*, 1 August 2005; Sebastian Rotella, "British Terrorism Case Parallels Others; Trial in a suspected plot to bomb a nightclub or mall in 2004 involves alleged home-grown Islamic radicals with ties to militants in Pakistan,"*Los Angeles Times* http://proquest.umi.com/pqdweb?RQT=318&pmid=7683&TS=1164637618&clientId=61650&VType=PQD&VName=PQD&VInst=PROD, 1 September 2006 http://proquest.umi.com/pqdweb?RQT=572&VType=PQD&VName=PQD&VInst=PROD&pmid=7683&pcid=33308581&SrchMode=3; and *BBC News*, "Man admits UK-US terror bomb plot," 12 October 2006 accessed at http://newsvote.bbc.co.uk/mpapps/pagetools/print/news.bbc.co.uk/2/hi/uk_news/6044.

[35] Ibid., p. 12. See also, the section of the Honourable House of Commons, *Report of the Official Account of the Bombings in London on 7th July 2005*, pp. 20–21.

More compelling, albeit for the moment necessarily circumstantial, evidence may be found in the "martyrdom" videos made by Khan and Tanweer sometime while they were in Pakistan between November 2004 and February 2005.[36] Like all Usama bin Laden's most important video taped statements and appearances, the Khan and Tanweer statements were both professionally produced and released by al Qaeda's perennially-active communications department, "Al Sahab [the Clouds] for Media Production."

The first of the two videos, of Khan, was broadcast on the Qatar-based Arabic-language news station, al Jazeera, on 1 September 2005. It is worth exploring the content of Khan's statement in some detail since it accurately encapsulates the essence of European Muslim radicalism today. Kahn's statement is especially noteworthy for the following reasons:

- He professes his preeminent allegiance to and identification with his religion and the *umma* – the worldwide Muslim community. Hence, unlike most Western conceptions of identity and allegiance that are rooted to the nation or state, Khan's is exclusively to a theology.
- Like all terrorists before him, Khan frames his choice of tactic and justifies his actions in ineluctably defensive terms. He describes his struggle as an intrinsically defensive one and his act as a response to the repeated depredations and unmitigated aggression of the West that have been directed against Muslims worldwide.
- The sense of individual empowerment and catharsis evident in Khan's words and demeanor.
- The intense desire for vengeance and martyrdom, with the latter regarded by him as "supreme evidence" of his religious commitment.[37]
- Khan's laudatory comments about bin Laden and his deputy, Ayman al-Zawahiri.

The relevant portions of Khan's statement are as follows:

> I and thousands like me are forsaking everything for what we believe. Our driving motivation doesn't come from tangible commodities that this world has to offer. Our religion is Islam – obedience to the one true God, Allah, and following the footsteps of the final prophet and messenger Muhammad... This is how our ethical stances are dictated.
>
> *Your democratically elected governments continuously perpetuate atrocities against my people all over the world. And your support of them makes you directly responsible, just as I am directly responsible for protecting and avenging my Muslim brothers and sisters* [my emphasis].
>
> Until we feel security, you will be our targets. And until you stop the bombing, gassing, imprisonment and torture of my people we will not stop this fight. We are at war and I am a soldier. Now you too will taste the reality of this situation . . . .
>
> I myself, I make du'a [calling] to Allah . . . to raise me amongst those whom I love like the prophets, the messengers, the martyrs and today's heroes like our beloved Sheikh

[36] Honourable House of Commons, *Report of the Official Account of the Bombings in London on 7th July 2005*, p. 20.

[37] Honourable House of Commons, *Report of the Official Account of the Bombings in London on 7th July 2005*, p. 19.

> Osama Bin Laden, Dr Ayman al-Zawahiri and Abu Musab al-Zarqawi and all the other brothers and sisters that are fighting in . . . this cause.[38]

Al-Zawahiri in fact appears at the end of the same tape, praising Khan for having brought the "blessed battle . . . to the enemy's land." In a subsequent video, aired on al Jazeera on 19 September, al-Zawahiri also claimed responsibility for the attacks in the name of al Qaeda.[39]

In July 2006, a similar martyrdom tape made by Khan's traveling companion and fellow bomber, Shahzad Tanweer, was released by al Sahab to mark the first anniversary of the London attacks. Titled, "The Final Message of the Knights of the London Raid," it showed Tanweer expressing similar views to those of Khan. "To the non-Muslims of Britain," he begins,

> you may wonder what you have done to deserve this. You are those who have voted in your government, who in turn have, and still continue to this day, continue to oppress our mothers, children, brothers and sisters, from the east to the west, in Palestine, Afghanistan, Iraq, and Chechnya. Your government has openly supported the genocide of over 150,000 innocent Muslims in Falluja.
>
> You have offered financial and military support to the U.S. and Israel, in the massacre of our children in Palestine. You are directly responsible for the problems in Palestine, Afghanistan, and Iraq to this day. You have openly declared war on Islam, and are the forerunners in the crusade against the Muslims.

Al-Zawahiri then appears on screen to explain that, "What made Shehzad join the camps of Qaeda Al-Jihad was the oppression carried out by the British in Iraq, Afghanistan, and Palestine. He would often talk about Palestine, about the British support of the Jews, and about their clear injustice against the Muslims." An unidentified narrator then continues:

> In order to remove this injustice, Shehzad [sic] began training with all his might and devotion. Together with the martyr Siddiq Khan, he received practical and intensive training in how to produce and use explosives, in the camps of Qaeda Al-Jihad. The recruits who join these camps do not have to achieve high averages or to pass entrance exams. All they need is to be zealous for their religion and nation, and to love Jihad and martyrdom for the sake of Allah. [40]

The video continues with Tanweer warning "all you British citizens to stop your support to your lying British government, and to the so-called 'war on terror,' and ask yourselves why would thousands of men be willing to give their lives for the

---

[38] Quoted in Honourable House of Commons, *Report of the Official Account of the Bombings in London on 7th July 2005*, p. 19.

[39] "London's blessed raid is one of the raids which Jama'at Qa'idat al-Jihad (Al Qaidah of Jihad Group) was honoured to launch." Quoted in Honourable House of Commons, *Report of the Official Account of the Bombings in London on 7th July 2005*, p. 19.

[40] Quoted in MEMRI, Clip No. 1186, "Al-Qaeda Film on the First Anniversary of the London Bombings Features Messages by Bomber Shehzad Tanweer, American Al-Qaeda Member Adam Gadan and Al-Qaeda Leader Ayman Al-Zawahiri: *Recorded message of London bomber Shehzad Tanweer and statements by Al-Qaeda leaders Ayman Al-Zawahiri and Adam Gadahn, which were posted on www.tajdeed.net.tc on 8 July 2006*" accessed at http://www.memritv.org/Transcript.asp?P1=1186.

cause of Muslims." Al-Zawahiri also again appears to emphasize how both Khan and Tanweer were "striving for martyrdom, and were hoping to carry out a martyrdom operation. Both of them were very resolute in this." Tanweer then calls upon his fellow British Muslims to rise and fight the "disbelievers, for it is but an obligation made on you by Allah." A statement is then heard from U.S.-born Muslim convert Adam Gadahn ("Azzam the American") before concluding with Tanweer threatening that:

> What you have witnessed now is only the beginning of a series of attacks, which, *inshallah*, will intensify and continue, until you pull all your troops out of Afghanistan and Iraq, until you stop all financial and military support to the U.S. and Israel, and until you release all Muslim prisoners from Belmarsh, and your other concentration camps. And know that if you fail to comply with this, then know that this war will never stop, and that we are ready to give our lives, one hundred times over, for the cause of Islam. You will never experience peace, until our children in Palestine, our mothers and sisters in Kashmir, and our brothers in Afghanistan and Iraq feel peace.[41]

Towards a New U.S. Policy Counterterrorism Policy[42]

> "Could we, could others, could the police have done better? Could we with greater effort, greater imagination, have stopped it? We knew there were risks we were running. We were trying very hard and very fast to enhance our capacity, but even with the wisdom of hindsight I think it is unlikely that we would have done so, with the resources available to us at the time and the other demands placed upon us. I think that position will remain in the foreseeable future. We will continue to stop most of them, but we will not stop all of them."
>
> Dame Eliza Manningham-Buller, Director-General, UK Security Service (MI-5)[43]

As this discussion of the 7/7 London bombings has shown, al Qaeda and the threat it poses cannot be defeated through military means alone. Yet, our policy to date has arguably been predominantly weighted towards the tactical "kill or capture" approach and metric: assuming that a traditional center of gravity exists whether the target is al Qaeda or the insurgency in Iraq and that this target simply needs to be destroyed so that global terrorism or the Iraqi insurgency will end. However, both our adversaries today and the threats that they pose, are much more elusive and complicated and, as the previous discussion of the London attacks clearly depicts, less amenable to kinetic solutions. As one U.S. intelligence officer with vast experience in this realm acerbically said to me nearly three years ago: "We don't have enough bullets to kill them all." Accordingly, a new strategy and new approach is vital. Its success will be predicated upon a strategy that effectively combines the tactical elements of systematically destroying and weakening enemy capabilities (the "kill or capture" approach) alongside the equally critical, broader strategic imperative of

---

[41] Ibid.

[42] I am indebted to Lieutenant Colonel Fred T. Krawchuk, U.S. Army Special Forces for his contributions to this section of my paper.

[43] Quoted in Intelligence and Security Committee, *Report into the London Terrorist Attacks on 7 July 2005*, p. 39.

breaking the cycle of terrorist and insurgent recruitment and replenishment that have respectively sustained both al Qaeda's continued campaign and the ongoing conflict in Iraq. A successful strategy will thus be one that also thinks and plans ahead with a view towards addressing the threats likely to be posed by the terrorist and insurgent generation beyond the current one.

At the foundation of such a dynamic and adaptive strategy must be the ineluctable axiom that effectively and successfully countering terrorism as well as insurgency is not exclusively a military endeavor but also involves fundamental parallel political, social, economic, and ideological activities. This timeless principle of countering insurgency was first defined by Field Marshal Sir Gerald Templer in Malaya more than 50 years ago. "The shooting side of the business is only 25% of the trouble and the other 75% lies in getting the people of this country behind us," Templer famously wrote in November 1952, responding to a terrorist directive from the previous year that focused on increasing appreciably the "cajolery" of the population.[44] Accordingly, rather than viewing the fundamental organizing principle of American national defense strategy in this unconventional realm as a GWOT, it may be more useful to re-conceptualize it in terms of a global counterinsurgency (GCOIN). Such an approach would *a priori* knit together the equally critical political, economic, diplomatic, and developmental sides inherent to the successful prosecution of counterinsurgency to the existing dominant military side of the equation.

Such a new approach would necessarily be built upon a more integrated, systems approach to a complex problem that is at once operationally durable, evolutionary and elusive in character. Greater attention to this integration of American capabilities would provide incontrovertible recognition of the importance of endowing a GCOIN with an overriding and comprehensive, multi-dimensional policy. Ideally, this policy would embrace several elements: including a clear strategy, a defined structure for implementing it, and a vision of inter-government agency cooperation, and the unified effort to guide it. It would have particular benefit with respect to the gathering and exploitation of "actionable intelligence." By updating and streamlining interagency counterterrorism and counterinsurgency systems and procedures both strategically as well as operationally between the Department of Defense, the Department of State, and the intelligence community, actionable intelligence could likely be acquired, analyzed and disseminated faster and operations mounted more quickly. A more focused and strengthened interagency process would also facilitate the coordination of key themes and messages and the development and execution of long-term "hearts and minds" programs.[45]

---

[44] Quoted in John Cloake, *Templer: Tiger of Malaya – The Life of Field Marshal Sir Gerald Templer*, (London: Harrap, 1985), p. 262.

[45] Facilitating this would doubtless go well beyond DoD's purview, necessarily involving the National Security Council or the National Counterterrorism Center, and would likely entail the development of an "operational arm" with the authority of the President to de-conflict, synchronize, and task the various agencies of the government involved in counterterrorism and counterinsurgency operations.

The U.S. government, in sum, will need to adjust and adapt its strategy, resources, and tactics to formidable opponents that, as we have seen, are widely dispersed and decentralized and whose many destructive parts are autonomous, mobile, and themselves highly adaptive. In this respect, even the best strategy will be proven inadequate if military and civilian agency leaders are not prepared to engage successfully within ambiguous environments and reorient their organizational culture to deal with irregular threats. A successful GCOIN transcends the need for better tactical intelligence or new organizations. It is fundamentally about transforming the attitudes and mindsets of leaders so that they have the capacity to take decisive, yet thoughtful action against terrorists and/or insurgents in uncertain or unclear situations based on a common vision, policy, and strategy. In addition to traditional "hard" military skills of "kill or capture" and destruction and attrition; "soft" skills such as information operations, negotiation, psychology, social and cultural anthropology, foreign area studies, complexity theory, and systems management will become increasingly important in the ambiguous and dynamic environment in which irregular adversaries circulate.

Arguably, by combating irregular adversaries in a more collaborative manner with key relevant civilian agencies, military planners can better share critical information, track the various moving parts in terrorist/insurgency networks, and develop a comprehensive picture of this enemy – including their supporters, nodes of support, organizational and operational systems, processes, and plans. With this information in hand, the U.S. would then be better prepared to systematically disrupt or defeat all of the critical nodes that support the entire terrorist/insurgent network, thus rendering them ineffective.[46] Achieving this desideratum, however, will necessitate the coordination, de-conflicting, and synchronization of the variety of programs upon which the execution of American counterterrorist and/or counterinsurgency planning are dependent. An equally critical dimension of this process will be aligning the training of host nation counterparts with GWOT/GCOIN operations: building synergy; avoiding duplication of effort; ensuring that training leads to operational effectiveness; and ensuring that the U.S. interagency team and approach is in complete harmony. In other words, aligning these training programs (among the different government agencies) with GCOIN operations to build indigenous capabilities in counterterrorism and counterinsurgency will be absolutely fundamental to the success of such a strategy.

---

[46] Battle against small, independent, and mobile formations change too rapidly to allow rigid, centralized command and control. The U. S. military will have to continue to adjust and fight accordingly. Fast and fluid bottom-up planning and execution, supported by top-down guidance, resources and support is an appropriate approach to counterinsurgency. Intelligence logistics, and communications must integrate horizontally and vertically with operations to support this innovative approach to fighting insurgents. Counterinsurgency forces, with clear guidance and appropriate technology, can be both responsive C4ISR and effective execution nodes, greatly shortening the decision-making loop while still allowing the passing of information on actions and results to higher levels for strategic analysis.

In sum, new times, new threats, and new challenges ineluctably make a new strategy, approach and new organizational and institutional behaviors necessary. The threat posed by elusive and deadly irregular adversaries emphasizes the need to anchor changes that will more effectively close the gap between detecting irregular adversarial activity and rapidly defeating it. The effectiveness of U.S. strategy will be based on our capacity to think like a networked enemy, in anticipation of how they may act in a variety of situations, aided by different resources. This goal requires that the American national security structure in turn organize itself for maximum efficiency, information sharing, and the ability to function quickly and effectively under new operational definitions. With this thorough understanding in mind, we need to craft an approach that specifically takes into account the following key factors to effectively wage a GCOIN:

1. Separating the enemy from the populace that provides support and sustenance. This, in turn, entails three basic missions:

    a. Denial of enemy sanctuary
    b. Elimination of enemy freedom of movement
    c. Denial of enemy resources and support;

2. Identification and neutralization of the enemy;
3. Creation of a secure environment – progressing from local to regional to global;
4. Ongoing and effective neutralization of enemy propaganda through the planning and execution of a comprehensive and integrated information operations and holistic civil affairs campaign in harmony with the first four tasks;
5. Interagency efforts to build effective and responsible civil governance mechanisms that eliminate the fundamental causes of terrorism and insurgency.

In conclusion, al Qaeda may be compared to the archetypal shark in the water that must keep moving forward – no matter how slowly or incrementally – or die. In al Qaeda's context, this means adapting and adjusting to our countermeasures while simultaneously searching to identify new targets and vulnerabilities. In this respect, al Qaeda's capacity to continue to prosecute this struggle is a direct reflection of both the movement's resiliency and the continued resonance of its ideology. Accordingly, if the threat we face is constantly changing and evolving, so must our policies and responses be regularly reviewed, updated and adjusted. In this struggle, we cannot afford to rest on past laurels or be content with security that may have proven effective yesterday and today, but could likely prove inadequate tomorrow given this process of terrorist change and evolution.

Al Qaeda's "operational durability" thus has enormous significance for U.S. counterterrorism strategy and policy. Because it has this malleable resiliency, it cannot be destroyed or defeated in a single tactical, military engagement or series of engagements – much less ones exclusively dependent on the application of conventional forces and firepower. To a significant degree, our ability to carry out such missions effectively will depend on the ability of American strategy to adjust and adapt to changes we see in the nature and character of our adversaries.

The Debate over "New" vs. "Old" Terrorism

Martha Crenshaw[1]

Since 9/11, many policy makers, journalists, consultants, and scholars have become convinced that the world confronts a "new" terrorism unlike the terrorism of the past.[2] Thus the government and policy elites have been blamed for not recognizing the danger of the "new" terrorism in the 1990s and therefore failing to prevent the disaster of 9/11.[3] Knowledge of the "old" or traditional terrorism is considered irrelevant at best, and obsolete and anachronistic, even harmful, at worst. Those who

M. Crenshaw
Stanford University
e-mail: crenshaw@stanford.edu

[1] I wish to thank Audrey Kurth Cronin and Bruce Hoffman for their comments, as well as participants in a seminar at the Center for International Security and Cooperation, Stanford University, at the conference at the University of Utah where papers in this volume were presented, and at the 2005 annual meeting of the International Society of Political Psychology. This paper was also presented at the Annual Meeting of the American Political Science Association, Chicago, Illinois, September 1, 2007. My research has been partially funded by the National Consortium for the Study of Terrorism and the Response to Terrorism, a Center of Excellence established by the Department of Homeland Security. The views represented here are my own.

[2] Examples include Bruce Hoffman, *Inside Terrorism* (New York: Columbia University Press, 1998), although Hoffman is sometimes ambivalent; Daniel Benjamin and Steven Simon, *The Age of Sacred Terror: Radical Islam's War Against America* (New York Random House, 2003); Walter Laqueur, *The New Terrorism: Fanaticism and the Arms of Mass Destruction* (New York: Oxford University Press, 1999); and Ian O. Lesser, et al., *Countering the New Terrorism* (Santa Monica: The Rand Corporation, 1999). Ambassador L. Paul Bremer contributed "A New Strategy for the New Face of Terrorism" to a special issue of *The National Interest* (Thanksgiving 2001), pp. 23–30. A recent post 9/11 overview is Matthew J. Morgan, "The Origins of the New Terrorism," *Parameters* (the Journal of the U.S. Army War College), 34, 1 (Spring 2004), pp. 29–43. However, not all proponents of this point of view are American. See the text of a lecture by (Professor Lord) Anthony Giddens, delivered at the London School of Economics November 10, 2004, "The Future of World Society: The New Terrorism" available at Columbia International Affairs Online (CIAO). Farhad Khosrokhavar also refers to "new" terrorism in *Les Nouveaux Martyrs d'Allah* (Paris: Flammarion, 2003).

[3] See, for example, Simon and Benjamin, *The Age of Sacred Terror*, p. 381. See also the 9/11 Commission report (Final Report of the National Commission on Terrorist Attacks upon the United States), Ch. 2, "The Foundation of the New Terrorism."

I.A. Karawan et al. (eds.), *Values and Violence*,

believe in a "new" terrorism think that the old paradigms should be discarded and replaced with a new understanding.[4]

For example, Bruce Hoffman concluded that "The growth of religious terrorism and its emergence in recent years as a driving force behind the increasing lethality of international terrorism shatters some of our most basic assumptions about terrorists and the violence they commit. It also raises serious questions about the continued relevance of much of the conventional wisdom on terrorism particularly as it pertains to potential future terrorist use of WMD."[5] He argued that assumptions that terrorism might be restrained might still apply to most secular terrorists, but they appear to be dangerously anachronistic with respect to religious terrorists.

In 2000, however, in responding to Simon and Benjamin, Hoffman adjusted his views to suggest that the idea of a "profound and potentially catastrophic change in the nature of terrorism today," is "by no means as certain or even convincing as it is often portrayed . . ."[6] He warned against threat exaggeration, since however fanatical or irrational the new terrorists might seem, they remained operationally conservative, and that the era of new terrorism had not in fact materialized. Simon and Benjamin in turn responded that they were "intrigued by Hoffman's heavy reliance on arguments based on historical inference at a time of dramatic change in the ideology of important terrorist groups and rapid technological advances. To be sure, history should be consulted, but it is by no means a foolproof predictor."[7]

Other analysts, primarily from the academic community, have challenged this interpretation.[8] For example, Thomas Copeland argues that the old terrorism never

---

[4] See Hoffman, *Inside Terrorism*, p. 196 and p. 205; Simon and Benjamin, *The Age of Sacred Terror*, p. 221 and p. 384; Lesser, *Countering the New Terrorism*, p. 2; Laqueur, *The New Terrorism*, p. 7.

[5] *Inside Terrorism*, pp. 204–205.

[6] Bruce Hoffman, "America and the New Terrorism: An Exchange," *Survival* 42, 2 (Summer 2000), p. 162.

[7] Hoffman, op cit. p. 171.

[8] See, e.g., David Tucker, "What is New about the New Terrorism and How Dangerous is It?" *Terrorism and Political Violence* 14, 3 (Fall 2001), pp. 1–14, Thomas Copeland, "Is the 'New Terrorism' Really New?: An Analysis of the New Paradigm for Terrorism," *The Journal of Conflict Studies* 21, 2 (Winter 2001), pp. 7–27, Isabelle Duyvesteyn, "How New is the New Terrorism?" *Studies in Conflict & Terrorism* 27, 5 (2004), pp. 439–454, Doron Zimmerman, *The Transformation Of Terrorism* (Zurich: Andreas Wenger, 2003), Rik Coolsaet, *Al-Qaeda: The Myth* (Gent: Academia Press, 2005), and Jonny Burnett and Dave Whyte, "Embedded Expertise and the New Terrorism," *Journal for Crime, Conflict and the Media* 1, 4 (2005), pp. 1–18. After the July 2005 bombings in London, Professor Richard Aldrich of the University of Nottingham criticized the idea in an editorial, "The new terrorism," in *The Independent*, July 10, 2005. Also see Olivier Roy, *Globalized Islam: The Search for a New Ummah* (New York: Columbia University Press, 2004), especially pp. 41–54, "Is Jihad closer to Marx than to the Koran?" and Frederick W. Kagan, "The New Bolsheviks: Understanding Al Qaeda," a National Security Outlook report from the American Enterprise Institute for Public Policy Research (November 2005). In addition, Audrey Kurth Cronin draws lessons from the past in "How al-Qaida Ends: The Decline and Demise of Terrorist Groups," *International Security* 31, 1 (Summer 2006), pp. 7–48. Both John Mueller, *Overblown: How Politicians and the Terrorism Industry Inflate National Security Threats, and Why We Believe Them* (New York: Free Press, 2006) and Ian S. Lustick, *Trapped in the War on Terror* (Philadelphia:

really went away, that it is too soon to declare a new paradigm, and that the idea of a "new" terrorism is a particularly American way of framing the threat.[9] Duyvesteyn argues for continuity rather than rupture. She also notes the lack of historical research to substantiate the claim that current terrorism is "new."[10]

If a new explanation of terrorism is necessary, what are the puzzles that the "old" paradigm cannot solve? The problem that stands out in the discussions is the increasing lethality of terrorism and the role of religion in motivating both terrorism and unusually deadly terrorism, extending to the deliberate pursuit of appropriately catastrophic weapons. The idea that the world confronted a "new" threat appears to have taken hold after the 1993 World Trade Center bombing, although Benjamin and Simon argue that the phenomenon began in 1990, with the assassination of Meir Kahane in New York.[11] The argument was well established, and had been criticized in turn, by the time of the 9/11 attacks. The idea that there was a distinctively "religious" terrorism began to develop with the growth of radical Islamic movements after the Iranian revolution, particularly as a reaction to the use of suicide bombings in Lebanon, which began in the early 1980s. The 1993 World Trade Center bombing and the discovery of subsequent ambitious plots instigated by Ramzi Youcef (such as the so-called "bojinka" plot, which involved blowing up airliners over the Pacific) caused alarm because of the prospect of large numbers of civilian casualties, but also because of the apparent inchoate nature of the source of terrorism. The fear that terrorism could cause mass casualties was exacerbated by the prospect of terrorist groups' acquiring nuclear, chemical, biological, or radiological weapons, especially considering the insecurity that followed the collapse of the Soviet Union.[12] The new terrorism idea gained momentum with the 1995 Aum Shinrikyo sarin gas attacks on the Tokyo subway and the bombing of the federal building in Oklahoma City by Timothy McVeigh. Growing awareness of the extent of the Al Qaeda conspiracy caused more alarm, especially after Osama Bin Laden moved from the Sudan to Afghanistan and called for jihad against the United States in 1996.[13] The 1998 bombings of American embassies in Kenya and Tanzania, the attack on the USS Cole in the port of Yemen in 2000, and the discovery of the millennium plots strengthened the perception of a new threat. After the September 11th attacks, the anthrax letters in the United States further heightened fears of the use of unconventional weapons. Since 2003, the global spread of suicide bombings

---

University of Pennsylvania Press, 2006) have argued that the United States has over-reacted to the threat.

[9] Copeland, "Is the New Terrorism Really New?"

[10] Duyvesteyn, "How New is the New Terrorism?"

[11] Simon and Benjamin, *The Age of Sacred Terror*, pp. 3–4. See Tom Morgenthau, "The New Terrorism," *Newsweek*, (July 5, 1993), p. 18.

[12] See Jessica Stern, *The Ultimate Terrorists* (Cambridge: Harvard University Press, 1999).

[13] See the review essay by Gideon Rose, "It Could Happen Here: Facing the New Terrorism," *Foreign Affairs* (March-April 1999). Accessed online. Ashton B. Carter and William J. Perry in *Preventive Defense: A New Security Strategy for America* (Washington, D. C.: Brookings Institution Press, 1999) warned of "catastrophic terrorism," defined as acts of an order of magnitude more severe than "ordinary" terrorism and unprecedented outside of warfare (p. 150).

against civilian targets has contributed to the feeling that terrorism has changed fundamentally.

It is critical to examine systematically the assumptions on which the appeal for the new paradigm is based and to question both their logic and empirical foundation before accepting them as self-evident. Accounts of a "new" terrorism have not always been grounded in sufficient knowledge of history or understanding of contemporary terrorism. The point is not that there has been no change in terrorism over the past century but that the changes that have occurred need to be precisely delineated. An assessment of change can be completed only by careful fact-based comparisons. What is needed in the argument for a "new" terrorism is careful specification of the concept of a "new" terrorism and of the distinction between "new" and "old." What are the specific definitional attributes of the "new" terrorism? How are they different from those of the "old"? Second, a satisfactory theoretical framework needs to clarify which groups or practices belong in which category and explain how these cases satisfy the requirements of the definition.

My contention is that the departure from the past is not as pronounced as many accounts make it out to be. Today's terrorism is not a fundamentally or qualitatively "new" phenomenon but grounded in an evolving historical context.[14] Much of what we see now is familiar, and the differences are of degree rather than kind. Contemporary terrorism shares many of the characteristics of past terrorism, dating back at least to the late 19th century and the use of terrorism by groups of Russian revolutionaries, European anarchists, and Irish nationalists.

For example, accounts of "new" terrorism cite the common characteristic of religious doctrine as motivation.[15] However, although the "new" terrorists are all supposedly religious, not all religious groups are deemed to be "new." The groups that are typically cited as examples of the genre are radical or jihadist Islamists in general (e.g., al Qaeda, al Qaeda in Mesopotamia, Jemaah al-Islamiya in Indonesia, the Abu Sayyaf Group in the Philippines, and the Salafist Group for Preaching and Combat in Algeria), the Christian Identity movement and its offshoots in the United States (including Timothy McVeigh, although it is not certain that he represented an organized group, and the attribution of a religious motivation to his violence is problematic), Ramzi Youcef and his cohort, Aum Shinrikyo, and the Jewish radical groups that plotted to blow up the Dome of the Rock and assassinated Israeli Prime Minister Itzhak Rabin. Hamas, however, is not included. The case of Hezbollah is treated with ambivalence; it is included by some (e.g., Hoffman) but not others

[14] For an argument about civil war that helped inspire this analysis, see Stathis N. Kalyvas, "'New' and 'Old' Civil Wars: A Valid Distinction?" *World Politics* 54 (October 2001), 99–118.

[15] The classic work on religion and terrorism is Mark Juergensmeyer's *Terror in the Mind of God: The Global Rise of Religious Violence* (Berkeley: University of California Press, 2000). Although he argues that religion adds a distinctive dimension to terrorism, he does not assume that the association between religion and violence is new. Instead he refers to its reappearance at a particular historical juncture (p. 7). See also *The New Cold War? Religious Nationalism Confronts the Secular State* (Berkeley: University of California Press, 1993). It should be noted that Juergensmeyer's analysis is based on a broad cross-cultural comparison of religious movements in difference societies.

(e.g., Simon and Benjamin). Laqueur includes Hezbollah, the LTTE, and the Taliban since he considers some nationalist groups to be in the "new terrorism" category.[16] Jessica Stern includes far-right groups and millenarian cults.[17]

Clarification of the distinction between categories is hard to find in the "new terrorism" literature. The National Memorial Institute for the Prevention of Terrorism's Terrorism Knowledge Base (TKB), which is based on event data collected by the Rand Corporation since 1968, lists 130 groups in the category of religious terrorism.[18] Of these 130 cases, 124 are linked to descriptive group profiles, which indicate that only 54 of the cases are labeled as exclusively religious. Almost all the others are simultaneously classified as national separatist groups, although reasons for classifications are not provided. Nevertheless, if it is the case, as Simon argues, that "the explicitly religious character of the 'new terrorism' poses a profound security challenge for the United States," are we to understand the statement to mean those groups that are only religious or those groups that are both religious and nationalist?[19] Which orientation will determine their actions? Why would Hamas be considered a nationalist group when it calls for the establishment of an Islamic state?

If "old" terrorism refers to secular groups or groups existing before 1990 and the end of the Cold War, we have over 400 examples, and more if we go back to the 19th century. Accounts of the new terrorism are not specific or comprehensive on this score. For example, Steven Simon lists only the Irish Republican Army, the Red Brigades in Italy, and the Palestine Liberation Organization as examples of "conventional" terrorist groups.[20] At another point, Simon and Benjamin associate the old terrorism with state sponsorship.[21]

There is a further problem. Even if a conceptual distinction between two types of terrorism can be established, it is not clear whether there is a chronological dimension. Should we assume that the "new" is replacing the "old"? When was the transition? If not, how do we explain the persistence of the "old" as well as the emergence of the "new"? David Rapoport has dealt with these questions in analyzing the historical evolution of terrorism in terms of "waves," which in his terms are "cycles of activity in a given time period" characterized by a common international

---

[16] See Laqueur, *The New Terrorism*, p. 82.

[17] Stern, *The Ultimate Terrorists*, p. 8.

[18] The Institute was established as a memorial to the victims of the 1995 Oklahoma City bombing. http://www.mipt.org/terrorism/MIPT-Mission-History.asp, *last visited* Oct. 9, 2007. For the period before 1998 the database only contains international incidents, not domestic. The classification of groups was done by DFI International, a Washington consulting firm. See http://www.tkb.org/AboutTKB.jsp, *last visited* Oct. 9, 2007.

[19] Steven Simon, "The New Terrorism: Securing the Nation Against a Messianic Foe," *The Brookings Review* 21, 1 (Winter 2003), p. 18. It is important to look closely at the Rand data, since it is the main source of the argument that religiously motivated terrorism is (1) increasing and (2) more lethal and indiscriminate than other forms. See Hoffman, *Inside Terrorism*, pp. 92–94.

[20] Simon, "The New Terrorism."

[21] Simon and Benjamin, "America and the New Terrorism," pp. 59–75.

"energy" or ideology.[22] All waves feature nationalist movements that take on different forms according to the nature of the "wave," whether driven by anarchism, anti-colonialism, "New Left ideology," or now religion. He sees each wave ebbing as the new wave gathers strength. Although Rapoport does not espouse the idea that the religious wave is qualitatively different from preceding waves, he does see a process of replacement rather than coexistence. Although Simon and Benjamin are among the leading proponents of the "new terrorism" point of view, they have at times referred to the old paradigm being "joined by" rather than replaced by the new.[23] Laqueur also thinks that new and old coexist.[24]

In order to make the argument that "old" and "new" have more in common than proponents of a "new" terrorism seem to think, I analyze the propositions of the "new terrorism" school concerning the goals, methods, and organizational structure and resources of groups practicing terrorism.

Goals

First, the *ends* of the "new" terrorism are presumed to be both unlimited and non-negotiable. These aims are also considered largely incomprehensible and amorphous. From the perspective of the "new" terrorism school of thought, the goals of "new" terrorists are derived exclusively from religious doctrines that emphasize transformational and apocalyptic beliefs, usually associated with Islam although they are assumed to be present in all monotheistic religions. Millenarianism is a key belief. Walter Laqueur, for example, characterizes the "new terrorists" as religious fanatics who suffer from delusion and persecution mania.[25] As his views indicate, some confusion exists over levels of analysis, since it is not clear whether it is individual motivation or group purpose that is being described.

In the world of politics, the "new" terrorists are presumed to hate Western and especially American values, culture, civilization, and existence. As Ambassador L. Paul Bremer expressed it, it is not that they do not understand us: "They hate America precisely because they *do* understand our society; they hate its freedoms, its commitment to equal rights and universal suffrage, its material successes and its appeals. . . ."[26] President Bush described the enemy thus: "we face an enemy which cannot stand freedom. It's an enemy which has an ideology that does not believe in free speech, free religion, free dissent, does not believe in women's rights, and they

---

[22] "The Four Waves of Modern Terrorism," in Audrey Kurth Cronin and James M. Ludes, (eds.), *Attacking Terrorism: Elements of a Grand Strategy* (Washington: Georgetown University Press, 2004), p. 47.

[23] See Simon and Benjamin, "America and the New Terrorism," p. 59 and p. 66.

[24] Laqueur, *The New Terrorism*, pp. 80–81.

[25] "Left, Right, and Beyond: The Changing Face of Terror," in James F. Hoge, Jr. and Gideon Rose (eds.), *How Did This Happen? Terrorism and the New War* (New York: Public Affairs Press, 2001), p. 80.

[26] Bremer, "A New Strategy," p. 24.

have a desire to impose their ideology on much of the world."[27] Further, "we're not facing a set of grievances that can be soothed and addressed. We're facing a radical ideology with inalterable objectives: to enslave whole nations and intimidate the world. No act of ours invited the rage of the killers – and no concession, bribe, or act of appeasement would change or limit their plans for murder."[28] The new terrorism threat is compared to the existential threat of Communism during the Cold War, not past terrorism.[29] In terms of this analogy, it is described as totalitarian and compared to the fascism that led to World War II.

The goals of terrorism are inextricably linked to the means, according to this point of view. The new terrorists are fanatics unconstrained by any respect for human life. Violence is at the heart of their beliefs. There is some ambiguity about whether violence is "strategic," since Simon and Benjamin argue that for the new actors terrorism is used strategically and not tactically, by which they mean killing is an end in itself.[30] If destruction is an end in itself rather than the means to an end, then it is not strategic but expressive. Nevertheless, the assumption of the "new terrorism" school of thought is that rather than choosing among alternative ways of achieving political ends, the new terrorists seek primarily to kill. Lethality is their aim rather than their means. As Benjamin and Simon explained in an editorial in the *New York Times* in early 2000, "The terrorists allied with Mr. bin Laden do not want a place at the table: they want to shatter the table. They are not constrained by secular political concerns. Their objective is not to influence, but to kill, and in large numbers – hence their declared interest in acquiring chemical and even nuclear weapons. It is just this combination – religious motivation and a desire to inflict catastrophic damage – that is new to terrorism."[31]

The goals of the "old" terrorism, by contrast, are thought to have been negotiable and limited. Their ambitions were local, not global.[32] The aims of "old" terrorists were understandable and tangible, typically related to issues of nationalism and territorial autonomy. Deals could be struck. The state could bargain with the "old" terrorists. Conflicts could be resolved. In effect, these were presumably sensible terrorists whose objectives were realistic and pragmatic. As Laqueur describes the comparison, even the most indiscriminate of the "old" terrorists, which he locates in the second half of the twentieth century, hesitated at true mass murder because they feared a backlash and because such actions were alien to their traditions.

[27] White House, Office of the Press Secretary, January 11, 2006, "President Participates in Discussion on the Global War on Terror," Kentucky International Convention Center, Louisville, Kentucky.

[28] Graduation Speech, United States Military Academy, West Point, New York, June 1, 2002.

[29] October 6, 2005, address to the National Endowment for Democracy, "The Nature of the Enemy We Face and the Strategy for Victory."

[30] See for example Simon and Benjamin, *The Age of Sacred Terror*, p. 419.

[31] "The New Face of Terrorism," *The New York Times*, January 4, 2000. This indicates perhaps that the new terrorists must be more than religious.

[32] Anthony Giddens, for example, explains that "old style terrorism is fundamentally local therefore because its ambitions are local" and that violence thus tends to be "relatively limited." Giddens, "The Future of World Society."

He continues, "They hated their enemies, but they had not been totally blinded by their hate. For the radical religious practitioners of the new terrorism, however, murder and destruction on an unprecedented scale did not pose much of a problem."[33] Hoffman explains that "Whereas secular terrorists regard violence either as a way of instigating the correction of a flaw in a system that is basically good or as a means to foment the creation of a new system, religious terrorists see themselves not as components of a system worth preserving but as 'outsiders,' seeking fundamental changes in the existing system."[34]

Is this an accurate depiction of the old terrorism? Unobtainable ends and flamboyantly bloodthirsty rhetoric are not unique to religion or to the contemporary political environment. The European anarchist movement of the late nineteenth century (of which the proponents of terrorism were a fringe) sought to abolish all government as well as capitalist society. Sendero Luminoso wished to establish a Maoist regime in Peru. Its leader, Abimael Guzman, launched the war in 1980 with a speech titled "We are the Initiators," which asserts that "we begin the strategic offensive for world revolution, the next 50 years will see imperialism's dominion swept away along with all exploiters. . . . The people's war will grow every day until the old order is pulled down, the world is entering a new era." The speech continues,

> The people rear up, arm themselves, and rise in revolution to put the noose around the neck of imperialism and the reactionaries, seizing them by the throat and garroting them. They are strangled, necessarily. The flesh of the reactionaries will rot away, converted into ragged threads, and this black filth will sink into the mud; that which remains will be burned and the ashes scattered by the earth's winds so that only the sinister memory will remain of that which will never return, because it neither can nor should return.[35]

In the 1970s, revolutionary organizations in Germany (the Red Army faction) and Italy (the Red Brigades), with little to no popular support, thought that they could overthrow well-established liberal democracies, bring down NATO, and deal a death blow to imperialism.[36] Separatist organizations are not immune from overreaching. ETA sought to establish a Basque state that would include regions of both France and Spain. It was not particularly reasonable of Palestinian groups such as the Abu Nidal Organization or the Popular Front for the Liberation of Palestine, or Libya, to believe that they could destroy the state of Israel or bring about revolution in the Arab world. Patrick Seale, in a biography of Abu Nidal, describes his terrorism as "fitful and purposeless," "incoherent, incompetent, and invariably counterproductive to Palestinian interests." There was no "strategic vision:"

> His claim that he wanted to prevent a compromise between the PLO and Israel so as to recover Palestine was not a credible objective. The vast imbalance of strength between

---

[33] Laqueur, "Left, Right, and Beyond," p. 74.

[34] Hoffman, *Inside Terrorism*, p. 95.

[35] Quoted in Gustavo Gorriti, *The Shining Path: A History of the Millenarian War in Peru* (Chapel Hill: The University of North Carolina Press, 1999), pp. 34–35.

[36] See the communiqués reproduced in *Europe's Red Terrorists: The Fighting Communist Organizations*, compiled and annotated by Yonah Alexander and Dennis Pluchinsky (London: Frank Cass, 1992).

> Israel and its opponents made such pursuit suicidal. By degrading the Palestinian liberation struggle to mere criminal violence, Abu Nidal offered Israel the pretext for refusing to negotiate and to giving the Palestinians nothing but the sword.[37]

Do the "new terrorism" proponents' assumptions about objectives describe the new terrorism? Are such groups led by apocalyptic visionaries with no appreciation of reality? Groups claiming to act in the name of religious doctrine may be more extreme in their rhetoric than in their preferences (although analysis of their rhetoric is certainly worthwhile). They have often shown themselves to be astute political strategists, using terrorism successfully to compel the withdrawal of foreign military forces or to disrupt peace processes. Hezbollah is an excellent example, having transformed itself into a political party as well as a resistance organization. Some regional experts have interpreted al Qaeda's activities in pragmatic terms.[38] Bin Ladin's stated goal of expelling American military forces from Muslim territories is quite specific. He cites the encouraging historical precedents of Vietnam, Somalia, and Lebanon, as well as the Soviet withdrawal from Afghanistan.[39] His interpretations may not be completely accurate, but they are not illogical. Many other examples of pragmatism can be found in internal al Qaeda documents captured by American forces.[40] Just as secular nationalist groups such as ETA and even the IRA took on a Marxist-Leninist veneer when it was ideologically fashionable to do so, nationalistic or revolutionary groups today may take on an Islamist cast. The Moro National Liberation Front became the Moro Islamic Liberation Front, and secular nationalist Fatah produced the Al Aqsa Martyrs Brigade as a rival to Hamas and Palestinian Islamic Jihad.

As noted above, whether these extreme motivations are individual or collective is not clear. For example, Walter Laqueur's account focuses more on the motivations or "mind-sets" of the individual than the objectives of the group. He says, for example, that the new terrorists, whose motivations include rage, aggression, sadism, paranoia as well as fanaticism, can be found on the fringes of any extremist movement.[41] At other times he is contradictory; he seems to imply that the motive for terrorism, fanaticism, has not changed but that the availability of weapons has. At yet other times he suggests that religious fanaticism is different. The "new breed" of terrorist is said to enjoy killing.[42]

---

37 *Abu Nidal: A Gun for Hire* (New York: Random House, 1992), p. 231.

38 See for example Michael Doran, "The Pragmatic Fanaticism of Al Qaeda: An Anatomy of Extremism in Middle Eastern Politics," *Political Science Quarterly* 117, 2 (Summer 2002), pp. 177–90. See also Quintan Wiktorowicz and John Kaltner, "Killing in the Name of Islam: Al-Qaeda's Justification for September 11," *Middle East Policy* X, 2 (Summer 2003), pp. 76–92. They analyze debates over the use of violence within the Salafi movement.

39 See *Messages to the World: The Statements of Osama Bin Laden*, edited and introduced by Bruce Lawrence (London: Verso, 2005).

40 Translations of a number of these documents can be found on the website of the Combating Terrorism Center at West Point: http://www.ctc.usma.edu.

41 Laqueur, *The New Terrorism*, p. 281.

42 Laqueur, *The New Terrorism*, p. 231.

Marc Sageman, while asserting that the world faces a new type of terrorism driven by networks of fanatics, actually describes the jihadists about whom he was able to acquire biographical information in terms that are not dramatically different from descriptions of secular revolutionary terrorists.[43] He concludes that "Members of the global Salafi jihad were generally middle-class, educated young men from caring and religious families, who grew up with strong positive values of religion, spirituality, and concern for their communities."[44] Like the groups in the West in the 1970s and 1980s, they did not come from poor backgrounds. Their education was largely modern. They exhibited no signs of psychopathology. As is the case with the "old" terrorism, the group mattered more than the individual: "Social bonds are the critical element in this process [of joining the jihad] and precede ideological commitment."[45] They were not transformed into terrorists out of hatred for the United States.

A finding that remains constant over time is that while some members of radical organizations are motivated by sincere beliefs in the cause, others are less committed to doctrine. Individual militants may be manipulated by their leaders. Undoubtedly all members of the groups designated as "new terrorists" are not religious "fanatics."[46] Within al Qaeda, the concerns of militants are often mundane and prosaic, such as salary disputes.

As Stephen Holmes observes with regard to the 9/11 attacks, "Many of the key actors in the 9/11 drama, admittedly, articulate their grievances using archaic religious language. But the very fact that the code involved is ancient while the behaviour we want to explain is recent suggests the inadequacy of causal theories that overemphasize the religious element."[47] Holmes argues instead for a political explanation. He notes that Bin Laden's public statements stress secular rationales for the 9/11 attacks and that historical circumstances rather than religion led al Qaeda to target the United States. Because the governments of Egypt and Saudi Arabia could not be overthrown by force, al Qaeda turned to the "far enemy."

---

[43] *Understanding Terror Networks* (Philadelphia: University of Pennsylvania Press, 2004).

[44] Sageman, *Understanding Terror Networks*, p. 96.

[45] Sageman, *Understanding Terror Networks*, p. 135. On the importance of the group in pre-jihadist terrorism, see Martha Crenshaw, "The Psychology of Political Terrorism," in *Political Psychology: Contemporary Problems and Issues*, pp. 379–413, edited by Margaret G. Hermann (San Francisco: Jossey-Bass, 1986) and "Decisions to Use Terrorism: Psychological Constraints on Instrumental Reasoning," in *Social Movements and Violence: Participation in Underground Organizations*, edited by Donatella della Porta. *International Social Movement Research*, Volume 4, pp. 29–42. (Greenwich, CT: JAI Press Inc., 1992).

[46] See Alan Cullison, "Inside Al-Qaeda's Hard Drive: A Fortuitous Discovery Reveals Budget Squabbles, Baby Pictures, Office Rivalries – and the Path to 9–11," *The Atlantic Monthly* (September 2004), pp. 55–70.

[47] Stephen Holmes, "Al-Qaeda, September 11, 2001," in Diego Gambetta, ed., *Making Sense of Suicide Missions* (Oxford: Oxford University Press, 2005), pp. 134–35. He presents a plausible argument that non-religious motivations were dominant. Steven Simon and Jonathan Stevenson admit this heterogeneity in "Thinking Outside the Tank," *The National Interest* 78 (Winter 2004–2005), pp. 90–98.

He concludes: "What hit the United States on 11 September was not religion, therefore. Instead, the 9/11 terrorists represented the *pooled insurgencies* of the Arab Middle East."[48]

Journalist Terry McDermott also investigated the backgrounds of the 9/11 hijackers.[49] He concluded that these men were ordinary. The Hamburg cell that provided the pilots was bound together by affiliation with the Al Quds mosque. The group had formed well before it was recruited to the Al Qaeda plot. All but one of the other hijackers were from Saudi Arabia. As McDermott points out, we know less about them because "Saudi Arabia has been parsimonious with the information in its hands, which is considerable, and has made the discovery of information by others difficult."[50] However, he notes that they were from an isolated province that was a stronghold of conservative religious belief. They were not poor and were relatively well educated. Jobs, however, were lacking, and the tradition of leaving home to participate in jihad abroad had been well established since the 1980s and the appeal to fight against the Soviet Union in Afghanistan. From a pragmatic point of view, it was easier for Saudi citizens to get American visas than it was for other nationalities from which hijackers might have been recruited.

Journalists Peter Bergen and Swati Pandey analyzed the 79 individuals responsible for the 1993 World Trade Center bombing, the 1998 bombings of the U.S. embassies in Kenya and Tanzania, the 9/11 attacks, the 2002 Bali nightclub bombings, and the 2005 London bombings. They confirmed that "History has taught that terrorism has been a largely bourgeois endeavor, from the Russian anarchists of the late nineteenth century to the German Marxists of the Bader-Meinhof gang of the 1970s to the apocalyptic Japanese terror cult Aum Shinrikyo of the 1990s. Islamist terrorists turn out to be no different."[51] The terrorists were neither poor nor undereducated. More than half of those studied had some university education. None had attended a madrassa, Islamic schools that American officials have often considered the hotbeds of Islamic extremism.

Methods

Second, the *means* of the "new" terrorism are also assumed to be radically different from the past. The premise is that because the ends of the new terrorism are unlimited, so, too, are the means that groups espousing these goals are willing and able to use. The "new" terrorists are supposed to be dedicated to causing the largest possible number of casualties among their enemies. According to Walter Laqueur, "The new terrorism is different in character [from the old], aiming not at clearly defined political demands but at the destruction of society and the elimination of

---

[48] Holmes, "Al-Qaeda, September 11, 2001," p. 168.

[49] Terry McDermott, *Perfect Soldiers* (New York: Harper Collins, 2005).

[50] McDermott, *Perfect Soldiers*, p. 217.

[51] "The Madrassa Scapegoat," *The Washington Quarterly*, 29, 2 (Spring 2006), p. 122.

large sections of the population."[52] According to Steven Simon, "Religiously motivated terrorism, as Bruce Hoffman of the Rand Corporation first noted in 1997, is inextricably linked to pursuit of mass casualties."[53] Presumably for the "new" terrorists the means have become an end in themselves, not a way of reaching an audience other than a deity. They are not concerned with public support. The "new" terrorists seek only to destroy, and their deaths will result only in the reaching of the millennium and a place in paradise, not political change in the here and now.

Thus the "new" terrorists are also thought to be significantly more inclined than secular groups to use "weapons of mass destruction." Jessica Stern, for example, argues that the risk of terrorist use of nuclear, chemical, or biological weapons against civilians is growing not only because of the increased availability of such weapons but because of changes in terrorist motivation: "A new breed of terrorists – including ad hoc groups motivated by religious conviction or revenge, violent right-wing extremists, and apocalyptic and millenarian cults – appears more likely than the terrorists of the past to commit acts of extreme violence."[54]

The "old" terrorism is considered to be much more restrained and specific in targeting. The traditional terrorist wanted people watching, not people dead, according to Brian Jenkins' now famous aphorism. Hoffman describes the old terrorists as selective and discriminating.[55] Benjamin and Simon say past terrorists used "carefully calibrated violence" because "they knew that excessive brutality would deny them the place they sought at the bargaining table."[56] These terrorists imposed restraints on their actions because they aimed to change the attitudes of audiences who could help them achieve their goals. Although capable of being more destructive, they chose not to be. Their audiences and reference groups were tangible and present. They were limited by their dependence on constituencies and by their political interests. Their pursuit of legitimacy, in effect, restrained their behavior.

However, the "old" terrorists were not always discriminating in their choice of targets. Levels of selectivity and restraint vary across groups and across time, but not according to a religious-secular or past-present divide. A few examples show that killing large numbers is not restricted to groups espousing religious doctrines, although no single attack was near as deadly as 9/11.[57] The French anarchists of the 1880s bombed restaurants frequented by the bourgeoisie in order to show the working class who the true enemy was. "No bourgeois is innocent" was their slogan.

---

[52] Laqueur, *The New Terrorism*, p. 81.

[53] Simon and Benjamin, *The Age of Sacred Terror*, p. 18.

[54] Stern, *The Ultimate Terrorists*, p. 8.

[55] Hoffman, *Inside Terrorism*, p. 197.

[56] In "The New Face of Terrorism," 2000.

[57] Also see the similar conclusions of Chris Quillen, "A Historical Analysis of Mass Casualty Bombers," *Studies in Conflict and Terrorism* 25, 5 (September–October 2002), pp. 279–302. The article provides a chronology.

The history of anarchism in Spain was particularly violent. Martin Miller refers to a "will to destroy" in the European anarchist movement.[58]

Nationalist groups have also caused mass casualties. In 1946, the bombing of the King David Hotel in Jerusalem by Zionist extremists killed 91 and injured 45.[59] During the Algerian war, the FLN attacked Europeans indiscriminately, leaving bombs in cafes, on beaches, in soccer stadiums, and at bus stops in Algiers during the famous "Battle of Algiers." Their bombs often killed Algerians as well as Europeans. (The FLN also considered bombing the Eiffel Tower, in a campaign to bring the war home to France. They did bomb oil refineries near Marseille.)

Would-be revolutionaries could also be extremely lethal. The Japanese Red Army's attack on the Tel Aviv airport in 1972 killed 24 and wounded 80 people, most Puerto Rican pilgrims. The secular regime of Colonel Qaddafi was responsible for the midair bombing of Pan Am Flight 103 in 1988, which left 270 dead.

Far right extremists have also been willing and able to cause mass casualties; for instance, 85 people were killed in the bombing of the Bologna railroad station in 1980.[60] As the Algerian war concluded, the OAS (Organisation de l'armée secrète) adopted a scorched earth policy of indiscriminate terrorism against Muslims. For example, on May 2, 1962, a car bomb on the Algiers docks killed 62 and wounded 110 among a crowd of Algerians waiting for day work.[61] It is also fair to say that Timothy McVeigh's actions should be placed in the category of rightwing extremism rather than religion.

The issue of possible resort to weapons of mass destruction is complicated. Aum Shinrikyo is the only group so far to have employed self-manufactured chemical weapons against a civilian population.[62] Terrorists have not used nuclear or radiological weapons to any serious destructive effect despite official concern over the prospect since at least 1976.[63] While both Aum Shinrikyo and Al Qaeda

---

[58] Martin A. Miller, "The Intellectual Origins of Modern Terrorism in Europe," in *Terrorism in Context*, ed. Martha Crenshaw (University Park, PA: Pennsylvania State University Press, 1995).

[59] J. Bowyer Bell, *Terror Out of Zion* (New York: St. Martin's Press, 1977), p. 172.

[60] Note, however, that some authors who think that there is a "new" terrorism, such as Stern, include the far right in that category.

[61] Bernard Droz and Evelyne Lever, *Histoire de la guerre d'Algérie, 1954–1962* (Paris: Seuil, 1982), p. 337. See also Alexander Harrison, *Challenging De Gaulle: The O.A.S. and the Counterrevolution in Algeria, 1954–1962* (New York: Praeger, 1989).

[62] Another possible example is the LTTE's use of chlorine gas in an attack on a Sri Lankan army base, but their use appears to have been circumstantial and opportunistic, not planned. See in general Jonathan B. Tucker (ed.), *Toxic Terror: Assessing Terrorist Use of Chemical and Biological Weapons* (Cambridge: MIT Press, 2000). According to this study, there had so far been only nine instances of what might be defined as chemical or biological terrorism, which included deliberate food poisonings. The anthrax mailings of 2001 could be added to the list. *See also* Richard A. Falkenrath, Robert D. Newman, and Bradley A. Thayer, *America's Achilles' Heel: Nuclear, Biological, and Chemical Terrorism and Covert Attack* (Cambridge: MIT Press, 1998) and Stern, *The Ultimate Terrorists*.

[63] See U. S. Central Intelligence Agency, "Research Study: International and Transnational Terrorism: Diagnosis and Prognosis" (April, 1976).

demonstrated a commitment to acquiring nuclear materials and devices, neither was successful despite their extensive resources, and, in al Qaeda's case, state sanctuary.[64] However, al Qaeda is known to have tested nerve gas in Afghanistan, and chlorine has been used opportunistically in Iraq, probably by al Qaeda-linked groups. al Qaeda also apparently planned to use chemical weapons in an attack on New York subways in 2003.[65]

While the September 11 hijackings caused the highest number of casualties of any single terrorist attack in history, other al Qaeda or al Qaeda-related terrorism has (fortunately) caused fewer casualties (overall and per incident) and has not involved such innovative methods or sophisticated planning. The bombings in Bali in 2002 (202 killed), Madrid in 2004 (191 killed), and London in 2005 (52 killed) were tragically destructive, but not fundamentally dissimilar to past bombings by secular groups in crowded public venues.[66] Simultaneous explosions may be a hallmark of al Qaeda, but such coordination was also characteristic of Palestinian nationalist groups in the 1970s. For example, the Popular Front for the Liberation of Palestine hijacked three airliners to Jordan simultaneously in 1970.

More evidence of strategic discrimination in targeting and practical concern for the future is found in the July 2005 letter from Ayman al-Zawahiri, former head of Egyptian Islamic Jihad and Bin Ladin's second in command in al Qaeda, to the late Abu Musab al-Zarqawi, leader of the Iraqi branch "al Qaeda in Mesopotamia." The document is sharply critical of indiscriminate terrorism against ordinary Shia in Iraq, especially attacks on mosques. Zawahiri warns that sectarian terrorism will undermine the popular support that is essential to seizing power in the Sunni areas of Iraq following an anticipated American withdrawal. He cautions that any action that the masses do not understand or approve must be avoided, and he notes numerous questions about the wisdom and rightness of anti-Shia terrorism that were circulating among even Zarqawi's supporters.[67]

Looking further at the purported association between religion and lethality, it is instructive to evaluate the twenty most lethal of the groups classified as religious in the MIPT Terrorism Knowledge Base. Each was responsible for over 100 total fatalities through December of 2005. However, only nine of the twenty are classified as *exclusively* religious. They include al Qaeda and al Qaeda affiliates in Europe, the Armed Islamic Group in Algeria, the Lord's Resistance Army in Uganda, Jemaah al-Islamiya in Indonesia, al-Gama'a al-Islamiya in Egypt, the

---

[64] Sara Daly, John Parachini, and William Rosenau, *Aum Shinrikyo, Al Qaeda, and the Kinshasha Reactor: Implications of Three Case Studies for Combating Nuclear Terrorism* (Santa Monica: The Rand Corporation, 2005).

[65] See Sammy Salama in the Martin Center for Nonproliferation Studies report "Manual for Producing Chemical Weapon to be Used in [2003] New York Subway Plot Available on Al-Qaeda Websites Since Late 2005," (2006). Ron Suskind describes the proposed use of the "mubtakkar device" in *The One Percent Doctrine* (New York: Simon and Schuster, 2006).

[66] Figures are from the BBC Online.

[67] Text accessed on the Office of the Director of National Intelligence website, where it was posted in October 11,2005: http://www.dni.gov/letter_in_english.pdf.

Taliban in Afghanistan, and, curiously, Ansar Allah, which is regarded as an offshoot of Lebanese Hizb'allah, an organization considered to have mixed motives. (Ansar Allah is thought to have used suicide bombings against Jewish and Israeli targets in Argentina in 1992 and 1994.) Ansar al-Sunnah in Iraq is considered purely religious, while other Iraqi groups are defined as national separatist as well. The other hybrid groups are (1) in Palestine, Hamas and Palestinian Islamic Jihad, (2) three associated with the struggle in Chechnya, (3) three originating in the war in Iraq, (4) Lashkar-e-Taiba in Kashmir and Pakistan, (5) the Abu Sayyaf Group in the Philippines, (6) Hizb'allah, and (7) the Moro Islamic Liberation Front in the Philippines. Thus purely religious groups killed a total of 6120 people, and hybrid or mixed groups killed 4657. Unfortunately the database does not explain the distinction between purely religious and hybrid groups. Most Africa specialists, for example, would not necessarily consider the Lord's Resistance Army in Uganda to be primarily a religious group.

There are other problems with the factual claim that religion is invariably associated with increased lethality.[68] The MIPT events database did not include domestic incidents until after 1998. Thus older groups that used extensive violence at home against local targets will be underweighted in the comparisons. For example, in 2003 the Peruvian Truth and Reconciliation Commission reported that between 1980 and 2000 Sendero Luminoso was responsible for 54% of the 69,280 total deaths in the conflict, thus over 37,000 people.[69] Although one might not define all of Sendero's violence as terrorism, the victims included in the tally were not from the security forces but from the civilian population. By contrast, the MIPT Terrorism Knowledge Base credits Sendero Luminoso with only 133 fatalities and 267 injuries from 1968 to the present. This discrepancy is significant. Furthermore, over time small group or individual access to destructive technologies as well as their knowledge of target vulnerabilities (i.e., capability rather than motivation) has increased. If most new groups are categorized as religious, the results will be biased because a number of factors come together to produce increased deadliness in the contemporary world. One cause of high numbers of civilian casualties, for example, is the adoption of suicide missions as a tactic of terrorism, which is practiced by both secular and religious groups.[70] The Liberation Tigers of Tamil Eelam in Sri Lanka are a prominent illustration.

---

[68] See, e.g., Hoffman, *Inside Terrorism*, p. 94: "The reasons why terrorist incidents perpetrated for religious motives result in so many more deaths may be found in the radically different value systems, mechanisms of legitimization and justification, concepts of morality, and world-view embraced by the religious terrorist, compared with his secular counterpart." Hoffman's calculations are based on Rand data, which is the basis of the MIPT database.

[69] For the text of the report see: http://www.cverdad.org.pe/ingles/ifinal/conclusiones.php.

[70] See Martha Crenshaw, "Explaining Suicide Terrorism: A Review Essay," *Security Studies* 6, 1 (Spring 2007), pp. 133–162.

Organization and Resources

The *organization* of the new terrorism is also thought to be fundamentally different from earlier structures of terrorist actors. The "new" terrorists are said to be decentralized, with a "flat" networked apparatus rather than a hierarchical or cellular structure.[71] Subunits are supposed to have substantial autonomy, if not complete independence, and the scope is transnational (global reach). Much of the new terrorism is thought to be inspirational rather than directed from the top; it is diffuse rather than concentrated. The American government now says that the war on terrorism is against an ideology rather than an organized entity. Laqueur says that the new terrorism uses smaller groups that, in his view, are more radical.[72] Hoffman adds that the new groups are likely to be composed of amateurs rather than professional terrorists who devote their lives and careers to the cause; they are likely also to be less well trained and to rely on information they collect themselves, primarily from the internet.[73] Simon and Benjamin add that the absence of state support is a key feature.[74]

By contrast, the "old" terrorist structure was considered to be centralized and top-down. As Hoffman described it, "In the past, terrorist groups were recognizable mostly as collections of individuals belonging to an organization with a well-defined command and control apparatus, who had been previously trained (in however rudimentary a fashion) in the techniques and tactics of terrorism, were engaged in conspiracy as a full-time avocation, living underground while constantly planning and plotting terrorist attacks, and who at times were under the direct control, or operated at the express behest, or a foreign government . . ."[75] Hierarchies operated. The classic cellular structure was paramount.

Although al Qaeda is a transnational actor, it is problematic to assume that it is entirely different from the past, that it is necessarily a model for the future, or that secular groups might not organize themselves similarly. First, among "religious" groups, al Qaeda is the only example of such a network or franchise/venture capital operation. Other "religious" groups are more traditional in form (Hezbollah, Hamas, or Egyptian Islamic Jihad). Aum Shinrikyo was extremely hierarchical; like Sendero Luminoso, it was dominated by a charismatic leader. Second, before the war in Afghanistan in 2001, al Qaeda was largely a centralized organization. Its functioning depended on extensive face-to-face communication. Apparently some actions were ordered by the top leadership, but there was also some local autonomy. The importance of the shared experience, socialization, and training in Afghanistan and

---

[71] According to Ian Lesser, "This new terrorism is increasingly networked. . . . As a result, much existing counterterrorism experience may be losing its relevance as network forms of organization replace the canonical terrorist hierarchies. . . ." In Lesser, "Countering the New Terrorism: Implications for Strategy," p. 87.

[72] Laqueur, *The New Terrorism*, p. 5.

[73] Hoffman, *Inside Terrorism*, p. 197, 203.

[74] See "America and the New Terrorism," pp. 59–75.

[75] Hoffman, *Inside Terrorism*, p. 197.

subsequent access to recruits from diasporas and from other conflict zones cannot be underestimated in the organizational development of al Qaeda. Its subsequent decentralization may not have been a choice but an adaptation to the loss of sanctuary in Afghanistan, pressure from security services around the world, and the war in Iraq.

Furthermore, the organization of the "old" or "canonical" terrorism was not always as tight and hierarchical as it might now appear. Peter Merkl, for example, has argued that the apparently monolithic quality of the Red Army Faction in West Germany was a myth.[76] The nineteenth century anarchists formed a transnational conspiracy, linking activists in Russia, Germany, Switzerland, France, Spain, Italy, and the United States. The essence of anarchism was antipathy to central direction, and much terrorism was locally generated or inspirational. Well-publicized trials of anarchists would invariably spark retaliation by sympathizers who were not members of any organization. The secular Palestinian groups of the 1970s and 1980s split, merged, resplit, and remerged. The relationship of Black September to Arafat and Fatah was one of indirection and deniability. West German and Japanese groups cooperated with Palestinians; in fact, the Japanese Red Army relocated to Lebanon after being driven from Japan. In addition, some of the more hierarchical groups in the past actually allowed significant local autonomy. The Active Service Units of the IRA, for example, sometimes acted independently, without the approval of the Army Council. The Italian Red Brigades were organized in independent "columns" in different cities. The French Action Directe was actually two groups, one limited to France and the other operating internationally and linked to groups in Belgium.

The Appeal of the "New Terrorism" Idea

Why is the idea of a fundamentally new terrorism attractive, if indeed it is as flawed as I claim? One reason may be that the conception of a "new" terrorism supports the case for major policy change – a justification for the global war on terrorism, the establishment of the category of "enemy combatant," brutal interrogation methods, reliance on a strategy of military preemption, and the use of tactics such as renditions, domestic surveillance activities, and other homeland security measures that restrict civil liberties. Defining jihadist terrorism as entirely new is a way of framing the threat so as to mobilize both public and elite support for costly responses that have long-term and uncertain pay-offs. The shock of the surprise attacks of September 11th was a turning point in the United States, especially for officials such as Richard Clarke (and including Simon and Benjamin as former staff members from the Clinton Administration National Security Council) who had long warned that terrorism could be a major danger and who felt that they had been ignored.[77]

---

[76] See Peter Merkl, "West German Left-Wing Terrorism," in Martha Crenshaw (ed.), *Terrorism in Context*, (University Park, PA: Pennsylvania State University Press, 1995).

[77] *Against All Enemies: Inside America's War on Terror* (New York: Free Press, 2004).

The effect of 9/11 may resemble the impact of the North Korean invasion of the South on American policy makers, in cementing the ideas behind interpretations of the threat of Communism and the militarization of containment.[78] It seemed and may still seem impossible to consider terrorism a "first order threat" justifying military action unless it is defined as unprecedented. Linking the idea of a "new" terrorism to the threat of "weapons of mass destruction" magnifies the danger even more.

Furthermore, the new terrorism model permits top-down processing of information. If policy-makers can rely on a set of simple assumptions about terrorism, they need not concern themselves with understanding a contradictory and confusing reality. In the presence of incomplete and ambiguous information, policy-makers are prone to rely on prior cognitive assumptions. Doing so saves them time, energy, and stress. They rely on metaphors, narratives, and analogies that make sense of what might otherwise be difficult to comprehend. For example, defining groups such as Hezbollah and Hamas as "terrorist organizations" with whom the United States cannot negotiate saves policy makers from having to cope with the troublesome problem of how to deal successfully with hostile but democratically-elected nonstate actors.

For similar reasons, terrorism "experts," especially newcomers to the field, might find it convenient not to have to take the time to study the long and complicated history of the terrorist phenomenon.[79] If analysts and pundits can focus only on the "new" terrorism of the post Cold War world, then they can safely disregard the record of terrorism that occurred from the late nineteenth century to the 1990s. The narrowed scope of their research streamlines the task of analysis. Furthermore, if analysts can safely assume that religion is the cause of terrorism, they need not look for other more complex explanations that necessitate linking religion to other political, social, and economic factors. The appeal of Islam in immigrant communities in the West, for example, is a political and social question involving issues of cultural assimilation and economic integration. Processes of radicalization cannot be understood without examining background conditions and individual propensities in particular societies. There is no generic "new terrorist."

Conclusions

Rejecting our accumulated knowledge of terrorism by dismissing it as "obsolete" is dangerous. A misdiagnosis of what the "new" actually entails could lead to mistakes of prediction and of policy as grave as those attributed to lack of recognition of the

---

[78] Indeed Simon (2003) calls for a policy of containment, as the U.S. contained the Soviet Union during the Cold War. Simon and Benjamin, *The Age of Sacred Terror*.

[79] Burnett and Whyte (2005) go further to say that "It is certain that some elite groups will make a great deal of political and social capital out of this war on terror. It is equally certain that state interventions against the terrorists will continue to be supported by a manufactured conception of 'new terrorism' that is founded upon a highly questionable knowledge base" (p. 15). They are particularly critical of the role of the Rand Corporation.

threat. For example, the assumption that the sort of catastrophic terrorism that many defined as "new" would necessarily involve the use of "weapons of mass destruction" turned out to be mistaken. Similarly, before the September 11, 2001, attacks, many observers thought that hijackings were an outmoded tactic. They believed that terrorists had abandoned the method because governments had erected effective defense measures such as passenger screenings at airports. They did not imagine that the old terrorism tactic could be combined with suicide missions (which began in the 1980s in Lebanon) to produce such a cataclysmic effect.

Differences among groups and differences in patterns of terrorism over time do exist, but many of these shifts are due to a changing environment, largely processes associated with what is termed globalization, in particular, such as advances in communications, access to weapons and explosives, and individual mobility. Differences can also be attributed to specific opportunity structures, such as Al Qaeda's emergence in protected spaces in Pakistan, the Sudan, and Afghanistan. The internet, for example, has proved an important resource for terrorists. It is a transnational means of communication, recruitment, indoctrination, instruction, propaganda, and fund-raising that largely escapes government control.[80] Jihadist websites, for example, have proliferated. Political and military conflicts provide further opportunities. The American invasion of Iraq and the insurgency it provoked, for example, have provided both a stimulus and a training ground for jihadi militants. Furthermore, the development of terrorism exhibits evolutionary progression, as groups learn from their own experiences and those of others. They are not driven solely by doctrine, whether religious or secular, but react to what governments and publics do. They seek the support of constituencies and are sensitive to changing attitudes and values. Their behavior is highly contingent.

Thus, analysis of what is new about terrorism needs to be based on systematic empirical research that compares a wide range of cases over extended time periods. Without knowing the contours of the "old" terrorism, the shape of the new cannot be identified. Comparisons must also take into account the historical context within which terrorism occurs. Otherwise we cannot understand adaptation and innovation in terrorist behavior.

The "new terrorism" viewpoint is bound to overestimate the effect of religious beliefs as a cause of terrorism and as a cause of lethality. It underestimates the power of nationalism. The distinction between religious and nationalist or secular revolutionary motivations is not clearly established or substantiated in fact. Few groups are classified as exclusively religious; most have mixed motives. The statistical data on which the association between religion and mass casualties is based are incomplete, excluding as they do domestic terrorism prior to the late 1990s.

In particular, analysts need to recognize that secular ideologies can also be fundamentalist, exclusive, and totalitarian and that secular groups can promote excessive killing. Sendero Luminoso (the Shining Path) in Peru in the 1980s is a case in point,

---

80 See Gabriel Weimann, *Terror on the Internet: The New Arena, the New Challenges* (Washington: United States Institute of Peace Press, 2006).

and it has inspired groups as distant as Maoist rebels in Nepal. According to Cynthia McClintock, Sendero Luminoso resembled the Khmer Rouge in ideology, strategy, and social base. Both emphasized political violence in the revolutionary process and systematically terrorized civilians. Only 17% of Sendero's victims were military or police: "Between 1980 and 1992, Sendero murdered at least 8 ecclesiastics, 9 foreign development workers, 44 grassroots leaders, 203 businessmen, 244 teachers, 303 students, 424 workers, 502 political officials (primarily local officials such as mayors), 1,100 urban residents, and 2,196 peasants."[81] Like contemporary jihadists, the attitudes of both the Khmer Rouge and Sendero Luminoso were characterized by emotional rage, complete confidence in the rightness of their cause, and hatred for the corruption they saw around them. Sendero Luminoso was politically uncompromising, ideologically rigid, and internally authoritarian. It wished to seize power and eliminate both the government and political rivals. It did not seek a place at the bargaining table or calibrate its violence judiciously, as the "new terrorism" proponents would predict of a secular "old terrorist" organization.

The "mechanisms of moral disengagement" that Albert Bandura described over fifteen years ago operate for all worldviews.[82] We should not assume that only groups claiming religious sanction will be capable of mass killing or that they are uniformly composed of irrational fanatics who seek only to destroy. Nor should we assume that all religiously motivated groups are dedicated to killing the largest possible numbers. We might note, for example, that the Egyptian Islamic Group, in contrast to Islamic Jihad, has abandoned terrorism although the two groups shared many of the same religious beliefs.

In sum, then, a close look at the objectives, methods, and organizational structures of what is said to be "new" and what is said to be "old" terrorism reveals numerous similarities rather than firm differences. It cannot really be said that there are two fundamental types of terrorism. The question should be reframed in broader terms, to ask why some groups choose to cause or try to cause large numbers of civilian casualties and others do not, rather than assuming that religious beliefs are the explanation for lethality. If we settle on religion as the answer, we are likely to misunderstand both religion and terrorism.

---

[81] *Revolutionary Movements in Latin America: El Salvador's FMLN and Peru's Shining Path* (Washington: United States Institute of Peace Press, 1998), p. 68.

[82] "Mechanisms of moral disengagement," in *Origins of Terrorism: Psychologies, Ideologies, Theologies, States of Mind*, ed. Walter Reich (Cambridge: Woodrow Wilson International Center for Scholars and Cambridge University Press, 1990).

Globalization, Social Capital and Networked Violence: The Role of Values

Benjamin N. Judkins and Stephen E. Reynolds

Introduction: Defining the Challenge of Franchised Violence

By most accounts terrorism is not a new phenomenon. Its saliency to daily politics is. While even a decade ago most policy makers were content to see terrorism as at best a minor threat, today calls are heard for the development of new strategies to contain its growth. Yet before a new approach to containing "terror" can be drafted it first is necessary to ask what kinds of opponents we are facing. Are they best understood as privatized appendages to state policy, international organizations or perhaps more broadly based social movements? In this respect modern "terrorism" shows a frightening degree of diversity that is not always reflected in subsequent policy discussions. By understanding why some groups adopt relatively horizontal, as opposed to vertical, organizational structures we hope to point out some potential pitfalls in traditional strategies to "contain" the growth of terrorist networks.

Al Qaeda and the current wave of Islamic extremism are interesting in this regard. Students of terrorism have noted that following the American reprisals in Afghanistan, al Qaeda began to redraw its organizational flow chart. Where as before it was fairly hierarchic and unitary in its structure, with extensive fixed assets in places like Afghanistan and Northern Africa, it now operates more like a franchised multi-national corporation. While it retains a "central board of directors" and an extensive "media wing," it has been content in recent years to loan its brand name to attacks planned or carried out by independent or previously unaffiliated groups around the globe.

This development raises a number of puzzles. We know from the literature in economics and business (as well as our daily experience as consumers) that once established firms are willing to expend huge amounts of energy and resources to protect the quality, image and ownership of their brand names. Nor are other agents allowed to use a brand name without paying substantial royalties. Yet these general principals do not seem to be observed in the current case.

B.N. Judkins
University of Utah
e-mail: benjamin.judkins@poli-sci.utah.edu

I.A. Karawan et al. (eds.), *Values and Violence*,

While not usually discussed in the same context this general strategy of a central group with global ambitions franchising out terrorism has in fact been employed in at least two eras of modern history, and by a number of very different groups. Most recently we have seen both white supremacists and radical environmental groups employ this same general tactic of developing an easily recognized brand name (such as the "Animal Liberation Front" or the "Klu Klux Klan") and then franchising it to a network of locally recruited, funded and organized cells who maintain communication with each other through an extensive system of web pages and chat rooms.

Yet it would be a mistake to assume that patterns of franchised or "networked" violence first emerged at the end of the 20th century. While al Queda and the ALF seem to have very little in common, both can be thought of as a reaction to the problems and opportunities created by the spread of trade, investment and communication technologies. In short, the existence of both of these groups is inexplicably bound up with the phenomenon popularly called "globalization."

The current period is not the only one in which globalization has emerged as a major social force. By most measures the period of 1880–1914 was almost as "global" as the world today and in some respects, such as labor mobility, much more so.[1] We should not then be surprised to see the emergence of other franchised groups in this period.

The anarchists and communists of the late 19th and early 20th centuries were no strangers to the idea that one could develop a reputation through acts of violence, spread your ideas through quickly expanding media outlets, and then let others begin to organize themselves and take up the cause in a new area of the world. The doctrine of world wide revolution practically demands a "networked" approach to political violence.

When presented in this broader ideological and historical context both a new pattern and puzzle begins to emerge. It is at the points of greatest "globalization" that we begin to see the emergence of franchises as a successful strategy for *some* antisystemic movements. How specifically does globalization advantage these strategies, and just as importantly, what costs do they impose on groups that employ them? What limits their utility? If they give some groups an advantage in getting their message heard, why don't other groups such as Hamas or the IRA adopt this strategy as well? Is this simply a matter of historical path dependency, or is there a logic to the organizational structure that different political groups adopt? Lastly, what can policy makers do to counter the spread of these deadly identities in an age of global struggle and instant communication?

In the following paper we argue that while globalization is a necessary condition for the success of these groups, it is not sufficient to understand their distribution throughout the international system. To better predict where franchised violence

---

[1] For an overview of the social and economic consequences of this early period see Kevin H. O'Rourke and Jeffrey G. Williamson, *Globalization and History: The Evolution of a Nineteenth-Century Atlantic Economy* (Cambridge: MIT Press, 1999).

will emerge we need to turn to the realm of identities, ideas and beliefs that individual actors hold about their relationships with their neighbors, their social groups and society at large. Networked movements can only expand by spreading their unique norms and identities through vulnerable communities. We ask what role a community's level of social capital can play in containing or hampering the growth of extremist groups.

While social capital and networks are often discussed in relation to a community's ability to absorb new norms and identities, we believe that they may also have a conservative character or bias. By imposing a substantial "entrance cost" to new identities certain communities may make themselves less vulnerable to the growth of fringe extremist movements.

This insight goes some way towards explaining why different sorts of terrorist structures are needed to succeed in different types of communities. It also implies that policy makers who are concerned about the spread of networked extremist groups should be very careful when crafting their policies to avoid systems that rely on heavy surveillance, or other forms of state cooptation of social groups, as these methods can actually destroy the social capital that is their first line of defense in the face of extremist ideologies.

Theory: Globalization, Social Capital and the Choice of Institutional Structure

For the purposes of this model, and following the general trend in the literature, a terrorist organization is defined simply as a group of non-state actors who attempt to use violence to accomplish an avowedly political aim.[2] Yet the label "terrorist" remains overly broad, obscuring more than it reveals about the variety of groups who may turn to violence to accomplish their political or ideological objectives. Outlining a more specific typology of actors is therefore the first step in developing our model of franchised violence.

While there has been a great deal of discussion of the socio-economic, ideological and even religious sources of extremist violence, this model begins by assuming that no matter what issues or values motivate group formation, the leaders of these organizations will act in a way that is basically rational, seeking to accomplish their goals, while protecting their institutions, not unlike the CEOs of for-profit multinational enterprises.[3] Thus our model subscribes to a "thin rational choice" perspective

---

[2] There has been considerable controversy as to how the term "terrorism" should be defined. The topic has been actively debated at the international level since at least 1937 when the League of Nations failed to resolve the dispute. For an overview of some of the commonly accepted definitions employed in UN documents see http://www.unodc.org/unodc/terrorism_definitions.html.

[3] For an argument as to how seemingly irrational acts of terrorism can be modeled as a more or less rational strategy see Richard K. Betts, "The soft underbelly of American primacy: Tactical advantages of terror," *Political Studies Quarterly* 117 (Spring 2002). An "eclectic theory of foreign investment" is developed mainly in the works of John Dunning, particularly in John H. Dunning,

in which shifting norms and values define a group's medium and long range goals, but we assume that the costs and benefits of various strategies will be weighed in this struggle. Our analysis is informed by the literature on the activities of the multinational for-profit enterprise (MNE), especially the widely used "eclectic theory of foreign investment" and the extensive empirical analysis of the MNE.

The "eclectic theory" emphasizes transaction costs and the interaction of three aspects (ownership, location and internalization) of a horizontally organized MNE, one carrying out the same activities or producing the same product in multiple national markets: (1) ownership or appropriation of a value-creating proprietary asset for which there are few close substitutes, e.g., reputation, synergies within the organization, unique technology, trust, etc., (2) processes that use that asset do so efficiently when distributed across several national markets, (3) the use of the asset is more efficiently managed, i.e., generates more value that is appropriable to the owning firm, when managed within the owning firm than by licensing its use to others. This hierarchical structure is in contrast to a structure characterized by franchising or licensing the use of the proprietary asset to others. Several propositions are derived from the theoretical and empirical literature on licensing versus direct foreign investment by a MNE. In fact the choice is not dichotomous but a continuum from direct control of a wholly owned subsidiary at one end to affiliates with varying contractual relations to franchises and finally arms-length licensing at the other end.

When licensing does take place, the market for the right to use, for example, proprietary technology or reputation or personnel for training typically (but not uniquely) leads to long term relationships in order to deter opportunistic behavior by the licensee that may reduce the value of the proprietary asset to its owners. Geographically dispersed, incomplete licensing contracts are more common for less complex processes and less differentiated products, i.e., when national variations, differentiation in a product or process that requires its reconfiguration or successful variations have little value in another location. Licensing of the proprietary asset is less beneficial to its owner and less likely to take place the more direct is the competition between the two entities; competitors or potential competitors in distant countries are more attractive licensees than are those near by. The owner is more likely to license use of the asset when it lacks knowledge of the foreign market, faces high entry barriers to establishment of direct operations in that market, or faces high opportunity costs on use elsewhere of its own complimentary assets. The owner will be deterred from licensing by risk of reduction in the value of its proprietary asset by the licensee. The licensee is attracted when costs of developing an asset similar to the one in question are high relative to the costs of operations using it or when it is diversifying from its core activities.

International Production and the Multinational Enterprise.(London: Allen and Unwin, 1980). Extensive review of the empirical literature on the multinational enterprise may be found in Richard E. Caves, *Multinational Enterprise and Economic Analysis* (New York: Cambridge University Press, 1996).

With respect to terrorist organizations the above observations from the "eclectic theory" literature imply that franchising or licensing of capabilities for violence, lending the use of reputation, technical expertise or trainers, would be attractive to the franchiser only if doing so builds, rather than undermining its reputation for competence and commitment to its putative values – and would lead to severing the relationship when opportunism or incompetence by the franchisee threatened that reputation. Capabilities for simple acts of violence would be more easily franchised or licensed when local variations in values, ideological justifications for violence and political ambitions do not have wider appeal.

An organization, with political ambitions focused on the Middle-east would be expected to find licensing to a distant competitor in political violence in Indonesia or the Philippines more attractive than to one nearer home. Local criminal gangs with newly developing political ambitions would be attracted by an opportunity to reduce their own costs of pursuing those ambitions through acquiring license to use an established reputation for competence (and expanded capability) in political violence, as well as, an articulated, recognized ideology as a source of political legitimacy. High entry cost barriers, including the social capital phenomena discussed in this paper, to carrying out terrorist activity in a particular location would encourage foreign entry there through franchise rather than through direct control.

Prior to accomplishing its long run policy goals there are two tasks that any organization must be able to accomplish. First, it has to be able to recruit members, investment and the human capital needed to build its organization, and second it has to protect these assets until its final goals can be accomplished. However, the optimal strategy for accomplishing these goals may vary according to policy demands or the environment that the group must operate in.

We begin by positing the existence of two "types" or archetypal modes of group organization. In real life these possibilities clearly exist on a continuum, with most groups combining some aspects of both types. Nevertheless it is still important to lay out the possibilities and ask how these different sorts of groups will seek to accomplish the two goals outlined above, and what modes of containment might be most effective in countering each type.

The first group of organizations has a relatively traditional organizational pattern in which a small ruling authority has clear lines of communications with all parts of the institutions and a basically hierarchical command structure. These lines of communication are often formalized to increase the efficiency of communication and lower transaction costs, and the organization itself often shows extensive specialization where the group seeks the efficiency gains to be had from trade by splitting itself either geographically, or by technical department.

Many of the national liberation movements, modeled on either traditional Marxist parties or military units assume this pattern of organization. In the current era and recent past groups like the IRA, the PLO, the Shining Path and the Tamil Tigers have exhibited this form of organization. Each one of these groups has run extensive political, military, and in some cases humanitarian missions through different wings of the organization. Prior to the 1960s the various inheritors of the Ku Klux Klan (also a non-state actor that sought to use violence and terror to accomplish political aims) was a powerful organization that basically shared the same institutional structure as other American fraternal or secret societies. They too would fall into this group of "institutionalized" actors prior to the advent of the civil rights movement and globalization.

Nevertheless, not all extremist groups today share this basic structure. "Franchised" groups differ from more highly institutionalized ones on a number of counts. First, the lines of communication linking the leadership of an organization are likely to be more tenuous, and in some cases non-existent. Rather than having internal and highly efficient means of communications these groups instead must rely on the media to not only build and spread an image, but to motivate and in some cases direct members of their far flung empires. Where as more institutionalized groups will likely fund and oversee any significant operations carried out in its name, a "franchised" approach instead depends on previously unaffiliated local groups to not only organize themselves, but also to select targets and raise the money necessary to fund the attacks, though a sort of "seed grant" program may be run by some groups.[4]

While al Qaeda has exceptional resources at its disposal by the standards of most extremist organizations, the really remarkable thing is that it does not need to use these to fund all of the operations carried out by its literally vast network of operatives working under the al Qaeda "brand name" around the globe. Drug dealing, white collar crime and identity theft are becoming an increasingly common funding solution for local cells of extremist groups.[5]

It is entirely likely that strategies that have been developed for dealing with "institutionalized" groups will be less effective when faced with a more "networked challenge." In order to understand why, we need to now turn our attention to the role of globalization and social capital in promoting and in hindering the emergence of each of these "types" of terrorist organizations.

The global spread of capital, technology, media, etc. has at least two aspects that need to be taken into account. First, by lowering the cost of communication technology we should expect that groups will utilize more of this input in the creation of their political networks. Second, and perhaps more importantly, as increased flows of trade, investment and information cross national boundaries we expect that both groups of winners and of losers will be created.

Standard economic theory informs us that the winners will win more than the losers will lose, and yet this oft quoted dictum does not tell the entire story. It must be remembered that while according to the Stolper-Samuelson Theorem the holders of scarce (in each isolated market) factors of production will be the big losers. In the prior autarchic system they will have been able to charge high prices for their resources, thus gaining not just economic wealth but often political power and social influence as well. A change in the economic fortunes of the various players threatens not just to upset the economic balance of power in a rapidly expanding

---

[4] Daniel Pipes, "Al-Qaeda's Limits." *New York Post*. March 28, 2003.

[5] Hayder Mili, "Tangled Webs: Terrorist and Organized Crime Groups." *Terrorism Monitor*. 4, 1 (2006). John P. Sullivan, "Terrorism, Crime and Private Armies." *Low Intensity Conflict & Law Enforcement* 1, 2 (2002), pp. 239–253.

economy, but the social and political one as well as new groups begin to move into positions of authority.[6] The patterns of general social disruption and degradation of traditional social and political power structures which accompanies globalization may also make some types of communities more susceptible to the new identities and set of values that are promised by networked terrorist organizations, especially if their ideology also promises increased social stability and material benefits.

Social Capital and Political Violence

Given that it is unlikely that this social disruption can be reversed, or even slowed without imposing huge costs on the consumers and other groups who do benefit from globalization, the question then becomes how does one instead contain the spread of certain value systems that support political violence? The process of social decay that globalization threatens would seem to indicate one possible method. Social capital, or the bonds of trust and reciprocity that exist in society, may act in at least two different ways as a "barrier to entry" to outside terrorist organizations seeking to expand their influence.

Social capital is a somewhat amorphous subject that has been discussed from many angles. In small primary communities characterized by intensive and repeated interactions overlapping networks of personal friendships and connections may form the web of trust necessary to facilitate cooperation in pursuing some public good. At stake in these networks is not material gain so much as identity, reputation and social standing.[7] As the size of the community increases the same volume of face-to-face interactions becomes impossible to maintain. Yet even a shared core identity may still facilitate the growth of certain norms and patterns of social trust that will be advantageous in a more complex society. While weaker in nature, even this "thin trust" can be an effective social lubricant in larger communities.[8] The basic thought is that groups with extensive reserves of social capital, or strong networks of trust, will be better able to work together to accomplish goals that would be unattainable for a control group that lacked this capital, but was otherwise identical.[9]

James Coleman has explored the elements of several types of social relations that may contribute to the formation of social capital. The first of these factors are

---

[6] W.F. Stolper and P.A. Samuelson, "Protection and Real Wages," *Review of Economic Studies*, 9 (1941), pp. 58–73. For a discussion of the further political implications of shifts in trade see Ronald Rogowski, *Commerce and Coalition: How Trade Effects Domestic Political Alignments* (Princeton: Princeton University Press, 1990).

[7] B. Williams, "Formal Structures and Social Reality" in D. Gambetta (ed.), *Trust: Making and Breaking Cooperative Relations* (Oxford: Basil Blackwell, 1988).

[8] M. Granovetter, "The Strength of Weak Ties," *American Journal of Sociology* 78 (May 1973), pp. 1360–1380.

[9] Corwin Smidt, *Religion as Social Capital* (Waco, TX: Baylor Univ. Press, 2003), p. 5; James Coleman, "Social Capital in the Creation of Human Capital," *The American Journal of Psychology* 94 (1988), pp. S95–S119.

expectations and obligations revolving loosely around norms of reciprocity. Under the norm of reciprocity if one member of the community does a favor for the second, an expectation of obligation is created. Such expectations may then become formalized in norms of correct behavior that are enforced with social sanctions.[10]

Note that by invoking social capital we are not necessarily banishing the egoistic or rational elements of our subjects. Rather than suddenly becoming irrational altruists, the use of reputation or social trust to reach deals in situations characterized by repeated interactions can lead to not only pareto optimal outcomes in individual bargaining games, but also to much more diffuse outcomes such as a generally improved contracting environment (which facilitates market growth) or an increase in institutional efficiency as the same norms begin to spill over into the bureaucratic and political realm. Discussions of social capital are not necessarily incompatible with a generally "rational" model of social or political analysis.

As such one would assume that a rational goal held by most groups or identity structures would be its own self-preservation. Social capital is usually discussed in relation to how it may spread the growth of certain democratic or liberal norms and identities. Putnam's work on the character of democracy in Italy and changing nature of American society are probably the two most widely read examples of this general approach.[11] But it does not logically hold that social capital would aid in the spread of all sorts of norms and value systems. In fact, it may have a very conservative bias from the perspective of an extremist group.

Much of the current literature makes a distinction between "bonding" and "bridging" capital. Small groups characterized by frequent repeated interaction among members may be thought of as having a large amount of bonding capital.[12] Some scholars have worried that the tight relationships formed within these groups (such as small fundamentalist religious congregations) might actually serve to insulate and cut their members off from the rest of society.[13]

The alternative arrangement is often referred to as "bridging capital." This basically refers to the stock of social trust and relationships that exists between a specific preexisting group and the rest of society. It is logically possible that some groups, such as an ethnic clan or tribe, may have very strong bonds between the immediate members of the group, but have weak relationships or feelings of trust towards

---

[10] James Coleman, *Foundations of Social Theory* (Cambridge MA: Harvard University Press, 1990), p. 311.

[11] R.D. Putnam, *Making Democracy Work: Civic Tradition in Modern Italy* (Princeton: Princeton University Press, 1993); R.D. Putnam. 2000. *Bowling Alone: The Collapse and Revival of American Community* (New York: Simon & Schuster, 2000).

[12] Putnam, *Bowling Alone*, pp. 22–23.

[13] Other scholars disagree with this received wisdom. For instance Campbell and Yonish have found that charitable engagement with the outside community increases as the level of religiosity of the parishioners in question goes up, regardless of their denominational identity. This would seem to indicate that individuals can be taught to value bridging social ties even if their interactions are dominated by a single institution. David E. Campbell and Steven J. Yonish, "Religion and Volunteering in America," in Corwin Smidt (ed.), *Religion as Social Capital: Producing the Common Good* (Waco: Baylor University Press, 2003), pp. 87–106.

individuals from other clans or tribes. In many cases, it is the presence or absence of this bridging capital that is central to understanding what types of terrorist groups are likely to emerge in a given environment.

We propose that in the abstract the leaders of terrorist organizations thinking of expanding their operations in new environments would prefer to construct traditional hierarchic organizations as this would give them the most control of operational strategies and the quality of the "product" to which their hard earned brand name is about to be attached. This may even be observed in the case of more traditional terrorist groups such as the Weathermen or the Covenant, Sword and Arm of the Lord (CSA) that specialized in recruiting relatively unattached and previously marginalized individuals into their organizational structure. In fact, Jessica Stern finds that these sort of terrorist organizations and leaders will sometimes go to great lengths to isolate their members from all social links outside the group precisely so that their leaders can exercise greater control over them.[14]

Yet the existence of a dense network of preexisting groups characterized by high levels of bonding capital would act as a barrier of entry to leaders attempting to establish new, and in many ways incompatible, organizations. This is especially true if some of the local groups, such as religious congregations, could be thought of as possible "peer competitors." In this case, the outside terrorist organization may decide that the most efficient course of action is to attempt to co-opt an entire existing social group, in effect offering a side payment to convince the local group to license its name and ideology. Since it is both more difficult and more expensive to recruit entire segments of society rather than picking off alienated and atomized individuals one by one, societies with high levels of bonding capital should be less susceptible to the spread of terrorist organizations. Nevertheless, if and when they do emerge these groups are more like to be "franchises."

The next question that must be addressed is the size of the side-payment to be made in the case of a franchised operation. Now it is the bridging, rather than bonding, capital that acts as the barrier to entry to outside terrorist organizations. If the social group they are attempting to recruit is relatively isolated with few bonds to the larger social fabric it stands to reason that their opportunity cost for switching their alliances to an extremist ideology would be fairly small. If on the other hand this group had many social connections with society its opportunity cost for switching its allegiance would be much higher. Suddenly the foreign terrorist organization would be forced to step in and replace many of the goods and services that society at large had previously provided if they wish to retain the loyalty of their newly acquired client.

Notice again that the greater the preexisting stock of social capital the more expensive it will be for some outside terrorist organization to penetrate this target

---

14 Jessica Stern, *Terror in the Name of God: Why Religious Militants Kill* (New York: Ecco, 2003), pp. 15–21. With regards to the question of social isolation within vertically oriented terrorist organizations it is interesting to note that Stern titled her first four chapters "Alienation," "Humiliation," "Demographics," and "History" as a way of summarizing those factors that make individuals susceptible to terrorist recruitment.

group, and the less likely they are to try. However, in cases where for whatever reason they do go ahead with these efforts social capital will once again impact the structure of the terrorist organization that emerges.

In the case of groups with high levels of bonding capital, but little bridging capital, the foreign terrorist organization can maintain a pretty sparse, highly networked, presence. Because a local group already exists it doesn't have to worry much about recruiting or funding the cell's day to day operations. And since this group feels highly marginalized or alienated extensive side payments are not necessary to turn them against other targets in society. Al Qaeda's operations in the United Kingdom and Spain, as well as the operations of ALF and various other environmental terrorists groups would seem to fall into this category.

However, if the desired group had previously been tightly connected with the broader social structure then it would be necessary to make extensive side payments, or to step in to fill a number of social functions. This then requires a group with much greater organizational capacity for raising, spending and overseeing money, as well as coordinating its various efforts. Thus Hamas was forced to compete against the influence of the PLO, UN and other social actors for the loyalty of certain groups of Palestinians by building hospitals, hosting youth soccer leagues, paying for weddings and even printing calendars. Such groups must develop a mixed organizational structure which incorporates both preexisting social units in a cell-like or networked structure, but also has highly hierarchic mechanisms needed to coordinate these much more complicated and expensive organizations. From the standpoint of a policy maker seeking to contain the terrorist organization this is actually an advantageous outcomes as it makes it much more expensive to maintain the organizational structure necessary to carry out terrorist attacks. Social capital has essentially altered the offense/defense balance between those that would promote extremist ideologies and the rest of society.

Policy Implications

The question then becomes, what sorts of impact can the state have on the creation of this social capital? Again, while much of the prior literature has focused on the impact of social capital on the ability of state sponsored development or social programs to run smoothly, we have every reason to expect that this is essentially a recursive relationship. In this paper, we propose that states in fact can choose policies the either help or hinder the creation of social capital, and hence can do much to either promote or dampen the susceptibility of society to franchised terror.

Consider the role of mosque in civil society.[15] We know for instance that religious congregation can generate impressive amounts of social capital in relatively short

[15] While space prohibits us from providing a full discussion for every type of franchised terrorist group that this model applies to its not hard to see how the same basic argument might apply to other sorts of small group social gatherings like political clubs, or environmental protest groups.

periods of time. Further, both relatively liberal and highly conservative groups show similar patterns of behavior on this score. And just as interestingly, the patterns of trust and reciprocity that these groups create spill well beyond their original boundaries and into the broader community as well. Both Dynes and Quarantelli and Wuthnow have found that membership and participation in religious groups is a good predictor of volunteerism in the community at large.[16] Likewise individuals who give money to religious causes are also more likely than the community at large to give charitably to secular causes.[17] Given these initial findings a number of students have concluded that the formation of social capital in religious communities does in fact lead to a greater degree of involvement in society at large.[18]

Yet none of this is automatic. It is important to consider the shape of the broader society that these groups are embedded in. In which communities might religiously generated social capital have the greatest marginal impact? It stands to reason that the largest effects would be observed in communities that in addition to having strong devotional institutions are also suffering from a lack of engagement with, and trust in, other key social institutions like the courts, law enforcement, the educational system, city hall or the markets. As such religiously generated social capital might have a particularly important impact on minority communities in general and, for the purposes of this essay, Muslim communities in Europe in particular.[19]

Many states around the globe are currently concerned about the spread of radical forms of Islam and are concerned with their own inability to monitor or control who preaches in the local mosque and what will be said. This has led to an explosion of proposals or laws seeking greater state involvement in areas like the licensing of Islamic clergy, centralizing their training or pay and even having the state move into the financing of officially sanctioned meeting places. Yet how successful will these steps ultimately be in reducing the attraction of radical value systems?

All of these attempts to establish a certain "approved" version of a new religious movement share a common strategy of (by either threat or inducement) reorienting the vision and loyalties of local religious leaders away from their communities

---

[16] R. Dynes & E. L. Quarantelli, "Helping Behavior in Large Scale Disasters," in D. H. Smith and J. Macauley and Associates (eds.), *Participation in Social and Political Activities* (San Francisco: Jossey-Bass, 1980). R. Wuthnow, *Acts of Compassion: Caring for others and helping ourselves* (Princeton, NJ: Princeton University Press, 1991).

[17] V. Hodgkinson, M. Weitzman & A. Kirsh, "From Commitment to Action: How Religious Involvement affects giving and volunteering," in R. Wuthnow and V.A. Hodgkinson and associates (eds.), *Faith and Philanthropy in America* (San Francisco: Jossey-Bass, 1990).

[18] A. Greeley, "Coleman revisited: Religious structures as a source of social capital," *American Behavioral Scientist* 40, 5(1997), pp. 587–594. See also more recent studies by Ram A. Cnaan, Stephanie C. Boddie and Gaynor I. Yancey, "Bowling Alone but Serving Together: The Congregational Norm of Community Involvement," in Corwin Smidt (ed.), *Religion as Social Capital: Producing the Common Good* (Waco, TX: Baylor University Press, 2003).

[19] S. Verba, K. L. Scholzman, and H. E. Brady, *Voice and Equality: Civic Volunteerism in American Politics* (Cambridge, MA: Harvard University Press, 1995); Frederick Harris, "Ties that Bind and Flourish: Religion as Social Capital in African-American Politics and Society," in Corwin Smidt (ed.), *Religion as Social Capital: Producing the Common Good* (Waco, TX: Baylor University Press, 2003).

and towards the state as their new benefactor, regulator or financier. When this happens the local leadership no longer finds itself forced to compete as fiercely within the religious marketplace as the state itself now has a greater impact on its survival. As such, religious organizations may scale back their involvement with extra-religious social, economic or political programs which were previously seen as an important mechanism for maintaining their visibility within the larger community. As a result of this decreased responsibility and interaction, the congregation loses its ability to generate the sorts of social and human capital that could be vital for addressing other social issues. Both bonding and bridging capital suffer in this situation.

We can only presume that a networked or franchised extremist group will have a easier time penetrating a weakened community in which worshipers have stopped attending mosques for fear of government surveillance, than vibrant and healthy communities in which local leaders have a stake in maintaining their own identity structure. Thus regulatory and surveillance measures that have proved successful in the past when dealing with hierarchic groups may actually make problems worse in the current era.

This then leads us to our first set of conclusions and hypotheses.

Hypothesis 1: During times of globalization with its attendant weakening of the social fabric we should see an increase in the success of networked or franchised terrorist groups. In more autarchic eras we should instead see the emergence of more hierarchic groups.

> **Corollary 1:** National response strategies that are effective in dealing with these more hierarchic groups will not necessarily be effective with other groups that are instead responding to different social and "market" conditions.

Hypothesis 2: Highly disrupted societies, or fringe areas within a society, the losers from globalization, will be most susceptible to networked or franchised groups. More cohesive elements of society will only be penetrated by more highly structured and specialized institutions.

> **Corollary 2:** National response strategies that encourage the growth of social capital within at risk communities should help to slow the spread of new radical identities. Policy responses such as increased surveillance, censorship or state intervention in civil society which tend to break down social capital may have an opposite effect of what was intended.

Conclusion and Directions for Further Research

The preceding model argues that two factors, the degree of globalization, and the level of social capital formation are key to understanding both what types of structures terrorist groups are likely to adopt, and what sorts of policy responses states may wish to consider when containing them. The results of this discussion are summarized in the following evolutionary diagram.

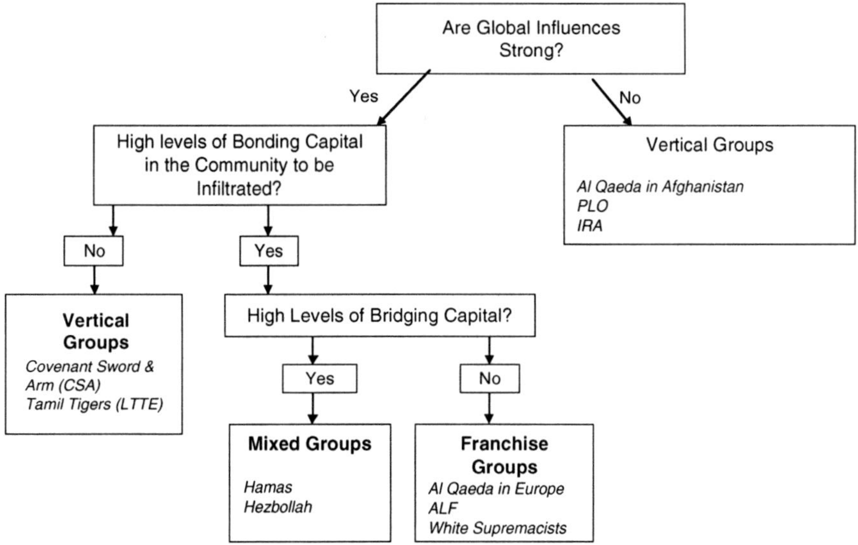

Fig. 1 Predicted effects of global and social structure

A number of possible research strategies present themselves for testing this model in the future. Perhaps most fruitful would be to focus on terrorist movements with a long longitudinal history and to examine how they have reacted to changing environmental conditions, or to do a comparative examination over time of their operations in different countries. For instance, racial hate groups like the Klu Klux Klan are interesting in that they encompass at least two periods of globalization and retrenchment. Therefore our model predicts that we should expect to see changes in Klan's organizational structure as communication technologies evolve and new social outlooks and law enforcement techniques make change necessary.

Likewise al Qaeda is interesting as it has carried out major operations in a number of different countries and communities in the past decade. These target states have often shown a great deal of variation in their stock of social capital. For instance, cells operating in Afghanistan, a country with minimal international exposure and low levels of bridging social capital, would have to be very different from those carried out in Europe, or even America. Groups indigenous to the highly networked societies of the advanced industrial world, such as radical environmentalists, would likely combine some of both elements.

A quick examination in the preceding chart seems to indicate that the model we have laid out in this paper has at least some ability to explain why certain groups adopted a franchised structure as well as when and under what conditions we are likely to see a change in a groups institutional character. This is important because not all terrorist organizations can be deterred in the same ways. Strategies that may be quite useful when dealing with hierarchic groups may actually exacerbate the underlying conditions that allow more networked groups to thrive. We intend to more fully explore the link between institutional structure and optimal containment strategy in additional papers.

Geospatial Analysis of Dynamic Terrorist Networks

Richard Medina and George Hepner

The emergence of global terrorism has given a new relevance to the study of social networks within global geographic space. Terrorists and their organizations, as non-state actors, are a great threat to the existing order, structures and people. However, as organizations, terrorist networks share an evolving correspondence to other organizational entities both in terms of their social network relationships, and the manifestation of these relationships across geographic space. This evolving correspondence is a fertile ground for description and investigation. While our knowledge of structure and operations of terrorist networks is presently limited, gaining this knowledge is a matter of global security and peace.

Generally, a network is visualized as a collection of vertices or nodes and the connections between them termed edges or links. In the study of terrorist networks in social space, nodes, or actors in the network can be individual terrorists, terrorist cells, or clusters, where the links are the relationships between those nodes. Various types of nodes and links can coexist. For example, nodes can represent different sex, nationality, location, etc., while links can vary by strength of relationships, geographic or social class proximity, etc. Nodes and links in a network can also be represented with varying degrees of importance or influence by different weights.[1] For example, if the nodes in question are individual people, Osama bin-Laden of al Qaeda will be a larger influence on the network than an actor of lesser status.

Nodes within a network typically vary in their connectivity. They can be classified based on their relative connectivity as hubs or non-hubs. Network hubs dominate connectivity, and are responsible for connecting nodes with fewer connections. An ideal example of a hub in a network is the wheel that contains a node at the center, and nodes at the outside end of each spoke. The hub in the center has optimal connectivity, as it is connected to each of the nodes through the spokes, while the outer nodes have the minimal connections; they connect only to the hub. It is easy

R. Medina
University of Utah
e-mail: richard.medina@geog.utah.edu

[1] M. E. J. Newman, "The Structure and Function of Complex Networks," *Society for Industrial and Applied Mathematics* 45, 2 (2003), pp. 167–256.

I.A. Karawan et al. (eds.), *Values and Violence*,

to see that the hub is responsible for the total connectivity of the wheel network described above. Since hubs play such an important role in network connectivity, it follows that the removal of hubs from a network will cause various levels of fragmentation. Hub and non-hub connectivity will be discussed in this paper as it applies to counterterrorism.

Network Models

There are two main network models that generally describe the organizational and authoritative structure of every real network: hierarchical and decentralized. In hierarchical network organization, a leader delegates tasks to lower levels and manages organizational activities. The delegation of authority is structured from top, down through the ranks, typically in a pyramidal shape. Hierarchical network organization can be seen throughout the business world in which corporations operate authoritatively from the top down, or from the CEO or Board of Directors down to the lower levels of the organization. An example of a hierarchically structured former terrorist organization is the Provisional Irish Republican Army, in which its authority flows from the Army Counsel at the top of the pyramid to the Active Service Units at the bottom.[2] In decentralized networks, there is no true organizational hierarchy. An extreme structural example of this is an all-channel or fully connected network in which each node is connected to all other nodes in the network.[3] Tasks and orders are not directed top to bottom in a pyramidal flow; rather nodes in the network determine their own path, albeit many times with a general direction. Examples of decentralized networks are the World Wide Web and the Internet. In both examples it is apparent that there are many connections from node to node (i.e., webpage to webpage or computer to computer, respectively), and both are lacking a pyramidal structure. Examples of decentralized terrorist organizations are al Qaeda and Hamas. Both groups, although they have a central authoritative core, also have cells that act autonomously for the good of the movement, or what seems in their eyes to be a beneficial step toward particular goal.

Aside from the hierarchical and decentralized network structures of terrorist or criminal activities, a completely decentralized structure exists, known as Leaderless Resistance. This structure, or lack of, can be described as a group of perpetrators acting out the wishes of an "inspirational leader." This leader offers no direction, support, funding, etc., only an overall goal. An example of this occurred in California when the White Aryan Nation (WAR) sought retribution after the

---

[2] J. Horgan and M. Taylor, "The Provisional Irish Republican Army: Command and Functional Structure," *Terrorism and Political Violence* 9, 3 (1997), pp. 1–32.

[3] J. Arquilla and D. Ronfeldt, "The Advent of Netwar (Revisited)," in J. Arquilla and D. Ronfeldt (eds.), *Networks and Netwars: The Future of Terror, Crime, and Militancy: Rand Report MR-1382* (Santa Monica: Rand Corporation, 2001), pp. 1–25.

barring of Proposition 187, which was written to end U.S. government services to immigrants. The WAR urged violent attacks from their followers.[4]

Terrorist organizational structure can be a hybrid of these three structures. For example, the network may include a central authoritative core, while the large majority of the organization is decentralized or in the process of decentralizing. An example of this occurs when organizations are the shifting from one structure to another, most likely when decentralization is required for security.

Terrorist networks are increasingly complex systems of people, finances, and technology, while at the same time striving for nodal (cell) isolation and a lack of interdependency that offers resiliency and tactical security benefits. Understanding this paradox is foundational to comprehending these networks and trying to anticipate activities. Deployed al Qaeda cells are required to be monetarily self sufficient. This ensures that if members of a cell are captured, information about organizational funding is not exposed. It also ensures that cells are not dependent on organizational funding. Financial self sufficiency is part of the operational doctrine of al Qaeda and is taught in the military training manual, *Declaration of Jihad against the Country's Tyrants*. To remain self sufficient, cells are to split finances for operations and investments, such that financial returns are generated. For security purposes funds are at times left with non-members of the cells so that those funds and their sources are not exposed if cell members are captured. Training for financial gain includes some illegal activities including credit card fraud and document forgery. Much of the financial planning in an al Qaeda cell is the responsibility of the cell commander.[5]

Decentralization

Terrorist organizations have been moving toward a network structure goal of increased security through social and geographic decentralization. One of the major strengths of decentralized networks is resilience. Decentralized structures cannot be destroyed by leadership decapitation as with hierarchical structures. Random attacks on a decentralized network will most likely not cause network failure. A directed attack on a relatively large number of the network's hubs is necessary for complete network failure.[6] This may be the greatest benefit of the decentralized network.[7] Another benefit of utilizing a network structure is the ability to quickly reconfigure when necessary, especially when given advance warning of threat to the

---

[4] C. Dishman, "The Leaderless Nexus: When Crime and Terror Converge," *Studies in Conflict and Terrorism* 28 (2005), pp. 237–252.

[5] M. Basile, "Going to the Source: Why Al Qaeda's Financial Network Is Likely to Withstand the Current War on Terrorist Financing," *Studies in Conflict & Terrorism* 27 (2004), pp. 169–185.

[6] M. Sageman, *Understanding Terror Networks* (Philadelphia: University of Pennsylvania Press, 2004).

[7] See Sageman, *Understanding Terror Networks*; P. Williams, "Transnational Criminal Networks," in J. Arquilla and D. Ronfeldt (eds.), *Networks and Netwars: The Future of Terror, Crime, and Militancy: Rand Report MR-1382* (Santa Monica: Rand Corporation, 2001), pp. 61–97; R. Albert,

organization. Since decentralized networks often have little concrete infrastructure and monetary investment in any specific place they can migrate within the geography of their socio-cultural activity space to avoid threats. Transcending national boundaries is becoming easier for decentralized organizations with the continuing shift toward globalization. Terrorist organizations can operate transnational to take advantage of more lenient laws and regulations, government tolerance of illicit activity, and the assistance of resident allies in one nation verses another.[8] Border regions have become places of meeting, planning, and support for terrorist and other criminal organizations. Islamic terrorist organizations such as Al-Gama'a al-Islamiyya, al Qaeda, Hizballah, and Hamas have utilized the sanctuary of the socio-cultural mix in the tri-border region of Paraguay, Brazil, and Argentina in South America.[9]

The process of network decentralization is furthered by the use of advancing information technologies. The ease of communication access along with electronic financial systems are fostering increased decentralization. There are three major ways in which information technologies are assisting terrorist network decentralization: (1) the reduction of transmission time, (2) the reduction of communication costs, and (3) an increase in the complexity of transmittable information.[10]

With transmission times reduced and technologies such as cell phones and global positioning systems (GPS), terrorist attacks can take place with the assistance of information in real time, and real location. These technologies assist in the assessment of target locations and temporal efficiency, as well as with early warnings, escape routes, and other logistical tactics. The reduction of communication costs will increase decentralization simply because it is relatively cheaper to decentralize as technology increases in the future. In the past, organizations centralized to reduce communication and coordination costs, while they are now free to spread out. While terrorists are able to transmit increasingly complex information, the complexity of their operations can also increase. This complex information may include air photo and satellite images, detailed maps, and weapons information transmitted in real time. It should also be noted that the quality and effectiveness of commercial encryption software is continually increasing, and already allows for information to be sent and received without the threat of interception. These new encryption technologies will soon be integrated into programs and servers, offering terrorists the ability to send encrypted, unbreakable communications without extra effort.[11]

H. Jeong, and A.-L. Barabasi, "Error and Attack Tolerance of Complex Networks," *Nature* 406 (2000), pp. 378–382.

[8] Williams, "Transnational Networks."

[9] R. Hudson, "Terrorist and Organized Crime Groups in the Tri-Border Area (TBA) of South America," *The Library of Congress – Federal Research Division* (2003).

[10] M. Zanini and S. J. A. Edwards, "The Networking of Terror in the Information Age," in J. Arquilla and D. Ronfeldt (eds.), *Networks and Netwars: The Future of Terror, Crime, and Militancy: Rand Report MR-1382* (Santa Monica: Rand Corporation, 2001).

[11] D. E. Denning and W. E. Baugh, "Encryption and Evolving Technologies as Tools of Organized Crime and Terrorism," *The National Strategy Information Center's US Working Group on Organized Crime (WGOC)*, (1997).

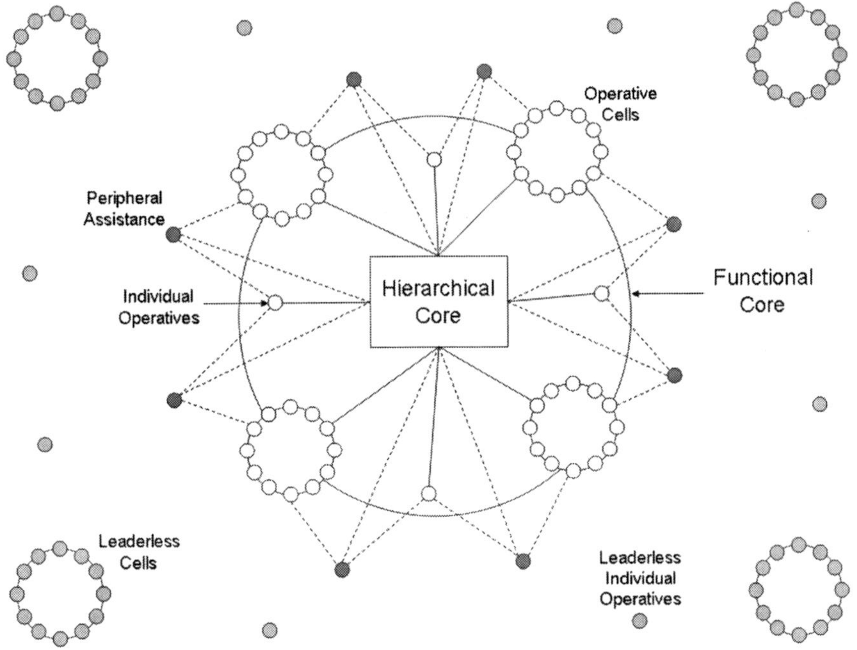

Fig. 1 Advanced terrorist network structure

Terrorist networks are social networks with specific and evolving structures and decentralized connectivity. An advanced terrorist network structure is displayed below in Fig. 1.

The network core contains the hierarchical core leadership, operative cells, and individual operatives, while the periphery contains peripheral assistance, and beyond the periphery are leaderless cells and individual operatives. It is assumed that the leaderless cells and operatives are not connected in the typical sense of connectivity between nodes in a network, but are connected by ideological/religious beliefs and/or purpose. Dotted lines are used to denote weak ties within the network, such as connections between terrorists in the network to those who offer assistance, but are not close ties. Weak ties in a social network typically refer to the connection between acquaintances.[12] These ties can connect nodes in the network to nodes in the periphery, such that they are not operational actors in the network, but are functional in the sense that they offer recruitment assistance, shelter and safe havens, monetary support, as well as other types of assistance. Core/Periphery connections can, and in many cases do refer to strong ties in a social network, however, here they are shown here as weak ties to emphasize the importance of making a distinction between strong and weak ties. Acquaintances in a social network can provide benefits by

[12] M. S. Granovetter, "The Strength of Weak Ties," *The American Journal of Sociology* 78, 6 (1973), pp. 1360–1380.

introducing nodes to new experiences and opportunities.[13] Weak ties in a terrorist network can assist nodes with funding, recruitment, shelter, etc.

Figure 1 illustrates a generalized version of the structure of a present day evolved terrorist organization. Depending on the organization, cells and operatives are more or less decentralized, and leaderless cells and operatives may or may not exist. There may also be less reliance on cells with dependence on branches of the hierarchical core. An example of this is seen with Hamas, which has four operational wings: "internal security (Jihad Amman), 'popular uprising' (stage violent protests, stone throwing, etc.), suicide bomber group (Al-Majahadoun Al-Falestinioun), [and the] professional killer group (The Izz al-Din al-Qassam Squads)."[14] Hamas uses operational cells which depend on the hierarchical structure of the organization (i.e., they take orders from and answer to a higher authority), whereas al Qaeda cells can operate self sufficiently and don't necessarily have to take orders from a higher authority.[15] Cells acting independently will have different connectivity patterns than cells that are operationally connected.

Networks in Social Space

Terrorist networks operate and, therefore, can be analyzed in social and geographical spaces. In social space, the two main social network components are connectedness and structure. Connectedness refers to the social links between nodes or actors in the network, while network structure refers to the shape of the network. Both social network components can be mapped in geographic space and visualized using various mapping techniques. Connectivity and structure can be analyzed using traditional social network analysis, small-world, and scale-free approaches. Traditional social network analysis (SNA) tends to focus on relationships within networks while non-traditional SNA, including small-world and scale-free analyses, focuses on the identification of network classes.[16] The fundamental concepts of traditional SNA focus on actors (nodes), and the social ties (linkages) that delineate relationships in subgroups, groups, and entire social networks. The term subgroup is used to define any subset of a network including nodes and links. Groups are actors and ties that make up an assumed bounded system. Traditional SNA uses graph theory and matrix operations to analyze social networks. The benefits of the use of graphs for SNA are (1) a vocabulary that is applicable in the description of social structure and connectivity properties, (2) quantitative methods that are used to analyze social networks, and (3) through the use of vocabulary and quantitative methods graph theory can

---

[13] Granovetter, "The Strength of Weak Ties," pp. 1360–1380.

[14] K. M. Carley, "Estimating Vulnerabilities in Large Covert Networks Using Multi-Level Data," in *Proceedings of the 2004 International Symposium on Command and Control Research and Technology* (2004), p. 1.

[15] Carley, "Estimating Vulnerabilities."

[16] F. Liljeros, C. R. Edling, and L. A. N. Amaral, "Sexual Networks: Implications for the Transmission of Sexually Transmitted Infections," *Microbes and Infection* 5 (2003), pp. 189–196.

be used to prove graphical theorems and make inferences about the social systems they represent. Graph theory uses metrics such as degree (number of connections per node), density (proportion of links present to links possible), geodesic distance (shortest path between two nodes), node eccentricity (largest geodesic distance between a given node and any other node in a graph), graph diameter (largest geodesic distance in a graph), and general connectivity.[17]

Small-World Networks

The small-world approach suggests that each of the nodes in a terrorist network is connected to any other node within a relatively small number of degrees. The growth of various terrorist networks can be attributed to the process of "preferential attachment," in which the probability of a node to gain connections to new nodes is determined by the number of connections that node has presently, simply meaning that the more connected a node becomes, the easier is will be for new nodes to find that node.[18] Networks that grow through this process eventually evolve into a small-world structure. This is the case with regard to two of the main network clusters involved in the present global jihad: the cluster of terrorists from the Core Arab states (Saudi Arabia, Egypt, Yemen, Kuwait), and the cluster of terrorists from the Maghreb (Morocco, Algeria, Tunisia).[19]

Although it has been stated that all social networks contain properties of clustering and the small-world effect,[20] there still remains question as to whether terrorist networks are small-worlds. Terrorist networks are social networks, but in these networks does there exist conscious effort to inhibit connectivity within the network for security purposes? And if the connectivity is purposefully inhibited, is it possible to stray from a small-world structure? The benefit would be the removal of links to more important nodes in the network by decreased connectivity. Even if terrorist networks are small-worlds, strong ties in the networks can appear as weak ties, which will inhibit the detection of the small-world structure.[21] Even with the highest level of security precautions, where cell members do not know each other until time of an operation, small-world connectivity may be unavoidable. An example of the use of small-world connectivity is given in Krebs, where the September 11th terrorists are described as using shortcuts in the network for planning efficiency. Additional analyses of real terrorist network data that reflect the decentralized nature of present day terrorist networks are required to understand the small-world issue more fully.

---

[17] S. Wasserman and K. Faust, *Social Network Analysis: Methods and Applications* (New York: Cambridge University Press, 1994).
[18] Sageman, *Understanding Terror Networks.*
[19] Sageman, *Understanding Terror Networks.*
[20] D. H. Zanette, "Models of Social Processes on Small-World Networks," Paper read at American Institute of Physics, at Bariloche, Argentina, 2–15 June 2002.
[21] V. E. Krebs, "Mapping Networks of Terrorist Cells," *Connections* 24, 3 (2002), pp. 43–52.

If one assumes that terrorist networks are small-worlds, there are many implications for security and defense. For example, the spread of information, money, and commodities throughout a small-world network may be relatively quicker than diffusion through other types of networks. The spread of infectious diseases has been shown to diffuse relatively fast in small-world networks.[22] Determining the speed and directions of covert network flows would be beneficial for counterterrorism. By viewing terrorist networks as small-worlds, the most connected nodes in the network may become more visible. In small-worlds, the most currently 'popular' nodes are not always the most connected. In the network of actors the most highly connected nodes are not simply the most recognizable. The "centers of the Hollywood universe" are determined by attributes, including length of time in the profession and types of movies made. The top five most highly connected (central) nodes based on appearances in movies are Rod Steiger (2.68), Christopher Lee (2.68), Dennis Hopper (2.70), Donald Sutherland (2.70), and Harvey Keitel (2.71).[23] Each actor listed above is followed by his "Bacon Number." The centrality of nodes in this network, which is the average number of hops to get from the "center" to any other actor, is determined by their Bacon Number. These five actors were found to have the lowest average number of hops to connect to any other node in the network.[24] A greater understanding of centrality in terrorist networks will assist in counterterrorism. Removing the most highly connected nodes will work to fragment a network by greatly reducing connectivity, and can cause network failure.

Small-world networks exhibit characteristics of rapid diffusion, such as with communicable diseases or information. One of the main characteristics of small-world networks is that any node is connected to any other node by a relatively few number of hops through the network. It follows that disease will diffuse through the network quickly. In an ideal model of disease (i.e. infection rates by contact are one hundred percent), a disease will spread as far and as fast as the measured degree for each node at each step through the network. The spread will increase first through time steps, then exponentially, and only slowing down as the network becomes saturated.[25] In countering terrorism, analysis of networks as small-worlds may assist in the redirection to the most central nodes for targeting, and also slow down the diffusion of necessary ideas, funding, and commodities through terrorist networks.

[22] D. Watts and S. H. Strogatz, "Collective Dynamics of 'Small-World' Networks," *Nature* 393 (1998), pp. 440–442.

[23] University of Virginia, Department of Computer Science (2006), *The Center of the Hollywood Universe* [cited Oct. 22 2006]. Available from http://oracleofbacon.org/center_list.html.

[24] The Internet Movie Database (IMDb) was used to build this small-world example, and can be found at http://www.imdb.com/.

[25] M. E. J. Newman, "Models of the Small-world: A Review," *Journal of Statistical Physics* 101, 3–4, (2000), pp. 819–841.

Scale-Free Networks

The scale-free property of various networks was first introduced in 1999 by Albert-László Barabási and Réka Albert. Contrary to their hypothesis, they found that the distribution of nodal connectivity of the World Wide Web was not that of a typical random network, but instead was scale-free, where some nodes "defied explanation." In the authors' words, it was "almost as if (they) had stumbled on a significant number of people who were 100 feet tall."[26] Many real networks have shown through analysis to be free of scale. These include: food webs, the internet, the World Wide Web, the network of actors made popular by the "six degrees of separation from Kevin Bacon" game, and the social network of human sexual contacts, among others.[27]

Growth of a network in a self-organized process of preferential attachment between nodes results in a scale free structure. Preferential attachment refers to network growth where the probability of an existing node to attain new links is proportional to the number of links the given node already has.[28] If a network grows by preferential attachment its primary nodes will have the most opportunity to attract new nodes, and therefore will eventually dominate the network because their probability to gain connections will increase with the growing number of connections.[29] In scale-free networks nodes have a relative amount of "attractiveness." Attractive nodes are generally highly connected while unattractive nodes are less connected. The concept of nodal attractiveness is explained in Mossa et al. where "new nodes want to connect to the existing nodes with the largest number of links – i.e., with the largest degree – because of the advantages offered by being linked to a well connected node."[30] Attractiveness in a network can be directed either from the less connected nodes to the hubs or from the hubs to the less connected nodes.

Plotting frequency on the y axis (the number of nodes that have a specified connectivity), against connectivity on the x axis (nodal degree) will result in a downward sloping curve that contains all points as shown below in Fig. 2. The points on the left side of the graph are representative of nodes that have low connectivity. Each point represents one or more nodes with the same number of connections in the first degree. The frequencies of low connected nodes in a scale-free network are relatively much higher than the frequencies of high connected nodes. In this figure, the point in the far right, which is representative of a relatively small number of nodes with relatively many connections, dominates the connectivity of the

---

[26] A. L. Barabási and E. Bonabeau, "Scale-Free Networks," *Scientific American* 288, 5 (2003).

[27] D. Cohen, "All the World's a Net," *New Scientist* 174, 2338 (2002), pp. 24–29.

[28] S. N. Dorogovtsev, J. F. F. Mendes, and A. N. Samukhin, "Structure of Growing Networks with Preferential Linking," *Physical Review Letters* 85, 21 (2000), pp. 4633–4636.

[29] A. L. Barabási, *Linked: They New Science of Networks* (Cambridge: Perseus Publishing, 2002).

[30] S. Mossa, M. Barthélemy, H. E. Stanley, and L. A. N. Amaral, "Truncation of Power Law Behavior in "Scale-Free" Network Models due to Information Filtering," *Physical Review Letters* 88, 13 (2002), pp. 138701–1.

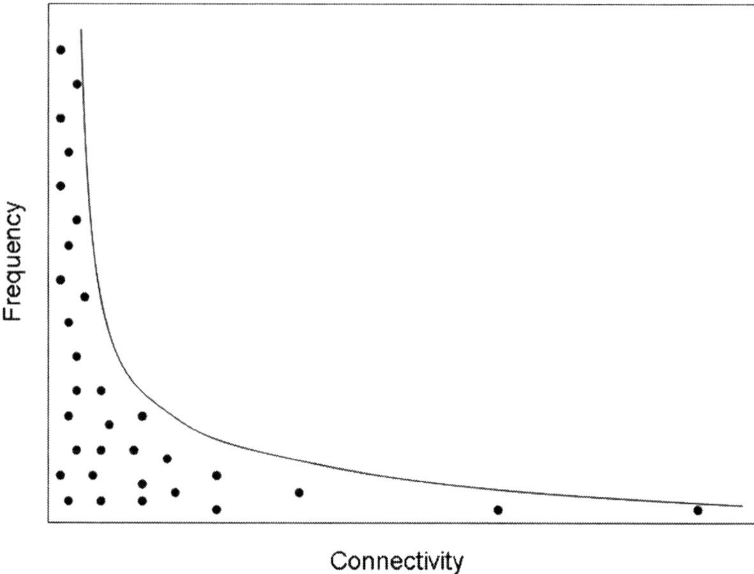

Fig. 2 Plot of scale-free conditions

hypothesized network. The few nodes represented by the graphical placement of this point have a very large number of connections.

When the log of the frequency (y axis) is plotted against the log of the connectivity (x axis) in this hypothesized network, the power law distribution becomes apparent. One of the main characteristics of this distribution is the linear downward sloping trend as seen below in Fig. 3.[31] The log-log plot is used to classify networks as being scale-free.

Preferential attachment, as discussed previously with small-world networks, is a key concept in scale-free networks. Scale-free networks follow a power law distribution (see Fig. 3), which simply means that the majority of nodes in the network have relatively few connections, while few nodes have relatively many. The power law distribution is reflective of the "hub" characteristic within a network. Relatively few nodes in a scale-free network dominate its connectivity. The two main attributes that determine whether a network is scale-free: growth and preferential attachment are properties of many real world networks. The random graph and small-world network approaches do not take these attributes into consideration. The scale-free network attributes, which are inherent in many real world networks, make these networks resilient to random attacks, but vulnerable to attacks directed toward the hubs. Examples of these are the internet and the al Qaeda terrorist network. In a scale-free network, a random attack will most likely target a node that is poorly connected and less influential in that network, while the hubs will remain unharmed.

---

[31] Barabasi, *Linked, the New Science of Networks.*

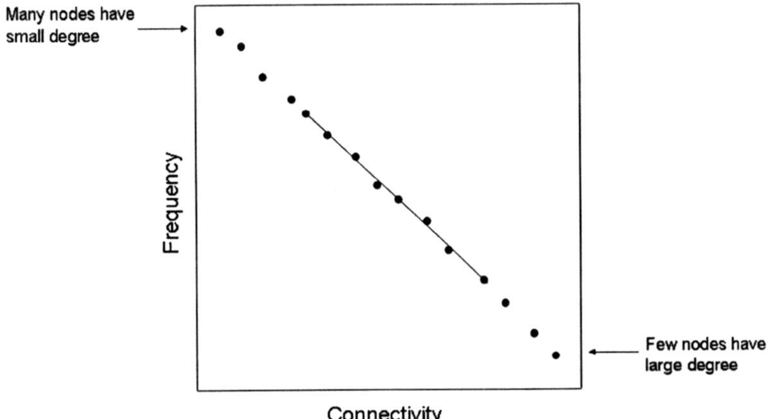

Fig. 3 Log-log plot of scale-free conditions

Real world networks display many examples of nodes that are connected by preferential attachment. In the case of the academic paper citation network, a new citation is more likely to be directed toward a previous paper with a relatively large number of citations. More citations imply that the author is a relatively well known peer in the academic community.[32] In the case of food web networks, predator species are the nodes responsible for the attractiveness property, because they prey on large numbers of varying species. In the case of sexual networking, people that have relatively more partners may be more attractive to others than people with fewer partners.[33]

Fateh Kamel is an example of a node with preferential attachment in a terrorist network. He acted as a hub of the network that was responsible for much of the nodal connectivity applied in the September eleventh attacks of 2001. Kamel was what may be referred to as a "typical hub," in that he was "a charming and handsome man with a knack for making friends and acquaintances."[34] His "attractiveness" then led to a process in which "the better known he became, the easier it was for newcomers to find him and the more people he met."[35] This is an example of the "rich-get-richer" structure, which is a characteristic of scale-free networks. It can be assumed that hubs similar to Kamel exist within the al Qaeda network, as well as within other terrorist networks. The growth of terrorist organizations can be attributed at least in part to preferential attachment.

If we assume that terrorist networks are scale-free, what implications does this have for countering these networks? First, and quite possibly the most important

[32] A. L. Barabási and R. Albert, "Emergence of Scaling in Random Networks," *Science* 286 (October 1999), pp. 509–512.

[33] Cohen, "All the World's a Net."

[34] Sageman, *Understanding Terror Networks*, p. 139.

[35] Sageman, *Understanding Terror Networks*.

characteristic is that scale-free networks are extremely resilient to random or "accidental" attacks. This is due to the existence of relatively many more, less connected nodes than hubs. A random attack will most likely damage or remove a node that is not essential to network flow. It is estimated that approximately eighty percent of nodes can be randomly removed from the Internet, and a connection between any two nodes in the network will still remain (internet defined here as the physical web of routers, servers, etc. that information travels through). While random attacks on a scale-free network will prove in most cases to be futile, a relatively few directed attacks on known hubs can successfully break up the network. It is estimated that the removal of as few as five to fifteen percent of all hubs within the network will dismantle it. The largest difficulty may lie in successfully identifying hubs within a terrorist network. It is more difficult to identify social network hubs than hubs of any other type of network.[36]

Diffusion of information and tactics throughout a scale-free network is quick to spread and very persistent.[37] This is due to the diffusion through highly connected hubs. Since these hubs have a relatively large number of connections, it only takes one node linked to a hub to diffuse to a substantial number of other nodes within the network. Borrowing from contagious disease literature, hubs in a network have also been termed "superspreaders," because of their ability to infect other nodes in the network (Barthélemy et al. 2004). With regard to terrorist networks, where propaganda can be used as a tool to gain and further support, the diffusion of information through the network can be selective and very efficient. It takes only one node to begin diffusion through the network, but to stop the diffusion almost every node in the network must be considered as a carrier. In the case of measles infections, approximately ninety percent of people within the social network must be vaccinated in order to effectively stop diffusion. The large majority of the hubs, if not all, must be reached.[38]

Scale-free networks also have the ability to allow nodal variation. Many nodes within the network can "mutate," change location, or leave the network without damaging it as a whole, as long as too many hubs aren't removed. This property adds to the robustness of scale-free networks. The networks are able to constantly improve by evolving.[39] By using the example of Fateh Kamel, one can see the ability of a node to change location. Kamel immigrated to Canada in 1997 from Algeria. In Canada, he assisted in the formation of a terrorist network for the Bosnian jihad. He then formed a logistical support network in Milan around the Islamic Cultural Institute.[40] Kamel's ability to attract other nodes proved to be beneficial for the Global Jihad. Because of his attractiveness, he had the ability to move from one region to

---

36 Barabasi and Bonabeau, "Scale-Free Networks."

37 Barabasi and Bonabeau, "Scale-Free Networks."

38 M. Barthélemy, A. Barrat, R. Pastor-Satorras, and A. Vespignani, "Velocity and Hierarchical Spread of Epidemic Outbreaks in Scale-Free Networks," *Physical Review Letters* 92, 17 (2004) pp. 178701–1–178701–4.

39 Cohen, "All the World's A Net."

40 Sageman, *Understanding Terror Networks.*

the next and form subgroups of networks along the way. Kamel had evolved from his training in the Afghan camp in the early 1990s, to an insurgent in Bosnia, then on to be a well-connected hub of the terrorist network.[41]

Networks in Geographic Space

In spite of less reliance by terrorist groups for a controlled geographic territory for generating operational revenue and providing a safe haven, there is a necessary physical presence in specific socio-cultural support areas, logistical supply points, training sites, and safe houses. Regardless of the advancement of information technologies there is a high level of spatial interaction by actors in terrorist organizations for recruiting, financial flows, and tactical support at various geographic scales. Network dynamics include the spatial interaction of ideas, innovations, orders, and tasks, flows of goods such as money, weapons, etc., and movement of actors throughout the network.

When geographic or geospatial information corresponds to the components of a social network, the network can be mapped to provide insights into the structure and dynamics of the network. The visual portrayal of information is used because humans "reason and learn more effectively in a visual setting than when using textual and numerical data,"[42] and also because visualization can offer implicit information about spatial data as well as non-spatial data. Activity based mapping can include locations of multiple activities as well as temporal variables (e.g., minute, day, month, year, etc.).[43] By using activity based mapping it is easier to discover spatial, temporal, and spatio-temporal patterns within data. Terrorists work in activity spaces which include necessities such as funding, targets, weapons, planning and education, etc., and their activities take place in time.

An example of accessibility visualization is given by the spatio-social network of Aafia Siddiqui in Fig. 4b below. In this example, important geographic locations for strategic operations or interactions can be found when the social network data is mapped (Fig. 4a).

In Boston, Aafia lived with other terrorists, while she was educated at MIT in Biology. The flow of funding begins to become apparent, as well as ties to Ibrahim Bah who was a gateway into funding through diamond trading in Africa and a leader of the Revolutionary United Front (RUF). Through the assumed case given by these data, Aafia Siddiqui is two degrees from Osama bin Laden through Khalid Shaikh Mohammed (KSM). It is possible that Aafia is directly linked to bin Laden but the relationship is not represented in these data.

---

41 Sageman, *Understanding Terror Networks.*

42 M. P. Kwan and J. Lee, "Geovisualization of Human Activity Patterns Using 3D GIS: A Time-Geographic Approach," in M. F. Goodchild and D. G. Janelle (eds.), *Spatially Integrated Social Science: Examples in Best Practice* (Oxford: Oxford University Press, 2003), p. 3.

43 Kwan and Lee, "Geovisualization."

(a)

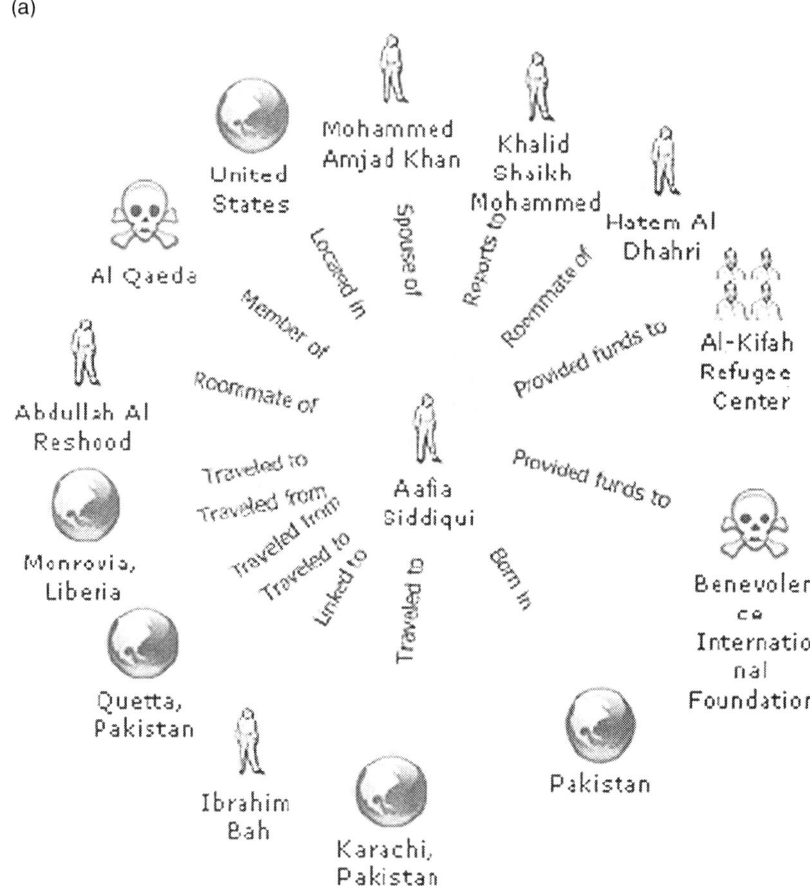

Fig. 4a Aafia Siddiqui social network as visualized at www.trackingthethreat.com

In order to conceptualize terrorist network activities and accessibilities both physical and virtual spaces must be considered. The action of decentralization is supported by information technologies such that geographically dispersed terrorist networks require the use of virtual interaction to operate efficiently, while they operate in physical spaces. When people or organizations use both physical and virtual activity spaces they are acting in what has been referred to as "hybrid space."[44] Operational cells of terrorist networks can now substitute physical interaction with virtual interaction, although they may choose to use physical space for planning at times to remove any risk of leaving a digital trail. While virtual interaction can be

[44] M. Batty and H. J. Miller, "Representing and Visualizing Physical, Virtual and Hybrid Information Spaces," in D. G. Janelle and D. C. Hodge (eds.), *Information, Place, and Cyberspace: Issues in Accessibility*, (New York: Springer, 2000).

(b)

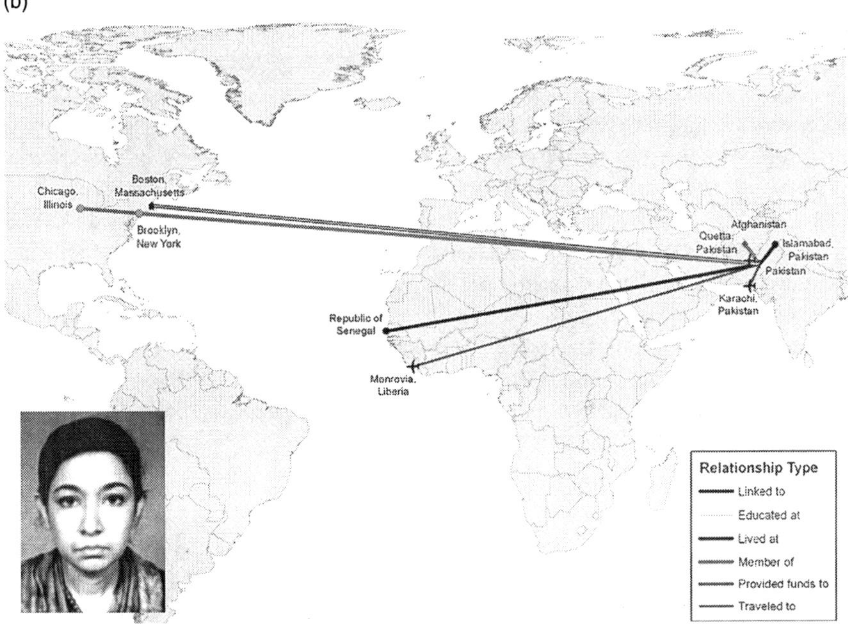

Fig. 4b Spatio-Social network of Aafia Siddiqui
DOB – 3/2/1972
Birthplace – Pakistan
Educated at MIT (Biology)
Founded the Institute of Islamic Research and Teaching
Linked to Ibrahim Bah (Diamonds)
Provided funds to the Benevolence International Foundation (Chicago) and the Al-Kifah Refugee Center (Brooklyn)
Member of al Qaeda
Believed to be in Pakistan
Data source: FMS www.trackingthethreat.com

used in the planning states of and operation, the actual operation must take place in physical space, unless the actors are planning a cyber-terrorist attack. For example, cells must be strategically placed such that access to targets or other objectives is maximized and access to monetary opportunities is minimized if the cell is not funded by the organization.

The location of terrorist bases, safe houses and support facilities, and cells involve several geographic factors. These facilities can only exist in areas of community support, and disorganized political authority. Proximity to international borders and favorable terrain for operations and security tend to be more suitable locations for facilities.[45]

[45] A. D. Lohman, "Insurgencies and Counter-Insurgencies: A Geographical Perspective," in E. J. Palka and F. A. Galgano (eds.), *The Scope of Military Geography: Across the Spectrum from Peacetime to War* (New York: McGraw-Hill, 2001), pp. 263–290.

Interaction can exist in virtual space using computers and cell phones, but the majority of operational goals require accessibility in physical space. Conceptualizing terrorist networks in hybrid space is required of any present day research on terrorism or counterterrorism, as the actions of terrorist organizations in both the physical world and the virtual world are equally important.

Examples of the geographic mapping and visualization of terrorist network dynamics using geographic information systems (GIS) are shown in Figs. 5 and 6.[46] In these figures, terrorist incidents in Iraq for 2004 are mapped. The vertical bars in Fig. 5 represent the number of incidents, with the cities receiving the most incidents labelled. In Fig. 6, the bars represent the number of fatalities per incident. It is apparent that the cities of Baghdad, Mosul, and Kirkut suffer the most incidents, but more people die per attack in Irbil, Mahhoudiya, and Anah. In this case the cities with high fatalities per incident had only one to two recorded attacks in 2004, but each of these attacks had a substantial number of fatalities. Incident, fatality, and fatality per incident data are provided below in Table 1.

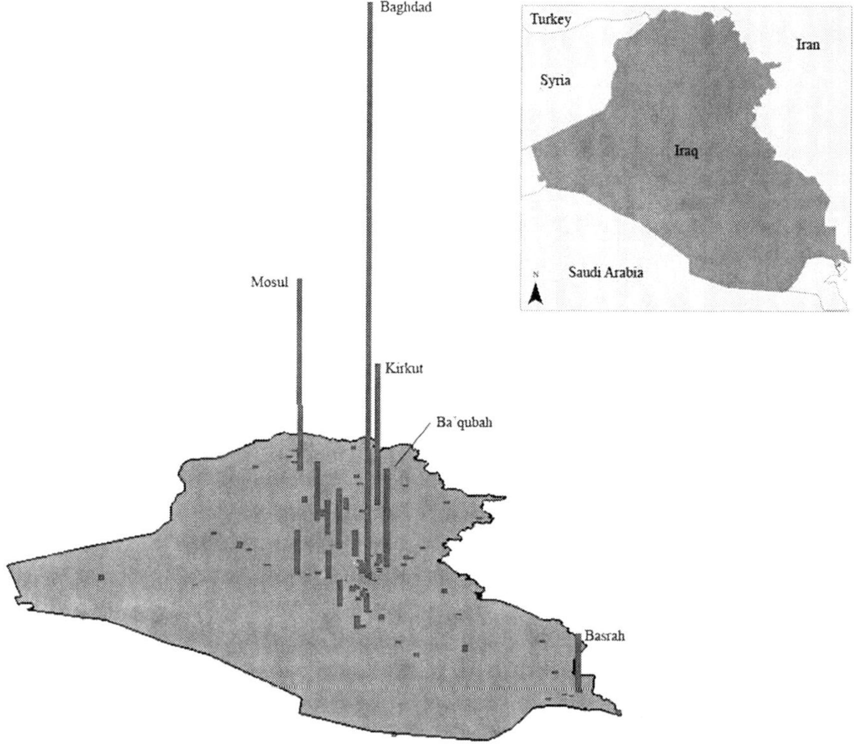

Fig. 5 Iraq – number of incidents by city (2004)

[46] Data for these maps were collected online from the National Counter Terrorism Center's Worldwide Incidents Tracking System (WITS) at http://wits.nctc.gov/Main.do.

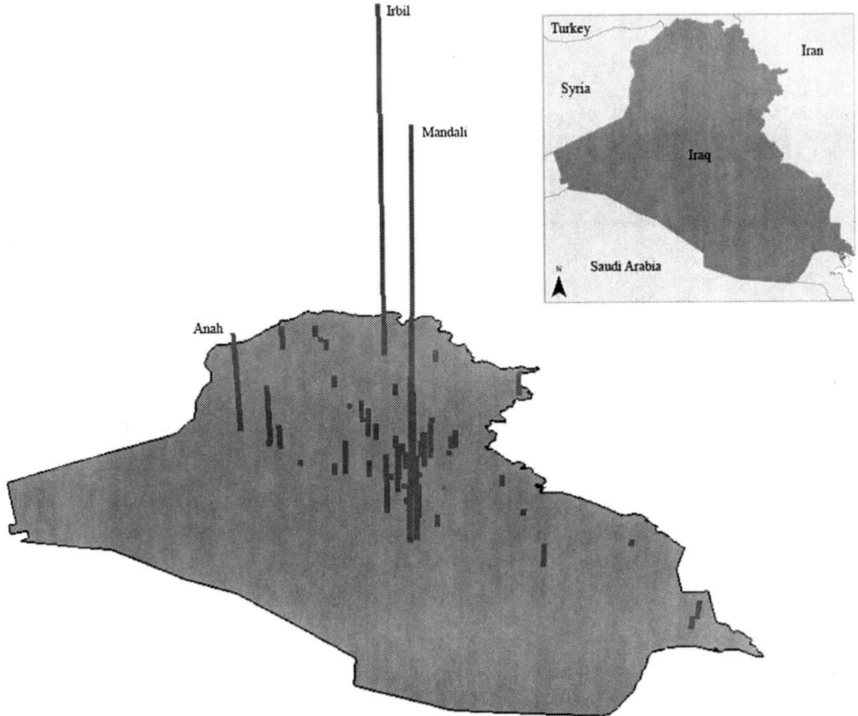

Fig. 6 Iraq – fatalities per incident by city (2004)

Table 1 Incidents, fatalities, and fatalities per incident for mapped cities in Iraq (2004)

City	Incidents	Fatalities	Fatalities per incident
Basrah	33	102	3.090909
Anah	1	16	16.000000
Baghdad	304	976	3.210526
Ba'qubah	53	193	3.641509
Irbil	2	110	55.000000
Kirkuk	75	156	2.080000
Mandali	1	54	54.000000
Mosul	102	251	2.460784

Networked organizations act in social and geographic space. Terrorist groups, while unique in several ways, share characteristics of many other more benign social networks. Analysis of these universal characteristics, with recognition of the unique qualities of terrorist networks allows for scientific analysis of their structure and dynamics. This is a necessary undertaking to analyze and deal effectively with these groups in the future.

Developing Moral Agency in the Midst of Violence: Children, Political Conflict, and Values

Cecilia Wainryb and Monisha Pasupathi

Introduction

As reported by the *UN Office of the Special Representative of the Secretary General for Children and Armed Conflict*, children in approximately 50 countries grow up in the midst of armed conflict and its aftermath. In the last decade alone, wars injured 6 million children, killed 2 million, and displaced nearly 30 million. While no precise figures exist distinguishing the number of children growing up under conditions of state-sponsored violence versus violence from non-state-sponsored groups or terrorism, the report also calls special attention to the approximately 300,000 children who are drawn directly into political conflicts as child soldiers and forced to serve in various military roles, including participation in killings and torture.[1]

The concern for the fate of child soldiers is of such proportions that it is now monitored directly by the United Nations. One of the most significant developments in more recent times on their behalf has been the intervention of the United Nations Security Council and the passing of resolution 1612 of 26 July 2005. Based on this resolution, the Office of the Special Representative has established a comprehensive monitoring and reporting process relating to grave violations against children in situations of armed conflict, in particular the recruitment and use of children as soldiers. In addition to taking measures for monitoring and reporting violations, the Special Representative has advocated for rigorous post-conflict rehabilitation and reintegration initiatives and programs for children, and has striven to ensure that children's protection, demobilization and reintegration needs are addressed in the initial planning and implementation of peacekeeping and peace-building operations. Finally, and in pursuit of the objectives outlined above, the Office of the Special Representative has also underscored the need for further research focusing

C. Wainryb
University of Utah
e-mail: cecilia.wainryb@psych.utah.edu

[1] U.N. (2006a). *The impact of armed conflict on children. Special Representative of the Secretary-General for Children and Armed Conflict.* Retrieved 3/10/2006, from www.un.org/special-rep/children-armed-conflict/index.html

I.A. Karawan et al. (eds.), *Values and Violence*,

on lessons learned and best practices, as well as other emerging areas of concern, including research on child soldiers, their needs and attitudes to violence, and successful strategies for their reintegration into society.[2]

A most serious concern arising out of this situation is the impact that exposure to political violence has on the wellbeing of children. In this chapter, we focus in particular on the impact that active involvement in political violence is likely to have on the long-term development of children who participate in armed groups, such as child soldiers – especially their ability to think of themselves as moral agents. Children's moral capacities have tremendous implications not only for their individual sense of identity, dignity, and well-being, but also for the possibility of breaking cycles of violence and the ultimate success of humanitarian and political interventions geared toward conflict resolution and social reconstruction.

The Impact of Political Violence on Children's Psychological Well-being

Psychologists have long been concerned with the effects that long-term exposure to political violence has on children's well-being. Most research efforts in this regard have used a trauma model and measured the consequences of exposure to violence in terms of mental health outcomes. Whereas findings concerning children's specific patterns of symptoms have varied across studies as a function of the domains of adjustment targeted and the characteristics of the samples studied, in general children's reactions to political violence have included anxiety, depression, dissociation, avoidance and numbness, psychosomatic disturbances, anger and hostility, and other symptoms that have come to be associated with post-traumatic stress, or PTSD.[3] Specific features of the conflict situation, such as the relative proximity (emotional and physical), intensity, and chronicity of violence, have been found to increase the likelihood of symptom development or play a protective role. As an example, it has been shown that children are minimally affected by isolated or short-term instances of violence, especially if parental support remains available, but repeated or long-term exposure to political violence, societal disintegration, and displacement constitute major risk factors. As indicated by risk accumulation models, multiple stressors compound the effects,[4] which are further amplified when the stressors are chronic. Research has also shown that child soldiers, who are directly engaged in

---

[2] U.N. (2006a). *The impact of armed conflict on children. Special Representative of the Secretary-General for Children and Armed Conflict.* Retrieved 3/10/2006, from www.un.org/special-rep/children-armed-conflict/index.html.

[3] D. Browne, "Examining the impact of terrorism on children," in A. Silke (ed.), *Terrorists, victims, and society: Psychological perspectives on terrorism and its consequences* (New York: Wiley, 2003), pp. 189–211; J. A. Shaw, "Children exposed to war/terrorism," *Clinical Child and Family Psychology Review*, 6 (2003), pp. 237–246.

[4] J. Garbarino, & K. Kostelny, "The effects of political violence on Palestinian children's behavior problems: A risk accumulation model," *Child Development* 67 (1996), pp. 33–45; G. Straker, "The

violence, exhibit much higher rates of PTSD than children who had been exposed to violence – rates that also vary with the severity and chronicity of their experiences.[5] (Findings from research on PTSD rates of war-affected children and child soldiers should be interpreted with caution, as the nature of armed conflict makes it unfeasible to adhere to methodological requirements such as control groups and pre-war baseline rates).

And yet, research suggests that the sorts of interpretations and meanings that children attribute to the violence to which they are exposed might mitigate symptom development. Political violence can be given different meanings in different communities and while no public discourse or ideology can fully remove suffering, it can shape what is experienced as either meaningful or hopeless.[6] In particular for those who become directly engaged in political struggle and fighting, ideology can bolster their sense of self-worth and integrity by offering a compelling narrative that renders their world comprehensible and their own violent behaviors justifiable. While systematic research relating in-depth assessments of children's ideological beliefs and the effects of political violence is scant, there is some evidence suggesting that ideological commitment may act as a protective factor against at least some of the negative outcomes associated with exposure to political violence. As an example, Palestinian youth, who are assumed to have available to them a wealth of religious and historical justifications for their engagement in political violence, have been shown to display less psychological distress (e.g., less depression, insecurity, anxiety) than, for example, Bosnian youth, who cannot rely on a similarly coherent belief system for explaining the violence to which they are exposed.[7]

This and similar findings relating ideological commitments to decreased symptomatology and increased subjective sense of wellbeing have received quite a lot of attention recently, in part because they suggest the possibility of resilience in the face of adversity. This potential makes for the kind of story that many people like to hear – one in which hardship and loss result in renewed meaning and strength

---

continuous traumatic stress disorder: The single therapeutic interview," *Psychology and Sociology* 9 (1987), pp. 48–79.

[5] M. Wessells, *Child soldiers: From violence to protection* (London: Harvard University Press, 2006).

[6] A. Dawes, "The effects of political violence on children: A consideration of South African and related studies," *International Journal of Psychology* 25 (1990), pp. 13–31.

[7] B. K. Barber, J. M. Schluterman, E. S. Denny, & R. J. McCouch, "Adolescents and political violence," in M. Fitzduff and C. Stout (eds.), *The psychology of resolving global conflicts: From war to peace* 2, Group and social factors (Westport, Conn: Praeger, 2006), pp. 171–190; see also N. Laor, L. Wolmer, M. Alon, J. Siev, E. Samuel, & P. Toren, "Risk and protective factors mediating psychological symptoms and ideological commitments of adolescents facing continuous terrorism," *The Journal of Nervous and Mental Disease*, 194, 4 (2006), pp. 279–286; R. L. Punamaki, "Can ideological commitment protect children's psychosocial wellbeing in situations of political violence?," *Child Development* 67 (1996), pp. 55–69; R. L. Punamaki, S. Quota, & E. El-Sarraj, "Models of traumatic experiences and children's psychological adjustment," *Child Development* 68 (1997), pp. 718–728.

of character.[8] Of course, it is absurd to conclude that persuading children to share the ideologies of combatants is a good solution, and in fact, this points to a broader issue. Namely, the tendency to ground questions concerning the effects of political violence on children within a mental health paradigm may be overly narrow, as clinical definitions of mental health in terms of the absence of symptoms does not include aspects of healthy personhood, such as children's ability to tell right from wrong and to view themselves as moral agents, or their capacity to function as members of a civil society in a moral sense. These aspects of psychological health are not only important for individuals, but are also critical for collective well-being. In fact, the very ideological belief structures that offer some measure of protection against the symptoms that typically accompany sustained exposure to violence (e.g., depression, anxiety, avoidance, numbness), may at the same time have serious deleterious long-term effects on precisely those capabilities.[9]

While serious psychopathology cannot be ruled out, especially in contexts in which children face extreme brutalization on a large scale, the sequellae of exposure to political violence are not likely to be limited to emotional distress. In fact, given the protracted nature of contemporary political conflicts, such that violence (injustice, violation of rights) is normalized, children's moral capacities are most vulnerable. Thus the question is not so much whether children cope emotionally – most do – but what price they (and ultimately society) pay, in terms of their long-term development, for their continued coping with and adaptation to such excruciating living conditions in which exigencies of mere survival may oblige them to breach moral values and codes. This is likely to be especially true for children who have been active participants in political violence – children who themselves have been combatants.

Even as a number of researchers have alluded to the potential importance of understanding the moral development of war-affected children,[10] systematic research in this area has been limited. In part this has been because, understandably, most research undertaken with children affected by armed conflict has tended to

---

[8] D. P. McAdams, *The redemptive self: Stories Americans live by* (USA: Oxford University Press, 2006).

[9] Dawes, "The Effect of Political Violence on Children," pp. 13–31; J. Garbarino & K. Kostelny, "Children's response to war: What do we know?," in L. A. Leavitt & N. A. Fox (eds.), *The psychological effects of war and violence on children* (Hillsdale, NJ: LEA, 1993), pp. 23–40; Loar et al., "Risk and Protective Factors," pp. 279–286; R. Posada, & C. Wainryb, "Moral development in a violent society: Colombian children's judgments in the context of survival and revenge," *Child Development* 79 (2008), pp. 882–898; Punamaki, op cit. note 7, pp. 55–69.

[10] See, e.g., E. Cairns, *Children and political violence* (Oxford: Blackwell, 1996); A. Dawes, "The effects of political violence on socio-moral reasoning and conduct," in A. Dawes & D. Donald (eds.), *Childhood and Adversity* (Cape Town, South Africa: David Philip Publishers, 1994), pp. 200–219; Garbarino and Kostelny, "The effects of Political Violence on Palestinian Children's Behavior," pp. 33–45; L. A. Leavitt & N. A. Fox, (eds.), *The psychological effects of war and violence on children* (Hillsdale, NJ: LEA, 1993); M. Macksoud, L. & Aber, "The war experiences and psychological development of children in Lebanon," *Child Development* 67 (1996), pp. 70–88; Punamaki, "Can Ideological Commitment Protect Children's Psychosocial Wellbeing," pp. 55–69.

accommodate the most pressing needs for immediate intervention.[11] Psychologists have made significant contributions in this regard, both to documenting the traumatic effects of political violence on children, and to adapting established treatments to local situations on the ground in conflict-torn regions of the world.[12]

Beyond the very pressing concerns guiding research, it is also likely that the type of research questions being examined has been constrained by available conceptual frameworks for studying moral development. One such limitation is that nearly all the moral development research conducted in war-torn countries has relied on assessments based on hypothetical moral dilemmas designed to rank-order the sophistication of children's moral reasoning. The findings of this research have been mixed, with some researchers reporting that children living in the midst of political violence evidenced lower levels of moral reasoning, and others suggesting that the moral development of these youths was not negatively affected.[13] The mixed nature of these findings may be associated with the fact that this evidence was obtained largely on the basis of assessments of global stages of moral reasoning, with the underlying question being whether children in communities characterized by political violence can be said to generally reason at lower (or higher) stages. Much research conducted in the last several decades with children developing in normative contexts has pointed to the limitations of global assessments of moral stages.[14] Furthermore, the assessments of moral stages typically used in moral development research do not tap into the unique types of conflicts and dilemmas associated with growing up in war-torn countries. Indeed, political upheaval, war, terrorism, displacement, and chronic violence are likely to produce a multitude of moral realities bearing little resemblance to most of the hypothetical situations used in moral development research. Thus findings such as that children growing up in a war-torn region reason at a lower (or higher) global stage of moral thinking than children growing up in a nonviolent region are likely to tell us little regarding how these children might make sense of their experiences and of themselves and others as moral beings.

---

[11] Dawes, "The Effects of Political Violence on Children," pp. 13–31; O. T. Muldoon, "Children of the troubles: The impact of political violence in Northern Ireland," *Journal of Social Issues* 60, 3 (2004), pp. 453–468.

[12] S. Stepakoff, J. Hubbard, M. Katoh, E. Falk, J. Mikulu, P. Nkhoma, P., et al. "Trauma healing in refugee camps in Guinea: A psychosocial program for Liberian and Sierra Leonean survivors of torture and war," *American Psychologist* 61, 8 (2006), pp. 919–932; M. Wessells, K. & Kostelny, *After the Taliban: A child-focused assessment in the northern Afghan provinces of Kunduz, Takhar, and Badakshan* (Richmond, VA: CCF International, 2002); M. Wessells, & C. Monteiro, "Psychosocial assistance for youth: Toward reconstruction for peace in Angola," *Journal of Social Issues* 62, 1 (2006), pp. 121–139.

[13] For a comprehensive review, see Cairns, *Children and Political Violence.*

[14] For reviews, see J. Smetana, "Social-cognitive domain theory: Consistencies and variations in children's moral and social judgments," in M. Killen & J. Smetana (eds.), *Handbook of moral development* (Mahwah, NJ: LEA, 2006), pp. 119–154; E. Turiel, "The development of morality," in W. Damon & N. Eisenberg (eds.), *Handbook of psychology, 5th Edition, Vol. 3, Social, emotional and personality development* (New York: Wiley, 1998), pp. 863–932.

Another limitation of the extant research is that it has overlooked the significance – for children's moral development – of how children make sense of experiences in which they were the agents of harm. However, the inferences that children draw about themselves as moral beings based on their real experiences of doing harm are likely to hold long-term implications for the development of moral identity, and ultimately, for moral conduct.[15] Thus the important, and more useful, questions bear on how these children think about the moral complexities and ambiguities within which they function, and how they reconcile themselves with their own experiences of both committing and enduring injustice and violence, and integrate them within a sense of themselves as moral – a sense deemed essential for sustained commitment to moral action.[16] Before we address these questions, it is necessary that we consider, as a starting point, the development of children's moral capacities under normative conditions.

The Development of Children's Moral Capacities

Moral development research conducted over the last 25 years has demonstrated that, starting at the age of 2 or 3 years, children are consistently bothered by injustice and are concerned with people being hurt, physically or psychologically. Indeed, in contrast to what was previously assumed,[17] research suggests that even young children develop basic prescriptive moral concepts – that is, ways of thinking about welfare, justice, and rights – and do so on the basis of their actual social interactions.[18] This is to say that while children generally attend to the rules and teachings of adults, it is not the internalization of rules per se that is at the basis of children's moral development, but children's own perceptions and interpretations of the features of social interactions (e.g., their construal of the consequences of an act of aggression or a violation of a promise), including – or perhaps in particular – those interactions involving conflicts, transgressions, injustice, and aggression.

Although the lion's share of this research has been conducted in Western societies, studies have also been conducted in South America, Africa, Asia, and the Middle East. This research has demonstrated that in spite of the considerable diversity in cultural practices and religious beliefs, the processes of moral development

---

[15] See S. Dwyer, "Reconciliation for realists," *Ethics of International Affairs* 13 (1999), pp. 81–98.

[16] A. Colby & W. Damon, *Some do care: Contemporary lives of moral commitment* (New York: Free Press, 1992); S. A. Hardy & G. Carlo, "Identity as a source of moral motivation," *Human Development*48 (2005), pp. 232–256; M. K. Matsuba, & L. J. Walker, "Young adult moral exemplars: The making of self through stories," *Journal of Research on Adolescence*, 15 (2005), pp. 275–297.

[17] See, e.g., L. Kohlberg, "Stage and sequence: The cognitive developmental approach to socialization," in D. Goslin (ed.), *Handbook of socialization theory and research* (Chicago: Rand McNally, 1969), pp. 347–480.

[18] For comprehensive reviews of this research, see Smetana, "Social-Cognitive Domain Theory," pp. 119–154; Turiel, "The Development of Morality," pp. 863–932; C. Wainryb, B. Brehl, & S. Matwin, "Being hurt and hurting others: Children's narrative accounts and moral judgments of their own interpersonal conflicts," *Monographs of the Society for Research in Child Development* 70 (2005).

are largely the same across cultures.[19] Across the world, children tend to reason that it is morally wrong to, for example, hurt or mistreat others, not because they may otherwise be punished, but rather because of their concerns with fairness and the well-being of persons, and they tend to bring these concepts to bear on actual social interactions.

Of course this is not to say that children never hurt others or that they never behave unfairly towards others. They certainly do. The concrete instances in which this happens hold in them an inherent tension between what children think and what they sometimes do.[20] One could regard morality as insisting on self-denial, such that the demands of morality are necessarily antagonistic to other interests that an individual may have. From this perspective one would view these instances as evidence that children (or people in general) find it difficult to live up to the demands of morality and are not, in general, very moral. Such a perspective is rooted in a conception of morality as radically "disengaged from the perspective of the individual agent – from the full range of concerns associated with the living of an actual human life."[21] Scheffler and other contemporary moral philosophers[22] have suggested, instead, that the discussion of the relations between morality and the interests of the individual requires consideration of the complexity of psychological reality. Importantly, they have underscored that morality is fully compatible with a realistic picture of human deliberation, including experiences of ambivalence and regret in the face of situations of moral conflict in which no act is available that is without pain, loss, or harm. This latter view is more closely aligned with our conception. Moral life is not about sainthood, and experiences of mistreating or inflicting harm on other people, as well as experiences of being mistreated or hurt, are part of children's *moral* lives. Being a moral person thus implies the need to negotiate not only the potential for being a very good person, but also the threats implicated in one's actions, that is, one's potential for also, sometimes, being a bad person or doing the wrong thing.

Given the inevitability of causing and experiencing harm in an interpersonal world, it is essential that we understand how people integrate such actions and make sense of themselves and others as moral agents. Thus in recent years we have moved away from the more typical approach to studying moral development in terms of children's judgments about hypothetical scenarios, toward a focus on how children understand and make sense of their own and other people's *real* harmful and unjust actions.[23] How do children grasp these situations? What sense do they make of

---

[19] For a review of research conducted across cultures, see C. Wainryb, "Moral development in culture: Diversity, tolerance, and justice," in M. Killen & J. Smetana (eds.), *Handbook of moral development* (Mahwah, NJ: LEA, 2006), pp. 211–240.

[20] Wainryb et al., op cit. note 18, "Being Hurt and Hurting Others."

[21] S. Scheffler, *Human morality* (New York: Oxford University Press, 1992), p. 18.

[22] S. Hampshire, *Morality and conflict* (Cambridge, MA: Harvard University Press, 1983); B. Williams, *Ethics and the limits of philosophy* (Cambridge, MA: Harvard University Press, 1985).

[23] C. Wainryb, "Is and ought: Moral judgments about the world as understood," in B. W. Sokol & J. Baird (eds.), *Mind, morals, and action: The interface between children's theories of mind and socio-moral development* 103 (San Francisco: Jossey-Bass, 2004), pp. 3–17; Wainryb et al., "Being Hurt and Hurting Others."

them? What do they think about themselves and others and whatever circumstances lead up to such hurtful interactions? How do they integrate these experiences into their understandings of themselves and others as moral beings? Existing findings point to the role of personal experiences, and of children's construction of meaning out of those experiences, as important forces in the development of a moral self. Indeed, it is in the struggle to make sense of their own actions that children are likely to further their sense of themselves as moral beings.

One of the ways in which we have learned about these processes in our research is by observing and analyzing how children talk about situations in which they have caused harm to others. This approach draws from narrative traditions for looking at self and identity development.[24] Such approaches, while heterogeneous, aim to capture the way people's experiences *and their subjective understandings of those experiences* are linked to their further development. In part, the narratives that result from children's talk about harmful (or indeed, any) events reflect the way they have experienced those events. But such narratives also reflect how children have made sense of the events at multiple levels – the way they have linked an event to their own intentions, goals, beliefs, and emotions. Further, such narratives may actually involve drawing connections between children's experiences and what children believe to be true of themselves and others, and ultimately, how they construe what it means to be a good person – their sense of themselves as moral agents.

Our research[25] has shown that even very young children consider their own needs and their own reasons for having acted the way they did, and they also consider the needs and feelings of the people they hurt. They think about how their actions affect others, and they think about how to repair relationships. It appears as though children find ways to integrate their own acts of perpetration – when they hurt others – within a sense of who they are and who they want to become. Indeed, for the most part children can acknowledge the consequences of their harmful actions without being devastated by what they did. There is a sense in which they take this "bad" part of themselves and integrate it into an understanding of themselves, and also rely on these experiences to draw conclusions about their future behavior – their future self. Empirically, that process is reflected in specific features of the contents of narratives, in particular a greater emphasis on subjective, interpretive, and psychological (intentions, goals, emotions) aspects of experience, relative to facts.

Because this perspective on moral development does not exclude the perpetration of aggression from the scope of moral life, it lends itself to asking how children who are exposed to and are themselves active participants in political violence might develop a sense of morality and a sense of being moral agents. Next, we consider

---

[24] M. Pasupathi, E. Mansour, & J. Brubaker, "Developing a Life Story: Constructing relations between self and experience in autobiographical narratives," *Human Development* 50 (2007), pp. 85–110; D. P. McAdams, *The stories we live by: Personal myths and the making of the self* (New York: Guilford Press, 1993); K. C. McLean, "Late adolescent identity development: Narrative meaning-making and memory telling," *Developmental Psychology*, 41 (2005), pp. 683–691.

[25] Wainryb, et al., op cit. note 18, "Being Hurt and Hurting Others."

what our approach has already suggested about the impact of exposure to political violence in children.

Moral Development of War-Affected Children: Exposure to Political Violence

Colombia has been in a state of civil war for more than 50 years, with leftist guerrilla groups and rightist paramilitary groups waging war against the government and against each other. The ongoing conflict has been characterized by widespread violence, resulting in one of the highest kidnapping and homicide rates worldwide.[26] As a result of this conflict, nearly 3 million people (out of a population of 44 million) have been forced to leave their homes and towns, seeking refuge in the big cities. More than 400,000 of these internal refugees have relocated in shanty-towns in the outskirts of Bogota – a startling number given that the capital's total population is 8 million – creating peripheral rings of squatter settlements characterized by high population density, poor housing, lack of public services, and inadequate nutrition. In the last several years, we[27] have been studying a group of displaced children and adolescents (ages 6–17) in Usme, one of southern Bogota's poorest slums (population 230,000) featuring one of the largest concentrations of displaced persons. Usme is a vast warren of concrete homes and plywood-and-aluminum shacks. Only some roads are paved, and in many places people have to walk through mud and sewage. Sanitation is poor and access to water and electricity sporadic (e.g., during the time we conducted interviews, the water supply was cut off for days at a time.) Usme is considered one of the most dangerous localities in Bogota, with a rate of 3.3 violent deaths per 10,000.[28] Although reliable figures could not be obtained, many of the children we studied had been separated from their parents or lost their parents; most lived in abject poverty and all of them reported having witnessed different forms of violence perpetrated on others, including events as severe as seeing someone being shot at or killed or finding a dead body.[29]

In general, we found that in spite of their appalling experiences, these children nevertheless develop basic moral concepts (e.g., that it is wrong to steal from others or to inflict harm on others). This is not an insignificant finding, given that

---

26 World Bank, *Violence in Colombia: Building sustainable peace and social capital.*(Washington, DC 2006).

27 Posada and Wainryb, *Moral Development in a Violent Society*; R. Posada, & C. Wainryb, "Narratives of violence: Making sense of interpersonal conflicts from a victim and perpetrator's perspective," paper presented at the biennial meetings of the Society for Research on Child Development, Boston, MA (March 2007); C. Wainryb, & R. Posada, *Moral development in Colombia: Children's judgments about what people should and will do in the context of survival and revenge*, Society for Research on Child Development, Boston, MA (March 2007).

28 Red Bogota, *Hacer publico lo publico*. http://www.redbogota.com/lopublico/index.htm, retrieved on 3/10/2006.

29 Posada and Wainryb, *Moral Development in a Violent Society.*

the circumstances of their lives would not seem to facilitate (explicitly or implicitly) such learning. We suggest that this finding, rather than the protective effects of ideology, may be a source of hopefulness about the long-term potential of war-affected children for developing a healthy sense of moral agency.

That said, our research also indicated that their conceptions of what is right and just were divorced from what they expected others and themselves to actually do, and were applied selectively to some groups of people but not others.[30] For example, the majority of children interviewed consistently predicted that they and others would actually steal and inflict physical harm on people in a variety of situations, despite acknowledging that these actions would be wrong. Also, they judged that while aggression is wrong, it is permissible when inflicted on those people they considered their enemies. While the distinctions drawn by children in these studies between moral prohibitions (oughts) and normative expectations can be seen as realistic and sophisticated, they also indicate a construal of the world as one in which nobody follows ethical principles. It is not difficult to imagine that, in such a world, the motivation to do the morally right thing may be undermined. It is also not difficult to imagine that in such a world, it might be hard to trust others, and indeed, oneself, to honor commitments and control aggressive impulses. Functional civil societies, however, rely on the assumption that their citizens possess precisely these capacities.

Another issue of importance is how these children might negotiate views of themselves and others as moral agents in relation to their specific experiences of victimization and perpetration. Previous work suggests that past moral experiences and what people make of those experiences, can further the moral self. How those events in which they could be seen as "bad" are explained or negotiated is critical for understanding how children come to evaluate themselves and others along moral lines and, even, how they understand their place in the world. These children's expectation that no one abides by moral rules appears to also translate into fairly "thin" views of themselves and others as moral agents – something that is clearly evident in how they talked about situations in which they had been the perpetrators of violence. In our research, we asked displaced Colombian children to tell us about a time when they hurt someone they knew. What follows is an excerpt from a story told by a displaced teenage boy about a time when he hurt someone:

> I remember a time when we were in the classroom and the teacher left. Then I tried to hurt one of my best friends with a rope that was hanging from the roof. I put it around his neck and started pulling. I don't know why I did it. Everybody saw that, and they called the principal . . . and she began to scold me and she told me that she might expel me from school. And then she told me that I was useless, and after that everybody avoided me and they made me feel like I don't belong in there. And so I felt really bad, I cried.

This narrative, which is fairly representative of the narratives given by this group of children, has two noteworthy features. First, as this teenage boy tells us about a time when he hurt his best friend (he put a rope around his neck and pulled – not an

[30] S. Opotow, "Moral exclusion and injustice," *Journal of Social Issues*, 46 (1990), pp. 1–20.

insignificant infraction!), he devotes a few short sentences to describing what he did to his friend, and devotes the rest of the narrative to describing how he himself had been victimized: he was scolded, he was told he'd be expelled, he was told he was useless, everyone avoided him, and he felt sad. This pattern was true of about 70% of the narrative accounts produced by displaced children. Indeed, one of the essential features of these children's perpetration stories was their focus on the idea that their perpetration had turned *them* into victims. This pattern, which was pervasive among displaced children, was never found in normative samples in the United States.[31]

The other important feature of this narrative is the prevailing emphasis on observable events and behaviors, and the near total absence of references to the meanings that these behaviors may carry. There is almost no inferential content in this account – no references to non-observable information, the type of information that requires the communication of internal states, desires, wants, feelings, thoughts. It is even devoid of emotional language, especially in the portion that is linked to this child's perpetration. Notably, the only reference to internality and emotions appears when he switches to describing how he had felt victimized: "I felt really bad, I cried." This feature, too, is inconsistent with the ways in which children and adolescents in normative samples speak about and think about times in which they had hurt others.[32] Notably, however, the narratives of juvenile delinquents and behaviorally troubled adolescents tend to exhibit patterns similar to those of displaced children.[33]

Should we be concerned about this? Yes.

By talking about mental states, emotions, interpretations, intentions – people make sense, more or less coherently, of complex situations. It is through this type of language that people connect a sequence of actions in a comprehensible way – by relating the actions to a sense of themselves as agents with beliefs, desires, and feelings. It is also through this kind of language that children (and adults) connect specific events to a more continuous sense of the type of person they think they are. When this type of language is missing from a narrative, actions are rendered incoherent; the actions simply stand in for internal character and agency is undermined. This teenager's narrative suggests avoidance and lack of integration. It is as though this child cannot integrate a sense of himself as a wrong-doer, but is fully aware of himself as a powerless weeping victim. In this narrative, the impoverished language leaves his behavior incomprehensible even to himself – the only clarity in this story involves the pain of his own exclusion after having attempted to hurt his friend.

This child's inability to make sense of his own behavior, and the juxtaposition of that senselessness with his much more coherent pain of victimization, is deeply problematic. It is deeply problematic for this individual's future welfare. But it is

---

[31] Wainryb et al., "Being Hurt and Hurting Others."

[32] Wainryb et al., "Being Hurt and Hurting Others."

[33] A. Sanderson, "A narrative analysis of behaviorally troubled adolescents' life stories," Doctoral dissertation, The University of Calgary, 2001, *Dissertation Abstracts International,* 62 (2001), p. 4076; C. Wainryb, M. Komolova, M. Coquillon, & P. Florsheim, "Youth offenders' and high-school teens' narrative accounts of their own aggressive behaviors," paper presented at the biennial meetings of the Society for Research on Child Development, Boston, MA, (March 2007).

also deeply problematic for us all to live in a world populated by hurting adolescents who cannot make coherent sense of their own dangerous behavior, but who can see themselves very clearly as victims. These data thus suggest that there is reason for concern. In fact, all this should leave us deeply concerned about the potential that political violence around the world has for undermining children's development as moral agents. The disruption in the development of moral capacities is likely to be even more severe for child-soldiers, who at an early age were forced to become instruments of killing and torture. Globally there are an estimated 300,000 child soldiers.[34] However, virtually nothing is known about their moral development. Next, we begin by reviewing what is known about the process by which children become actively involved in armed groups, and then consider the implications for their moral development.

Moral Development of War-Affected Children: Involvement in Political Violence

It is not surprising that living in the midst of social disarray and poverty, having been displaced and often separated from their parents and families, children become easy targets for recruitment into violent organizations. Nowadays, given the availability of lightweight automatic weapons, even young children can become fighters. Children are recruited by both government forces and non-state groups. In some cases children are coerced into joining armed groups through forced conscription or abduction. Even when not coerced, children's "voluntary" decision to join an armed group is typically informed by the adverse conditions in the midst of which they grow up: children join armed groups to escape abject poverty or family violence, to remain with a family member who had recruited or enlisted, to acquire skills or education that cannot be had elsewhere, or to gain prestige, power, or excitement. It is also the case that in social contexts characterized by injustice and lack of opportunity, youth may become highly politicized and volunteer to join armed groups out of ideological conviction. While some of the children who join armed groups engage only in the more peripheral activities, serving in roles such as porters, cooks, or spies (with many girl soldiers serving in the role of "wives" or sexual slaves), many become fighters, participating in killings, torture, and destruction.[35]

There is evidence that, across the world, many armed groups target young children for indoctrination into programs that glorify violence and self sacrifice.[36] One of the consequences of such indoctrination processes and of those ideologies that ascribe meaning to the violence in their lives, is that children in politically violent

---

[34] S. McKay, "Girls as "weapons of terror" in Northern Uganda and Sierra Leonean rebel fighting forces," *Studies in Conflict and Terrorism* 28 (2005), pp. 385–397; Wessels, *Child Soldiers: From Violence to Protection*.

[35] Wessles, *Child Soldiers: From Violence to Protection*.

[36] Browne, "Examining the Impact of Terrorism on Children," pp. 189–211; Cairns, *Children and Political Violence*.

worlds become identified with an in-group and develop a clear sense of the out-group as *Other*. This process, it should be noted, is part of normal human development. In fact, the tendency to glorify the in-group and to denigrate the *Other* is so robust and compelling that it can be triggered with even trivial laboratory psychological experiments.[37] Thus it is not surprising that in the context of political violence, and even without explicit training, children would acquire, often from a young age, belief-systems concerning the presumed goodness of the in-group and the badness of the *Other*, as well as collective narratives concerning their group's mistreatment at the hands of the *Other.* While these communal ideologies aid children in making sense of their bewildering and distressing lives, they also tend to disallow or dismiss ambiguities and contradictions,[38] thereby leading children to develop polarized understandings of the complex realities within which they operate, dehumanize the *Other*, and ultimately justify violence and revenge. Strongly held ideological beliefs can also lead youth to higher risk taking and acceptance of future loss, or an increased "willingness to sacrifice"[39] which, when combined with a distorted image of the *Other*, might contribute to continuing cycles of violence. It has been argued, for example, that the phenomenon of suicide bombers is shaped by such communal beliefs. The target group is portrayed as so evil and threatening that killing its members is seen not as murder but as justified revenge or admirable self defense. As the language of "martyrdom" replaces the language of "suicide," the larger purpose and nobility of those who carry on the attacks are reframed. Note, indeed, that the distinction between suicide and martyrdom is given in the belief system, as martyrs exist only in the minds of those who confer their status.[40]

It is also well known that many fighting groups have developed brutal and perversely sophisticated techniques, explicitly calculated to isolate children from their communities, harden and numb them to violence, dehumanize their victims, and prepare them for killing. Children are often forced at first to witness violence, and subsequently are made to join in and brutally beat and kill others. Sometimes they are compelled to participate in the killing of family members, because it is understood by these groups that there is "no way back home" for children after they have committed such crimes.[41]

How do such appalling and abhorring experiences affect the development of child soldiers? While it is possible that psychopathology and severe mental illness characterize some of them, this is unlikely to be the case across the board.[42] Speaking about arrested moral development in global terms is similarly unlikely to do justice

---

[37] See, e.g., T. M. Ostrom & C. Sedikides, "Out-group homogeneity effects in natural and minimal groups," *Psychological Bulletin* 112 (1992), pp. 536–552.

[38] Punamaki, "Can Ideological Commitment Protect Chilren's Psychosocial Wellbeing," pp. 55–69; Wessels, *Child Soldiers: From Violence to Protection.*

[39] Loar, et al., "Risk and Protective Factors," 279–286.

[40] B. Hoffman & G. H. McCormick, "Terrorism, signaling, and suicide attack," *Studies in Conflict and Terrorism* 27 (2004), pp. 243–281.

[41] McKay, "Girls as "Weapons of Terror," " 385–397.

[42] Wessels, *Child Soldiers: From Protection to Violence.*

to the complexity of these youths' experience. The more useful questions are how child soldiers reconcile themselves with their own experiences of both committing and enduring injustice and violence, and how they integrate these experiences within a sense of themselves as moral.

One possibility is that in attempting to make sense of their experiences, whether before or after joining (voluntarily or involuntarily) an armed group, child soldiers carve up the world in Manichean terms, as "us" and "them" or "good" and "evil," thereby construing their actions as the desirable and justifiable means for ridding the world of the evil enemy and exacting revenge for perceived past wrongs. This process, which is surely aided by ideology and indoctrination, tends to exclude certain groups of people from the moral universe[43] and increases the probability of continuing cycles of violence.

Another possibility is one that actually prevents or precludes meaning-making. Even normal, healthy adults report avoiding disclosing troubling events in order to attempt to forget those experiences.[44] So it is not surprising that children faced with extreme experiences, that run counter to their values and principles, might also respond with numbness and more extreme kinds of repression or dissociation. While this strategy may be adaptive in the short term, inasmuch as it facilitates children's self-preservation, it is far from clear whether children (or adults, for that matter) are capable of leaving awful experiences "to the side" – forgetting them on purpose, if you will – without serious consequences for their functioning. In our normative samples, it is noteworthy that despite attempts to forget everyday troubles, people are still reporting them in the research setting, even many years later. And in samples of people with documented, true recovered memories, there is evidence that such memories are capable of resurfacing years later with troubling consequences for those individuals.[45]

To date, there is no systematic evidence about how prevalent each of these strategies may be, and whether some strategies may be predictive of better developmental outcomes in the short-term – for example, during the conflict and in its immediate aftermath, and in the long-run, as children need to return to functioning in a post-war society. The sort of narrative examinations and analyses that we described in relation to war-affected children in Colombia are useful for understanding how child soldiers (or former child soldiers) go about integrating, or not integrating, their own experiences of victimization and perpetration into a sense of themselves and others as moral agents. This approach has the advantage of preserving a sense that child soldiers are active constructers of their own experiences. Furthermore,

---

[43] Opotow, "Moral Exclusion and Injustice," pp. 1–20; S. Opotow, J. Gerson, & S. Woodside, "From moral exclusion to moral inclusion: Theory for teaching peace," *Theory into Practice* 44 (2005), pp. 303–318.

[44] M. Pasupathi, K. C. McLean, & T. Weeks, *The told and untold narrative self*, Unpublished manuscript, University of Utah (2007).

[45] J. W. Schooler, M. Bendiksen, & Z. Ambadar, "Taking the middle line: Can we accommodate both fabricated and recovered memories of sexual abuse?," in M. A. Conway (ed.), *False and recovered memories* (Oxford, Oxford University Press, 1997), pp. 251–292.

because narratives are social constructions,[46] focusing on child soldiers' narratives also leaves open the possibility for guiding or aiding them into reconstruing the same experiences in alternative ways – construals that may help in both short- and long-term ways.

How *do* child soldiers talk about their experiences? While, to our knowledge, we are the first to propose these kinds of systematic narrative examinations and analyses, existing records of conversations with former child soldiers can be used to illustrate our approach. Between 1995 and 2005, psychologist and child-protection practitioner Michael Wessells interviewed more than 400 former child soldiers between the ages of 7 and 18 years in Afghanistan, Angola, Kosovo, northern Uganda, Sierra Leone, and South Africa. In a groundbreaking book, Wessells departs from the more traditionally simplistic and sensationalist approach to this phenomenon, and sets the stage for understanding the complex and multifaceted experiences of child soldiers.[47] In fact, one of the most important contributions of Wessells' book is the attention and respect it gives to child soldiers' own subjective construals of their experiences. In what follows, we refer to some of the compelling narratives reported by Wessells to illustrate how children's own words – what they do and do not include in their subjective construals – can be used to understand the psychological mechanisms underlying their interpretations and sense-making of their realities, as well as what that might mean for their moral development.

The following narrative, by a Philippine boy who had joined the Moro Islamic Liberation Front (MILF) at age 13, is where we begin:

> It feels great to kill your enemy. The MILF does not initiate attacks. If the military didn't attack us, there would be no trouble. They are the ones who are really at fault. They deserve to be killed. The other children, they are happy too. They are not sad. I really do not regret killing. If they are your enemies, you can kill them. But if they are not your enemies, you shouldn't kill them.[48]

This narrative differs from the type that we would normally examine in that it does not refer to a specific event experienced by this child but rather to the child's views about the generic experiences of killing. Nevertheless, this narrative illustrates an extraordinarily polarized universe, in which there are good people (the MILF) and enemies (the military); killing of the enemy is associated with positivity and the high moral ground. It is difficult to know for certain how this boy might tell a story about a specific time when he killed an enemy person, but we speculate that, given this starting point, he might tell a story involving very little subjective content (other than happiness for the killing of the enemy), little sense of moral struggle, and perhaps even a sense of righteous self-defense – the kind of reversal of victimhood that we observed in the Colombian displaced youth's story, earlier.

---

[46] M. Pasupathi, "The social construction of the personal past and its implications for adult development," *Psychological Bulletin* 127 (2001), pp. 651–672.

[47] Wessels, *Child Soldiers: From Violence to Protection*.

[48] Wessels, *Child Soldiers: From Violence to Protection*, p. 81.

Whereas the boy in the narrative above seems to exist in a straightforward moral world, the language in the following two narratives, which are much closer to the type of data we employ in our work, points to much less clarity, certainty, and integration. In the narrative below, a boy who had been abducted by the LRA in northern Uganda told about the way in which this group dealt with escapees.[49] The narrative after next, pertains to a 12-year-old Colombian girl who had joined the FARC-EP and recounts how she was forced to administer punishment on her friend.[50]

> One boy tried to escape and was caught, tied up, and marched back to camp. All the recruits from the various companies were told that we were never going home, that we were fighting now with the LRA so as a symbol of our pledge to fight on, this boy would be killed and we would help. Soldiers then laid the boy on the ground and stabbed him three times with a bayonet until the blood began seeping from the wounds. Then the new recruits approached the boy and beat him on the chest. Each one has a turn and could only stop once the blood from the body splashed up on to you. This boy was 16 years old. We were beating him with sticks, each recruit was given a stick.
>
> I had a friend, Juanita, who got into trouble for sleeping around. We had been friends in civilian life and we shared a tent together. The commander said that it didn't matter that she was my best friend. She had committed an error and had to be killed. I closed my eyes and fired the gun, but I didn't hit her. So I shot again. The grave was right nearby. I had to bury her and put dirt on top of her. The commander said "You did very well. Even though you started to cry, you did well. You'll have to do this again many more times, and you'll have to learn not to cry."

In both these narratives, there is a near complete absence of psychological, interpretive language. Virtually every sentence contains only observable information. The boy reports things that could be seen (the escapee being tied up and marched to camp, being laid on the ground, etc.) or heard (told we would never go home...). There is no mention of what the boy himself felt, thought, wanted, or did not want, in relation to these actions. In the girl's narrative, the references to emotion, and the evaluations that are provided (crying, doing well), are contained in reported speech. Without constructing links between actions and thoughts/feelings, even when those links involve a sense of coercion, ambivalence, or fear, it is likely to be difficult for each of these children to integrate their own experiences – experiences which are horrifying even to read about – with their own autobiography. One noteworthy feature in the girl's narrative is that the one piece of information in the text that is not directly observable is her statement about her friendship with the victim. That claim is, of course, incoherent with the act of killing; again, this experience poses serious problems for integration with a sense of the self as a moral agent. And again, this narrative provides little evidence that any integration has occurred.

Not all the narrative accounts given by child soldiers are devoid of internality and interpretive language. In the following narrative, a Colombian boy explains how he was forced to watch and participate in the killing of captives:

> They bring the people they catch, guerrillas and robbers, to the training course. My squad had to kill three people. After the first one was killed, the commander told me that the next

---

[49] Wessels, *Child Soldiers: From Violence to Protection*, p. 59.

[50] Wessels, *Child Soldiers: From Violence to Protection*, p. 64.

> day I'd have to do the killing. I was stunned and appalled. I had to do it publicly, in front of the whole company, fifty people. I had to shoot him in the head. I was trembling. Afterwards, I couldn't eat. I'd see the person's blood. For weeks, I had a hard time sleeping... some of the victims cried and screamed. The commander told us we had to learn how to kill.[51]

This narrative's content and structure are closer in some ways to those obtained in normative samples with much less severe types of harm. For this boy, there are statements of mental states – stunned, appalled. There are reports of flashback experiences, difficulty with sleeping. And the victims remain human beings who express terror and pain – crying, screaming. While the pain experienced by the boy is clearer in this narrative, this narrative also reflects a remaining sense of moral agency that is lacking in the other narratives. That agency is somewhat constrained, given the coercion involved, but it is there. It is because of this tension between experiencing pain and retaining a sense of agency that child soldiers will struggle to reconcile these events within a sense of themselves as moral beings.

Indeed, for child soldiers, the task of reconciling themselves with their experiences is a difficult task, because they must integrate their violent and aggressive experiences without denying their own moral agency and without adopting a sense of themselves as amoral or immoral. That is, they need to end up with a sense that they *are* moral agents (and were moral agents even when they engaged in violence), and also that they are capable of *also* doing the right thing. Both are necessary for them to be able to make different choices in the future.

Not surprisingly, it is common for those who come into contact with returning child soldiers, to want to exonerate them. What follows is an excerpt from the autobiographical book *A long way gone: Memoirs of a boy soldier*, by Ishmael Beah, who as a 12-year-old in Sierra Leone was abducted by the Revolutionary United Front. In this excerpt, Beah speaks about his experiences 3 years later, when he entered a rehabilitation camp for returning child soldiers:

> When I finished telling Esther the story, she had tears in her eyes, and she couldn't decide whether to rub my head or hug me. In the end she did neither, but said: "None of what happened was your fault. You were just a little boy" ... I became angry and regretted that I had told someone, a civilian, about my experience. I hated the "It is not your fault" line that all the staff members said every time anyone spoke about the war.[52]

Such anger may seem puzzling. But consider that the statement "it was not your fault," while heartfelt and well-intentioned, acts so as to deny Ishmael's sense of agency. This type of statement also denies whatever positive consequences this child perceives may have resulted from his participation in this armed group. Child soldiers often are or become committed to the ideology of their group, believing strongly in the validity of what they did.

---

[51] Wessels, *Child Soldiers: From Violence to Protection*, p. 70.

[52] Ishmael Beah, *A long way gone: Memoirs of a boy soldier* (New York: Farrar, Strauss & Giroux, 2007), pp. 159–160.

On the Reclamation of Moral Agency

Having raised the alarm about the implications of collective violence in general and participation as soldiers in particular for children's moral development, one might ask whether there is any hope at all. In closing, we focus on two areas in which there may be reservoirs to call on, for rehabilitating children's sense of moral agency. One of those ways involves the fact that these children retain what we might call reservoirs of moral sentiment – their relationships to others. Indeed, one common thread in very diverse accounts given by child soldiers, is the depiction of strong friendships developing among child soldiers. Beah depicts developing and nurturing those very friendships, and as we have noted above, the girl soldier's account of killing her friend did not in itself deny the friendship and its meaning.[53] These relationships maintain the kinds of sentiments of care and concern that can be used to remind child soldiers that they *also* acted as positive agents, and that they can do so again.

A second route involves helping former child soldiers, as well as the communities from which they come, to make sense of their own actions with regard to the larger political and historical conflict. Children and communities naturally attempt at making sense of their actions and of the events endured. Unfortunately, this often happens by calling upon entrenched ideologies and in-group/out-group dynamics. There is little doubt that the presence of a truly evil enemy makes one's own killing sensible and right. Sadly, this kind of ideology also makes one more likely to pursue violence again. But there are ways to place one's own and other people's unthinkable actions within the context of a more complex understanding of the political and historical conflict, one that acknowledges the culpability and atrocities on all sides. This type of context can help to make sense of a child soldier's actions without relying on a polarized view of self and *Other* that justifies the killing. In some sense, this is the ideal pursued by the Truth and Reconciliation Commission in South Africa – the notion that a sufficiently comprehensive understanding of the blood on everyone's hands will reduce the potential for renewed conflict.[54]

Many children participating in terrorist and armed groups are beyond our reach, but increasing numbers can be helped, as when they participate, in the aftermath of conflict, in programs of disarmament, demobilization, and reintegration (DDR) under the auspices of the U.N. and child protection agencies. Gargantuan DDR efforts have been tremendously aided by needs-assessment studies carried out by DDR officers and related personnel.[55] These studies have worked to uncover the

---

[53] Beah, *A Long Way Gone;* see also J. Boyden, "The moral development of child soldiers," *Peace and Conflict: Journal of Peace Psychology* 9 (2003), pp. 343–362; Michael Wessels, *Child Soldiers: From Protection to Violence* (Cambridge, Mass.: Harvard Univ. Press, 2006).

[54] See, e.g., C. Villa-Vicencio, & W. Verwoerd (eds.), *Looking back reaching forward: Reflections on the Truth and Reconciliation Commission of South Africa* (Cape Town, South Africa: University of Cape Town Press, 2000).

[55] See, e.g., Wessels and Kostelny, "After the Taliban;" Wessels and Monteiro, "Psychosocial Assistance for Youth," pp. 121–139.

many psycho-social needs of this group of children. It has been suggested[56] that, of the entire DDR process, the task of reintegrating children into civilian life, whether their communities and families of origin or some newly reconstituted community, presents the most challenges. This is because returning child soldiers bring with them the residues of their war experiences. They have learned to use violence as a means for achieving goals, and because they have been the instruments of brutality, often forced to commit atrocities in their own communities, many communities fear, resent, and reject former child soldiers. Thus, reintegration often requires community negotiation and healing as well as help for the individuals.

Ultimately, of course, the question is how to help these children reconcile or integrate their experiences with victimization and transgression in ways that help both individuals and groups to heal. The answers to these questions will not come easily, and moving from these answers towards a significant positive impact in conflict-torn regions around the globe will be even more complicated. It is our belief that these children's stories – their narrative accounts of their own experiences – are not only a key to seeing what is going wrong with children exposed to violence, but they are also likely to be a way to put things right. But not all stories will put things right in a sustainable way. The more sustaining stories will be those that embrace everything about these children and their place in the world – the good, and the bad. The best stories will be the complicated, full ones, those that encompass where the children started and where they have been.

Relying heavily on accounts and interviews given by former child soldiers from around the world, Uzodinma Iweala, an American writer from Nigerian descent, created a character he called Agu – a child soldier in an unnamed West African country, who is abducted and forced to commit murder, rape, and other atrocities. The book, *Beasts of No Nation*, ends with Agu foreshadowing that kind of complicated, encompassing story:

> And every day I am talking to Amy. She is white woman from America who is coming here to be helping people like me... She is telling me to speak speak speak... I am saying to her sometimes, I am not saying many thing because I am knowing too many terrible thing to be saying to you. I am seeing more terrible thing than ten thousand men and I am doing more terrible thing than twenty thousand men. ... So I am saying to her, if I am telling this to you it will be making you to think that I am beast or devil. Amy is never saying anything when I am saying this... And I am saying to her, fine. I am all of this thing, but I am also having mother once, and she is loving me.[57]

As implied in this story, child soldiers, like Agu, are complex individuals, with histories, relationships, desires, regrets, and hopes. It is by construing and telling stories in which they recognize themselves as such, that they can hope to survive the brutality and insanity they experienced and further their own sense of self as moral beings.

---

56 See, e.g., Wessels, *Child Soldiers*, note 53.

57 Uzodinma Iweala, *Beasts of No Nation* (New York: Harper, 2005), pp. 140–142.

Violent and Non-violent Responses to State Failure: Papua New Guinea and Ecuador

Ken Jameson and Polly Wiessner

Treatments of the failed state in the current world economy abound, coming from the right,[1] from the left[2] and from everywhere in between.[3] There is even a "failed states index"[4] that ranks 177 states on their degree of failure in terms of 12 indicators.[5]

Underlying the reality of state failure is the conflict between globalization and the continuation or resurgence of indigenous political structures and cultural traditions. On the one hand is the claim of the apostles of globalization that the "world is flat"[6] or that the triumph of liberal democracy had brought us to "the end of history."[7] On the other hand, events of the 1990s and 2000s dealt the final blow to predictions of modernism, to wit, that the process of globalization would raze indigenous political structures and cultural traditions to produce a homogeneous global village, governed by nation states and guided by principles of capitalism. Cultural institutions and traditions of many forms have persisted or resurged, amongst them "tribalism."

One result of these contradictory historical processes has been state failure. One important manifestation of state failure has been an upsurge in violence and terror within and between countries, though not uniformly. This chapter attempts to understand why the contradictory trends have led to violence in some cases but not

K. Jameson
University of Utah
e-mail: jameson@economics.utah.edu

[1] Stephen Krasner and Carlos Pascual, "Addressing State Failure." *Foreign Affairs* 84, 4 (July/August 2005), pp. 153–163.
[2] Noam Chomsky, *Failed States: The Abuse of Power and the Assault on Democracy.* (New York: Metropolitan Books, 2006).
[3] Alexandros Yannis, "State Collapse and Its Implications for Peace-building and Reconstruction," *Development and Change* 33, 5 (November), pp. 817–836.
[4] Fund for Peace, "The Failed States Index." http://www.fundforpeace.org/web, accessed October 17, 2007.
[5] For 2007, the index goes from #1, Sudan, the most failed state, to #177, Norway, the most successful state. The U.S. ranks 160 out of 177 countries in the failed states index, between Chile and Singapore. Ecuador is number 73, between Nicaragua and Venezuela. Papua New Guinea is number 52, between Belarus and Angola.
[6] Thomas Friedman, *The World Is Flat* (New York: Farrar, Straus and Giroux, 2005).
[7] Francis Fukuyama, *The End of History and the Last Man.* (London: Hamish Hamilton, 1992).

I.A. Karawan et al. (eds.), *Values and Violence*,

in others. The argument has three parts. The first examines the attack on the state that crystallized in the policies of the Reagan administration and then was adopted by much of the rest of world's policy makers as part of the neo-liberal push for globalization. We then turn to two case studies in which tribalism and indigenous movements have come to embody the main resistance to the failed state that globalization created. The first, Papua New Guinea (PNG) and in particular the Enga, provides an example of how state failure results in an upsurge of violence as a result of tribalism's commitment to provide for its members. The second, Ecuador and the indigenous movement, provides an experience in which the indigenous have grown in influence through a studied use of their traditions and through non-violent political action.

What accounts for the different outcomes in Papua New Guinea and in Ecuador? In the first, tribalism resulted in horizontal competition between tribes, whose tactics have become increasingly violent and merit the term terror. In Ecuador, a resurgent indigenous movement has unified the "tribes," or different indigenous groups, and has succeeded in the vertical competition for resources. Indigenous organizations have become viable competitors for the resources that the state controls and participants in setting social and economic policy. Their success has come from unifying indigenous groups and avoiding horizontal competition among them. They have taken their place alongside traditional power groups such as industrialists and exporters. The tactics have been confrontational but non-violent and there has been no recourse to terror to attain tribal aims. The final section sums up the article and contrasts the PNG and Ecuador. In that regard, the resurgence of tribalism provides reason for optimism, justifying a "bias for hope."

The Contemporary Attack on the State

The current form of argument against the state was cast in the early 1980s under the Reagan administration, with its implementation of a particular set of anti-state policies, best termed "conservative economic individualism (CEI)."[8] From that starting point, the expanded attack on the state progressed in a series of steps:

- the successful effort of the Reagan administration in the US and the Thatcherites in England to reduce the role of government, particularly its regulatory functions;
- the monetarist stance of the Federal Reserve under Paul Volcker designed to reduce discretionary monetary policy by targeting the money supply;
- the "Washington Consensus" which successfully advocated reducing the role of the state in developing countries, particularly in Latin America;
- increased international concern with failed states, because their weakness could become destabilizing to the entire international system through their domestic turmoil or by exporting disorder;

[8] Charles K. Wilber and Kenneth P. Jameson, *Beyond Reaganomics: A Further Inquiry into the Poverty of Economics* (Notre Dame, In.: University of Notre Dame Press, 1990).

- advocacy of second generation reforms that seek improvements in institutions and in governance. This is actually another assault on the state, since the state is assessed on its governance ability through the perceptions of external private sector actors, many of whom naturally see a strong state as inimical to their interests. The implication is that the state that is most accommodating to the private sector governs best.[9]

As a result of this globalization of economic policy, the market, transnational corporations, and individualism constituted the new recipe for economic and political progress. States in the periphery could only interfere, with negative consequences, and had to be limited to controlling inflation and maintaining stable international economic relations. The attack on the state has largely succeeded, but with many consequences unforeseen by its exponents. The vacuum created in many states has threatened not only the well-being of their citizens, but of the world as a whole. People in these states have searched for new mechanisms to gain power and to substitute for the inadequacy of the current institutional arrangements.

State failure will differ between a newly created country such as Papua New Guinea, and a long independent country such as Ecuador. However, the changes over the last twenty years in the international economy and in the set of institutions deemed acceptable are the common factors of the state failure in each case. Nonetheless, their historical experience, economic reality, and role in the world economy have determined the particular direction that each country's state has evolved.

On one end of the spectrum is Papua New Guinea, one of the newest "states" (1975). There the main indicators are at the "micro" level. The state and the macro level never functioned well enough to even be considered viable, and thus the failure is seen most clearly in the lives of individuals and in their primary identification, the tribe. On the other end is Ecuador, with a much longer experience of independence and of the developmental state. It fails through a combination of factors, micro and macro, national and regional, and at the level of the population and of ethnic groups. The differences among the types of state failure will affect their citizens' responses and the degree to which they result in violence.

In Papua New Guinea, tribal institutions and sentiments can impact the state at a number of points during its development or during its demise. In states established by colonial powers that became independent when indigenous "tribal" political institutions were still the primary means of local governance, "tribal" institutions and sentiments often penetrate the state and use its machinery for pursuit of their own ends. In such cases intertribal competition is horizontal with tribes competing for the resources of the post-colonial state and thereby weakening it (e.g. island nations of Oceania). This has been the case in Papua New Guinea. By contrast, in states such as Ecuador that over time developed a sense of nationhood, central governance, and

---

[9] Critics suggest that the governance focus is part of an effort to create a "global governance model" that finally and successfully marginalizes the state in developing countries (Emre Özçelik and Eyüp Özveren, "An Institutionalist Perspective on the Future of the Capitalist World-Economy," paper presented at the AFEE Meetings, Boston, Mass., 6 January 2006).

whose citizens have links to the broader world economy, indigenous society is often colonized by the state and global forces. This has been the case in Latin America and in Ecuador in particular, where local institutions atrophied and homogenization of identity grew. In these cases, tribal institutions take second place, and only resurge when the state weakens and can no longer enforce order, protect property, uphold contracts, and care for the basic needs of citizens. Competition is vertical with tribal units opposing the state.

The response to the successful attack on the state is much less definable in this case. It will be determined by the interplay of micro and macro effects. Good macro performance can stabilize the situation and maintain existing structures and relations. On the other hand, mobilization of existing civic organizations or resurgence of traditional ones, such as "tribes," can alter the direction of evolution and bring about a new relation of state and individual. Whether this development results in violent attacks on the existing state apparatus or on domestic competing interests depends heavily on how important the tribes become and how they gain access to the residual power of the weakened state. In some cases, such as Papua New Guinea, tribal institutions have led to an increase in patterned violence. "Tribes" call on traditional means, warfare, to challenge the state's monopoly on legitimate sanctioned violence as a means of keeping order. In other cases, such as Ecuador, indigenous movements that have had an impact at the national level have grown peacefully. The contrast between the resurgence of indigenous institutions in Papua New Guinea and Ecuador can provide insights into the implication of state failure for violence.

State Failure and Violence in Papua New Guinea

Papua New Guinea (PNG) provides a case study of a post-colonial state where indigenous "tribal" institutions and sentiments have persisted and, together with globalization, have had a strong impact on democracy, institutions, and governance. The population of Papua New Guinea is approximately 5.3 million today and is growing at a rate of over 3% per annum. Its 800 different linguistic groups are spread out over islands, coastal regions, and the Highlands of the main island, where the majority of the population lives in fertile mountain valleys. The estimated GDP of PNG in 2003 was US$1.3 billion. Mineral resources account for 25% of the GDP and make up 75% of exports; agriculture, timber and fish make up 30% of the GDP and support 85% of the population; industry makes up only 9% of the GDP. Eighty-five percent of the population is rural and only 10% of the population is employed in the formal sector.[10] A 0.7% per capita income growth is not sufficient to match a population growth of 3.1% per annum.

From the late 19th century, the south east portion of Papua New Guinea (PNG) was annexed by Britain and another portion by Germany. After WWI, PNG was

[10] See Australian Government, AusAID (www.ausaid,gov.au/country/png) and "Background note: Papua New Guinea," Bureau of East Asian and Pacific Affairs, Sep.2004. (www.state.gov/r/pa/ei/bgn/2797.htm).

administered by Australia under a UN mandate that lasted until 1974. Social and economic change accelerated in the 1960s with the expansion of health and educational facilities. Local and district courts were established in the mid 1960s and the first general election for the House of Assembly took place in 1964. Its seats were dominated by official European members. Australia granted Papua New Guinea independence in 1975 in response to growing domestic and international pressures, but without a broad-based anti-colonial movement. The discourse of nationalism, where it existed at all, was to promote "The Melanesian Way," that is, indigenous forms of social and political development. With independence, opposition between colonizers and colonized was replaced by competition between local divisions.[11] It was difficult for a poorly trained police force, which had little support from the people, to collect sufficient evidence to sentence offenders under British law. Moreover, the sometimes brutal measures used to execute justice or punish tribal fighters meted out by Colonizers could not be used by a government against its own people. Crime rose rapidly and intertribal fighting resurged in the Highlands.

At independence, Papua New Guinea was not a nation, but a state in the making. Since independence 25 billion dollars have been invested in PNG by Australia and substantial funds have come into the country from mining and forestry. Nonetheless, PNG is on the verge of economic collapse and government services are much poorer than they were at independence.[12] A good deal of this can be attributed to the colonization of the emerging state by local "tribes" vying for funds that are seen as coming from the outside, not from local production and taxation, and thus are regarded as being up for grabs.

Tribalism is a term wrought with negative connotations in the world of today – primitive sentiments of aggression, intolerance, nepotism, and xenophobia. In anthropology, the concept of the tribe is seen as an imprecise notion encompassing formations from small flexible social groups to large scale political entities constructed by colonial powers to serve their interests. Nonetheless, indigenous tribes share important positive characteristics. First and foremost they are social institutions defined by descent from a putative common ancestor that are validated and integrated by ritual. Kinship is the social glue that binds members.[13] The sub-units of tribes, for example, clans, lineages sub-clans, constitute social security systems from the cradle to the grave. Members receive assistance in finding spouses, subsistence activities, the education of the young, care of the sick and elderly, dispute settlement, and protection of rights. Larger units provide defense. Shared norms and values within tribes and obligations of kinship reduce the transaction costs of social and economic exchange by fostering equality, loyalty, and trust. Definitions of boundaries between social units lay down the rules that facilitate inter-group

---

[11] T. Otto, and N. Thomas (eds.), *Narratives of Nation in the South Pacific. Studies in Anthropology and History* 19 (Amsterdam:Harwood Academic Publishers, 1997).

[12] R. Stella, "PNG in the New Millennium: Some Troubled Homecomings," *Building a Nation in Papua New Guinea: Views of the Post-Independence Generation* (Canberra: Pandanus Books, 2003), pp. 11–22.

[13] Frank Salter, (ed.), *Risky Transactions: Kinship, Trust and Ethnicity* (New York: Berghahn Books, 2002).

interaction.[14] Relations are largely egalitarian; and competition in tribal societies is horizontal, that is to say, it takes place between parallel social units and is often ritualized or rule bound to limit destruction.

Important features of democracy are inherent in most tribal systems. Relations are largely egalitarian; positions of leadership and status are achieved through actions that return benefits to the group. When leaders fail to serve the group, their demise is rapid. Even those holding inherited positions are kept in check and disposed of should they be incompetent or despotic. Transparency and accountability are assured by constant vigilance, gossip, rumor, and application of sanctions. There is usually widespread participation in "policy" decisions involving major problems confronting the group, though men are largely responsible for presiding over public events and decisions while women exert influence in and through private realms.

Colonial powers and capitalistic enterprises attempt to break down tribal institutions because their nepotistic foundation demands that wealth be distributed, inhibiting capital accumulation. The void left by the dissolution of local indigenous political units is to be taken over by the state: education, health, protection of rights, care of the elderly, protection of contracts and rights, law and order, and defense. This means that when the state fails to deliver basic goods and services to the population, people have little choice but to revert to former tribal institutions to fill the vacuum or to form an opposition to regimes that do not meet their interests and needs. This includes removing the state's monopoly on sanctioned violence.[15]

This can be illustrated by the Enga who inhabit the highlands and make up 8% of the population of PNG. Though situations vary greatly in different areas of PNG, the Enga case provides a good example of how the state can be undermined by horizontal competition on the part of tribes to procure its resources and how the weakening of the state leads to further chaos as the result of competition.

The Enga[16]

The social, economic and political situation in Enga at first contact with Europeans in the 1930s was not long-established.[17] Some 300 years earlier, the sweet potato had been introduced to the island of New Guinea from Indonesia and made

---

[14] E. Barth, *Ethnic Groups and Boundaries* (Boston: Little Brown & Co. 1996).

[15] In many cases this involves "reinventing" the tribe through shared symbols and bonding rituals to create an institution in which the negative attributes of ethnicity are accentuated – prejudice, xenophobia, and violent action. In the PNG case, this was not necessary as the state had not succeeded in breaking down former clans and tribes. In Ecuador, the negative attributes have been muted.

[16] For ethnographic works on the Enga see Feil (1984); Kyakas and Wiessner 1992; Meggitt (1965, 1972, 1977). For a superb discussion of law and order in Papua New Guinea, see Dinnen (2001).

[17] Polly Wiessner and A. Tumu, *Historical Vines: Tracing Enga Networks of Exchange, Ritual and Warfare among the Enga of Papua New Guinea* (Smithsonian Institution Press, Washington, D.C., 1998).

its way into the highlands along local trade routes. There it released constraints on production and made ample surplus production possible for the first time – in the form of pigs on the hoof. Within a century of its introduction, the population had undergone major shifts in subsistence production, and was growing steadily. Elaborate ceremonial exchange and religious rituals were developing in response to new potentials and problems. Amongst these was the Tee Ceremonial Exchange Cycle, which linked approximately 400 clans and involved the exchange of tens of thousands of pigs and valuables.[18] At the heart of the Tee Cycle was the quest to assemble as much wealth as possible in one place and then distribute it in public, bringing fame to both prominent individuals and the clan. Ritual and exchange were orchestrated by "big-men," skilled orators and mediators who achieved their status by mediation, organizing large events, negotiating peace and war reparation payments, and attracting outside wealth to the clan and distributing it to their supporters. Exchange networks crossed many clan boundaries; warfare was endemic as local groups jockeyed to maintain the matrix of equality between clans that was necessary for long distance exchange to flow.

First contact with Europeans occurred in 1932. In the 1960s local government councils were established in Enga as part of an effort to install local democracy. Though free elections were held, people did not show great interest in voting. When they did, they elected respected big-men who were former leaders appointed by the Australian Administration. There was little interest in council affairs,[19] for the Enga felt that they did not depend on the government for anything other than to keep the peace. They had plenty of food in their gardens, substantial warm houses, relatively good health, and clan support for daily problems and life crises. Only a small percentage of those elected were modernizers.

Politics imposed by the Australian regime was not of great interest to the Enga as long as projects were funded by a head tax and budgets were small. This was to change dramatically around independence when the provincial government budget increased greatly, with up to 90% provided by the PNG national government.[20] The amount of wealth that could be obtained from provincial and national governments was unmatched by any other source. The government was then seen as a source of wealth for distribution, not an instrument of development. The questions at hand were not what should be developed, but in whose tribe development should take place. Emphasis was on the man and not the issues. The secret ballot was rejected as being contrary to "the Melanesian way," for how could leaders know to whom they were to return wealth if they did not know who voted for them? Either clan leaders took all the ballots and filled them in for their candidate of choice or the name of the candidate of choice for each voter was announced at the polls so that

---

[18] Weissner and Tumu, *Historical Vines*.

[19] Robert J. Gordon and J. Meggit Mervyn, *Law and Order in the New Guinea Highlands: Encounters with Enga.* (Hanover. N.H.: Published for University of Vermont by University Press of New England, 1985).

[20] B. Carrad,"The Economy," in D. Lea Carrad and K. Talyaga, (Armidale: Dept. of Geography, University of New England, 1981).

the candidate could reciprocate with favors. The goal of politics was one and the same as in the former Tee Ceremonial Exchange Cycle: to divert as much wealth as possible into one's own area.

With independence and the establishment of the provincial and national assemblies, a new problem arose – the upscaling of democracy from the clan level to the regional level. In the former system, each clan chose its own leaders and some rose to have influence at the level of the entire tribe. After independence, one candidate represented people from many clans and people soon found that there was not enough wealth to repay supporters. Jealousy mounted over gifts favoring some individuals and clans and the resulting unequal development. Ever more candidates entered the race as small local groups sought to get their man into office. Votes became commodities. By 2002, elections in Enga were out of hand; 156 candidates ran for six provincial seats. On the final day, the full ballot boxes were brought to the police station at Wabag for safe-keeping. At 5 AM a group of 30 heavily armed men stormed the police station and blew up the shipping containers of ballots with two tons of jet fuel. Despite this destruction, twice as many ballots counted in as there were registered voters.[21]

Local problems with democracy are repeated at the National level. Since political office has become a means of securing wealth for public distribution to supporters, there is little interest in political parties and their policies. Aspiring prime ministers must "buy" a majority through offering individual members large "discretionary funds." Policy making and implementation becomes secondary. Wealth diverted to the slush funds of Members of Parliament supporting the Prime Minister greatly reduces the financial capacity of the government to deliver services.[22] The National economy is largely maintained by Australian foreign aid and income from the export of gas, oil and minerals. But hand in hand with economic growth comes increased corruption and local competition for government wealth, for there are no local sources of wealth comparable to what can be obtained from the state.

The weakening of the state, together with increasing involvement in the local cash and global economies, has accentuated the greatest challenge in PNG since Independence: maintaining law and order. This is largely due to two factors. First, shortly after independence, the state lost control of law and order because they could not use the same brutal measures to repress crime and tribal fighting that had been used by the Colonial Administration. Moreover, little effort has been made to control the circulation of modern weapons, many of which are stolen or purchased from the police or defense force by business men or politicians seeking to "assist" their clans people or supporters.[23] As a result, criminals and warriors of today have the same arms as the police. Second the weak state has been unable to provide adequate education, to build infrastructure, or to stimulate economic growth and employment

---

[21] J. Frankham, *Tanim* (Aukland: Faraway Pictures, 2003).

[22] Sinclair Dinnen, Sinclair, "Law and Order in a Weak State: Crime and Politics in Papua New Guinea," *Pacific Islands Monograph Series* 17, (Honolulu: University of Hawaii Press, 2001).

[23] P. Alpers, *Gun-Running in Papua New Guinea: From arrows to assault weapons in the Southern Highlands*, Small Arms Survey, Geneva, Graduate Institute of International Studies (2005).

opportunities for youth. Less than 10% of youth make it through grade 12 and get jobs or continue on to higher education. Those who make it often end up in high positions. For the majority, education creates discontent with village life. This is in stark contrast to the past when any young man could work hard, raise pigs, develop economic exchange ties, and make a name for himself. The result is a cohort of unemployed, angry youth who feel disenfranchised from the modern world. They have little to lose and so seek name, legitimization, or wealth through crime and tribal fighting.

As a result of the collapse of law and order enforced by the police in Enga, tribes and clans have moved into the vacuum and taken violence back into their hands as a means to redress insult or injury, protect rights and property, and level inequalities created by politicians favoring their supporters. The cohort of disenfranchised youth provides warriors who contribute to their groups and make a name by redressing wrongs to their clans in this "culture of honor." Owing to unequal development, emerging social equalities and tension generated by election competition in Enga, tribal fighting has increased from but a handful of fights a year during the colonial period to 138 tribal wars between 1991 and 2000, to 202 tribal wars between 2001 and 2006.[24]

With high-powered weapons provided by wealthy businessmen and politicians to their fellow tribesmen, wars that previously led to a couple of deaths and minimal destruction have become extremely destructive. Many are killed, populations of entire valleys are displaced for months or years, houses burned, gardens destroyed, pigs slaughtered, trees razed, and schools, health centers, and churches burned to the ground. Projects of successful politicians benefiting supporters are destroyed to level the playing field. A new profession of "Rambo" or mercenary has arisen, further fueling the arms race.[25] Mercenaries band into opposing teams of fighters from several clans, and when a war is over, seek to colonize the troubles of other clans to continue to fight out their inter-team vendettas.[26]

Attempts to restore democratic practice have been made since the 2002 elections by cleaning up the electoral role and introducing "preferential voting" so that candidates must appeal to and serve a broader portion of the electorate. Moreover, party politics are playing an ever-greater role in the PNG even though they are still tied to people, not platforms.[27] No doubt these efforts will enhance democratic elections and governance. However, the shift from "one clan one vote" towards "one man one vote" is also brewing internal tensions within tribes and clans. Clans and tribes are dividing between *nenge* and *nanenge,* those who have eaten benefits from the

---

[24] Polly Wiessner, "Report on Enga tribal fighting: from pre-history to the new millennium," *Report to the Enga Provincial Government* July 2007.

[25] Polly Wiessner, "From Spears to M-16s: Testing the Imbalance of Power Hypothesis among the Enga," *Journal of Anthropological Research* 62 (2006), pp. 165–191.

[26] Weissner, "Report on Enga Tribal Fighting."

[27] Alphones Gelu, "A Democratic Audit for Papua New Guinea," in D. Kavanamur, C. Yala, and Q. Celments (eds.), *Building a Nation in Papua New Guinea: Views of the Post-Independence Generation* (Canberra: Pandanus Books, 2003), pp. 11–22.

candidate and will vote for him versus those who have not and will support another candidate. The growing force of party politics has led opponents not only to bring down the reputation and accomplishments of single competitors, but of all members of the party. Whether these fault lines will generate an increase in warfare remains to be seen in the years following the 2007 elections.

Four years ago, the Lai Valley of Enga was the home of some 60,000 Enga and was bustling with agricultural enterprise and roadside markets. Now after tribal fighting with high-powered weapons, it is an empty wasteland "cared for by the birds, rats and snakes," as the Enga say. All agree that everybody has lost and nobody has won. What is going wrong? Is this the product of poor infrastructure, policy, and governance or can it be attributed to the lack of imagination in designing post-colonial states.

At independence Papua New Guinea rejected nationalism and sought to maintain culture and identity. "The Melanesian Way" is a phrase heard frequently in the political discourse of today. The Melanesian way resists standard democratic voting procedures, the upscaling of democracy to provincial and national levels, the privatization of tribal land, obedience to law over obligations of kinship, emphasis on accumulation of wealth rather than its distribution, and national interest over local agendas. Foreign imports from western democracy as ideals have left citizens baffled. Unable to make the new rules of the game work in their society, which focuses on community above individual, people take important issues back into their hands. On the positive side, a few Enga "tribes" (*tata*) have formed foundations or associations to try to combat the spread of HIV/AIDS and to take care of the afflicted. On the negative side, many "tribes" of Enga have taken law and order back into their own hands through applications of violence. A state can take many forms and still meet basic democratic ideals. Institutions and cultural sentiments and practices differ from society to society. Accordingly, strengths must be harnessed in different ways to yield a strong state that can reclaim a monopoly on sanctioned violence to redress wrongs.

State Failure and Non-violence in Ecuador

The challenges faced by the Latin America state differ fundamentally from those faced in other geographic areas. The differences are rooted in their histories. The failure of the state has both macro and micro dimensions, though their interaction characterizes both the present and the future. This also offers reason to hope that Ecuador can find creative responses at the micro level that avoid the chaos and violence of PNG.

The isolation of Latin America during the Depression and the boom of WWII, combined with "Latin American structuralism," provided the most coherent and successful period of state led development, from the 1930s through the 1960s. Almost without exception, growth rates of GDP in the 1950s were higher than during the 1913–1950 period, and they increased further during the 1960s (Bruton 1998,

Table 1 Ecuador – GDP growth rates

ECUADOR	MACRO		
	71–80	81–90	91–97
Per Capita GDP Growth	6.3	–0.6	1.5
Per Capita GDP (US$)*	1378	1264	1392
Average Inflation	13.8	36.6	34.9
Gr. Dom. Invest. Growth	10.7	–5.1	2.3
Gov't Exp.(% of GDP)	14.2	15.6	18.5
Govt Deficit(% of GDP)	–1.4	–2	–1.3

*-end of period.
Sources: IDB, Economic and Social Progress in Latin America, 1998; World Bank, World Development Report, 1984, 1990, 1992, 1994; ECLAC, Statistical Year book for Latin America and the Caribbean, 1988, 1999.

Table 1). Success bred confidence in the developmental state; the centrifugal tendencies that we call tribalism diminished as more of the population was incorporated into the modern economy; domestically driven growth was undertaken on national terms, not primarily globally conditioned; and the creation of the institutions of the modern economy advanced.[28] Unfortunately the problem of governance was less successfully addressed, largely because of the continued high level of inequality that characterized Latin America, including Ecuador. By the 1960s and 1970s rising expectations and willingness to challenge existing political power spawned military governments across Latin America. Ecuador's was a modernizing military, with impulse given to industrialization and to an agrarian reform to modernize the rural sectors. This began the process of incorporating the indigenous.

The military government of the late 1970s was nationalist in its international policy and developmentalist in its domestic policy. It was able to attain "state participation on the order of 80 percent of all revenues generated by concessionary (oil) companies... (and) to acquire significant portions of the shares belonging to foreign firms operating in the country's Oriente oilfields."[29] The oil exploitation took place in territory that was home to many of the Amazon indigenous. There was little concern for their welfare, forcing them to become active opponents of the modernization process. Nonetheless, macro performance in the decade was excellent (Table 1).

Successful integration of marginalized populations into the state structure presumes supportive macroeconomic performance. The weakness of the macro performance of the 1980s reflected state failure and gave rise to a resurgent indigenous

[28] Indigenous identity, and tribalism, is quite complex in Ecuador. The highland Kichua are the most numerous. There are thirteen indigenous nationalities, four on the coast, eight in the Amazon, and the Kichua in both highlands and Amazon. Within these nationalities are different cultural and language groups and "other indigenous peoples that claim their own identities or are in the process of recovering their identities" (Sánchez, 2005). The groups also differ significantly on their degree of integration with the national economy and society.
[29] Osvaldo Hurtado, *Political Power in Ecuador* (Boulder, Colorado: Westview Press, 1985).

movement. The lost decade of the 1980s truncated the integration process and forced the indigenous into opposition to the state and a search for mechanisms that could preserve their gains and counter the flailings of an ever weakening central state.

The military, under civilian governments in the 1980s, were willing to use violent repression to repress the small "Alvaro Vive, Carajo!" insurgent group. But the level of violence was low and was not directed against indigenous demonstrators. This allowed space for increased mobilization of the indigenous population. They were successful in getting legal recognitions, e.g. the creation of a Directorate for bilingual education in the Ministry of Education in 1988. More importantly, they found direct action mechanisms such as road blockages that allowed them to have a tangible but non-violent effect on the entire country.

The imposition of neo-liberal Washington Consensus policies in the 1990s shifted power from the state and implicitly increased the importance of indigenous organizations. The anemic macroeconomic performance of the decade and the first years of the 21st century amplified these tendencies (Tables 1 and 2). The promise of faster growth and improved overall economic performance, which could have revalidated the state, was not realized.

Instead, micro level processes were unleashed that further weakened the state and provided sources of strength to the indigenous movement. The neo-liberal period of the 1990s was characterized by increasing inequality, a slight decrease in urban inequality offset by a much larger increase in rural inequality.[30] This generated discontent in the country-side that came to be an important problem for the state.

Table 2 Ecuador-recent macro performance

	1997	1998	1999	2000	2001	2002	2003	2004	Average
Per Capita GDP Growth(%)	2.4	0.6	–7.6	1.3	3.6	1.9	1.2	5.4	1.1
Average Inflation(%)	30.6	43.4	60.7	91.0	22.4	9.3	6.1	1.9	33.2
Govt Deficit(% of GDP)	–1.2	–4.1	–2.9	0.1	–1.1	–0.8	–0.4	–1.1	–1.4
Urban Unemployment(%)	9.3	11.5	15.1	14.1	10.4	8.6	9.8	11	11.2
Current Acct. Balance($billions)	–427	–2001	877	921	–599	–1398	–472	–166	–408.1
Capital Acct. Balance($billions)	745	1378	–1485	–950		1275	591	447	90.8
Net Resource Transfers	–316	467	–2715	–2020	–776	28	–841	–1050	–906.4
Foreign Investment($ millions)	724	870	648	720	1330	1275	1555	1160	875.9
Change in Reserves(–=Incr.) ($billions)	–251	460	492	–307	106	66	–152	–277	16

[30] Miguel Szekely and Marianne Hilgert, "The 1990s in Latin America: Another Decade of Persistent Inequality," Inter-American Development Bank, Working Paper#410 <http://idbdocs.iadb.org/wsdocs/getdocument.aspx?docnum= 788229>. Accessed June 13, 2007, p. 33, Table 2.

Sánchex presents a detailed and insightful treatment of the micro elements of the resulting "social disorder."[31]

Second, one result of the economic turmoil was an acceleration of emigration from rural indigenous areas to the U.S. and Europe. Over ten percent of the population left the country since the late 1990s, and they are the largest Latin immigrant group in Spain.[32] As a result, remittances have grown concomitantly and now constitute the second largest source of foreign exchange, exceeded only by oil. From 1994 to 2005, remittances grew from $273 million to $1.7 billion.[33] The remittances provide a source of revenue and support that is independent of Ecuadorian economic performance and is outside of the control or influence of the state.[34] They provided the indigenous an independent economic base.

As a result, the state and its mechanisms of decision-making have been paralyzed. Not only has the executive become weak and prone to removal, the Congress barely functions and the effort to create institutions that are familiar in the new globalized world has foundered.[35] The traditional political institutions arguably function worse than they had in previous decades. As the developmental state becomes less successful, the very institutions that were central to its functioning attenuate as well. This leaves a vacuum that has been filled by external institutions such as the World Bank and the IMF. It has also made the country less able to resist pressure from the United States on free trade agreements, respect for desires of US multinational enterprises, and the military aspects of the drug war.[36] In addition, the role of non-governmental Organizations (NGOs) has grown significantly. They have come to play the central role in providing social capital and responding to needs at a local level. In doing so, they further undercut the state.

This combination of failures at the macro and then micro levels is the background for the growth in the influence of the indigenous movement in Ecuador. "Tribalism," or the substitution of national identity by a sub-national identity, has become a key factor in Ecuador's political and economic life. The movement's trajectory is complex[37] though the political context simplified when the Confederación

---

31 Jeanette Sánchez, "Inequality, Ethnicity and Social Disorder: The Ecuadorian Case," Quito: Typescript (October 2005).

32 ILDIS. *Análisis de Coyuntura Económica: Una Lectura de los Principales Componentes de la Economía Ecuatoriana durante el año 2005.* Quito (2006).

33 ILDIS. *Análisis de Coyuntura Económica: Una Lectura de los Principales Componentes de la Economía Ecuatoriana durante el año 2005.* Quito (2006).

34 Bendixon and Associates, "Receptores de Remesas en Ecuador: Una Investigacion del Mercado," Quito, Typescript, (2003).

35 President Rafael Correa succeeded in gaining approval for a Constituent Assembly designed to transform the governmental institutions. This was strongly resisted by powerful political players, particularly in the Congress. This device allowed President Hugo Chavez to consolidate power in Venezuela, though President Evo Morales in Bolivia has been less successful in a similar effort.

36 Correa was elected President in large measure for his promise to revisit these issues and to reassert Ecuadorian sovereignty. His election caused consternation in international financial markets for Ecuadorian debt instruments.

37 Melina Selverston-Scher, *Ethnopolitics in Ecuador* (Miami: North-South Center Press, 2001).

de Nacionalidades Indígenas del Ecuador (CONAIE)[38] was formed in 1986 as an umbrella for existing indigenous organizations. It led the successful 1990 uprising that paralyzed the country and showed the strength of the indigenous movement. The indigenous became king makers through their political party, Pachakutic, and king breakers through demonstrations that overthrew Presidents Bucaram and Mahuad.[39] It is not by accident that the movement grew precisely at the time that the developmental state reached its limits and could no longer satisfy the aspirations that had been raised.

In contrast with PNG, the indigenous movement has engaged in vertical competition for the resources of the state. For the most part the indigenous movement has unified its tribal elements and represents them all in political affairs. In PNG the tribes compete with each other, horizontally, for the meager resources the state can provide.

One main implication of the difference is that the violence that has characterized the PNG tribes' efforts to gain resources has not appeared in Ecuador. Rather, the indigenous movement has been able to find a series of strategies to press their demands and defend their rights. These have ranged from participation in the Congress and in presidential coalitions to peaceful but forceful street demonstrations. Ecuador's indigenous movement has undertaken a successful "vertical" competition for government resources by becoming a powerful constituent based organization that can deliver politically. In the run up to the constituent assembly, they have created a variety of alliances in support of their candidates.

Equally importantly, the movement has been guided by reclaimed indigenous principles such as family, community, collective work, dialogue, consensus, and environment.[40] It is a movement that is both returning to its traditional roots and inventing and adapting them in the process of applying them to the challenges of modern society. Reclaiming and revitalizing the Kichua language has been a fundamental step, facilitated by the national recognition of bilingual education noted above. This has opened the way to notable political power and has given the indigenous key roles in major events of the last fifteen years. However, indigenous organizations have always entered with a healthy skepticism about existing structures and processes.

For example, the indigenous were central to Col. Lucio Gutierrez's electoral victory in 2002 and received three ministerial positions as a result. However, when he reneged on his platform promises and reversed his positions, they quickly left the government rather than compromise their principles. The head of CONAIE, Luis

---

[38] CONAIE, Home page: <http://conaie.org> Accessed 12 July 2005.

[39] The Bolivian indigenous, combined with the coca producers, forced the resignation of Pres. Mesa in Bolivia, on an anti-globalization agenda. They were opposed to granting greater autonomy to the two richer areas of the country, a sub-rosa issue between the coast and sierra in Ecuador. They then elected Evo Morales President and he is attempting to chart a new and different course for the country.

[40] Luis Macas, "Foreword," in Melina Selverston-Scher (ed.), *Ethnopolitics in Ecuador* (Miami: North-South Center Press, 2001), pp. xi–xx.

Macas, reaffirmed that it is a social movement, not simply a political movement. This allows them to play a role that is much broader than simply pressing the government for resources. For example, they have positions on the major issues facing the country that often go beyond the narrow indigenous interests. The positions of CONAIE are trenchant: rejection of free trade agreements, rejection of the U.S. base in Manta, which is the forward observation point for "Plan Colombia," rejection of the "neoliberal model and privatizations."[41]

While the indigenous movement has ensured it will be a force to be reckoned with, its current and future role is not clear. Under Gutierrez, the movement split between the evangelicals and the secular groups; they played little role in the overthrow of Gutierrez, which resulted from a middle class urban insurrection. In the recent Congressional and Presidential elections, they again played an important role in the victory of the "leftist" candidate, Rafael Correa. Their positions are for the most part the positions of Correa. However, their experiences in the Congress and as coalition partners of Gutierrez have forced a reconsideration of their role in the political life of the country.

Ecuador's experience in recent decades is quite familiar. The promise of the developmental state has not been realized, the state has failed to provide the growth and stability that had been seen in the 1960s and 1970s. This has been one major contributor to the revitalization of indigenous identity and the creation of an indigenous movement, complete with an organizational structure and set of policies and strategies to attain them. So tribalism has resurged and the earth looks anything but flat from the perspective of Ecuador. Most importantly this has occurred without significant increases in violence within the indigenous movement nor by the state against the indigenous, nor by the indigenous against those outside its movement. The ability of the movement to compete vertically within the existing structures has been a central factor in this outcome.

Conclusions

The concerted attack on the state since the 1980s has been successful, and the two cases examined indicate the dimensions of the state failure. In Papua New Guinea, the horizontal competition between groups for state resources inhibited its development and ability to provide critical services: economic development, opportunities for youth, and law and order. In Provinces like Enga, "tribes" have taken control in the vacuum left by the weak state. Some of their efforts have been positive, for example, organizing communities to fight HIV/AIDS and care for the afflicted; others are negative, reverting to warfare to avenge insult or injury, to restore balance, or to bring about an equal distribution of modern resources. In the absence of effective government enforcement of law and order, former tournament-like warfare has

[41] CONAIE, Home page: <http://conaie.org> Accessed 12 July 2005.

fallen into the hands of youth with modern weapons who feel they have nothing to lose becoming every more lethal and destructive of property.

In Ecuador, deteriorating macro performance provided the impulse for the formation of indigenous organizations. The micro aspects of state failure are present in Ecuador in terms of inequality and emigration. The resurgence of tribalism in its modern form of CONAIE has generally been positive in addressing these issues for the indigenous population. Rather than adopting a distorted, violent and counterproductive direction, the indigenous movement has found strong positive values to guide it, drawing upon indigenous traditions.

Despite some splits engineered by the Gutierrez government, at the macro level the indigenous movement has become an important player in Ecuadorian politics. It has joined the competition for the diminished resources available through the national government. In addition, and more importantly, the movement has been able to exert considerable influence over political and social policy. In this vertical competition for resources and of ideas, the indigenous movement has been, and continues to be, quite successful. On the negative side, this very success contributes to the weakness of the central state. In any case, the movement has been careful to avoid compromising its principles in an effort to hold onto power and has maintained a non-violent stance in pressing demands. It remains to be seen how far this new tribalism can go toward redefining the relation of the micro and macro and reconstituting a viable state in Ecuador. But the possibilities exist and they may embody a process that could lead to such a state in Ecuador in the future.

Part III
Values and Policy Choices

Terrorism, Islam and America: In Search of a Disarming Narrative

Tom Farer

If anything is uncontroversial in the envenomed setting of contemporary American political debate, it is the proposition that the struggle to protect the United States against violent Muslim extremists is in part a struggle to influence "hearts and minds." Though it has deployed the nation's resources as if terrorism were essentially a nail that could be flattened by the military hammer, the Bush Administration itself has conceded the importance of ideas, for instance, by sending one of the President's closest political advisors to the State Department in a misconceived hence futile effort to invigorate its essays in public diplomacy.[1]

Intellectual fellow travelers of the Administration, like the writers Paul Berman[2] and Jean Bethke Elshtain,[3] even as they vilify a notional "left" for seeking to "understand" Muslim rage, note the risk of multiplying recruits to terrorist networks faster than we can unravel them. In doing so they display a kind of schizophrenia. On the one hand, they call for merciless war against a phenomenon they variously characterize as Islamic fundamentalism or Islamo-Fascism and vituperatively indict as naïve or worse anyone who proposes to explain the ferocious militancy of groups like Al Qaeda in part as a reaction to U.S. policies. On the other hand, they concede that there is a hierarchy of militancy with suicide bombers and their handlers at the narrow top and below them broad layers of persons experiencing various degrees of antagonism toward the United States in particular or Western governments and peoples in general. More importantly they seem to concede that violent measures alone, at least measures of the kind they are willing to countenance, are unlikely to block movement of a dangerous number of people into the top level where the armed and intractable militants reside.

T. Farer
University of Denver
e-mail: tfarer@du.edu

[1] See Tom Farer, *Confronting Global Terrorism and American Neo-Conservatism: The Framework of a Liberal Grand Strategy* (Oxford: Oxford University Press 2008) Chapter 6.
[2] See Paul Berman, *Terror and Liberalism* (NY: Norton 2004) pb. And see critique in Tom Farer, ibid.
[3] See Jean Bethke Elshtain, *Just War Against Terrorism*, (NY: Basic Books 2003).

I.A. Karawan et al. (eds.), *Values and Violence*,

Their dilemma stems from their notional liberal values, as well as from the strategic circumstances in which the United States finds itself. To more fully appreciate that dilemma it may be useful to recall the somewhat analogous but revealingly different experience of those Latin American countries in which during the global Cold War left-wing insurgents challenged entrenched conservative regimes. The threatened regimes, composed by civilian and military elites organized in various political forms, regarded the insurgents as irreconcilable enemies of the established order, as "terrorists" who needed to be exterminated. While they too saw the insurgency as the armed tip of alienated segments of society, they were not schizophrenic.

Between so-called "moderates" and "hard-liners" in these regimes, the main policy difference was not over methods for defending the status quo, but over how wide to cast the net of repression. To hard liners the armed insurgents, those who gave them logistical support, those who sympathized with their aims if not their methods, and those who criticized the regime's methods were all of a piece, a view famously summarized in words attributed to an Argentine general: "First we will kill all the terrorists; then we will kill all who helped them; and then we will kill all who did not help us." As far as methods rather than scope of application were concerned, policy differences vanished. Interrogation by beating, water boarding and other tools of the torture repertoire followed by murder was the standard method of operation in countries otherwise as different as Argentina and Guatemala.[4] Uruguay was exceptional in that rather than killing most suspects, it imprisoned them indefinitely with or without a risible legal process in conditions carefully calibrated to break their minds and shatter their will.

Except in the special case of Nicaragua, where a peculiar conjunction of circumstances produced regime failure, state terror generally succeeded. In Argentina and Uruguay, it broke the back of insurgent movements and silenced civil society. In Chile, where conservative elites backed by the United States had first to overthrow a democratically-elected government, it preempted armed opposition not only to the coup d'etat, but to radical economic policies initiated by the triumphant elites that initially traumatized much of the working class. In Guatemala it liquidated urban enemies of the regime and reduced the rural insurgency to the status of a nuisance paradoxically beneficial to the enrichment and entrenchment of the military elite. And in El Salvador, though not without massive assistance from the United States, it thwarted a powerful coalition of insurgents with a large popular base.

Even if the broad strategic conditions of the conflict with Muslim militants were similar, political leaders like President George W. bush or intellectuals like Bethke Elshtain, who believe that we are under attack simply because the United States exemplifies a liberal democratic society, could not *coherently* endorse state terrorism

---

[4] During much of this period, I served as a member and ultimately as President of the Inter-American Commission on Human Rights of the Organization of American States and helped to author reports on the condition of human rights in Argentina and Guatemala, among others, reports based on first-hand observation.

as a means of self defense.[5] In any event, the strategic conditions are very different indeed. Latin American insurgents were hierarchically organized groups largely circumscribed by national frontiers. They did cooperate to some degree, particularly where they operated in contiguous countries; nevertheless they were vulnerable to containment and decimation within national envelopes as militant insurgents have been in countries like Egypt and Saudi Arabia. Moreover, operating in urban, middle-class countries like Argentina and Uruguay, they had no grounds for believing that their Marxist-inspired ideologies connected them to a large potentially supportive social base alienated by virtue of ideas or ethnicity from the general population. Furthermore, they themselves shared many of the cultural habits and values of the general population. Thus both their cultural conditioning and their need to cultivate support in the general population precluded recourse to mass-casualty terrorism.

What have the few successful and the larger number of aborted attacks on targets in the United States and Europe, occurring *after* the United States deprived Al Qaeda of its base in Afghanistan, drove Bin Laden into remote concealment and decimated the organization's leadership, confirmed? They have confirmed what President Bush and his colleagues had implicitly conceded when they spoke of a war that could last for generations: We are faced not with a single organized conspiracy, but rather with an organizing narrative and a geographically diffuse, constantly renewing, potentially metastasizing social network of individuals and groups and grouplets resonating to that narrative, even as they respond to local grievances and what one expert calls "biographical triggers,"[6] that is personal or vicarious experiences that accelerate estrangement to the point where they are transformed into armed militants.

For most Latin American Marxist-insurgents, their political faith was not a total identity differentiating them from the great bulk of the civilian population. On the contrary, they shared a broad cultural identity with it. Moreover their strategic theory presumed a gradual broadening of revolutionary consciousness and belief in the possibility of achieving radical political change through a combination of political and insurgent actions and a corresponding isolation of the target elites. Selective acts of violence committed against members of the military or civilian elites or against American officials seen to be supporting them were compatible with this strategy. Indiscriminate attacks on civilians designed to kill the largest number possible were not. By contrast, it appears that for a consequential number of Muslims, religious identity bars feelings of sympathetic connection with persons outside the community of faith. And for a much larger number it generates susceptibility to a narrative of victimization that justifies violence in terms of self defense.[7]

---

[5] What the President has authorized to be done in practice is another matter, see generally Tom Farer, *Confronting Global Terrorism and American Neo-Conservatism,* Chapter 3.

[6] Quoted in George Packer, "Knowing the Enemy," *The New Yorker*, December 18, 2006, p. 60, at 68.

[7] To be sure, this phenomenon is not peculiar to the Islamic community and its theological sub-sets, principally the Sunni and Shia ones. It appears also among Christian, Jewish and Hindu militants,

Again in a converse manner, for Muslim militants, strategic theory reinforces cultural estrangement. Insofar as the United States is concerned, the proximate goal of Islamic militants is to force its withdrawal as a political-military actor from the Middle East and West Asia. To that end they seek to ramp up the costs of staying. Because of the radical asymmetry between their military resources and those of the United States and because their diffuse network structure and clandestine character protects them from a crippling military riposte, to Muslims who embrace without reservation the narrative of victimization mega-terrorism is likely to continue appearing as a coherent tactic until events prove otherwise. What would seem to follow as a strategic necessity for the United States is an effort to create reservations in the minds of Muslims who might otherwise become recruits to or at least facilitators of terrorist conspiracies or at the very least will not help in exposing and eliminating incorrigible militants. We need to propose an alternative narrative that could find traction in the broad Islamic world. We need to change the frame of our relationship.

Given the transparency technology now imposes on the actions of states, a new narrative must describe credibly the world of material fact; it must constitute a plausible account of the way our audience experiences, whether directly or vicariously through textbooks, folk history, and the media, quotidian life. And in order to have a chance of overcoming the human instinct to resist challenges to a long-accepted understanding of the way the world works, it is most likely to gain traction if it can integrate elements of the toxic narrative it seeks to displace and if it appears less as an insistent reinterpretation of the past then as a projection of what is possible in the future. It must appear, in other words, as an invitation to a new and better beginning. And because of the huge disparity in power between the United States and the countries where Muslims are preponderant and the history associated with that disparity, it must have in it something of the tone of an act of contrition.

I have tried to imagine both the content of a new narrative with any prospect of acceptance and the circumstances of its public birth. Widely shared narratives are tenacious at the best of times. These are not the best of times. States in which Muslims clearly predominate are not strongly placed in the global hierarchy of influence. Tens of millions live in states (India, various countries in Western Europe) where they are deemed a problematical minority. Their third most Holy City is governed by a non-Muslim state and the country of their two holiest cities, the country of origin, is a transparent client of the West. Western troops occupy Iraq, a part of their territorial heartland, and have turned it into a bloody shambles. Political participation and economic opportunity are thin in most countries where they form the majority and many of those countries are governed by corrupt and harsh regimes supported by the West Their own intellectuals publicly admit a broad failure in the Islamic world to contribute in proportion to its population or historical successes to the intellectual and economic life of the contemporary world and to its governance. Their culture and faith have not yet proved comfortably adaptable to the

---

even among Buddhist ones notably in Sri Lanka. But for contingent historical reasons, their animus is generally directed at non-Western targets, so they are not a strategic threat to the United States and its allies.

consumption-driven ethos of a post-industrial, world. Under the circumstances, a narrative of victimization is a comfort, a salve for psychic wounds. It will not yield easily.

All the more need, then, for a dramatically staged birth of . . . well, not a counter-narrative but rather a new one assimilating much that in its predecessor corresponded to notorious facts. The American President may not be a sufficient but he or she, as the case may prove to be, is a necessary mid-wife of this birth. Birth must assume the form of an appeal directly to the various components of the Islamic World, an appeal for a new beginning. Heralded with great fanfare in the world media, I see it embedded, ideally, in an iconic setting like a special meeting of the General Assembly or the Security Council or a joint meeting of the Organization of the Islamic Conference and the European Union and the United States and held in a symbolic place like Jerusalem or an indisputably Muslim capital like Cairo or Jedda or Kuala Lumpur, and broadcast through every medium of real-time communications that can be temporarily appropriated by money or interest (in its double sense) from the BBC to Al Jazeera and available through streamed video to computers around the world and immediately thereafter transmitted globally through CDs and DVDs to allow endless collective contemplation in bazaars and villages and offices and schools of this epochal appeal for a new beginning in the relations of the great faiths and the multitude of peoples embracing one or another of them, but above all in the relationship between the United States and the peoples of Islam.

What message would do justice to the setting and venue and the carefully cultivated worldwide anticipation of a statement by the President of the Superpower that would be unlike any Presidential statement in modern history about American power and purpose?

One proposal for such a message comes from that *enfant terrible* of the American Right, Dinesh Da'Souza. In the latest of his anti-Liberal polemics, *The Cultural Left and its Responsibility for 9/11*,[8] he argues that the God-fearing majority of Americans and the traditionalist majority in the Islamic community of faith actually have a common enemy which is liberal (and, *a fortiori,* European social democratic) secularism and the sensually uninhibited, indiscriminately tolerant, socially *laissez faire* culture he associates with liberalism (rather than post-industrial capitalism). The proposed message, then, is that rather than being natural antagonists, God-fearing Americans and their Islamic counterparts are natural allies.

In her risibly unsuccessful foray into the Middle East after being dispatched by her long-time political master, President George W. Bush, to head the State Department's torpid public diplomacy program, Karen Hughes seems to have tested this message albeit in much diluted form. According to press accounts, she met with Saudi women not as a champion of women's liberation from the constraints of fundamentalist Islam, but rather as a fellow God-fearing Mom. According to the same accounts, she found her audience unreceptive.

---

[8] (New York: Doubleday 2007)

There are a number of reasons why this narrative seems unlikely to have a positive effect on Muslim hearts and minds. In the first place, its premise is that Muslims rage at the cultural intrusion of the United States rather than its political-military one. Yet it is the latter which Bin Laden and other violent Islamists have indicted, even as they disparage the West's tolerance and sensuality and gender equality. At least in theory, Islamists could limit the cultural intrusion by seizing political power and employing state power to isolate their societies as a country like North Korea has done. But they have little hope of seizing power in Egypt, Tunisia, Algeria, Oman, Pakistan, and other Islamic states in part (or so it no doubt appears to them) because local autocracies enjoy Western political, economic and military support. And there is no evidence that Western political-military intrusion is driven by D'Souza's fantasized cultural left rather than garden variety *real politicians*, men like Donald Rumsfeld and Vice-President Dick Cheney and President George W. Bush himself, men not widely identified with support for gay rights or ebullient public sexuality. Moreover, the Republican Party, the carrier of American conservatism, inclines toward free trade and, since the United States is above all a producer of services including the provocatively erotic movies and television programs against which D'Souza inveighs, a conservative government in the United States is implicitly a defender of cultural intrusion at least to the same degree as a centrist or liberal one.

A second difficulty with this alternative narrative is that rage against Islam and support for Western domination of the Islamic world is nowhere more intense than among U.S. Christian fundamentalists many of whom support Israeli domination of the entirety of old Palestine and the permanent subordination even exclusion of its largely Muslim, Arabic-speaking inhabitants. Nor is there anything anomalous in this fact. After all, as any Muslim with the slightest historical memory will appreciate, the bloodiest encounters of Islam and the West, the crusades preeminent among them, were clashes between believers on both sides.

The third difficulty is that D'Souza's claim does not pass the laugh test. We are asked to believe that fundamentalist Muslims decided to murder thousands of unknown people living oceans away because they did not like some American movies imported by their fellow Muslims. One is reminded of the possibly apocryphal story about the Duke of Wellington's response to a man who came up to him in Hyde Park one day and said "Mr. Smith, I presume." "If you believe that," the Duke is recorded as saying, "you will believe anything."

What other narratives are available for deployment in the struggle to win hearts and minds among Muslims presently committed to a narrative in which the West, led by the United States, is victimizing Islamic peoples and dominating Muslim states? Not, surely the Neo-conservative one which presents the United States as a philanthropic hegemon committed to liberating the Arabic peoples from autocratic regimes and thus opening their way to self-government and market-driven affluence. Having been and now being the supporter of autocratic regimes in most of the Middle East and in Pakistan and of a colonial regime in the occupied territories of former Mandate Palestine, the United States is not a plausible orchestrater of a democratic renaissance for the Islamic peoples. Nor, having let loose the hounds of hell in Iraq and failed from the first moments of the invasion to safeguard the country's museums and libraries, the Iraqi peoples' historical legacy, and having previously championed a sanctions regime that, with help from Saddam, dramatically increased infant mortality in Iraq, and having responded to post-invasion insurgency with the time-honored means of mass roundups and cruel and humiliating interrogations, is the United States likely to appear to Arab peoples as history's first philanthropic superpower. Moreover, even if the claimed priority of the U.S. commitment to democratic government were credible in the light of history, the narrative would still not appeal to fundamentalists like the Saudi religious establishment or Bin Laden and other traditionalists who dismiss democracy as the substitution of the transient laws of men and women for the unchanging laws of God.

As I suggested above, it appears to me that one revised narrative that might find traction among alienated Muslims is one that speaks of the recent past in a spirit of contrition and projects a new relationship centering on respect for the doctrine of mutual non-intervention, in other words a U.S. disclaimer of intention to continue employing its strategic power for the purpose of shaping the Arab and the wider West Asian world to its geo-strategic or ideological ends. The contrite historical accounting would be easy to write but hard for any President to adopt without crippling political damage, since it would claw cruelly right across the face of the country's historic self-conception as a blessed city on the Hill of righteousness. The President would have to say frankly that since the middle of the twentieth century, when the United States replaced Britain and France as the dominating Western presence in the Middle East heartland of Islam, American policy, like that of all great powers in history, has been guided by no principle more exalted than perceived national interest as defined by the politics of a pluralist society and a democratic system of government. To advance its several ends, it has helped underwrite and protect from effective international sanctions Israel's colonization of the Occupied Territories after the 1967 War, organized the overthrow of a democratically elected government in Iran (1953), assisted Iraq after it launched a naked war of aggression against Iran following the fall of the Shah, smashed up Iraq after it launched a naked war of aggression against Kuwait, left the Shia inhabitants of southern Iraq to die at the hands of Saddam after encouraging revolt, and cooperated with autocratic client regimes when they served American purposes. None of this will be astonishing news to the peoples of the region. The astonishing thing will be the unprecedented confession and contrite tone of a great power.

Obviously confession alone will not constitute a new narrative able to compete with the *jihadist* one. The confession would only be the prelude to defining a new American policy toward the Middle East, a policy of strategic withdrawal and continued commercial and cultural presence on terms negotiated with Arab governments treated as equals and with Washington adopting a posture of indifference to the etiologies, ideologies and domestic policies of those governments. Hence the condition for launching the narrative is a decision that the policies it envisions serve American interests and values. Whether it is conceivable that any hegemonic power, much less one so self-imagined and politically organized as the United States, *could* actually adopt this self-restraining posture in any part of the world where internal developments will surely engage its interests and its values, well that is another matter.

Surely this is a case where the imaginable is not conceivable. Nor am I persuaded that a policy of determined non-involvement in the political-military affairs of the Middle East – a policy that would find at least rhetorical support in the left and Neanderthal Right fringes of American politics – would serve either the American interest or the human one. I believe that an affective new narrative can be developed in line with less dramatic but still profound change in American grand strategy toward the area. Its main features would probably have to include the following:

- A commitment to promoting internationally recognized human rights through its support for economic development and indigenous human rights and development organizations and providing asylum to persons victimized for asserting their human rights or defending the rights of others.
- A commitment to provide bi-lateral economic assistance and political and intelligence support only to democratic governments that respect basic human rights.
- A commitment to become involved militarily in the area only within the framework of the United Nations Charter or in response to massive Crimes Against Humanity.
- A commitment to maintain ordinary diplomatic and commercial relationships with governments and not to manipulate private flows of goods, services and capital between the United States and those countries, regardless of their ideologies, as long as they do not commit grave violations of human rights.
- A commitment to the establishment of a Palestinian State in all of the territories occupied by Israel during the 1967 war except as borders may be marginally revised through uncoerced agreement of the Israelis and Palestinians.[9]

Those elements would constitute a good deal less than disengagement from the Middle East. But they would be an extraordinary departure from American policy over the past sixty years and thus give life to a new narrative about America in the Middle East and hence about its relations with the wider Islamic community of faith.

---

[9] For a discussion of transitional scenarios and security issues, see my *Confronting Global Terrorism and American Neo-Conservatism: The Framework of a Liberal Grand Strategy* (Oxford: Oxford University Press 2008) Chapter 5.

The Importance of Values in the Fight Against Terrorism

Amos N. Guiora

Introduction

The Democratic Party's success in the 2006 Congressional campaign will be much interpreted and oft discussed. However, one critical fact cannot be forgotten: five years post 9/11, American forces are fighting and dying in Iraq, Afghanistan is far from quelled (as marked by recent Taliban victories) and the next terrorism act is a question of when, not if.

The Iraq Study Groups' report takes the President to task for a number of critical issues related to the war in Iraq. One of the most important recommendations – albeit troubling in its very essence – is that the President speak the truth to the American public.

In the spirit of that troubling recommendation, this article is written. Government 101 requires truth-telling, especially in the information age. Perhaps in the days of radio and newspapers, it was easier for government to deceive and feint the public. Today, with bloggers, instant messaging by phone or computer, web cameras and cell phones with cameras, government is under greater – *and more immediate* – scrutiny than ever before. The information age combined with extraordinary technological breakthroughs directly impact how governments develop, implement and articulate policy. A Tonkin Gulf type resolution[1] predicated on a President (Johnson) and Secretary of Defense (McNamara) deliberately misleading Congress[2] would be, given modern means of personal communication (not to speak of sophisticated satellites available to the media), nearly impossible to duplicate.

While some observers might suggest that the Congressional resolution[3] supporting President Bush's decision to invade Iraq is tantamount to a modern day Tonkin Gulf resolution, I would suggest it reflects a fundamental lack of oversight and

A.N. Guiora
University of Utah
e-mail: guioraa@law.utah.edu

[1] http://www.isop.ucla.edu/eas/documents/tonkin.htm (last visited February 4, 2007).

[2] http://www.bartleby.com/65/to/TonkinGu.html (last visited February 4, 2007).

[3] http://archives.cnn.com/2002/ALLPOLITICS/10/11/iraq.us/ (last visited February 4, 2007).

I.A. Karawan et al. (eds.), *Values and Violence*,

inquiry. Subsequent back-tracking reflects a disturbing lack of curiosity by some of those who voted in favor of the resolution (Senators Clinton and Kerry are two prominent examples).

How is the above introduction relevant to the issue at hand, "The Importance of Values in Fighting Terrorism?" It is my basic premise that the two most important issues facing our generation – Iraq and terrorism – require not only the public's undivided attention but also government veracity. The concept of "values" is predicated on an educated, moral public demanding that its elected leaders recognize not only the "limit of power" but the obligation to come forth with the truth. However, as the executive branch inherently and invariably seeks greater, unfettered power for itself, it is the role of the Courts, Congress and media to assume active roles of review, oversight and skeptic. The U.S. Constitution clearly articulates the principle of the separation of powers and checks and balances. The Founding Fathers' profound concern of an unchecked executive was based on their historical experience with a British monarchy whose power was unlimited.

In analyzing the two issues – Iraq and terrorism – it is important to note that though the issues are not directly related, there are threads that connect them. While this chapter seeks to engage in a discussion regarding how executives of five different nations (US, Israel, Russia, India and Spain) balance civil rights and national security rights, it is important to examine the war in Iraq in the context of values and executive power.

Understanding terrorism and counter-terrorism requires that we address two critical issues: how to balance the rights of the individual with the equally legitimate national security right of the state and how to resolve complex legal, moral and policy dilemma facing the public and decision makers alike.

To most effectively balance these two equally legitimate competing interests and address the legal, moral and policy dilemma in the age of what the Israel Supreme Court refers to as "armed conflict short of war" (a term initially suggested by the Israel Defense Forces Judge Advocate General Corps) it is proposed that we must establish a new paradigm. The criminal law and international law paradigms are equally inapplicable to this new conflict which has replaced war as traditionally understood. To bridge the two existing paradigms, I have coined the phrase "the hybrid paradigm" defined as being not quite a criminal law paradigm or a prisoner of war ("POW") paradigm, but rather a true "hybrid" of the two.[4]

---

[4] Specifically, the hybrid paradigm is "a true mix of both the criminal law and prisoner of war paradigms without [either] full Constitutional or criminal procedure rights." *See* Amos N. Guiora, *Quirin to Hamdan: Creating a Hybrid Paradigm for the Detention of Terrorists*, 19 Fla. J. Int'l L. 2 (forthcoming 2007); and Amos N. Guiora, Where *are Terrorists to be Tried – A Comparative Analysis of Rights Granted to Suspected Terrorists*, — CATHOLIC UNIV. L. R. (forthcoming 2007). However, the establishment of procedures does not imply that the full panoply of domestic criminal law rights, such as those articulated in *Arizona v Miranda*, be granted to the detainees in the trial process. The hybrid paradigm proposes a regime establishing the parameters of criminal law rights to be granted the detainees. The hybrid paradigm is comprised of seven policy recommendations that balance between the rights of the detainee and the equally legitimate rights of the state.

However, before engaging in a discussion regarding terrorism it is important to address Iraq. As previously noted though the two issues are not *naturally* related, they have been *artificially* linked by President Bush's actions. A consequence of the Bush Administration's false premise that Sadaam Hussein was linked to al-Qaeda and 9/11 is that an article discussing global counter-terrorism addresses Iraq. Regardless of any ties Iraq may (better stated, may not) have had to terrorism in the past, today it serves as a breeding ground for terrorists. As such, today's discussion of terrorism and counterterrorism must also address Iraq.

Iraq

While Iraq and terrorism are joined at the hip, they are not one and the same. A successful Iraq policy does not guarantee effective counter-terrorism. Similarly, preventing a terror attack in New York does not promise success in Mosul. The lumping of the two *related but distinctly separate issues,* may be politically convenient, but is also disingenuous. The two great issues of the day – and of our children's day – require sober analysis, deep reflection and are uniquely inappropriate for the "twenty second sound bite" that defines much of our contemporary public debate. The time for bluster – "bring 'em on" is but the most egregious example of rhetorical excess – is long gone.

While pundits, commentators, bloggers, spin masters and politicians from both sides of the aisle are discussing these issues, America's servicemen and women are in "harms way." It is for them that this article is written. They do not have time for us to "spin." They demand responsible decisions by our nation's leaders predicated on viable, implementable and responsible foreign policy. This is extraordinarily difficult when numerous Presidential hopefuls are positioning themselves and President Bush's approval rating is 28%.[5] Nevertheless, we are obligated to debate these issues, particularly when the President orders deployment of additional forces (the so-called "surge") with broad hints that the measure is not "one time."

Foreign policy must be viewed as a continuum where previous decisions and events impact on future courses of action; it is impossible to start anew. Rather, policy makers must play the hand they have been dealt. Is it a great hand? No. Is it a terrible hand? No. It is the best hand available as it is the *only* hand.

Going forward, decision makers *must* provide a coherent, concise answer to the following question: why are we in Iraq? Over the past three years, the Administration has suggested a variety of reasons for our presence in Iraq, ranging from weapons of mass destruction to Vice President Cheney's insistence of a connection between 9/11 and Iraq to the President's "bring democracy to Iraq." Now the Democratic leadership of the Congress is morally and politically obligated to ensure that the White House articulates *the* mission.

---

[5] http://www.cbsnews.com/stories/2007/01/22/opinion/polls/main2384943.shtml (last visited February 5, 2007).

Hand in hand with mission articulation is the absolute requirement to define the nature of the conflict. Who are the parties involved? What are their interests? What is the basis for mind boggling hatred between Shia's and Sunnis? The February 2, 2007 suicide bombing aimed at Shi'ites that killed 135 Iraqis is but the latest example. Are the Kurds a separate people? Is Iraq a monolithic nation or a 21st century Yugoslavia: a patchwork of different ethnic groups held together under a strong ruler (Tito, Sadaam Hussein) only to be partitioned after the relevant dictator has exited the scene? Is this an insurgency conducted by Iraqi's or by foreigners with their own agenda?

Only after we have answered the above, is it possible to address the following two questions: how many troops do we *really* need in Iraq and when can we begin returning them home.

Today there are three viable options as to what our mission is in Iraq: (1) assisting the Iraqi people (or at least those who are interested) to restore normalcy and to facilitate the development of civil society; (2) driving the non-Iraqi insurgents out; (3) a domino theory suggesting that withdrawal from Iraq signals American weakness to Iran and emboldens the Bin-Laden's of the world.

While those of age shudder when hearing the domino theory which harkens them back to the Vietnam War, the truth is that looming over Iraq, US, Europe and the Middle East is a significant Iranian threat. Policy makers must understand that the mission in Iraq has significant geo-political ramifications that extend beyond Iraqi borders. While this does not suggest that the domino theory is an absolute certainty, it does imply that realistic threat assessment is the critical byword. While the Iranian threat must be taken seriously and an America-less Iraq may well be a tempting target for the expansive minded mullahs, the domino theory also need not be accepted blindly. It must be carefully considered.

With respect to the two additional missions, the intensity of the insurgency clearly caught America's political and military leaders by absolute and total surprise. That reflects a break-down in intelligence gathering and analysis, failure to appreciate enmity to foreign presence and disconcerting naiveté regarding the international perception of the United States. Working with the Iraqi government, either in facilitating their ability to rebuild the nation or in ridding Iraq of foreign insurgents also requires significant time and resources commitment. It is tragically clear that we are light years away from accomplishing either.

Whichever of the three missions is adopted, we must continue the extraordinarily difficult process of recruiting and training Iraqi security forces. Re-building the Iraqi army has proven difficult because insurgents regularly attack and kill potential recruits. Nevertheless, the U.S. literally has no choice for the decision to disband the Iraqi army was an American one; therefore the responsibility to rebuild it also lies with the U.S. Once an Iraqi army is re-formed, the new recruits must be trained not only for traditional combat but for the far more difficult military assignment of counter-terrorism or counter insurgency. For this too, the U.S. bears responsibility as insurgency came to Iraq only after America entered the country. Counter-insurgency training is complicated and requires significant resources; however, there is no choice. Without the training and resources the Iraq of tomorrow will continue to be the zone of combat it is today.

Criteria for determining when the newly formed and properly trained Iraqi army has reached operational capability thus enabling U.S. withdrawal must be established. The criteria must be determined by both Iraqi and U.S. leadership with an eye towards realism, rather than hope, and with a clear means for measuring progress.

To accomplish the above requires time, patience and realism. It requires truth telling and courage on the part of senior military officials and an Administration willing to listen to honest reporting. Both have been sorely lacking these past six years. The Administration is obligated to consult with senior military leadership regarding the number of forces required. In consulting with the leadership, the Administration must encourage "truth-telling" on the part of the Joint Chief of Staffs. The reported malleability of General Richard Meyers, the "desire to please" mentality that seems to best define General Tommy Franks and the stifling of the honest reporting of General Shinseki by Secretary of Defense Rumsfeld ill-serves the men and women in uniform. As these lines are written, it is too early to comment on the tone and substance of Secretary of Defense Gates and Lieutenant General David Petraeus relationship.

What does all this mean? It requires articulating a mission, understanding societal realities, determining appropriate troop levels and developing criteria enabling U.S. withdrawal from Iraq. Announcing a pre-determined departure date today is irresponsible and impractical. Spinning responses to these issues does a disservice to those in uniform. Realistic analysis predicated on truth telling to the public, encouraged by active Congressional oversight and a skeptical and knowledgeable press corps, will enable the U.S. to *begin* the process of *responsibly* addressing the Iraqi question which will hopefully contribute to eliminating a current breeding ground for terrorism.

Counterterrorism

In developing a viable counterterrorism policy, the following fundamental must be internalized: the so-called "war on terrorism" cannot be "won." Terrorism can perhaps be marginalized and terrorists killed, but the reality is that civil democratic society must appreciate that terror threats are not episodic. They comprise the daily grind of contemporary life.

Accordingly, counter-terrorism policy must be based on long-term, geo-political considerations. This means developing and implementing operational counter-terrorism measures while simultaneously providing economic assistance and educational programs to the very areas of the world where potential terrorists are so easily recruited. Be it the modern day Marshall Plan or the contemporary version of Radio Free Europe, the requirement to reach out to the "swayables" – those millions of individuals who have yet to decide whether they and their children will follow the path of Osama Bin Laden or the path of economic development – is mandatory.

Operational counter-terrorism measures, running the gamut from detaining suspected terrorists to conducting more sophisticated checks at the nation's airports to ordering the targeted killing of a senior al-Qaeda operative must meet a stringent three part test before implementation: they must be subservient to the rule of law, they must be moral and they must meet a definition of effective.

Herein lie three of the major dilemmas facing policy and decision makers alike: what laws are to apply to operational counter-terrorism, what is morality in armed conflict and how is "effective" to be defined. In determining what laws are applicable, the status of terrorists must be articulated: are they common criminals entitled to full constitutional and criminal law protections and privileges, are they prisoners of war entitled to full Geneva Convention protections or are they a "hybrid" of the two, requiring the development of laws and procedures specific to terrorism?

A belief in the philosophical underpinnings of civil, democratic society implies the following: we can not kill everybody we would like to kill; we can not arrest everybody we would like to arrest. Decision makers must root their policies on Constitutional principles while respecting customary international law and signed conventions.

Similarly, the word "effective" escapes simple definition. Does a successful attack tomorrow morning on Salt Lake City International airport suggest "ineffective" policy? Similarly, does the fact that a successful attack has not occurred on American soil since 9/11 suggest an "effective" policy? Are long lines at the nation's airports an indication of thorough scrutiny and sophisticated checking or reflective of largely untrained people, overwhelmed with their mission?

Counterterrorism strategy also implies articulating the limits of personal freedom. If the Constitution, to quote Justice Jackson "is not a suicide pact," where is the line to be drawn and who is to draw the line? Is the warrantless wire-tapping of phone conversations in the name of national security acceptable and lawful? Are Americans' to feel comfortable in granting the President the power to classify a legal alien an "enemy combatant" and thereby deny *habeas* rights? How are internal threats to be balanced given America's abhorrence of profiling? How is separation of powers and active checks and balances to be guaranteed when the public feels threatened and under attack? How are the Courts and Congress expected to engage in active judicial review and strong oversight when the President emphatically argues for executive power in the face of the unseen enemy (internal and external)?

In answering these and other questions we must at all times recall the fundamental rule of counter-terrorism: terrorists have rights. Think of them what we may; find them repulsive and abhorrent, but until proven otherwise, an individual suspected of involvement in terrorism is no more than that – he or she is only a suspect. Forget that fundamental principle and America's stake to be the "beacon on the hill" will be significantly impacted.

In addressing the absolute supremacy of the rule of law while defining effectiveness, the critical buzzword is balancing. A civil, democratic society *must* be able to balance the legitimate rights of the individual with the equally legitimate national security considerations of the state. Without a balance between these two tensions, democratic societies lose the very ethos for which they fight. As Benjamin Franklin once said, "those who would give up essential liberty, to purchase a little temporary safety, deserve neither liberty nor safety."[6] Indeed, it is imperative for democracies to avoid infringing on political freedoms and civil liberties. Yet, the ultimate responsibility of government is to protect its citizenry. Given that terrorism cannot be defeated, the means and methods civil democratic society implements to marginalize the threat must be predicated on the balancing requirement.

Articulating the limits of power is an enormously painful and difficult challenge for decision makers. However, as counter-terrorism explicitly requires appreciating the limits of power, counter-terrorism policy must reflect that reality. How does that translate into policy that meets constitutional muster?

It means that decision makers look the public in the eye and tell them the following truths:

> *There will be good days and bad days in our effort to combat terrorism. In order to ensure the nation's collective security, the government may need to restrict your freedoms in response to particular threats. The decision to restrict your freedom of movement and imposition on liberty will be premised on reliable and corroborated intelligence information that will not be made available to the public. However, that information will be made available in full prior to implementation of particular, specific plans to the relevant Congressional committees and to an independent judiciary that will exercise checks and balances precisely as our Founding Fathers intended. The Constitution is a living, breathing document that enables the government to protect the people, while simultaneously protecting the people from the government. We will take the fight to terrorists while upholding the rule of law. That is our promise.*

Whether the independent judiciary will be the Supreme Court or an amended FISA court is an issue that must be addressed by academics, jurists, decision makers and the public. What is important is that the government's decision to impose on individual liberties must be subject to procedure, process and strict scrutiny in real time. The somnolent Congress and largely acquiescent Supreme Court of the past five years have not served America well.

Global Terrorism

Understanding, integrating and implementing policy premised on the rule of law while addressing balancing and effectiveness requires an interdisciplinary approach. To understand the practical application of this proposal, counter-terrorism must be understood to be comprised of four legs: law, policy, operational counter-terrorism and intelligence gathering.

In discussing the four legs, decision makers are faced with the challenge of implementing lawful, operational counter-terrorism. In doing so, decisions range from when a suspected terrorist may be arrested to when killing a suspected terrorist is lawful, self-defense. The fourth leg is perhaps the most difficult as, ultimately, counter-terrorism can be succinctly summarized as follows: *whether or not decision*

---

[6] Benjamin Franklin, Pennsylvania Assembly: Reply to the Governor, Nov. 11, 1755, in Leonard W. Labaree (ed.), *The Papers of Benjamin Franklin*, 6 (1963), p. 242.

makers know when the bad guys are going to do what it is believed they are going to do and if it possible to identify who the bad guys are.

Only by addressing all four distinct – yet joined – legs can counter-terrorism be understood. However, that is but step one in developing an understanding for and sensitivity to counter-terrorism. There is an absolute requirement to understand cultures. Without understanding why somebody wants to be terrorist, leaders will be hard-pressed to identify potential, future terrorists and therefore will be grasping at straws when attempting to neutralize terrorists. Needless to say, cultural sensitivity is but one side of the "cultural" coin; the flip side is the overwhelming requirement to develop linguistic sensitivity.

It is an open secret that one of the failures of pre 9/11 America was a disconcerting absence of foreign language competence, particularly Arabic and Farsi. This issue *must* be addressed. Without the ability to understand the language of the terrorists, or their supporters, countering their ideology, mission and goals will be extraordinarily difficult.

It is critical that efforts – academic, policy, economic, cultural – be made to understand what motivates terrorists. This requires developing economic development models relevant to regions of the world such as South Asia. Economic modeling must be combined with additional academic disciplines including anthropology, psychology and religious studies. Only then can civil, democratic society take the initial step of *beginning* to understand terrorism.

The problem is, as society takes that initial step, terrorists are at least one-step ahead because they have a clear mission predicated on a deeply rooted cause. Terrorist leaders have been able to articulate to themselves and their followers the causes' goals and means to achieve them. The relevant question for policy makers is how best to go forward.

In adopting the interdisciplinary approach discussed above it is incumbent that decision makers understand that policy is subservient both to the rule of law and morality in armed conflict. Otherwise, civil democratic society will lose its moral superiority which if lost, will prevent leaders and the public alike from looking themselves in the moral compass mirror.

Global counterterrorism means the following: that nations learn from each other because no one country has the answer; no one country knows exactly what needs to be done. By adapting other paradigms and models it is possible to begin developing and implementing a counter-terrorism policy. What this requires is globalization of counter-terrorism in response to the internationalization of terrorism. By undertaking a comparative analysis of how societies respond to terrorism it is possible to take the good and the bad from others, because otherwise, we will never learn.

United States

Let us begin this journey by examining the Bush Administration's response in the immediate aftermath of 9/11. The discussion will be facilitated by an examination of the Administration's initial treatment of aliens which can best be summarized by the timeless line from "Casablanca" – "round up the usual suspects."

Any alien who even looked like a potential terrorist – whatever that expression means – was rounded up, held in secret detention, and deprived of the right to consult an attorney and to contact family members. That is not how to respond to a significant act of terrorism, no matter how significant. I define that as a panic response.

The Supreme Court addressed the unconstitutionality of "guilt by association" in a number of cases, including *Korematsu v United States*,[7] *NAACP v. Claiborne Hardware Co*[8] and *Yick Wo v. Hopkins*.[9] Nevertheless, in the aftermath of 9/11 the Bush Administration implemented just such a policy. The detention of thousands of immigrants, the decision to interview thousands of others is but a modern-day "round up the usual suspects." 9/11 is undeniably a major terror attack designed and implemented by non-U.S. citizens. Nevertheless, the Administration was and is unable to demonstrate that *all* immigrants were involved in, much less supported, that act of terrorism.

Effective counter-terrorism strategy must be based on sophisticated risk assessment; an equal risk approach (viewing all threats equally) is both operationally unfeasible and ineffective.[10] The Bush administration's policy post 9/11, as reflected in the detention of immigrant policy, is implemented at the nation's airports where all travelers are subjected to the same check with little if any differentiation, just as all immigrants are treated with little, if any, differentiation. Just as that policy does not better protect America, detention predicated on belonging to a particular group rather than on an individualized basis does not best serve the public. In the context of the question that this article addresses, the alien policy adopted by the Administration in the aftermath of 9/11 reflects an improper value balance between national security and individual rights. Furthermore, as clearly articulated by the Supreme Court in previous cases, the policy is unconstitutional.

One of the problems of a panic mode response is a loss of proportion and sense of balance. A government's failure to balance the rights of the State with the rights of the individual suggests the slippery slope from which it is extremely difficult to get off. This is the primary issue American policy and decision makers' face in developing and implementing counter-terrorism policy.

---

[7] 323 U.S. 214 (1944).

[8] 458 U.S. 886 (1982).

[9] 118 U.S. 356 (1886).

[10] Amos Guiora, Airport Security: Time for a New Model at the American Enterprise Institute for Public Policy Research (Feb. 15, 2006), *available at http://www.aei.org/events/eventID.1260,filter.all/event_detail.asp*.

Israel

For better or for worse, Israel is the world's model for counterterrorism policy. In analyzing Israel's counterterrorism policy it is helpful to address a particular policy whose implementation I was intrinsically involved with. In the aftermath of a terrorist attack, the General Security Services would recommend to the IDF Area Military Commander to demolish the suspected terrorist's home in accordance with Article 119 of the Defense Emergency Regulation (1945). The policy rationale argued by the State before the High Court of Justice was deterrence – demolishing the house would deter other individuals in the terrorists' community from committing similar acts. The High Court of Justice, in a seminal case, ordered the IDF to establish a process whereby the affected family would be guaranteed the following rights: notice of the commanders' intent to demolish the family home, the right to petition the commander and if the commander denied the petition, the family could petition the Court. Upon the filing of a petition, the Court would issue a restraining order until a hearing would be convened. At the hearing the State would have to convince the Court that the measure was neither arbitrary nor punitive, but rather premised on deterrence.[11] Therefore, the issue before us is not the legality of the policy; that has been decided by the High Court of Justice.[12] Rather, our focus must be on the policy's effectiveness.

For years the State argued that the deterrence theory was effective. While the act may have violated international law principles of collective punishment, the legal paradigm articulated by the State was premised on self defense. Problematic? According to many international jurists, yes. Effective? Recently, a high level IDF commission recommended to the Minister of Defense that the policy be frozen. The commission concluded that the policy did not deter individuals in the terrorists' community from committing acts of terrorism and therefore did not meet its stated purpose. Subsequently, Prime Minister Sharon accepted the recommendation, though he indicated that the policy could be reactivated if there was an extreme change in circumstances.[13]

Many of the above questions are open-ended and reflect the enormous uncertainty involved in developing a counterterrorism strategy in the face of terror attacks. The balancing required, while difficult to implement, must reflect both a mature legal analysis and an equally sober, realistic policy analysis. While some would argue

[11] *See, e.g.,* Association for Civil Rights in Israel v. Central District Commander, HCJ 358/88.

[12] Over the years, Israeli, Palestinian and international human rights organizations have argued that the policy is illegal. The criticism has focused on the collective punishment argument; on issues related to actions the occupier may take and Geneva Convention violations. *See, e.g.,* B'Tselem Information Sheet, Nov. 2004, *available at* http://www.btselem.org/download/200411_Punitive_House_Demolitions_Eng.pdf and Palestinian Centre for Human Rights, Sweeping Reports, Reports on Destruction of Palestinian Land and Property by Israeli Forces in the Gaza Strip, *available at* http://www.pchrgaza.org/files/Reports/English/pdf_sweeping/sweepingr_reports.htm.

[13] Greg Myre, "Israel Halts Decades-Old Practice of Demolishing Militants' Homes," *New York Times*, Feb. 18, 2005, at A1.

"better late than never," the ultimate question in light of the commissions findings, is whether this policy and the legal arguments designed to explain it, failed?

The cost paid by Palestinian families, whose homes were demolished in response to the actions of a family member, is unquestioned. The development of an effective, balanced counter-terrorism strategy that does not collectively punish, but deters others while minimizing "blow back," is the true test facing policy and decision makers who must be sensitive to active judicial review during armed conflict.[14]

Over the years, while the High Court upheld commanders' decisions to demolish the family homes of suspected terrorists, human rights organizations strenuously argued that the policy was a collective punishment and therefore, imbalanced. It is indisputable that family members "paid a price" for the terrorist activities of a son, father or brother. If, as according to the internal IDF commission, the house demolitions did not deter others then the "price paid" would ultimately represent imbalance and a failed policy.

What is the good news and what is the bad news? The good news is that governments must constantly strive to examine their policy; otherwise action will be routine driven rather than effectiveness determined. There is nothing more dangerous than routine. That is the good news. The bad news is that there are hundreds of Palestinians whose homes were blown-up because of a now discounted theory.

Russia

In analyzing how the Russian government balances legitimate national security considerations with the rights of the individual, it is important to understand that the executive is clearly the dominant branch in what is referred to as a "managed democracy." The lack of life time appointments for high judges[15] suggests that the judiciary is beholden to the executive. Accordingly, Russian judicial review in armed conflict will obviously be weaker than the American model and, without doubt, the Israeli model is significantly stronger. In the context of understanding how the executive balances, it is apparent that the Russian executive has greater "freedom" than either the American or Israeli executive branches.

The Russian policy in Chechnya is characterized as aggressive operational counter-terrorism. This is a problematic as it is questionable whether or not the Russians are actually defeating Chechen terrorism. Secondly, even if the Russians are making some gains, it is important to ask at what cost. Is it worth the cost of committing severe human rights abuses? Are the Russians going to convince the Chechen population to put down their guns and pick-up the tools of peace? The jury is clearly still out.

---

[14] Amos N. Guiora and Erin M. Page, *The Unholy Trinity: Intelligence, Interrogation and Torture*, 37 Case W. Res. J. Int'l L. 427 (2006).

[15] Dana Dallas Atchison, *Notes on Constitutionalism for a 21st-Century Russian President*, 6 Cardozo J. Int'l & Comp. L. 239, 282 (citing Article 121 of the Constitution).

The terrorist attack on the Beslan schoolhouse in 2004 was the worst attack in modern Russian history and lead to increasing erosion of fundamental rights.[16] Even as the conflict in Chechnya entered its sixth year, the Russian government insisted that "it was successfully restoring peace in the republic."[17] However, allegations surfaced that Russian troops "committed hundreds of enforced disappearances and extrajudicial executions, and tortured detainees on a large scale."[18] Despite the wide scale abuses, only twenty-two Russian servicemen are serving "active prison terms for crimes committed against civilians" since the beginning of the Chechen war in 1999.[19]

The balance between national security and individual rights is clearly not the emphasis. Only a few days after the Beslan massacre, President Putin announced new political measures designed to "give the president de facto power to appoint governors, even more sway over the parliament, or State Duma, and increase the executive's influence over the judiciary."[20] Many Russians disagreed with the new measures, but the checks and balances system had already eroded to the point that no branch or institution could stop the implementation of the measures.[21]

The willingness of President Putin to forego "balancing" does not appear to have contributed to the success of the Russian campaign in Chechnya. Rather, the Chechen conflict continues and human rights violations still occur. The managed democracy principle, while perhaps "convenient" from the perspective of President Putin, enables the Russian executive to ignore international norms regarding individual rights. However, ignoring these norms does not seem to have substantively benefited Russia's counterterrorism efforts.

Measuring effectiveness in the context of balancing national security considerations and the rights of the individual also requires sensitivity to international law and the court of international opinion. An analysis of the Russian government's conduct in Chechnya suggests a willful disregard of the values of the larger international community. The Bush administration, as well as other nations, was very critical of the conduct of Russian forces in Chechnya prior to 2001.[22] Nevertheless, President Putin is clearly determined to pursue the policy that has been implemented in the past few years; a policy characterized by imbalance.

An objective assessment would suggest that the policy that President Putin implemented has not contributed to the defeat of Chechen terrorism. The "blow-back"

---

[16] Human Rights Watch, World Report 2005, p. 406.

[17] Human Rights Watch, World Report 2005, p. 409.

[18] Human Rights Watch, World Report 2005, p. 409.

[19] Human Rights Watch, World Report 2005, p. 409.

[20] Open Letter to the UN Counter-Terrorism Committee, Human Rights Watch, Jan. 25, 2005, http://hrw.org/english/docs/2005/01/25/uzbeki10074_txt.htm, (last visited March 26, 2006).

[21] Open Letter to the UN Counter-Terrorism Committee, Human Rights Watch, Jan. 25, 2005, http://hrw.org/english/docs/2005/01/25/uzbeki10074_txt.htm, (last visited March 26, 2006).

[22] *In the Name of Counter-Terrorism: Human Rights Abuses Worldwide*, Human Rights Watch Briefing Paper for the 59th Session of the U.N. Commission on Human Rights, March 25, 2003, p. 18.

is undeniable, the desire of the Chechens to continue their struggle is well documented and the resulting human rights abuse by both parties is all but inevitable. Weak domestic institutions, in clear contrast to the Israeli model of active judicial review in armed conflict, clearly contribute to the present state of affairs. Even an American model of circumspect judicial review could conceivably contribute to a more balanced and therefore more effective Russian counter-terrorism strategy.

Spain

In the aftermath of the March 11, 2004 Madrid train bombings, the Spanish government decided to do the following: one, to withdraw Spanish forces from Iraq and two, to not respond to the act of terrorism. Spanish policy, if compared to American, Israeli and Russian policy can be best defined as acquiescing to terrorism rather than conducting significant counterterrorism operations.

Has this policy been effective? In the past two-and-a-half years, no acts of terrorism have been committed in Spain or against Spanish targets, other than by ETA. Does that mean that Spain will not be a target of counter-terrorism down the road? Easy question, difficult answer.

The only measure the Spanish government has implemented is incommunicado detention whereby detainees can be held for an extended period of time without the right to counsel of their choice or to contact family members.

Incommunicado detention reflects a policy of firmness verging on denial of basic human rights. In denying a detainee basic rights, such as informing family members about the detention, the Spanish government is taking measures reflective of an imbalance of values. When the Israel Defense Forces invaded the West Bank (Operation "Ebb and Flow"),[23] the relevant military order decreed that detainees must be brought to a judge within eight days of their detention. Though the military commander reached the conclusion that operational circumstances dictated extending the time period to 18 days, the High Court of Justice held that logistic considerations are irrelevant and that basic rights may not be violated *even* during conflict.[24] Conversely, the Presidential Order creating the military commissions in Guantanamo Bay and the Department of Defense instructions subsequently promulgated were heavily criticized since detainees were denied the right to be brought before a judge.[25]

The Spanish policy of implementation of incommunicado detention, though legislatively enacted, raises concern from the perspective of a detainee's basic rights. Furthermore, an analysis of incommunicado detention from a policy perspective suggests that the benefits are unclear. What has the policy done? Largely, what

---

[23] Following the Passover massacre (March, 2001), thousands of Palestinians were detained.

[24] HCJ 3239/02 Marab v. IDF Commander in the West Bank (2002).

[25] *See, e.g.*, U.S., Human Right Watch, World Report 2003 and *Guantanamo and Beyond: The Continuing Pursuit of Unchecked Executive Power*, May 13, 2005, Amnesty International, *available at* http://web.amnesty.org/library/Index/ENGAMR510632005.

it has done is significantly irritated the international legal community who accuse Spain of depriving detainees of their rights. While rights are denied, the question is whether the policy positively contributes to counter-terrorism. As the values balancing equation requires that national security not outweigh civil liberties, the holding of a detainee under such conditions suggests an imbalance. While Spain has not suffered from a terrorist attack since the Madrid train bombings, there is no evidence suggesting that the incommunicado policy contributed to this. The Spanish response of incommunicado detention has been in contrast with harsher measures implemented elsewhere. Is it effective? Is it justified? Time will tell. Nevertheless, detention without the right to counsel or right to contact family members is extremely problematic in the context of balancing the rights of the individual with the rights of the state.

India

India confronts the most complicated threats: purely internal; internal that is Pakistani driven; and external emanating from Pakistan's nuclear viability. The question, then, given the political and historical circumstances that are unique to India, is whether balancing between national security and individual rights is realistic. India's historic religious tensions and strict policies in the wake of terrorism attacks[26] make balancing difficult.

In response to terrorist attacks over the past 10–15 years, Indian legislation has imposed harsh measures depriving individuals of civil rights. Even after a repeal of the strongest legislation, human rights abuses have occurred, largely resulting from an apparent free hand granted to the security forces by an executive subject to minimal scrutiny. While Public Interest Litigation[27] increasingly enables a citizen aggrieved by the action of the government to petition the Supreme Court, the Indian judiciary is still not engaged in active judicial review during armed conflict. Similarly, the Indian legislature has not significantly addressed the issue of human rights abuses by the military.

Does this policy prevent acts of terrorism? The answer is obviously, no. Recently, a sophisticated bombing on a train in Mbombai claimed 50 lives.

An examination of effectiveness based on an analysis of the five countries raises the following questions: does imposing harsh operational counter-terrorism

---

[26] *See, e.g.*, Jammu and Kashmir Public Safety Act, Assam Prevention Detention Act, National Security Act, Essential Services Maintenance Act, Anti-Hijacking Act, Armed Forces (Punjab and Chandigarh) Special Powers Act, Punjab Disturbed Areas Act, Chandigarh Disturbed Areas Act, Suppression of Unlawful Acts Against Safety of Civil Aviation Act, Terrorist Affected Areas (Special Courts) Act, National Security Ordinance, Terrorist and Disruptive Activities Act, National Security Guard Act, Criminal Courts and Security Guard Courts Rules, Terrorist and Disruptive Activities Rules, and the Special Protection Group Act, http://www.sscnet.ucla.edu/southasia/History/Independent/anti_terr.html.

[27] *See*, S. Muralidhar, *India: Public Interest Litigation*, 33–34 Annual Survey of Indian Law 525 (1997–1998), *available at* http://www.ielrc.org/content/a9802.pdf.

measures deter terrorists? I think the jury is still out. Question number two: does imposing legislative constraints on the executive impede effective counter-terrorism? Here too, I would suggest, the jury is out. What does that mean? Does that mean we can now sit and wait for terrorists to act, rather than for governments to act proactively? The answer is absolutely no.

From the perspective of policy makers the over-riding question is to more effectively and successfully counter terrorism. In developing policy, the primary consideration must be an acknowledgement that the rule of law is supreme and that policy must be beholden to a nation's constitution or Basic Laws.

Rights

On the other hand, are we to grant terrorists all the rights granted to non terrorists? The answer here, is also no. We must establish a paradigm that reflects these two potentially contradictory realities.

I recently wrote a paper proposing the adoption of a hybrid paradigm which integrates certain constitutional and international law guarantees for the terrorist or the terrorist suspect. From the general to the specific: Osama bin Laden will not be Mirandized upon capture, but when brought to the interrogation cell he will be granted certain constitutional rights. The following rights are to be granted: The 5th Amendment privilege against self-incrimination and the 8th Amendment privilege against cruel and unusual punishment. In contrast, the 6th Amendment right to confront one's accuser will not be granted.

So what does that mean for us in the context of interrogating suspected terrorists? The base line is that torture is illegal, immoral, and, according to interrogators, does not result in actionable intelligence. A November 2002 legal opinion approved by Secretary of Defense Rumsfeld authorized the U.S. waterboarding of suspected terrorists. When a detainee is waterboarded he is held down on a gurney while water poured is into his throat, thereby simulating imminent drowning. Is that torture? According to the 1984 Convention against Torture, to which the U.S. is a signatory, absolutely yes. That policy was in effect until January of 2003.

So while torture is out, coercive interrogation is permissible. I have previously suggested that the following five coercive interrogation measures are permissible: sleep deprivation, modulation of room temperature, placing a hood over the detainee's head, sitting in an uncomfortable position and the playing of loud, cacophonous music. The measures are permissible only if two critical safeguards are met: guidelines authorizing coercive interrogation are clearly written and senior command approves implementation.

Conclusion

Where does all this lead?

We must, at all times, understand that the individuals who comprise terror organizations have a clear sense of mission. Suicide bombers are but the most obvious manifestation of that reality, reflecting total commitment to a cause. To counter this, our leaders must be able to clearly articulate a mission and the truth, however unpleasant it may be.

In developing a global counter terrorism strategy, the preeminence of the rule of law has been previously alluded to. In practical terms, that means not every suspect can be detained and those who have been detained, cannot be held indefinitely. Indefinite detention goes against the values and mores on which this country was founded.

Not only is indefinite detention illegal, but in terms of policy, it is also ineffective as terrorist organizations modify operational plans. Therefore, a detainee held over a number of years will be of no practical use to his interrogators. In essence, the detention centers would be filled with people who possess no actionable intelligence.

Developing operational counterterrorism requires distinguishing the good guy from the bad guy. This demands reliable and timely intelligence information. Ultimately, intelligence information is the engine that drives operational counterterrorism.

Intelligence is gathered through three means: human intelligence (HUMINET) based on live sources; signal intelligence (SIGNET) which is technology driven; open sources which range from the New York Times to the internet. Once the information is gathered, analysts can begin providing policy and decision makers with intelligence – hopefully corroborated – the accuracy and reliability of which is extraordinarily difficult to ascertain.

Pre 9/11, the U.S. was largely unable to develop human sources in Afghanistan and Iraq. Human sources strategically placed in terrorist organizations are absolutely critical, without them it is extraordinarily difficult to prevent terrorism. If decision makers are unable to develop intelligence regarding the planned actions of terrorist organizations, the result will be "round-up the usual suspects" and the indiscriminate and arbitrary killing of individuals since commanders will be unable to distinguish innocent civilian from terrorist. Failure to respect the international law principles of proportionality, alternatives, collateral damage, and military necessity suggests the slippery slope is right around the corner.

A final thought: as legal advisor to the Gaza Strip, I provided senior military commanders with real time legal advice regarding targeted killing decisions. The advice was process and criteria driven. The requisite checklist was predicated on the following: the sanctity of the rule of law; an understanding that there are individuals who, because of the threat they pose to national security and an operational inability to arrest them, are legitimate targets from the perspective of self-defense; the need to be beholden to a moral compass.

There is no issue more important today facing the international community world than counter-terrorism in its broadest possible context. This means not only addressing terrorism as we know it, but also addressing its breeding grounds, such as Iraq.

These two great issues – Iraq and counterterrorism – demand our utmost attention. They require us to be skeptical with respect to government pronouncements, vigilant regarding the curtailment of rights and wary of committing our forces without a clearly articulated mission. We must demand clear, thoughtful responses from our nation's leaders and those who wish to lead us. To do otherwise tells those serving our nation the following: "you may have our back, but we sure don't have yours."

There are no easy answers in counterterrorism. Operational mistakes will be made; innocent civilians will be killed and detained. Policy decisions will not always reflect balancing and effectiveness as discussed above. However, decision makers are legally and morally obligated to articulate and implement strategies beholden to the rule of law and a moral compass.

Benjamin Franklin's wise words serve as warning, for if we fail then we shall "deserve neither liberty nor safety."

"Terrorism": Reflections on Legitimacy and Policy Considerations

M. Cherif Bassiouni

Introduction

"Terrorism"[1] can be defined as a strategy of violence designed to instill terror in a segment of a population or society in order to achieve a power outcome, propagandize a cause, or inflict harm for a vengeful purpose.[2] Both state and non-state actors resort to such a strategy, whether in the context of war or peace. In the case of states, a state can direct terror-violence either against its own population, non-nationals under its control, or the population of another state. Similarly, non-state actors may target individuals or groups within their own state or those of another state, as well as states' interests.

M.C. Bassiouni
DePaul University
e-mail: cbassiou@depaul.edu

[1] The term "terrorism" is referred to in quotes because of the lack of an internationally agreed-upon definition of the term and its contents. The more neutral term of "terror-violence" is also used throughout this article.

[2] *See* M. Cherif Bassiouni, *Perspectives on International Terrorism, in* International Terrorism: Multilateral Conventions (1937–2001) 1 (M. Cherif Bassiouni ed., 2001).

The U.S. Government defines domestic terrorism as "activities that involve acts dangerous to human life that are a violation of the criminal laws of the United States or of any state; appear to be intended to intimidate or coerce a civilian population; to influence the policy of a government by mass destruction, assassination, or kidnapping; and occur primarily within the territorial jurisdiction of the United States." 18 U.S.C. § 2331(5). It defines international terrorism as that which "involves violent acts or acts dangerous to human life that are a violation of the criminal laws of the United States or any state, or that would be a criminal violation if committed within the jurisdiction of the United States or any state. These acts appear to be intended to intimidate or coerce a civilian population; influence the policy of a government by intimidation or coercion; or affect the conduct of a government by mass destruction, assassination or kidnapping and occur primarily outside the territorial jurisdiction of the United States or transcend national boundaries in terms of the means by which they are accomplished, the persons they appear intended to intimidate or coerce, or the locale in which their perpetrators operate or seek asylum." 18 U.S.C. § 2331(1).

The Code of Federal Regulations states that "Terrorism includes the unlawful use of force and violence against persons or property to intimidate or coerce a government, the civilian population, or any segment thereof, in furtherance of political or social objectives." 28 C.F.R. Section 0.85.

I.A. Karawan et al. (eds.), *Values and Violence*,

Thirteen specialized conventions on "terrorism" exist – each one dealing with a different type of conduct.[3] None of them comprehensively defines "terrorism,"[4] and none of these conventions applies to states.[5] These conventions are part of an international criminal law regime applicable primarily to individuals acting as nonstate actors. Another legal regime applies to some aspects of terror-violence, namely, international humanitarian law and is primarily directed at combatants and nonstate actors.[6] In addition, the international regime of human rights law also is designed to protect persons from terror-violence in times of war and peace. The first two legal regimes apply to the control of violence, while the third applies exclusively to

---

[3] Convention on Offences and Certain Other Acts Committed on Board Aircraft [Tokyo Hijacking Convention], U.N. Doc. A/C.6/418/Corr.1, Annex II; 704 U.N.T.S. 219; 20 U.S.T. 2941; 2 I.L.M. 1042 (14 Sept. 1963); Convention for the Suppression of Unlawful Seizure of Aircrafts [Hague Hijacking Convention], U.N. Doc. A/C.6/418/Corr. 1, Annex II; 860 U.N.T.S. 105; 22 U.S.T. 1641; 10 I.L.M. 133 (16 Dec. 1970); Convention for the Suppression of Unlawful Acts Against the Safety of Civil Aviation [Montreal Hijacking Convention], U.N. Doc. A/C.6/418/Corr.2, Annex III; 974 U.N.T.S. 177; 24 U.S.T. 564; 10 I.L.M. 1151 (23 Sept. 1971); Protocol for the Suppression of Unlawful Acts of Violence at Airports Serving Civil Aviation [Montreal Protocol], ICAO Doc. 9518; 27 I.L.M. 627 (24 Feb. 1988); Convention on the High Seas, U.N. Doc. A/Conf/13/L.52-55 & 56 & 58; 450 U.N.T.S. 11; 13 U.S.T. 2312 (29 Apr. 1958); Convention on Law of the Sea, U.N. Doc. A/Conf.62-121 & Corr.1-8; 1833 U.N.T.S. 3; 21 I.L.M. 1261 (10 Dec. 1982); Convention on the Prevention and Punishment of Crimes Against Internationally Protected Persons, Including Diplomatic Agents [Diplomats Convention], U.N. Doc. A/Res/3166; 1035 U.N.T.S. 167; 28 U.S.T. 1975; 13 I.L.M. 41 (14 Dec. 1973); Convention on the Safety of United Nations and Associated Personnel [U.N. Personnel Convention], U.N. Doc. A/Res/49/59 (17 Feb. 1995); Convention for the Suppression of Unlawful Acts Against the Safety of Maritime Navigation, IMO. Doc. Sua/Con/15; 27 I.L.M. 668 (10 Mar. 1988); Protocol for the Suppression of Unlawful Acts Against the Safety of Fixed Platforms Located on the Continental Shelf, IMO. Doc. Sua/Con/16/Rev.1; 27 I.L.M. 685 (10 Mar. 1988); Convention Against the Taking of Hostages [Hostage-Taking Convention], U.N. Doc. A/Res/34/146; 1316 U.N.T.S. 205; 18 I.L.M. 1456 (17 Dec. 1979); Convention for the Suppression of Terrorist Bombings [Terrorist Bombing Convention], U.N. Doc. A/Res/52/164 (9 Jan. 1998); Convention for the Suppression of the Financing of Terrorism [Terrorism Financing], U.N. Doc. A/54/109 (9 Dec. 1999).

See also International Instruments Related to the Prevention and Supprression of International Terrorism (United Nations, 2001); International Terrorism: Multilateral Conventions (1937–2001) (M. Cherif Bassiouni ed., 2001); 1, 2 International Terrorism: A Compilation of U.N. Documents (1972–2001) (M. Cherif Bassiouni ed., 2002).

[4] In 1996, the U.N. General Assembly established an Ad Hoc Committee to elaborate a draft comprehensive international convention on terrorism, *see* U.N. G.A. Res. 51/210 (17 Dec. 1996). *See also* Declaration on Measures to Eliminate International Terrorism, G.A. Res. 49/60 (9 Dec. 1994) and Declaration to Supplement the 1994 Declaration on Measures to Eliminate International Terrorism, G.A. Res. 51/210 (17 Dec. 1996). *See also* Ben Saul, *Attempts to Define "Terrorism" in International Law*, 52 Netherlands Int'l L. Rev. 57 (2005).

[5] Thus, kidnapping for "extraordinary rendition" and torture is argued by the Bush Administration to be lawful, even when it violates both the 1984 Hostage-Taking Convention, *supra* note 3, and the 1984 Torture Convention, Convention Against Torture and Other Cruel, Inhuman or Degrading Treatment or Punishment art. 19, Dec. 10, 1984, 1465 U.N.T.S. 85. *See* M. Cherif Bassiouni, *The Institutionalization of Torture under the Bush Administration*, Case W. Res. J. Int'l L. 389, (2006) 411–16.

[6] *See* Howard S. Levie, The Code of International Armed Conflict (1986); Howard S. Levie, Terrorism in War: the Law of War Crimes (1993).

protection of persons from state action. They all differ as to *inter alia*: their subjects, their legally defined contexts, and modalities of enforcement and sanctions. Thus, even though these three regimes are based on the same commonly-shared values, the gaps, overlaps, and ambiguities that characterize them give rise to competing claims of legitimacy, which are used by state and non-state actors to rationalize their acts of violence, leaving the victims of violence exposed as if they were the acceptable collateral damage of these competing claims.

The international criminal law and international humanitarian law regimes are designed to control violence by prohibiting certain means of violence and by protecting certain groups and places from being targeted by violence. This approach is intended to be neutral as to its prohibitions and as to protected targets and persons. It does not take into account the asymmetry of forces of those engaged in conflicts, irrespective of their legal characterization. The international criminal law which includes "terrorism" as defined by the thirteen United Nations Conventions applies in times of war and peace. The international humanitarian law regime applies exclusively to the contexts of conflicts of an international character and conflicts of a non-international character. It supersedes the international criminal regime applicable to "terrorism" in respect of these conflicts and in their contexts. The international human rights regimes applies to the contexts of war and peace but is regarded as secondary in its application to the other two legal regimes.

Legitimacy

Two-thousand years ago, the Zealots Sicarii assassinated Romans in Judea and Jerusalem in order to bring an end to the Roman Empire's rule of Judea and Samaria.[7] The Roman pro-consul of Palestine retaliated against these "terrorists" of the time by ordering the death of all Zealots, banning Jews from Jerusalem, and destroying the Second Temple in 70 C.E.[8] For the Jews, the Zealots were freedom fighters; for the Romans, they were brigands and outlaws – today's equivalent to terrorists.[9] Today, the Palestinians fighting the Israelis are labeled by their supporters as freedom fighters and by their opponents as terrorists.[10] Throughout these two millennia, opposing characterizations of those who believe that they are fighting for

---

[7] *See, e.g.*, M. Cherif Bassiouni, *Foreword: Assessing "Terrorism" in the New Millennium*, 12 DePaul Bus. L. J. 1 (1999/2000).

[8] For a description of the abolishment of the Roman decree by Umar ibn al-Khattab, the Second Caliph of Islam), *see* Arthur Tritton, Caliphs and Their Non-Muslim Subjects: A Critical Study of the Covenant of Umar (1970). Its text is in 2 Al Watha'eq Al-Dawli Al-M'neia bi Huquq Al-Insan: Al-Wasta'eq Al-Islamiya Wal-Iqlimia (2 International Protection of Human Rights: Islamic and Regional Instruments) 36 (M. Cherif Bassiouni ed., Dar El Shorouk, Cairo, Egypt, 2003).

[9] *See* Bassiouni, *supra* note 7, at 1–2.

[10] *Id.* at 2.

a righteous cause[11] have perpetuated the dilemma reflected in the dictum: "What is terrorism to some, is heroism to others."[12]

Whether to characterize a given conduct which produces human harm as "terrorism" or not still has to do with differing conceptions and perceptions of legitimacy; all too frequently, subsuming the illegitimacy of the means employed within the legitimacy of the ends pursued.[13] This reflects the perennial dilemma of whether the ends can justify the means.

The dichotomy between ends and means raises a number of questions. The first is whether legitimacy is indivisible and thus whether the ends and the means must be co-extensively legitimate. The second question is whether the legitimacy of the ends overrides the legitimacy of the means, or conversely, whether the legitimacy of the means overrides that of the ends. The third is whether the legitimacy of the ends is irrelevant so long as legitimate means are adhered to. Each of these foundational questions leads to different answers and diverse outcomes, particularly when it comes to designing an appropriate legal control regime. However, it should be noted that not all forms of violence are characterized by generally accepted goals deemed to be legitimate. Moreover, even when these goals are deemed legitimate, they are not necessarily characterized by a universally accepted legitimacy of recognized means. The international community has, however, recognized certain means as being unlawful, and attacks upon certain persons and targets as also being unlawful. However, it has not applied these norms and standards in an equal manner to state and non-state actors, frequently justifying for some what it condemns for others.

The legitimacy issue is both constant and recurring in the debate on "terrorism." It reflects in part the Machiavellian maxim, "the ends justify the means,"[14] which is

---

[11] Both groups engaged in assassinations and wanton killings of persons they saw as foreign occupiers, perceiving legitimacy to be the basis of their actions. Both groups fail to see that their means are not legitimate when it comes to killing innocent civilians. Their rationalization is that no one belonging to the group that they are legitimately fighting fall under the category of innocent civilians.

[12] This phrase was first used by this writer at an international conference on terrorism held at the International Institute of Higher Studies in Criminal Sciences in Siracusa, Italy in 1973. *See* International Terrorism and Political Crimes (M. Cherif Bassiouni ed., 1975). *See also* Bassiouni, *supra* note 7, at 2. Since this time, the phrase has been commonly used as a term for the dilemma of law, legitimacy, and morality.

[13] On the legitimacy debate, *see* M. Cherif Bassiouni, *Terrorism: The Persistent Dilemma of Legitimacy*, 36 Case W. Res. J. Int'l L. 299 (2004); M. Cherif Bassiouni, *Legal Controls of International Terrorism: A Policy-Oriented Perspective*, 43 Harv. Int'l L.J. 83 (2002); Mark A. Drumbl, *Lesser Evils in the War on Terrorism*, 36 Case W. Res. J. Int'l L. 335 (2004); Thomas Franck, *Profiry's Proposition: Legitimacy and Terrorism*, 20 Vand. Transnat'l L. 195 (1987); Richard R. Baxter, *A Skeptical Look at the Concept of Terrorism*, 7 Akron L. Rev. 380 (1974); The Morality of Terrorism: Religious and Secular Justifications (David C. Rapport & Yonah Alexander eds. 1989).

[14] *See* Niccolo Machiavelli, Il Principe: Le Grandi Opere Politiche (1532) (G. M. Anselmi & E. Menetti trans., 1992).

advanced as a legitimizing argument by both state and non-state actors who engage in terror-violence.

Saint Augustine reflected upon the double standard of "terrorism" in the case of a pirate who was captured by Alexander the Great. In response to the question of how he dared to molest peaceful commerce on the high seas, the pirate replied to the Macedonian leader, "[h]ow dare you molest the whole world? Because I do it with a little ship only, I am called a thief; you, doing it with a great navy, are called an emperor."[15]

The rationale is explicitly or implicitly present in Osama bin Laden and Ayman el-Zawahiri's messages which ask how the U.S. can claim legitimacy when it commits this or the other acts, such as: aggressive military invasions of countries, killing of innocent civilians, torturing persons, and destroying private and public property. Implicit in this argument and the arguments of many others similarly situated is the primacy of the comparative merits of legitimacy or the lack thereof. This argument is advanced either on the merits or as estoppel to the claims that their violent actions are illegitimate and illegal. On the merits, it is tantamount to concluding that certain wrongs warrant others, even though not of a similar type or nature. Proponents of this view conclude that terror-violence is justified even if it is unrelated in nature or in kind.[16] The estoppel argument is more akin to *tu quoque*.[17] Since World War II, both of these arguments have been held to be contrary to international law.[18] However, the comparative legitimacy arguments seldom address the harm done to the victims, as if it is an inconsequential result not deserving of its own legitimate recognition and thus, de-legitimizing the very claim which is based on comparative legitimacy.

Legitimacy arguments, whether by states or non-states, are riddled with double standards, self-serving rationalizations, and consistency gaps. Most particularly, they ignore victims' rights.[19]

Legitimacy is a pre-condition to the use of force. Thus, aggression is a violation of international law.[20] When self-defense becomes an elastic concept, which permits

---

[15] *See* Noam Chomsky, Pirates and Emperors: International Terrorism in the World 1 (1986).

[16] International humanitarian law prohibits reprisals. *See* Frits Kalshoven & Lisbeth Zegveld, Constraints on the Waging of War: An Introduction to International Humanitarian Law (3d ed. 2001).

[17] For a historic discussion of tu quoque and its application before the International Military Tribunal at Nuremberg, *see* Robert K. Woetzel, The Nuremberg Trials 120–21 (1962). *See also* Sienho Yee, *The Tu Quoque Argument as a Defence to International Crimes, Prosecution or Punishment*, 3 Chinese J. Int'l. L. 87 (2004).

[18] *See supra* notes 16 and 17.

[19] Basic Principles and Guidelines on the Right to a Remedy and Reparation for Victims of Gross Violations of International Human Rights Law and Serious Violations of International Humanitarian Law, G.A. Res. 147, U.N. GAOR, 60th Sess., U.N. Doc. A/Res/60/147 (21 March 2006); M. Cherif Bassiouni, *International Recognition of Victims' Rights*, 6 Human Rights Law Review 203 (2006).

[20] *See* M. Cherif Bassiouni & Ben Ferencz, *The Crime Against Peace, in* 1 International Criminal Law: Crimes 313 (M. Cherif Bassiouni ed., 2d rev. ed. 1999).

pre-emptive use of force and other exceptions to aggression that only a few states can get away with, its legitimacy withers away.[21]

Some Considerations on the International and National Legal Systems

From a victim's perspective as well as a national or international social interest perspective, all forms of violence are on the same continuum, even though their legal distinctions are based on policy considerations. The distinction between legitimate and illegitimate forms of violence is in part arbitrarily established by law at the international level. The absence of commonly-shared values and the existence of diverse state interests have resulted in three legal regimes applicable to the international control of violence. Under these regimes, the prescribing and proscribing norms and their enforcement mechanisms are different. This is in part a reflection of states' interests, which are also manifested in double standards with respect to the international legal regimes' applicability to certain subjects, namely, individuals and non-state actors who are the subjects of international humanitarian law and international criminal law,[22] while excluding states and sometimes state-actors.[23]

National criminal justice experiences are relevant to the shaping of international policy on preventing "terrorism," though they are frequently overridden by states' interests. These experiences, which are relevant to international and national legal control of "terrorism," include the following:

1. National experiences over the last seven thousand years of recorded legal history[24] reveal that criminal laws, which embody commonly-shared social values, are most likely to be voluntarily observed and effectively enforced. Among the reasons for that outcome is that the criminalization of transgressions against these types of protected interests is based on society's assessment of the intrinsic value of the social interest, which in turn reflects the individual and social harm sought to be averted. Among the unarticulated premises of a society's assessment of the protected social interest are: the individual harm's impact on society; the social perceptions of the transgressor's future capabilities of furthermore engaging in such harmful conduct; and the very transgression of a norm reflecting the commonly shared values of a given society. However, where there is doubt as

---

[21] *See* Yoram Dinstein, War, Aggression and Self-Defense (3d ed. 2001), favoring the elastic approach; Thomas M. Franck, *The Power of Legitimacy and the Legitimacy of Power: International Law in an Age of Power Disequilibrium*, 100 Am. J. Int'l L. 88 (2006) (questioning the elastic approach); *see also* Jonathan Charney, *The Use of Force Against Terrorism and International Law*, 96 Am. J. Int'l L. (2001).

[22] *See* M. Cherif Bassiouni, Introduction to International Criminal Law 57 *et. seq.* (2003).

[23] *Id.* at 85. Admittedly, crimes are not committed by states, but the state shield often helps to protect individuals who commit international crimes.

[24] *See, e.g.*, Jean Imbert et al., I, II Histoires des institutions et des faits sociaux (1957); Henry Wigmore, A Panorama of World Legal Systems (1936).

to the legitimacy of the protected social interest and/or when there is a claim of higher legitimacy in transgressing the protected social interest in question, the level of individual compliance with the social norm is reduced. Moreover, social solidarity with the victim or the transgressor increases or decreases in proportion to the legitimacy of the protected interest and the validity of the transgressor's legitimacy claims.

2. The sanctions for transgressing a protected interest are a reflection of that social interest's significance to society. Thus, when the protected interest lacks in legitimacy, or when the transgressor has some valid claims of legitimacy, then the effectiveness of the sanction's deterring and preventing effects declines and that enhances the likelihood of transgressions.
3. Theories of general deterrence have never been very convincing because it is difficult to quantify how the threat of punishment has an impact on individual decision-making. But anecdotal and experiential data reveals that with respect to conformity or lack thereof to norms prescribing certain forms of violence, legitimacy is a strong factor. When it comes to ideologically motivated perpetrators of acts of violence, the legitimacy factor is even more significant. This includes the legitimacy of the perpetrator's motives, the ends to be attained, the nature of the attacked target, and the legitimacy or lack thereof of the proscribing regime.
4. Implicit in all of the above is a comparative legitimacy assessment by the perpetrator and by segments of society as to the preponderance of competing legitimacy claims. In other words, the question is whether those seeking to prevent certain persons from engaging in acts of terror-violence have lesser or no "clean hands" than the perpetrators of the acts of terror-violence.[25]
5. Just as criminal laws are assumed to reflect social values, their applications are assumed to be equal, fair, and impartial. Without these considerations, law is nothing more than an instrument of power, selectively wielded by those who have an interest in certain outcomes. When that happens, the assumption of voluntary compliance and the expectation of public support disappear and law fails to achieve its intended purposes – in the end, it becomes meaningless. It is not therefore the law that makes justice, but the perceived justice reflected in the law and evidenced in its application that brings justice to the law.[26]

National legal regimes are different, but they belong to only a few families of law.[27] However, these families of law belong to a system that is different from the international legal system.[28] The peculiarities of self-defense are illustrative of a set of

[25] The Common Law maxim describes that precondition for those seeking equity.

[26] For different perspectives on the concept of law, *see* Immanuel Kant, The Philosophy of Law (W. Hastie trans., 1887); George W.F. Hegel, The Philosophy of Right (S.W. Dyde trans., 1996); Carl J. Friedrich, The Philosophy of Law in Historical Perspective (2d ed. 1990).

[27] *See* René David, Les grands systèmes de droit contemporains (1973).

[28] However, they have an impact on the international legal system through "general principles of law." *See* ICJ Statue, art. 38; M. Cherif Bassiouni, *A Functional Approach to "General Principles of International Law,"* 11 Mich. J. Int'l L. 768 (1990).

problems relating to differences in legal regimes at the national and international levels.

The national laws on self-defense are established on the identifiable value of the individual's right to self-preservation. The international law of self-defense applies to the territorial and political integrity of a state. Whereas no national law on self-defense allows for preemptive self-defense, the international law of self-defense is sufficiently elastic to permit it. The national laws of self-defense are predicated on the assumption of some symmetry between the protagonists and allows for limited use of other means to redress imbalances of forces. The international law of self-defense makes no distinction as to the asymmetry of forces and means available to the protagonist. Last, but not least, individual self-defense is in part premised on the assumption that agents of the state will intervene on behalf of the victim, defend him or her, uphold the victim's rights, and pursue the perpetrator, eventually punishing him/her for the transgression. Thus, self-defense is only a temporary or stop-gap measure until state-actors intervene to take over. None of this exists at the international level.

Another major difference between national legal systems and the international one is that rights and obligations under national legal systems are enforced by the state, while this is rarely the case in the international legal system. On the contrary, this system raises expectations, but fails to fulfill them – leaving those with such expectations without any other recourse than the use of force.[29] For example, the international system recognizes certain principles, rights, and claims pertaining to self-determination, but fails to resolve conflicts between protagonists who rely on these principles, rights and claims. Since most of the claimants of these rights are non-state actors engaging in national liberation, or ethnic and religious groups seeking to obtain self-determination and secession from a larger national context, they are left with few if any peaceful choices as alternatives to violence. Because of the asymmetry of forces between national governments and their armies and non-state actors claiming certain rights, the latter compensate with terror-violence.

The wars of national liberation between the 1950s–1980s evidence the proposition that there were legitimate rights in dispute which the international system did not address and that there was an imbalance in power between proponents of these rights and those who opposed them, respectively, the national insurgents and the colonial powers. Resort to terror-violence thus became the only available means to achieve the legitimate end of liberation from foreign colonial domination. As a result, Mao Tse Tung guerilla tactics described in his *Red Book*[30] became the guerilla forces' equivalent of conventional armies' field manuals. Admittedly, this is not the only means of redressing wrongs or of asserting valid claims. The history of civil

---

[29] *See* M. Cherif Bassiouni, *Self-Determination and the Palestinians*, 1971 Proceedings of the American Society of International Law 31 (1971); Hurst Hannum, Autonomy, Sovereignty, and Self-Determination: The Accommodation of Conflicting Rights (1996).

[30] Quotations from Chairman Mao Tse-Tung (Stuart Schram ed., 1967).

disobedience movements throughout the world has also evidenced that non-violent means are not only possible, but also effective.[31]

Interestingly, the use of terror-violence during all conflicts since World War II[32] has been resorted to by both state and non-state actors. Both arguing some aspects of legitimacy to the exclusion of the other and both ignoring the harmful consequences inflicted on civilians and inhumane treatment inflicted on combatants.[33]

If effective peaceful resolution of conflict mechanisms existed to determine the validity of certain legal claims and to enforce those claims ascertained to be valid, there would be no room for questioning the legitimacy of international legal regimes applicable to "terrorism." However, the absence of legal or other means to redress wrongs and the absence of effective peaceful opportunities to assert valid legal claims leads to the resort to violence. When asymmetry of forces between the protagonists exists, violence tends to become terror-violence as a means of redressing the imbalance.[34] This is why the question of legitimacy of claims cannot be removed from consideration in assessing the "terrorism" legal control regime.

The International Legal Control Regimes

Three international legal regimes, share the same values, namely the protection of human interests. They are international humanitarian law, international human rights law, and international criminal law. To a large extent, these three regimes overlap and at the same time, evidence ambiguities in the prescriptions and proscriptions, as well as gaps between them.[35] Differences exist between these three legal regimes with respect to their structures, enforcement modalities, and more particularly, the contexts to which they apply. These issues are beyond the scope of this article.

The most significant issue in respect to the applicability of the three legal regimes is their legal contexts. International humanitarian law applies in conflicts

---

[31] Mohandes Gandhi's non-violent resistance Satyagraha movement was effective in ending the rule of the British Raj in India. Martin Luther King's civil rights movement in the 1960s, and the latter stages of South African transformation from an apartheid state to a democratic one under the leadership of Nelson Mandela, F.W. De Klerk, and Desmond Tutu, are also examples.

[32] For the quantum of harm resulting out of these conflicts *see infra* note 72.

[33] For the legal aspects of conflicts of a non-international character, *see* Lindsay Moir, The Law of International Armed Conflict (2002); Michel Veuthey, *Non-International Armed Conflict and Guerilla Warfare, in* 1 International Criminal Law: Crimes 417 (M. Cherif Bassiouni ed., 2d ed. 1999).

[34] "Revolutions have never lightened the burden of tyranny: they have only shifted it to another shoulder." George Bernard Shaw, Man and Superman (1903).

[35] As evidenced by the International Court of Justice decision, Legal Consequences of the Construction of a Wall in the Occupied Palestinian Territory, 2004 I.C.J. 131 (July 9), in which it discusses the applicability of the international human rights and international humanitarian law regimes, but without indicating how these overlapping regimes apply simultaneously and in what way they cumulatively enhance the protection goal sought to be achieved. *See also* M. Cherif Bassiouni, *The Normative Framework of International Humanitarian Law: Overlaps, Gaps, and Ambiguities*, 8 Transnat'l L. & Cont. Probs. 199 (1998).

of an international and non-international character;[36] international human rights law applies in times of war and peace, although subject to suspension of some of its rights in situations where "states of emergency" are declared; and international criminal law applies in times of war and peace. However, if the prohibited act is committed by combatants in times of war, they are lawful and therefore not subject to that regime.[37] It should also be noted that while international human rights law presumably applies in times of war and peace, international humanitarian law, which is considered the *lex specialis*, has priority in its application.[38]

Violations of international human rights law are not criminalized, as are "grave breaches" under international humanitarian law.[39] The international criminal law regime applicable to "terrorism" remains fragmented, both in terms of its norms and enforcement mechanisms. As to the former, it is evidenced by the lack of a legislative policy whereby there is no single comprehensive convention and where "terrorism" is not defined, instead there are thirteen conventions dealing with different topics, which are mostly means by which acts of terror-violence take place outside the context of armed conflicts. All of these conventions rely on the indirect enforcement scheme,[40] whereby states have the obligation of criminalizing these acts under their domestic legislation and prosecuting and eventually punishing those

---

[36] Even within the international humanitarian law regime there is a distinction between conventional and customary international humanitarian law and there is also a distinction as to the legal norm applicable to conflicts of an international character and conflicts of a non-international character. International humanitarian law excludes purely domestic conflicts and internal hostility.

[37] For example, taking of prisoners in time of war is subject to the Third Geneva Convention of 12 August and is not therefore kidnapping in accordance with U.N. Hostage-Taking Convention, *see supra* note 3. Similarly, the seizure or destruction of an aircraft in the course of an armed conflict is not a violation of the three relevant conventions in the international criminal law (the Hague Hijacking Convention, Montreal Hijacking Convention, and the Montreal Protocol), *see supra* note 3. Instead, these acts are subject to the conventional and customary law of armed conflict.

[38] It should also be noted that transgressions of the norms of international humanitarian law in conflicts of an international character are "grave breaches." The four Geneva Conventions of August 12, 1949 apply to both types of conflict and prohibit acts of terror-violence, as does the 1907 Hague Convention on the Customary Laws of Armed Conflicts. *See* The Hague Convention Respecting the Laws and Customs of War on Land, art. 18, 1907, 36 Stat. 2277 (1907); and the four Geneva Conventions: Geneva Convention Relative to the Protection of Civilian Persons in Time of War, of August 12, 1949, arts. 3, 4, 13, 16, 17–33, 147, 6 U.S.T. 3516, 75 U.N.T.S. 287; Geneva Convention for the Amelioration of the Conditions of the Wounded and Sick in Armed Forces in the Field, of August 12, 1949, 6 U.S.T. 3114, 74 U.N.T.S. 31; Convention for the Amelioration of the Conditions of the Wounded, Sick and Shipwrecked Members of Armed Forces, of August 12, 1949, [1955] 6 U.S.T. 3317, 755 U.N.T.S. 85; Convention Relative to the Treatment of Prisoners of War, of August 12, 1949 6 U.S.T. 3316, 75 U.N.T.S. 135 (article 33 which applies to noncombatants as defined in article 4). These conventions apply to 'conflicts of a non-international character' as defined in Common Article 3, where the transgressions equivalent to "grave breaches" are referred to as "violations." *See also* Protocol I Additional to the Geneva Conventions of August 12, 1949, *opened for signature* Dec. 12, 1977, U.N. Doc. A/21/144 Annex I; Protocol II Additional to the Geneva Convention, *opened for signature Aug. 12, 1949,* U.N. Doc. No. 32/144 Annex 2.

[39] The exception is if a specialized convention exists. such as in the case of torture. *See supra* note 5.

[40] *See* M. Cherif Bassiouni, Introduction to International Criminal Law 333 *et. seq.* (2003).

found guilty of the commission of these acts and to extradite persons accused or convicted of such crimes, as well as lend legal assistance to a state seeking to investigate or prosecute or carry out a sentence with respect to persons accused or found guilty of committing such crimes. In addition, the Security Council has established a special Counter-Terrorism Committee (CTC), whose task it is to coordinate international activities in preventing and suppressing international terrorism.[41] The CTC has the function of coordinating the many different international agencies involved in one aspect or another of violations of any of the thirteen conventions mentioned above, as well as in monitoring the flow of funds to prevent terrorism financing and to facilitate the flow of information between intelligence and law enforcement agencies.[42] The activities of the CTC, however, do not include situations falling within the meaning of armed conflicts. In that context, international humanitarian law applies.[43]

It is clear from this very brief description of these three legal regimes that their overlap as well as the differences they have contribute to a lack of clarity as to the applicable norms and sanctions for their transgressions. It also shows lack of effective coordination between them with respect to their applicability, both in regards to the rights and obligations of the subjects protected and of the subjects of the transgressions.

Since the enforcement of all three regimes is essentially left to states, even though there are a number of international organizations directly involved with enforcement, not the least of which is the Security Council, the responses by states vary. This depends in part on every state's legislative scheme, but also on the capabilities and effectiveness of the state's criminal justice system. More significantly, however, enforcement through states essentially means that states' interests will play a role in the way in which enforcement is carried out.[44] In some situations, states will over-react, as has been the case in the U.S. after September 11th, by curtailing well-established civil rights and even violating international law and human rights.[45] An

---

41 Security Council Resolution S/RES/1373 (28 September 2001); *see also* The United Nations Global Counter-Terrorism Strategy, U.N. G.A. Res. 60/288 (20 Sept. 2006).

42 For such information, *see* the United Nations Counter-Terrorism Online Handbook of the United Nations Counter-Terrorism Implementation Task Force, available at http://www.un.org/terrorism/cthandbook/http://www.un.org/terrorism/cthandbook/.

43 *See* Thomas M. Franck, *Criminals, Combatants, or What? An Examination of the Role of Law in Responding to the Threat of Terror*, 98 Am. J. Int'l L. 686 (2004).

44 One such example is the Lockerbie situation which pitted Libya against the U.S., the U.K., and the Security Council for nearly 10 years. *See* Order with Regard to Request for Indication of Provisional Measures in the Case Concerning Questions of Interpretation and Application of the 1971 Montreal Convention Arising from the Aerial Incident at Lockerbie (Libyan Arab Jamahiriya v. U.K.), 1992 I.C.J. 3 (Apr. 14); (Libyan Arab Jamahiriya v. U.S.), 1992 I.C.J. 114 (Apr. 14). *See also* Sean Murphy, *Verdict in the Trial of the Lockerbie Bombing Suspects*, 95 Am. J. Int'l L. 405 (2001); Michael P. Scharf, *Terrorism on Trial: The Lockerbie Criminal Proceedings*, 6 ILSA J. Int'l & Comp. L. 355 (2000); Peter H.F. Bekker, *Questions of Interpretation and Application of the 1971 Montreal Convention Arising From the Aerial Incident at Lockerbie, Preliminary International Court of Justice, February 27, 1998*, 92 Am. J. Int'l L. 503 (1998).

45 *See* Bassiouni, *Institutionalization of Torture Under the Bush Administration*, *supra* note 5.

over-zealous government, such as in the case of the Bush Administration, causes a champion of human rights such as the US to lose the high moral ground and thus provide those who engage in terror-violence with claims of illegitimacy on the part of their adversaries, which they can also argue bolsters their claims of legitimacy.[46] It has well been established that the best way of defeating spurious legitimacy claims is to act within legitimacy.[47]

These three legal regimes are premised on the assumption that no matter how legitimate the ends may be, certain means are impermissible. By implication, international humanitarian law and international human rights law are neutral with respect to the legitimacy of the ends, focusing instead on another presumed value-neutral concept of protecting certain persons and targets. Because neither one of these two legal regimes addresses the question of legitimacy of the ends, they draw an artificial legal barrier which avoids facing the reality of why terror-violence is resorted to. They do so in the name of ideological neutrality in an area that is almost entirely permeated with ideological considerations.

One of the main distinctions between these two legal regimes is that international humanitarian law does not differentiate between its violators, namely, between state and non-state actors. The international criminal law regime of "terrorism" control applies only to individuals and non-state actors, thus by implication excluding states and in some cases state agents acting on behalf of states.[48] This asymmetry between perpetrators creates another layer of legitimacy issues with respect to a legal order that purports to protect certain persons and targets from being victimized, but which discriminates as between state and non-state actors by excluding states from responsibility for the same crimes for which individuals are held responsible. This diversity undermines the moral legitimacy of the international control regime of "terrorism" and contributes to the claims of legitimacy by non-state actors who perpetrate certain prohibited acts.

The phenomenon of "terrorism" has only marginally been impacted by law whether national or international, even though states have devoted much of their resources and efforts to create new law and legal institutions to address this phenomenon. Technology, such as the metal detector, has done more to secure the safety of international civil aviation,[49] than have the four conventions dealing with aircraft

---

[46] On the proposition that if your adversary does not have "clean hands," it is possible to act in the same vein. This is reminiscent of reprisal and *tu quoque* arguments, see *supra notes* 16 and 17.

[47] *See* International Terrorism: Legal Challenges and Responses (Report of the International Bar Association's Task Force on Terrorism, October, 2003).

[48] *See* Bassiouni, *supra* note 7 at 4; M. Cherif Bassiouni, *A Policy-Oriented Inquiry into the Different Forms and Manifestations of International Terrorism*, *in* Legal Responses to International Terrorism: U.S. Procedural Aspects XV (M. Cherif Bassiouni ed. 1988); W.T. Maillison Jr. & S.V. Mallison, *The Concept of Public Purpose Terror in International Law: Doctrines and Sanctions to Reduce the Destruction of Human & Material Values*, 18 How. L. J. 12 (1973).

[49] *See* Paul Dempsey, *Aerial Piracy and Terrorism, Unilateral and Multilateral Responses to an Aircraft Hijacking*, 2 Conn. J. Int'l L. 42 (1987); *Measures to Prevent International Terrorism*, U.N. GAOR 6th Comm, 51st Sess., U.N. Doc. A/51/336 (1996).

hijacking and sabotaging.[50] Since no technology can protect against hostage-taking, the U.N. Convention on Hostage-Taking[51] has almost become an irrelevant legal footnote to contemporary events, such as the extensive kidnappings in Iraq and Afghanistan by state and non-state actors.[52]

The unstated assumptions in all of the thirteen international conventions on terrorism[53] are that the violators of their norms are few in number and that they operate in a context where legal and social controls are effective. Thus, necessarily, these conventions become irrelevant when these two assumptions are not met, as in the case of almost all the conflicts of a non-international character that have been witnessed since the end of World War II. The same is true for the norms of international humanitarian law, which assume their applicability to military organizations characterized by command and control structures capable of enforcing that body of law, and, also likely to observe it because of the mutuality of interests that opposing military forces have in ensuring observance of these norms. These assumptions are mostly inapplicable to conflicts of a non-international character where relatively smaller militias operate outside a well-established command and control system, and where no mutuality of interest exists with respect to their opponents. This explains in part why both legal regimes based on the same values have nonetheless substantially failed when their unarticulated assumptions do not exist in fact. However, more significant to the legitimacy of these regimes and thus to the voluntary compliance and public support that they engender are the double standards, which governments apply in regards to state-actors and non-state actors.

Legitimacy and Policy

As indicated above, there are three distinct international legal regimes applicable in whole or in part to the control of terror-violence and to the prevention of victimization. The latter, by the very nature of the term victim, cannot be considered participants in the processes of violence irrespective of whether these processes are deemed lawful or unlawful. Also as indicated above, the overlap of these three regimes without much indication in international law as to how their diverse prescriptive and proscriptive norms, enforcement modalities, and sanctions are to be applied, creates conflicts of laws in search of a hierarchical theory for their application. Customary international law has so far settled on the hierarchical priority of international humanitarian law in the context of conflicts of an international character on the basis of a general principle of law recognized by most legal systems, namely, the theory of the *lex specialis,* which prevails over the *lex generalis* (international

---

[50] *See supra* note 3.

[51] *See supra* note 3.

[52] There are daily reports in the mass media about individual incidents, but no single source which has cumulative numbers or statistics.

[53] *See supra* note 3.

human rights law being in the category of the *lex generalis*). The problem, however, arises with respect to international criminal laws' conventions on "terrorism," which are a *lex specialis*. Thus, there is a conflict with international humanitarian law. Presumably, international criminal law conventions on "terrorism" apply in times of peace, and when they apply in times of war, it excludes combatants.

Each of these three legal regimes has ambiguities as to the meaning and contents of its prescriptive and proscriptive norms and standards. Moreover, its enforcement mechanisms vary from what may be akin to administrative and civil enforcement in regards to international human rights law to criminal law enforcement mechanisms and sanctions for transgressions of international humanitarian law and international criminal law. It is to be noted that while transgressions of international humanitarian law are considered war crimes, whether the legal source of the violation is conventional or customary international law, and irrespective of whether it is a conflict of an international or non-international character. Thus, these transgressions can be enforced on the basis of universal jurisdiction and also by international tribunals, including the International Criminal Court. However, international humanitarian law excludes purely domestic conflicts and internal hostilities. In that respect, international human rights law applies to these types of conflicts, but that regime does not have enforcement mechanisms and sanctions of the criminal law types as in the case of the other two legal regimes.

With respect to all three regimes, the assumption is that they will be enforced by states. However, the distinction between these international legal regimes also carries out in their domestic enforcement. International humanitarian law is applied in almost every country in the world through its military laws, and these laws are usually limited to military personnel in accordance with the domestic law on military criminal jurisdiction. International criminal law is enforced through the criminal laws and procedures of states which are different from national military justice systems, their laws and procedures. International human rights law is enforced administratively or through limited civil procedures. Consequently, the diversity of these three international legal regimes is reflected in their national application which emphasizes the gaps that exist between them.

It is therefore hard to see how this approach can be effective when both at the international and national levels it has the flaws that necessarily pertain to three distinct legal regimes. These flaws evidence ambiguities in prescriptive and proscriptive norms and standards unsettled conflicts and issues of applicability and jurisdictional overlaps, and gaps which allow double standards of application.

These legal or technical flaws give states the opportunity to be selective in the application of the prescriptive and proscriptive norms and standards contained in these three legal regimes. The double standards employed in interpreting these norms and their unequal application, exceptions and exceptionalism claimed by states, as well as the repressive measures engaged in by states as part of their perceived preventive and punitive measures, combine to create a legitimacy gap which undermines the very foundation of any legal regime, let alone the three in question which are predicated on the same human values and social interests. The undermining of the legitimacy of any legal regime not only weakens voluntary compliance therewith, but also public support for it, thus enhancing the prospects of the numerical and qualitative increased terror-violence.

The use of any examples to illustrate these points would necessarily be *sui generis*, and to a large extent, subject to debate since none of them would be predicated on single or linear factors devoid of a significant number of variables. Purely for illustrative purposes, the following examples are offered, which fall into four categories.

1. Responses by states to internal acts of terror-violence. They range from the restrained attitude of Italy for a period spanning a decade between the late 1960s and late 1970s, whereby new legal measures, as well as expanded authority given to intelligence and law enforcement remained within the bounds of constitutionality, thus attracting significant public support. The trade-off was a perceived limitation on the discretionary authority of intelligence and law enforcement in exchange for preservation of the rule of law. The outcomes, initially difficult from a political perspective, were ultimately exceptionally successful. In Italy, "Terrorism" by the Red Brigades and other extremist groups dwindled and ultimately end because they were contrary to the people's commonly-shared values. Those who engaged in such acts realized that if their goal was to achieve a transformation in Italy's society, they would have to use different methods, because the vast majority of Italians were opposed to their methods.

In contrast, the Bush Administration reacted to the September 11th attacks by curtailing constitutional rights and engaging in anti-Arab and anti-Muslim discrimination; institutionalizing torture, and engaging in acts of violence against the civilian population of Afghanistan and Iraq in violation of international humanitarian law. In so doing, the Administration not only violated the U.S. Constitution and U.S. laws, but also international humanitarian law, international human rights law, and international criminal law. Whether these measures are likely to ensure the successful outcome of effectively deterring prospective "terrorists" is something which only time will tell. However, if historic experiences in different contexts can be used as analogy, they cannot be used here. Even if they could, however, the loss of legitimacy and legality can hardly be said to equal the gains of prospective security. As Benjamin Franklin said, "[t]hey that can give up essential liberty to obtain a little temporary safety deserve neither liberty nor safety."[54]

2. Repressive measures against occupied populations. The harsh measures carried out by Israel against Gaza and the West Bank, as well as attacks directed against Palestinians as a form of collective punishment, have only resulted in stiffening opposition against Israel among Palestinians, which in turn led to suicide bombings. Israel's responses include targeting Hamas and Hezbollah in Lebanon. These violations reduce the legitimacy of Israel's claims of legitimacy, which places it at the same level as those who engage in violations of international humanitarian law against it. In so doing, Israel has abandoned the high moral road of being the victim, upholding legality by observing international humanitarian law, and instead

[54] Benjamin Franklin, Reply of the Pennsylvania Assembly to the Governor (Nov. 1755).

has placed itself in an analogous position to its opponents by committing similar, though different, violations of international humanitarian law. Yet, while committing violations of international human law, Israel still advances the same claims of legitimacy of its actions as do its opponents.

3. The transformation of the international law doctrine of self-defense. This new elastic concept justified pre-emptive attacks and the elimination of proportionality in the use of force. This approach undermines the legitimacy basis of self-defense. This is in part the case of the U.S. in Afghanistan and Iraq, and also the case of Israel in Lebanon.[55]

4. Domestic repression of internal groups seeking regime-change by violent action. This varies from country to country. The conflicts that took place in El Salvador, Argentina, Chile, and Colombia best exemplify this, but there have also been destabilizing efforts in other countries such as Morocco, Egypt, Syria, Jordan and Lebanon – the last resulting in a protracted civil war. In all of these cases, but more particularly in those which only faced low-level violence and no armed insurrection, such as Argentina and Egypt, to name only a few, the result by the threatened regimes was to engage in brutal repression manifested by extrajudicial executions, disappearances, and torture. The outcomes in all of these cases have demonstrated the weakening of claims of legitimacy in these regimes and the strengthening of the claims of legitimacy of their opponents.

The significance of these issues in all of the above contexts is that they enhance the claims of legitimacy of those who engage in terror-violence, and they weaken the claims of legitimacy of those who oppose them. If, in the final analysis, it is only a question of the rule of force, which is to dictate outcomes, then a given civilization's progress is only skin-deep. As history has continually evidenced, the difference between a civilized society and an uncivilized one is that the former relies on the rule of law and the latter relies on the rule of force.

Some of the Actors' Characteristics

The characteristics of state and non-state actors engaging in terror-violence strategies and tactics differ. State actors usually consist of military, paramilitary, police, intelligence forces, and civilian militias that support of the state. At times, all of the above may act openly or covertly, or both, depending upon the goal or impact they

---

[55] Israel invaded Lebanon and occupied parts of it between July 12 and 27, 2006 on the proposition that Hezbollah's military wing took two of its soldiers as prisoners. In the course of the attack and occupation, it destroyed a significant portion of Lebanon's infrastructure and the estimated number of killed and injured is 40,000. *See* Fatal Strikes: Israel's Indiscriminate Attacks Against Civilians in Lebanon (Human Rights Watch, August 2006). Consequently, it is difficult to recognize the legitimacy of Israel's claim in light of the disproportionate harm that it has caused. The same was true during that same period of time when it invaded Gaza after one of its soldiers was kidnapped, causing disproportionate damage and casualties than the one soldier held prisoner by the group that kidnapped him. In turn, Hezbollah and Hamas will then claim legitimacy in retaliating against Israel, relying on Israel's previous unlawful conduct.

seek to achieve. This in turn depends on the overall purposes of whether a given state actor seeks to occupy another state's territory, subjugate a civilian population in occupied territories, preserve and maintain domestic power, repress a segment of their own domestic population, or extend political influence into other territories.

Non-state actors do not have the same organizational and cohesive structures that state actors have. Their groupings vary in size, as do their resources and capabilities. Their purposes are also heterogeneous. Larger groups may have the same characteristics of state actors, having military and paramilitary forces whose capabilities rise to the level of challenging the state's counterpart forces. Their methods vary according to their means, beliefs, command structure, discipline, and goals. Thus, it is necessary to assess the characteristics of actors engaged in terror-violence to design an appropriate legal regime to address such threats. This is reflected in the debate as to whether "terrorism" is a war in the conventional or unconventional meaning of the term to be addressed in military terms, or whether it is a crime which is to be addressed by criminal law's traditional enforcement means.[56]

Globalization brings a new dimension to terrorist operations. This is evident in connection with money laundering and arms purchasing. What is less evident is the connection between terrorism and organized crime and vice versa.[57] Ideologically motivated groups can engage in activities similar to those of organized crimes groups even though the two types of organizations have significantly different goals and interests. The former, who seek power outcomes, may nonetheless resort to organized crime groups' tactics to fund their activities or to establish strategic alliances with these groups to advance their purposes.[58] During the civil war in the former Yugoslavia in 1992–1994, some of these groups, such as Arkan's Tigers, engaged in contraband and after the civil war ended, morphed into drug trafficking.[59] At present in Iraq, some of the militias engaging in sectarian violence, particularly on the Shi' side, engage in racketeering, extortion, and embezzlement of government funds.[60] It is possible that they too may morph into full-fledged organized crime activities after order and stability is reinstated in that country.

Unlike state actors who depend on the resources of their respective states, non-state actors have to find ways of funding their existence and activities. The smaller the group, the less resources it needs, but then its political public impact may be

---

[56] This does not exclude enhanced methods of international cooperation and also enhanced law enforcement and intelligence cooperation, provided they are subject to legal and judicial controls. *See* Steven Becker, *Cave Janus: Increased cooperation Between Law Enforcement and Intelligence Agencies after September 11, 2001*, 76 Revue Internationale de Droit Pénal 57 (2005).

[57] *See* M. Cherif Bassiouni & Eduardo Vetere, *Organized Crime and its Transnational Manifestations, in* 1 International Criminal Law: Crimes 883 (M. Cherif Bassiouni ed., 2d ed. 1999).

[58] *Id.* at 894.

[59] *See* Final Report of the Commission of Experts Established Pursuant to Security Council Resolution 780 (1992), U.N. SCOR, Annex, U.N. Doc. S/1994/674 (27 May 1994), Annex III.A.

[60] *See* M. Cherif Bassiouni, *America's Iraq Policy*, ABA Int'l. L. News 6 (Spring 2006); M. Cherif Bassiouni, *Post-Conflict Justice in Iraq*, ABA Human Rights 15 (Winter 2006).

lessened.[61] This explains why in some conflicts, like Sierra Leone and Liberia, the rebels were quick to rush to the diamond mines to fund their activities in order to fund larger militias. However, had these groups not found those in the Western business establishment who would purchase the 'blood-diamonds' and those who would money-launder the funds which then went to pay off arms traffickers, this would have been a futile effort.[62] Economic interests, which, in this case, include the interests of states producing small weapons, trump the need for other effective legal controls of these trades and of money laundering.[63]

Funding is the key to "terrorism" control.[64] However, controlling "terrorism" financing[65] is too narrowly conceived. Large-scale terror-violence operations, such as guerilla warfare require significant funding, but limited funds are needed to cause significant damage by small groups against larger, wealthier, and stronger societies because of their high vulnerabilities. September 11th was such an example. Nineteen individual actors with a still-undetermined number of external supporters were able to inflict significant damage on the United States with an estimated $250,000–500,000.[66] Consequently, international measures on "terrorism" financing can hardly be said to be an effective method of control.[67] High impact consequences can easily be funded by private-fund sources which are likely to elude international control.

---

[61] Unless it can commit acts whose consequences are far greater than the groups' expected capabilities, as in Al-Qa'eda's case in connection with their U.S. September 11th attacks and their attacks on the Dar El-Salaam, Tanzania, Nairobi, Kenya attacks on U.S. embassies and on the U.S.S. Cole in Yemen.

[62] This experience raises a number of normative legal questions pertaining to the absence of an international regime to control the diamond trade, which, the Kimberley Process notwithstanding, is still quite open to trafficking in blood diamonds and other illegally obtained ones. In this case, economic interests trump the need to have an effective control system. The same can be said with respect to the international small arms trade, which is substantially unregulated and substantially un-enforced leading to what is probably the biggest cache proceeds of illicit international traffic.

[63] Notwithstanding national and international efforts with respect to money laundering, the gaps in these systems are still sufficiently wide to permit a fairly substantial sum from being used for illegal purposes. Suffice it to recall that the illicit traffic in drugs produces billions of dollars which are recycled with such ease that it is estimated that the cost of recycling such illegal proceeds are less than ten percent. Surely, if national and international controls were more effective, the volume of seizures and the cost of recycling would have been higher. Funding sources for non-state actors can also vary significantly. *See* Suppressing the Financing of Terrorism, A Handbook for Legislative Drafting (International Monetary Fund, 2003); Paul Allan Schott, Reference Guide to Anti-Money Laundering and Combating the Financing of Terrorism (International Monetary Fund, 2003).

[64] The FARC in Colombia taxes the cocaine traffickers; while in Iraq, the sectarian militias engage in racketeering, extortions, and embezzlement of government funds, which go to the financing these groups as well as funding their expansion. *See* Bassiouni & Vetere, *supra* note 57, at 889.

[65] *See supra* notes 61–63 and accompanying text.

[66] The attacks on U.S. embassies in Nairobi, Kenya, and Dar-al-Salaam, Tanzania, and the U.S.S. Cole in Yemen also indicate that terrorism-financing is not a high-cost operation, though there are no reported estimates of the costs publicly available.

[67] *See supra* notes 61–63 and accompanying text.

The Quantum of Harm and Its Impact

The attacks mentioned above indicate that it is not so much the actual harm produced as it is the national and international impacts which motivates non-state actor terrorist-groups in selecting their targets. While comparative statistics of human tragedies are distasteful, they are nonetheless instructive.[68] The September 11th attacks produced nearly 3,000 victims,[69] compared with over 16,000 annual homicides in the U.S. and another 15,000 persons killed in drunk-driving accidents per year.[70] It is not therefore the number of causalities or victims that was significant in September 11th, but the vulnerability of the U.S. and particularly the symbolism of the targets. The World Trade Center was a symbol of U.S. economic power, and the Pentagon was a symbol of its military power. The reactions in the U.S. reflected the fears of a vulnerability gap as well as a hurt national pride. Examples such as this one are numerous in the history of European terror-violence in the 1960s and 1970s. Suffice it to recall that the kidnapping of the Italian Prime Minister Aldo Moro in the 1970s caused more of a national crisis than the 1,000 victims of Red Brigades terrorism in that country over a decade. What is more telling as described below is the quantum of harm caused by "terrorism" in contexts left outside the international legal control regime of "terrorism." This artificial distinction is reminiscent of Shakespeare's "that which we call a rose by any other word would smell as sweet."[71] Terror-violence, no matter by whom it is committed, is still terror-violence.

The following facts illustrate the above-mentioned propositions. Between 1948 and 1998, there have been an estimated 251 conflicts of a non-international character or purely internal character, both of which involve state as well as non-state actors.[72] In these conflicts, casualties are estimated at between 70 and 170 million, mostly among innocent civilians, not including the millions of refugees that these conflicts have created and the millions of dollars in property damage that has occurred.[73] Not only have these crimes remained outside of the purview of what is called

---

68 *See, e.g.*, Patterns of Global Terrorism (Department of State Office of Counterterrorism, 2003).

69 *See Report of the National Commission on Terrorist Attacks Upon the United States* (commonly known as the 9/11 Commission Report), *available at* http://www.9-11commission.gov. http://www.9-11commission.gov/.

70 *See* Crime in the United States, annual report of the U.S. Federal Bureau of Investigation, *available at* http://www.fbi.gov/ucr/ucr.htm#cius. http://http://www.fbi.gov/ucr/ucr.htm#cius.

71 William Shakespeare, Romeo and Juliet (II, ii, 1–2).

72 *See* Jennifer Balint, *An Empirical Study of Conflict, Conflict Victimization and Legal Redress*, 14 Nouvelles Etudes Pénales 101 (M. Cherif Bassiouni ed., 1988); *see also* SIPRI Yearbooks 1975–1996. There were two reported studies in the PIOOM Newsletter and Progress Report in 1994 and 1995: A.J. Jongman & A.P. Schmid, *Contemporary Conflicts: A Global Survey of High and Lower Intensity Conflict and Serious Disputes*, 7 PIOOM Newsletter and Progress Report 14 (Winter 1995) (Interdisciplinary Research Program on Causes of Human Rights Violations, Leiden, The Netherlands); *PIOOM World Conflict Map 1994–1995*, 7 PIOOM Newsletter, *supra;* Rudolph J. Rummel, Death by Government 3, 9 (1994) (reporting a total of 72.5 million casualties); *see also* Bassiouni, *supra* note 7, at 4; M. Cherif Bassiouni, *Searching for Peace and Achieving Justice: The Need for Accountability*, 59 Law & Contemp. Probs. 9 (1996).

73 *Id.*

"terrorism," they have also resulted in substantial impunity for its perpetrators.[74] In very few of these cases have the world's major powers militarily intervened, and even then, seldom in a timely manner.[75] And yet, not in any one of these conflicts, many of which involve genocide,[76] crimes against humanity,[77] war crimes, torture, slave-related practices, and other international crimes,[78] has the international community, and in particular the Security Council, accepted a responsibility to protect.[79]

The volume of harm produced is so enormous and so egregious, that one cannot help ask of which "terrorism" do governments speak. In very few of these conflicts have governments been moved, if not by the legality then by the morality of acting to prevent or mitigate the harm in progress. Compare for example September 11th and its consequences to what has happened in Darfur and the Democratic Republic of the Congo during the last three years. The estimates of the Darfur victims include over 200,000 killed and over two million refugees,[80] while in the DRC, more than three and a half million casualties are estimated.[81] In both of these cases, the international community has done little more than verbal condemnations.[82] Thus, legitimacy claims compare the double standards of neglect in the case of the crimes which produce the most significant harm, while elevating crimes which produce significantly lesser harm to a high level of counteraction.

"Terrorism" and the Media

The quantum or level of violence, as well as the harm that state and non-state actors can bring about, is in direct proportion to their resources and means. Thus, the harm produced by state-actors is significantly higher than that committed by non-state

---

[74] *See* M. Cherif Bassiouni, *Accountability for Violations of International Humanitarian Law and Other Serious Violations of Human Rights*, *in* Post-Conflict Justice 3 (M. Cherif Bassiouni ed., 2002).

[75] This was the case in the former Yugoslavia and Rwanda.

[76] *See* Samantha Power, A Problem from Hell: America and the Age of Genocide (2003); William A. Schabas, Genocide in International Law: The Crimes of Crimes (2000); Matthew Lippman, *Genocide*, *in* 1 International Criminal Law (M. Cherif Bassiouni ed., 2d ed. 1999).

[77] *See* M. Cherif Bassiouni, Crimes Against Humanity in International Criminal Law (2d rev. ed. 1999).

[78] Such as in the former Yugoslavia, Cambodia, Rwanda, Sierra Leone, and Liberia, to name only a few.

[79] *See* U.N. Doc. G.A. Res. A/60/1 (24 October 2005), at 30; U.N. General Assembly Res., A/Res/60/1 (24 October 2005).

[80] *See* Human Rights Watch, *Crisis in Darfur*, January 29, 2007, *available at* http://www.hrw.org/english/docs/2004/05/05/darfur8536.htm.

[81] *See* Anneke Van Woudenberg, *Democratic Republic of Congo: On the Brink* (Human Rights Watch, August 2006).

[82] Thus, while these acts of "terrorism" receive only verbal condemnation, the September 11th attack in the U.S. warrants a presidential declaration of war against Al-Qaeda and the invasion and occupation of Afghanistan and Iraq, with all its attending harmful consequences on the civilian population of these two countries. *See* Sean Murphy, *Terrorism and the Concept of "Armed Attack" in Article 51 of the U.N. Charter*, 43 Harv. J. Int'l L. 41 (2002); W. Michael Reisman, *International Legal Responses to Terrorism*, 22 Hous. J. Int'l L. 3 (1999).

actors.[83] Those with the least means necessarily engage in the type of terror-violence acts most likely to obtain the most public impact. In that respect, they have to depend on the terror-inspiring impact of their act as disseminated within a given societal context or at the international level.

The sensationalism of the media disseminating the terrorizing impact does not reflect the actual quantum of harm produced by the act. There is no correlation between the actual harm produced and its socio-psychological impact.[84]

Terror-violence, whether by state or non-state actors, is largely dependent upon the socio-psychological impact of the act and the resulting harm. The selectivity of the target depends on the socio-psychological and political impact that derives from its attack and the mass media's dissemination.[85] Democratic societies are particularly vulnerable in this respect. They face the value-based choice of curtailing freedom of the press or mitigating the social, political, and economic consequences of mass media dissemination of such tragic events. The mass media are essentially business enterprises. The more sensational and dramatic the event, the more likely it is that they will be covered and disseminated. The competitiveness of news and media coverage also depends on other factors. But its political impact in any society is something that political leaders cannot ignore. Thus, the temptation is inevitable for such leaders at the highest level to be drawn into responses and reactions, thus contributing to the public perception's enhancement of the crisis. At times, this suits the political leaders' purposes in enhancing their powers. In the aftermath of September 11th, President Bush and his administration were able to appear as the defenders of the nation and its people, and thus acquire powers not contemplated by the Constitution.

In a perverse sense, just as there is a symbiotic relationship between the mass media and "terrorism," there is also a symbiotic relationship between politics and "terrorism." Each one feeds upon the other, though for different purposes. It is a perverse relationship, because at times it also blurs legitimacy distinctions.

In the age of globalization, small groups of terrorists can be very effective, particularly when, as a result of a few dramatic acts, they are able to acquire an unprecedented status. Almost overnight, after September 11th, Osama bin Laden became the person capable of attacking the U.S. and his small group of followers in Afghanistan and Pakistan referred to as Al-Qaeda, became an organization deserving of the U.S.'s declaration of war against them.[86] Considering that the Al-Qaeda operatives in Afghanistan and Pakistan are relatively few in numbers, and that for

---

[83] *See supra* note 57 and accompanying text.

[84] *See* M. Cherif Bassiouni, *Terrorism, Law Enforcement and the Mass Media: Perspectives, Problems, Proposals,* 72 J. Crim. L. & Criminology 801-51 (1981); M. Cherif Bassiouni, *Media Coverage of Terrorism*, 32 J. Comm. 128 (1982); Abraham Miller, Terrorism, Media and the Law (1982); Media, Terrorism and Theory: A Critical Reader (Anandam Kavoori ed., 2006); Terrorism and the Media (David Paletz & Alex P. Schmid eds., 1992).

[85] *Id.*

[86] *See* The National Security Strategy of the United States of America (The White House, September 17, 2002).

> The United States is fighting a war against terrorists of global reach. The enemy is not a single political regime or person or religion or ideology. The enemy is terrorism – premeditated, politically motivated violence perpetrated against innocents.

all practical purposes, Al-Qaeda is at best a network of contacts whose strength, capabilities, and reliability cannot be assessed. One can only speculate as to the wisdom of having elevated this individual and his small band of followers to the status given to them by the Bush Administration. Small wonder that when Zarqawi, who had been rejected by bin Laden's organization found his way into Iraq and organized a group of volunteers to engage in acts of terror-violence against U.S. forces and the local population mostly by inciting sectarian violence between Shi' and Sunni, he was given a franchise by bin Laden to operate in Iraq under the Al-Qaeda name. Thus, Osama bin Laden's small Al-Qaeda organization with its newly acquired status moved into the franchise business and significantly increased his threat capabilities worldwide.

Both the media's impact and politicians' reactions to acts of terror violence evidence how frequently they have triggered unintended consequences which have only benefited the public goals of terrorist groups. This is an extension of the perversity of the relationship between the legitimate structures of democratic societies and "terrorism." Not only is it a question of the media's freedom of speech rights and society's right to know, but it is also an inevitable consequence of democratic forms of government that its leaders must show high visibility and strong reactions to such events in order to preserve their elected positions. Experience thus reveals that overreactions necessitated by domestic politics produce unintended effects, which ultimately serve the goals of terrorist groups.

Because of these factors, "terrorism" will always seek the type of targets which are most likely to generate a significant terror-inspiring effect in order to maximize the power-outcomes they seek. Considering that so many such targets have been identified and attacked in the last forty years, it is plausible to consider the use of weapons of mass destruction as a likely next stage of "terrorism" threats.[87]

> In many regions, legitimate grievances prevent the emergence of a lasting peace. Such grievances deserve to be, and must be, addressed within a political process. But no cause justifies terror. The United States will make no concessions to terrorist demands and strike no deals with them. We make no distinction between terrorists and those who knowingly harbor or provide aid to them.
>
> The struggle against global terrorism is different from any other war in our history. It will be fought on many fronts against a particularly elusive enemy over an extended period of time. Progress will come through the persistent accumulation of successes – some seen, some unseen.
>
> Today our enemies have seen the results of what civilized nations can, and will, do against regimes that harbor, support, and use terrorism to achieve their political goals. Afghanistan has been liberated; coalition forces continue to hunt down the Taliban and al-Qaida. But it is not only this battlefield on which we will engage terrorists. Thousands of trained terrorists remain at large within cells in North America, South America, Europe, Africa, the Middle East, and across Asia.

Id. See also David Abramowitz, *The President, the Congress, and the Use of Force: Legal and Political Considerations in Authorizing Use of Force Against International Terrorism*, 43 Harv. J. Int'l L. 71 (2002).

87 *See* Walter Laqueur, The New Terrorism, Fanaticism, and the Arms of Mass Destruction (1999); Barry Kellman, *Biological Terrorism: Legal Measures for Preventing Catastrophe*, 24 Harv. J.L. & Pub. Pol. 417 (2001).

Conclusion

The President of the United States after September 11th vowed to pursue Osama bin Laden until killed or captured, and yet most of those responsible for the 70–170 million casualties since World War II have benefited from impunity. The very government that vowed to pursue justice with respect to bin Laden has also vowed to oppose the International Criminal Court, whose intended goal is international criminal justice for persons responsible for such crimes as genocide, crimes against humanity and war crimes. These and other double standards mentioned above have created a crisis of credibility and legitimacy in the efforts to prevent, mitigate, and control terror-violence as it is conventionally understood, namely those acts contained in the thirteen international conventions and whose perpetrators are non-state actors. However, even in the context of that legal construct, one cannot help note that nothing has been done to criminalize the use of biological weapons and nuclear weapons.

In 2005, the National Counterterrorism Center in its Report on Incidents on Terrorism which was released on April 11, 2006, indicated that fifty-six American civilians were killed in terrorist attacks in 2005 including in Iraq and Afghanistan.[88] This rather limited number of victims means that terrorist attacks upon U.S. citizens are low, or that the U.S.'s anti-terrorism measures are particularly effective, or both. When the Bush Administration urges the enactment of legislation giving it more powers with which to curtail civil rights and justify violating the Geneva Conventions in Guantanamo and elsewhere, and in invading Iraq, it is relying in part on faulty premises. But, it is also in part relying on the psychology of the absurd, arising out of its own generated social fears. In other words, if there are only fifty-six Americans (excluding combatants in U.S. forces) killed, mostly in Afghanistan and Iraq, it means that the Administration's anti-terrorism measures are successful. There is an example in absurd psychology that goes as follows, "did you know that elephants hid in cherry trees? Answer: No. Response: It goes to show you that it works," namely, that elephants can hide so well in cherry trees that no one can see them.

For sure, it must be acknowledged that greater vigilance works, and nothing stated above should be interpreted as meaning that vigilance should be reduced. However, it is equally necessary to separate the wheat from the chaff – namely what is lawful and what is not. One of the consequences of the U.S.'s unlawful actions has been in denying P.O.W. status to Guantanamo and other detainees, engaging in torture, and violating the law of armed conflict in Afghanistan and Iraq. This is de-legitimizing U.S. anti-terrorism measures, and thus reinforcing the legitimacy claims of those who wish to retaliate against the U.S. by acts of terror-violence and who can easily advance a comparative legitimacy argument.[89]

---

88 *See* Report on Incidents of Terrorism 2005 (U.S. National Counterterrorism Center, 11 April 2005).

89 *See* Harold Koh, *The Spirit of the Laws*, 43 Harv. J. Int'l L. 23 (2002).

Terror-violence exists and will continue to exist, much like crime exists in every society. However, "terrorism" threats are enhanced because so many injustices remain un-redressed. The resort to terror-violence is also enhanced when double standards of legitimacy are applied by governments for their benefit. In the age of globalization, tragic events of different sorts reach peoples all over the world. When those who are socially, politically, and economically oppressed see the double-standards applied in connection with violence, their hope for a more justice-oriented world diminishes. Instead, they are encouraged to follow Mao Tse Tung's advice that "power grows out of the barrel of a gun."[90] That is why democracy based on the rule of law and respect for human rights is one of the most effective ways of combating "terrorism." John F. Kennedy wisely remarked in 1961 that "those who make peaceful evolution impossible, make violent revolution inevitable."[91] These words are reminiscent of Abraham Lincoln's first Inaugural speech, in which he said, "This country, with its institutions, belongs to the people who inhabit it. Whenever they shall grow weary of the existing government, they can exercise their constitutional right of amending it, or exercise their revolutionary right to overthrow it."

---

[90] *See supra* note 30, at 33.

[91] Speech made at the OAS Heads of State Summit, Pinta del'Este, Uruguay, 1961.

Values Implicated in the Struggle with Terrorism: War, Crime, and Prevention

Wayne McCormack

Why does terrorism so dominate the public psyche? In terms of loss of life, it pales by comparison to traffic fatalities and gun deaths – even just counting U.S. fatalities in the latter two categories.[1] Deaths and suffering from natural disasters impact thousands, almost always the poorer regions and persons of the globe.[2] Human trafficking enslaves thousands of persons every year, most of them children exploited in sex markets but also many desperate immigrants and refugees.[3]

Values can tell us much about the terrorist choice of tactics as well as about its impact on us. Values are critical to understanding the policy choices that are available for addressing the problem of terrorism. Values reflect shared experience that has been solidified into principles that do not need to be revisited in time of crisis. Closer attention to value-driven policy making will go far in restoring order to the American policy chaos of the early 21st century and rebuilding U.S. credibility in the global community.

W. McCormack
University of Utah
e-mail: mccormackw@law.utah.edu

[1] Worldwide terrorism deaths for the year 2001 as reported by the U.S. State Department, including the 3000 deaths on September 11, were about 3400. For the year 2006, the State Department classified 20,498 deaths worldwide as attributable to terrorist incidents, 13,000 of which were in Iraq. Traffic deaths in the U.S. recently have hovered at about 42,000 per year following a peak of almost 50,000 in the late 1980s. Deaths from guns in the U.S. consist of about 16,000 suicides, 10,000 homicides, and 6,000 accidents per year.

[2] The year beginning in December 2004 was particularly devastating – 220,000 dead in the Christmas tsunami, 20,000 or more in the October 2005 earthquakes, thousands left homeless from a record-setting hurricane season in the U.S. and Caribbean. Predictions of the consequences of global warming are even more dire.

[3] Information about the extent of human trafficking is difficult to come by. The United Nations Office on Drugs and Crime reports that hundreds of thousands of women, children, and men are ensnared in nonconsensual sex, domestic, or other undesirable work settings, http://www.unodc.org/unodc/en/trafficking_victim_consents.html#facts. One credible author estimates that there are 27 million persons held in some form of forced labor today. Kevin Bales, Disposable People: New Slavery in the Global Economy (1999).

I.A. Karawan et al. (eds.), *Values and Violence*,

Values Threatened by Terrorist Tactics

Terrorism, other than the genocidal practices of some recent civil wars, may not have the physical impact of automobile traffic nor handguns, yet it captures the attention of the public in astonishing degrees. Why? The terrorist uses the tactic for the very reason that it will generate passion and fear. The values threatened by terrorist activity include the credibility of government, self-confidence of the citizenry, and the viability or at least productivity of social institutions.

First, the act is "in your face;" it was never more dramatically so than on 9/11. The symbolism embodied in graphic television coverage of two towering structures collapsing in the heart of the capitalist West's financial center substantially exceeded the death toll itself. The symbolism oddly trivializes the pain and loss of the relatives of those who died, and the psychological effect goes far beyond the physical consequences.[4] The psychological effect is designed not just to intimidate but also to demand retaliation; in the terrorist's ideal scenario, the victim will over-react and get drawn into an untenable position, such as invasion of another country.

Second, many terrorist acts are designed to appear random – a bomb on a bus in the middle of the day or in a shopping area or a nightclub on a quiet evening creates the impression that death can stalk in the most mundane of circumstances. A fearful populace is a tense populace, and the terrorist's hope is that a tense populace eventually will yield to some demands just to ease the tension.

Third, the perpetrators fall into either of two camps, persons who appear to have the official imprimatur of the victim's own government or faceless unidentifiable persons who could be standing next to you on the next street corner. Because they are not uniformed personnel of another nation's military, there are no ready avenues for seeking them out or guarding against their next act.

Fourth, modern terrorism challenges the very legitimacy of government itself. To the extent that the terrorist can create the impression that government is helpless to protect its citizenry, the government loses not just credibility but authority itself. This creates pressure for the government to over-react and enforce severe restrictions on its citizenry, further undermining confidence and trust between government and citizen.

It has been said in many political settings that we are "confronting a new threat" or a "new type of enemy." That is simply not true. Terrorism, patterned violence against civilians for political ends, has been part of the human condition since people first started to gather in communities and maybe even before. Is there something new about the international or globalization of terrorism? Certainly, just as the communication, economic, and military capabilities of states have become global, so the capabilities and network structures of terrorist collectives have become globalized. But the threat of violence against civilian populations remains the same set

[4] To use a truly trivial analogy, the effect is much the same as the way in which a ferocious slam dunk trivializes the scoring of two points in an NBA game. The slam dunk attempts to impose intimidation that will be remembered by the opponent the next time down the floor, causing the opponent to tense up and make a mistake. Similarly, the terrorist attempts to cause the victim to overreact and make a mistake.

of challenges regardless of the scale or complexity of their operations. Because of the globalized nature and loose-knit structure of terrorist operations today, there is a clear need for international cooperation in their pursuit and prosecution, but that does not mean that society should curtail or abandon any of its long-standing values under a threat that is no different in kind than what has been faced for centuries.

The "Global War on Terrorism" is a tragic misnomer, although it is also true that the normal processes of domestic criminal law enforcement are not adequate to the task of confronting international terrorism. There is an interlocking set of "communities" devoted to public safety within government today. Similarly, there are interlocking legal controls or restraints that operate both on the individual or group who contemplates terrorist action and on the government agencies attempting to respond. The essence of the government framework is a tripod consisting of protective services, law enforcement, and the military. In the wake of a major event, whether large terrorist attack or natural disaster, the proper balance of the three functions is naturally called into question. Following 9/11, the U.S. has heavily emphasized the military option while European nations emphasized both prevention and law enforcement.

The choice of how to use each of the available resources and how much to allocate in each area depends on a calculus that is itself value-driven. For example, planning a major international event such as a World Cup soccer game starts with evaluating the likelihood of various risks and the degree of impact that would be felt if each were realized. Knowing that not all risk can be eliminated, the planner decides on a reasonable allocation of resources to meet the most likely levels and types of threat. At each stage, these calculations place a weight on human life and balance it against the resources available for protection.

Each of the countermeasures carries costs that can be measured in terms of human values – impositions on privacy, on liberty to move around, or on freedom of expression are often called into play in the name of security. Countermeasures also present value choices in how they interact with cultural norms and values of other societies. Some of the most obvious blunders of the U.S. in the past five years have come from failures to understand or show concern for values inherent in other cultures.

Thus, the interlocking network of contributive factors and countermeasures presents opportunities for identifying cultural and universal values at work in each level of choice or decision-making. Paying attention to what kinds of values are implicated with various policy choices will be critical in making the rational allocation of resources required by counter-terrorism planning.

Structure and Values of Public Safety

Although the political world and the popular press tend to lump all responses to terrorism together under the heading of "counter-terrorism," that label is more appropriately used for prosecutorial and military-type responses while preventive measures are more aptly characterized as "anti-terrorism." The difference corresponds roughly to reaction versus prevention.

The U.S. government, unlike many governments in history or even in the world today, has divided and separated various units which deal with aspects of public safety. The three principal divisions with which we will be concerned are protective services, law enforcement, and the military. These are the three arenas of government that comprise society's monopoly on the legitimate use of force.[5]

The prevention, enforcement, and military approaches can be analogized to how individuals deal with their own home safety. Think about the steps you take to guard against intrusions on your own space. First, you lock your doors. This is a phenomenon of relatively recent vintage itself, and there are many societies in the world today that still do not have locking doors. If this is not enough, and you have the money, you install an electronic security system, and maybe you have that system wired to call armed guards at a signal of intrusion, or maybe you even go so far as to build a gated community with guards at the entrance. All these are progressive steps of increasingly aggressive preventive measures that you can take on your own or in conjunction with immediate neighbors.

Second, if you have been the subject of an intrusion, you may want to apprehend and punish the intruder. In early stages of society, this might have been done by the individual acting alone, but in most societies this function has been turned over to law enforcement agencies. Whether the purpose is to disempower the specific intruder or to deter others, punishment is the province of communal groups. Finally, if the community feels threatened as a group by some outside group, it may move to the level of armed conflict between politically defined groups. Again, in more "primitive" societies these conflicts were often less deadly and widespread than is likely to be the case today, but the concept of an organized military response that operates across more or less defined borders between recognized political groups is ancient.

These three steps reflect roughly the three divisions of prevention, enforcement, and military action. Each stage not only carries its own culture and modes of operation, but also is constrained by a set of limiting rules. The civil liberties implications of prevention (such as limits on demonstrations or searching persons entering an airport) may differ somewhat from the civil liberties aspects of criminal law enforcement. The limitations on military action are among the most elusive of legal concepts because they arise rather infrequently and because the enforcement mechanisms for those limits themselves are somewhat tenuous.

This article deals with the values at stake in society's monopoly on the legitimate use of force – preventive services, law enforcement, and military operations.

---

[5] There are many other agencies involved in public safety, primarily those that deal with public health and response to emergencies.

The Intelligence Community

By both Executive Order and statute, the Intelligence Community (IC) is defined as consisting of the eight intelligence agencies within the Department of Defense (DIA, NSA, NRO, NIMA, and the IA's of the four uniformed services), the CIA, and portions of five executive departments (State, Treasury, Homeland Security, Energy, and FBI).

Until recently, under the National Security Act,[6] the CIA was formally the lead agency for coordination of all intelligence. About 80% of the total intelligence budget of the U.S. is in the Defense Department, which first emphasized technological intelligence to track and identify military targets and then shifted that technology to monitoring communications traffic. That factor, plus budget cuts at the end of the Cold War, plus the fact that most CIA personnel were trained in the ways of Soviet intelligence rather than the distinctly different culture of terrorist organizations, all combined by the late 1990s to leave the U.S. less than adequately prepared to infiltrate or monitor terrorist organizations.[7]

The 9/11 Commission made specific recommendations addressing the structure of the Intelligence Community, including "unifying strategic intelligence and operational planning against Islamist terrorists across the foreign-domestic divide" and "unifying the intelligence community with a new National Intelligence Director."[8]

The Commission's recommendation to "unify across the foreign-domestic divide" raises two concerns, each of which has both policy and value dimensions. First, it would run counter to the mandate of EO 12333, which was based on the work of the so-called "Church Commission" in 1973–1976. Although a major focus of the foreign-domestic divide was the protection of civil liberties of U.S. persons, another aspect was the belief that the accumulation of too much power in one place could make that agency inefficient by reducing the need for it to justify its actions to other actors and policy makers. Second, and related to the first, the unification of all intelligence gathering would eliminate competition within the government for attention and resources. Not all competition is good, but Judge Posner makes a strong argument that some competition would be a good thing in this context.[9]

These are critical issues for the structure and control of intelligence gathering, which will in turn dictate legal arguments over the validity of investigatory techniques. Some serious value questions arise from the sheer difficulty of gathering reliable intelligence about terrorist groups and their actions.

To illustrate some of the values involved in acquisition of intelligence information, I can summarize an extensive e-mail conversation between myself and my friend Jeff Breinholt, a very senior counter-terrorism lawyer, over a decision in a

---

6 50 U.S.C. § 401 et seq.

7 *See* 9/11 Commission Report at 86–91.

8 *Id.* at 399–400 (http://www.9-11commission.gov/report/911Report_Ch13.htm).

9 Richard Posner, Preventing Surprise Attacks (2005).

case called *Doe v. Ashcroft.*[10] In *Doe*, the district court held that FBI issuance of National Security Letters (NSL)[11] was unconstitutional. An NSL seeks to obtain information about a third party, in this instance information from electronic communications providers about subscribers and their billing records (the phone numbers they have called, for example). At the time, NSL's were authorized by a statute that required the Director of the FBI to certify that the records were "relevant to an authorized investigation to protect against international terrorism or clandestine intelligence activities."

A key issue in the case was what effect could be given to an NSL. Although the statute said the FBI could "request" subscriber information, it also said that the provider "shall comply" with a request. The statute and letter went on to say that the recipient of the letter could not disclose to anyone the receipt of the letter. To the court, this combination of factors meant that the recipient was led to believe that she had a legally enforceable obligation to turn over the information without even being allowed to consult with an attorney. Read in that fashion, the NSL amounted to a judicially unreviewable search and seizure that violated the fourth amendment.

To my friend Jeff, the court had overreacted. Jeff argued that an NSL was unenforceable and thus little more than an official-looking request for informal assistance. The court argued that the NSL, at least as drafted at the time of the decision, did not appear to be a request. The liberal watchdogs (along apparently with the classic conservatives) would also respond that the mere collection of that much information on citizens is a very bad idea. Although it is true that there is nothing wrong with asking, the way in which the "request" is made or the way in which the data is stored could lead to problems.

To all of this, Jeff responded that the FBI is entitled to lie in order to get information, for example by using undercover informants. He didn't understand why creation of a climate for cooperation was excessively coercive. He argued that eliminating law enforcement deception would be like extending the fourth amendment to enemy-controlled property located overseas. "That would mean we can, consistent with international law, bomb this property, but we can't search it without a warrant. Surely that's anomalous, right?" My response to that was that it's primarily a question of degree – too much information with too little controls is just as bad as coercion.

The dispute here is a philosophic one at a rather deep level. It's the dilemma of running an open society that is also a highly complex system with various threats of "butterfly effect." The 20th century liberal lived in a constant state of internal tension, wanting government to organize collective solution to social problems – reallocating wealth being the primary mechanism. But the liberal wanted government to stay out of his or her "private" life because it is the privacy of thought and feeling (and some behavior) by which, as Justice O'Connor put it, we "define one's own concept of existence, of meaning, of the universe, and the mystery of human life." The conservative, of course, was just as bad, wanting government to keep everybody

---

[10] 334 F. Supp. 2d 471 (S.D.N.Y. 2004).

[11] 18 U.S.C. § 2709.

else in line to protect his/her "private" property "rights" and wealth. The only consistent philosophy of that era was libertarianism, and we know what Einstein said about consistency and small minds. I don't mean to be flippant about this – each of the three has a solid basis for its position and they are all worried about the same thing. The very fact that every position of political philosophy worries about big government is itself a signal of something important.

I fully understand the frustration of law enforcement faced not just with a physical threat but with a clandestine threat to their very integrity and professionalism. The terrorist is no more clandestine than organized crime, but the threat is to the very community in which the law enforcement professional exists. It is the "in your face" aspect that the terrorists use to make their point, and it is the "in your face" that ramps up the public pressure to do something. I want them shut down, but ultimately the fabric of an open society is the goal of our protective efforts. If they send us too far in the direction of controlling our own populace, then they have won.

This exchange illustrates some of the values at stake in attempting to prevent clandestine violence. Prevention requires information that the holder wants to keep private. The more information government acquires, the more likely it can prevent violence before it occurs. But the intrusion into our lives at some point becomes intolerable to an open society. Moreover, the behavior of government officials who are encouraged to lie, cheat and steal information leads to the proverbial slippery slope on which an open society does not want its government officials to step.

Similarly, prevention requires interference with our freedom of movement. During the security planning for the 2002 Olympic Winter Games in Salt Lake, the University of Utah was preparing to host the Olympic Village and Olympic Stadium on our campus. Many faculty and staff were insistent that they wanted extreme measures taken for their safety – and that they wanted no interference with their ease of access to their places of work. Impossible – safety limits access.

Finally, prevention implies a great deal of secrecy on the part of government. The Freedom of Information Act and the related "right to know" concepts embedded in the first amendment reflect an understanding that the citizenry needs information about the government as much or more than government needs information about us. Every demand for governmental secrecy, legitimate and reasonably appearing as each might be in its own context, threatens the long-term credibility of government. Stack up too much government secrecy and we have a government in which no citizen can trust and ultimately one which few citizens will support.

Thus, the values threatened by preventive counter-measures include citizen privacy and mobility along with government transparency. These values are hauntingly similar to the values threatened by terrorist activity itself.

The Law Enforcement Approach

The U.S. had successfully prosecuted a number of terrorism cases prior to 9/11. Among the most famous were the first World Trade Center cases and the conspiracy case against Sheikh Rahman and some of his followers. The WTC prosecution resulted in conviction of four conspirators.[12] Although the alleged mastermind Ramzi Yousef fled the country, he was later apprehended in Pakistan and prosecuted for other crimes. In a separate prosecution, Sheikh Rahman and nine of his followers were prosecuted for conspiracy to blow up tunnels and bridges in the New York area.[13]

In the year 2000, there was a pending indictment in the Southern District of New York against Osama bin Laden and a number of others for the bombing of the Embassies in Kenya and Tanzania.[14] Several defendants in the embassy bombing case eventually pleaded guilty, offered differing levels of cooperation, and were sentenced to various terms in prison.[15] El-Hage and three other defendants were convicted after trial and sentenced to life imprisonment. In failing to come to a unanimous recommendation for the death penalty, the jury noted that some of its members believed that life imprisonment was a worse punishment than death.

Other successful prosecutions of terrorists had included Fawaz Yunis, who hijacked Royal Jordanian Flight 402 in 1985 and blew up the plane after letting the passengers go.[16] The only apparent connection between this incident and the U.S. was that two American citizens were on board the plane and thus were held hostage for a period of time during the incident. Omar Rezaq was prosecuted for air piracy in which death resulted, a potential capital offense, on the basis of an overseas hijacking in which an American passenger was murdered.[17] Ramzi Yousef was involved in the first World Trade Center bombing, indeed was probably the mastermind of the operation, but was arrested in Pakistan after attempting to orchestrate a bombing of several airplanes in the Philippines. He was brought by U.S. authorities to the U.S. and charged with conspiracy to destroy U.S. commercial airliners as well as one count of completed bombing of a Philippines Airline craft bound for Tokyo.[18]

Despite this history of successful prosecutions and the presence of well-trained prosecutorial teams within the U.S. Justice Department, on September 11, 2001, President Bush used the language of war in response to the attacks on the World Trade Center. Secretary of State Colin Powell cautioned that it would be a protracted effort rather than a single military operation.

---

[12] United States v. Salameh, 152 F.3d 88 (2d Cir. 1998).

[13] United States v. Rahman, 189 F.3d 88 (2d Cir. 1998).

[14] United States v. Bin Laden, 109 F. Supp. 2d 211 (S.D.N.Y. 2000).

[15] United States v. El Hage, 213 F.3d 74 (2d Cir. 2000).

[16] United States v. Yunis, 924 F.2d 1086 (D.C. Cir. 1991).

[17] United States v. Rezaq, 134 F.2d 1121 (D.C. Cir. 1998):
In 1985, Rezaq hijacked an Air Egypt flight shortly after takeoff from Athens, and ordered it to fly to Malta. On arrival, Rezaq shot a number of passengers, killing two of them, before he was apprehended. Rezaq pleaded guilty to murder charges in Malta, served seven years in prison, and was released in February 1993. Shortly afterwards, he was taken into custody in Nigeria by United States authorities and brought to the United States for trial.

[18] United States v. Yousef, 927 F. Supp. 673 (S.D.N.Y. 1996).

The Transactional Records Access Clearinghouse (TRAC) monitors investigatory reports and prosecutions by the federal government in a number of fields. In 2006, TRAC issued a report containing these observations:

> In the twelve months immediately after 9/11, the prosecution of individuals the government classified as international terrorists surged sharply higher than in the previous year. But timely data show that five years later, in the latest available period, the total number of these prosecutions has returned to roughly what they were just before the attacks. Given the widely accepted belief that the threat of terrorism in all parts of the world is much larger today than it was six or seven years ago, the extent of the recent decline in prosecutions is unexpected.[19]

What might explain a decline in prosecution of terrorism cases in the U.S.? a lack of interest? movement of resources and personnel to other matters? that there have been no terrorist acts in the U.S. to prosecute? that suspected terrorists have been the subject of rendition to other countries? that federal priority has shifted dramatically to military action? Perhaps a combination of all of these factors, and others unknown, has been at work. The question for me is whether the criminal justice system is prepared to deal with prosecution of terrorist plots.

It is often said in the Anglo-American legal system that it is better that a guilty person go free than that an innocent person go to prison. The entire structure of our system is loaded to protect the accused against government over-reaching. This tilt starts with the burden of proof (beyond a reasonable doubt), extends through the manifold procedural protections of trial (right to counsel, confrontation of witnesses, right against self-incrimination, right to a jury, double jeopardy), includes some more substantive protections (protection against *ex post* facto legislation, freedom of expression), and is subsumed under the general heading of due process of law. There is an interesting debate that can be had over the question of the degree to which the single phrase "due process" subsumes all the other specific guarantees of the Bill of Rights, but for present purposes it is enough to emphasize that due process is the expression of a tradition stretching back to Magna Carta.

To avoid due process, the current administration has attempted to imprison suspected terrorism accomplices without trial by sending them to military prison. Others have been charged before an ad hoc species of military commission (not a regular court martial) that provides two shortcuts in procedure that would not be available even in an ordinary court martial – the ability to exclude the accused from the courtroom and to keep some evidence secret from the accused.[20] As discussed below, both civilian and military judges are now showing a distinct lack of patience with attempts to circumvent or modify both systems to allow for summary imprisonment or trial without complete trial procedures.

The principal values emphasized in all criminal justice systems are these:

- presumption of innocence
- public trial

---

[19] http://trac.syr.edu/tracreports/terrorism/169/.

[20] *See* Hamdan v. Rumsfeld, 126 S. Ct. 2749 (2006).

- trial fairness (e.g., confrontation of witnesses and right to counsel)
- rule of law precepts (such as the ban on *ex past facto* laws)
- protection of liberal values (such as freedom of expression)
- resistance to inchoate crimes

All of these values weight toward protection of the accused, making it difficult for the state to be unduly repressive. The basic difference between a "police state" and an "open society" lies in the processes of the criminal justice system.

The Military Option

The most powerful physical institution known to humanity is the military. In essence, it is the instrument by which a nation-state or other large group attempts to assert or maintain control of territory. Curiously, it is not that easy to arrive at a coherent definition of military or armed forces that distinguishes it clearly from law enforcement.

In modern western practice, the military is the armed force that operates against foreign enemies while law enforcement (or police) is the armed force that operates domestically. That distinction, however, neither holds true in many nations nor describes the differences in function between the two.

A second distinction could be that the role of the military is to destroy a threat while the role of law enforcement is to neutralize a threat. This distinction emphasizes the different regimes of law that apply to the use of force by a state actor, but it is more semantic than capable of practical application.

A third method of distinguishing law enforcement and military operations is that the military wields violence based on status while the police use force based on conduct. This distinction gets closer to the heart of Western political values that emphasize free will and immunity of the individual from state control. In classic Western liberalism, the individual is free to think and do as he or she wishes until the point at which harm occurs to another. By contrast, the military is mandated to kill others on the basis of nothing more than their wearing of an opposing uniform or appearing to represent a threat.

There are some limitations on these statements under the Law of Armed Conflict. An opposing combatant cannot be killed if he or she has attempted to lay down arms or otherwise make a symbolic statement that one is *hors de combat*. Combatants who are wounded or captured must be treated in humane fashion under the terms of the Geneva Conventions. And civilians are protected under all circumstances unless they take steps that justify the use of self-defensive force by another.

The use of force in a given situation is controlled by the "rules of engagement" for that particular place and time. They may be designed in a given situation to keep troops short of encroaching on unlawful use of force, for example by clarifying the general norms of protection of civilians, limiting force to what is militarily necessary, and preventing mistreatment of those who are *hors de combat*.

The norms regarding justification for deployment of military force are contained in the *jus ad bellum* branch of the law of war, while rules for the permissible methods and tactics of warfare are contained in the *jus in bello* branch. The U.S. invaded Afghanistan in November 2001 without a whisper of dissent either domestically or internationally. By contrast, the invasion of Iraq in March 2003 was preceded by intense debate and has met with increasing levels of hostility both at home and abroad, at least partly because the purported justifications for the invasion have become transparently fallacious.

The norms and values at stake in military operations are manifold. No credible decisionmaker would consider deploying military force without considering these norms and values. The impacts of organized violence are often summed up in phrases such as "unchain the dogs of war" or "war is hell," phrases that call to mind the devastation of warfare: loss of life, displacement of families from their homes, destruction of the infrastructure of a nation. On the domestic front, even if the war is being fought on someone else's territory, there are impacts: family and social disruptions, communal spirit (either positive or negative, depending on the popularity of the war), trust in government policy makers and ultimately trust in government itself.

Domestic Implications of Military Engagements

I want to focus here on the impact of military language and policy on the domestic legal system. President Bush's order authorizing military commissions for the trial of suspected terrorists and collaborators was promulgated on November 13, 2001. It is patterned on the orders issued during World War II to deal with suspected spies in *Ex parte Quirin*.[21] Similar orders were issued following WWII for war-crimes trials of both German and Japanese officials.

The order allows the Secretary of Defense to establish a military commission for trial of "all offenses" alleged to be committed by any person who the President finds "is or was a member of the organization known as al Qaida" or "has engaged in, aided or abetted, or conspired to commit, acts of international terrorism, or acts in preparation therefor, that have caused, threaten to cause, or have as their aim to cause, injury to or adverse effects on the United States, its citizens, national security, foreign policy, or economy." The order does not appear to attempt creation of any new crimes but refers instead to "offenses triable by military commission" and "penalties under applicable law."

The order was first met with some skepticism but very little open criticism.[22] No prosecutions were begun under the order until after the Supreme Court decided in

---

[21] 317 U.S. 1 (1942).

[22] Professor Paust (a former faculty member at the JAG School) has been the most vigorously outspoken academic critic of the order. Jordan J. Paust, *Antiterrorism Military Commissions: Courting Illegality*, 23 Mich. J. Int'l L. 1 (Fall 2001). An early response to the criticisms was provided by Curtis A. Bradley and Jack L. Goldsmith, *The Constitutional Validity of Military Commissions*, 5 Green Bag 2d 249 (2002).

Rasul v. Bush[23] in 2004 that alien military detainees were entitled to some determination of their status by a neutral decision maker. The first prosecution then was derailed by the D.C. District Court in *Hamdan v. Rumsfeld*,[24] a position that was upheld by the Supreme Court on the basis that the tribunals had not been authorized by Congress to proceed without the protections of the Geneva Conventions.[25]

Following *Hamdan*, the Bush administration went to work on legislation to authorize the use of military commissions for alleged terrorists, to provide a list of offenses triable by commission, to protect classified information, and a variety of other provisions. In the Military Commissions Act of 2006 (MCA), Congress has endorsed a new terminology that has pervaded post-9/11 rhetoric, that of the "unlawful enemy combatant." Until now, there have been enemy combatants who violated the law of war and could be punished through military tribunals, and there have been civilians who violated both domestic law and international humanitarian law and could be punished through civilian processes. Now the administration has attempted to create a third category, one that is very difficult to define and may be elusive for the very reason that the concept violates some fundamental values. The key provisions in the Act that apply to unlawful enemy combatants is that classified information may be summarized or redacted when introduced into evidence.

The definition in the statute of "unlawful enemy combatant" is:

> a person who has engaged in hostilities or who has purposefully and materially supported hostilities against the United States or its co-belligerents and is not a lawful enemy combatant.

A lawful enemy combatant is defined in the statute as a person who is a member of a regular armed force of a state or a recognized militia. The definition throws wide open the question of how to draw the line between criminal activity that would belong to the civilian authorities and "hostilities" that place a suspect into the realm of military operations. The question must be asked whether we can continue to maintain the separation between civilian and military operations and what values are at stake in doing so.

The phrase "unlawful enemy combatant" originated in the opinion of the Supreme Court in the trial of the German saboteurs during World War II.[26] But as explained by the Court, the concept referred to persons who had been adjudicated (sometimes summarily on the field of battle) to have violated the law of war:

> By universal agreement and practice, the law of war draws a distinction between the armed forces and the peaceful populations of belligerent nations and also between those who are lawful and unlawful combatants. Lawful combatants are subject to capture and detention as prisoners of war by opposing military forces. Unlawful combatants are likewise subject to capture and detention, but in addition they are subject to trial and punishment by military tribunals for acts which render their belligerency unlawful. The spy who secretly and without uniform passes the military lines of a belligerent in time of war, seeking to gather military information and communicate it to the enemy, or an enemy combatant who without

[23] Rasul v. Bush, 542 U.S. 466 (2004).

[24] 344 F. Supp. 2d 152 (D.D.C. 2004).

[25] Hamdan v. Rumsfeld, 126 S. Ct. 2749 (2006).

[26] Military parlance had used the phrase "unlawful belligerent."

uniform comes secretly through the lines for the purpose of waging war by destruction of life or property, are familiar examples of belligerents who are generally deemed not to be entitled to the status of prisoners of war, but to be offenders against the law of war subject to trial and punishment by military tribunals.

The phrase has been used in the Bush orders and in the MCA to make it seem as if there is a certain status in which one can be placed and thus lose what would otherwise be rights of personhood. This is sheer nonsense – there is no room in American law for the executive to make a classification of a person and thus determine what rights that person has or does not have. Due process does not allow this and has not since the time of Magna Carta.[27]

The MCA gives law enforcement power to the military with regard to any noncitizen who is found to have engaged in "hostilities" against the United States. But the Act nowhere defines "hostilities." If the concept were limited to insurgent activities in situations such as Afghanistan or Iraq, where U.S. troops are actively deployed in combat gear in the field, then there would be nothing unusual about the statute's coverage at all. At the other extreme, if the term embraces one such as Jose Padilla, who was arrested in the U.S. on allegations of planning to bomb civilian facilities, then the statute is a direct contradiction to the "posse comitatus" statute and its underlying philosophy of keeping the military out of domestic law enforcement. In between are a range of actors, none of whom by traditional law-of-war standards would have gone before a military tribunal unless they were in a zone of combat or zone of occupation.

For example, the MCA allows any suspected terrorist "captured" (or "arrested"?) in any country to be brought before a military commission. Why? What value does this serve? Is it expressing a lack of trust for the civilian justice system? a lack of trust of the country in which the person was apprehended? It is very difficult to perceive the justification for taking the concept of "hostilities" out of its traditional notion of combat or occupation.

Moreover, the MCA embraces the concept of "unlawful enemy combatant" as if it were a status that depends on mere executive whim. The combination of these definitions and coverage provisions could be a claim of power on the part of the executive to classify a person arrested on U.S. soil as an "unlawful enemy combatant" and detain that person offshore with no judicial review. Preventive detention is fundamentally at odds with western traditions dating from Magna Carta and enshrined in the concept of due process. We can only hope that the attempt to extend executive power to such extremes will fade rapidly.

In two significant developments in June 2007, both civilian and military judges rebuked the President and the complicit Congress with regard to the Military Commission Act. In proceedings at Guantanamo on June 4, 2007, Army Colonel Peter Brownback dismissed charges against Omar Khadr[28] while Navy Capt. Keith Allred dismissed charges against Salim Hamdan.[29] In both cases, the judges ruled that the

[27] Hamdi v. Rumsfeld, 542 U.S. 507, 555 (2004) (Scalia, J., dissenting).

[28] http://www.defenselink.mil/news/newsarticle.aspx?id=46281.

[29] http://www.defenselink.mil/news/newsarticle.aspx?id=46288.

commissions had no jurisdiction over the defendants because their CSRT panels had merely found them to be "enemy combatants" rather than "unlawful enemy combatants." The MCA jurisdiction extends to crimes committed by "unlawful enemy combatants" and the judges held that this requires a prior determination of unlawfulness. These rulings are rather transparent slaps at the administration's placing the military in unprofessional situations.[30] The whole purpose of the commission trial is to determine whether the defendant acted unlawfully – a finding to that effect by another tribunal would be either prejudicial or meaningless. The jurisdictional facts for any tribunal are often intertwined with the merits and can be determined at the trial over which the tribunal has taken jurisdiction. As some commentators put it, a tribunal has inherent jurisdiction to determine its own jurisdiction.[31] So the explanation for these rulings must be the disgust that professional military lawyers are feeling over the unprofessional way in which the entire military detention matter has been handled.

One week later, the Fourth Circuit ruled that the MCA did not remove habeas corpus jurisdiction on behalf of an alien arrested in the U.S. and held without any CSRT or other determination of his status.[32] With regard to the statutory argument, the MCA did not create a suspension of the writ, at least not in the absence of the CSRT process.[33] On the merits of the habeas claim, the court was adamant that the President could not authorize the military to imprison a person indefinitely with no hearing whatsoever.[34] The court expressed shock at some of the arguments made on behalf of the Government.[35]

---

[30] *See* Dahlia Lithwick, *Line in the Sand*, Slate Magazine (June 5, 2007), http://www.slate.com/id/2167691/.

[31] *See* Charles Alan Wright, Federal Courts 94 (5th ed. 1994).

[32] Al-Marri v. Wright, 487 F.3d 160 (4th Cir. 2007).

[33] *Id.* at 169:

> The statute's use of the phrase "has been determined ... to have been properly detained" requires a two-step process to remove § 2241 jurisdiction: (1) an initial decision to detain, followed by (2) a determination by the United States that the initial detention was proper. The President's June 23 order only constitutes an initial decision to detain. To read the statute as the Government proposes would eliminate the second step and render the statutory language "has been determined ... to have been properly detained" superfluous – something courts are loathe to do.

[34] *Id.* at164:

> Even assuming the truth of the Government's allegations, the President lacks power to order the military to seize and indefinitely detain al-Marri. If the Government accurately describes al-Marri's conduct, he has committed grave crimes. But we have found no authority for holding that the evidence offered by the Government affords a basis for treating al-Marri as an enemy combatant, or as anything other than a civilian.

[35] *Id.* at 190:

> [A]ccording to the Government, the President has "inherent" authority to subject persons legally residing in this country and protected by our Constitution to military arrest and

The civilian judges wrote with restrained but outraged language about the history of civil liberties.[36] The military judges spoke with even more restraint but with an apparent regard for a similar history. The role of warrior is an honorable profession with a long history. It contemplates strict adherence to discipline and a code of behavior for the very reason that the military's ability to inflict violence must be kept in check for society to survive. That code translates into a respect for legal limits on the use of force and respect for the processes of military justice. When this administration asks the military to engage in an unjustifiable invasion of another country, fails to give it the resources needed and fails to supply a coherent rationale by which the occupying forces can hand over governance to a native entity, decrees that the military shall detain persons in life imprisonment with no showing of wrongdoing – when the administration does all this and more to the integrity of the military profession, the professionals ultimately will rebel.

There are three statutes that authorize the President to use military force in time of insurrection or other emergency. These statutes are not, however, a standing delegation of the power to declare martial law. That power remains implicitly within Congress unless it cannot meet.[37] In the few cases decided under these statutes,[38]

> detention, without the benefit of any criminal process, if the President believes these individuals have "engaged in conduct in preparation for acts of international terrorism." This is a breathtaking claim, for the Government nowhere represents that this "inherent" power to order indefinite military detention extends only to aliens or only to those who "qualify" within the "legal category" of enemy combatants.

[36] *Id.* at 163:

> For over two centuries of growth and struggle, peace and war, the Constitution has secured our freedom through the guarantee that, in the United States, no one will be deprived of liberty without due process of law. Yet more than four years ago military authorities seized an alien lawfully residing here. He has been held by the military ever since – without criminal charge or process. He has been so held despite the fact that he was initially taken from his home in Peoria, Illinois by civilian authorities, and indicted for purported domestic crimes. He has been so held although the Government has never alleged that he is a member of any nation's military, has fought alongside any nation's armed forces, or has borne arms against the United States anywhere in the world. And he has been so held, without acknowledgment of the protection afforded by the Constitution, solely because the Executive believes that his military detention is proper.

[37] Some observers believe that distinction was breached in the Defense Authorization Act of 2007 when Congress tinkered with the language of 10 U.S.C. § 333 to broaden the President's powers. In essence, the amendments broaden the occasions for domestic military operations from "insurrection, domestic violence, unlawful combination, or conspiracy" to include "natural disaster, epidemic, or other serious public health emergency, terrorist attack or incident" as well as any other condition that overwhelms state authorities. The motivation for this change came from Hurricane Katrina as well as from 9/11. Senator Leahy saw the amendment as a quiet but dangerous enhancement of executive authority. He has introduced legislation to repeal the 2006 amendments, describing his proposal as "legislation to repeal these unwarranted and perilous changes." http://leahy.senate.gov/press/200702/020707.html.

[38] The Prize Cases, 67 U.S. 635 (1863); Martin v. Mott, 25 U.S. (12 Wheat.) 19 (1827).

the Supreme Court has held that the President's determination on appropriate use of military force was conclusive on the courts as well as on military personnel.[39] In these cases, however, the Court's deference to the President was based on an unquestioned state of armed conflict – the War of 1812 and the Civil War.[40]

Common sense would indicate that a judge would be loathe to intervene in the face of any genuine threat of imminent violence. On the other hand, the statutes and cases all reflect a strong tradition that the military should have no role in domestic law enforcement. Indeed, the Framers reflected a strong antipathy toward even having a standing army and attempted to ensure that the military would be under control of the civilian authorities.

Distrust of a standing military and its strength is consistent with the basic western value system of limited government, the general premise being that the individual can lead a better life with only limited government involvement. By contrast, recent decades in the U.S. have reflected a growing trend toward a strong central government beginning with the "Imperial Presidency" of the Nixon years and running to the "unitary executive" of the Bush years.

Military Engagements Abroad

On the global scene, the United States' military involvement in Iraq has cost the U.S. untold levels of credibility and influence. That invasion was promoted on three grounds: preemptive self-defense against a perceived threat, spreading democracy and self-governance, liberating people from a brutal regime.

By contrast, the invasion of Afghanistan created not even a ripple of dissent from the world community. There are two theories under which the U.S. invaded

---

[39] *Id.* at 30–33:

> We are all of opinion that the authority to decide whether the exigency has arisen, belongs exclusively to the President, and that his decision is conclusive upon all other persons.... He is necessarily constituted the judge of the existence of the exigency in the first instance, and is bound to act according to his belief of the facts.... The law contemplates that, under such circumstances, orders shall be given to carry the power into effect; and it cannot therefore be a correct inference that any other person has a just right to disobey them. The law does not provide for any appeal from the judgment of the President, or for any right in subordinate officers to review his decision, and in effect defeat it.... It is no answer that such a power may be abused, for there is no power which is not susceptible of abuse. The remedy for this, as well as for all other official misconduct, if it should occur, is to be found in the constitution itself. In a free government, the danger must be remote, since in addition to the high qualities which the Executive must be presumed to possess, of public virtue, and honest devotion to the public interests, the frequency of elections, and the watchfulness of the representatives of the nation, carry with then all the checks which can be useful to guard against usurpation or wanton tyranny.

[40] The Court's review of the Executive power to conduct a war was essentially the same as the judicial role in determining whether to award payment of compensation for wrongful takings. For example, landowners obtained compensation for some damage to their holdings in the Philippines during World War II.

Afghanistan. One is that Afghanistan "harbored" terrorists to the extent that the terrorists became essentially the agents of that government, thus moving from the class of mere criminal to agents of war. Because those agents violated the rules of war by taking aggression, by striking civilian targets, and by blending back into civilian populations, other nations were justified in using military force to retaliate and prevent further attack.

The second theory harkens back to the piracy and slave trading of the 18th and 19th centuries. "From the Halls to Montezuma to the shores of Tripoli" salutes the actions of Marines who rooted out pirate strongholds located in other nations. Other nations of the world were never called on to decide whether our actions were legitimate. Similarly, the European-American nations were in disarray over whether it was legitimate to strike militarily against slave depots and slave trading ships within the boundaries of other nations. Suffice to say that time and history are on the side of the victors in those cases. Today there is near, but perhaps not conclusive, consensus that it is permissible to make "surgical" incursions into another country to root out a pirate or slave trader to an extent that would not be permissible with a "mere" criminal.

The initial arguments for the Iraq invasion were (1) humanitarian intervention, on the basis that the Saddam Hussein regime was a brutal dictatorship committing multiple crimes against its own people, (2) self-defense, on the basis that Iraq was harboring elements of al Qaeda engaged in an ongoing campaign against western nations, and (3) preemptive self-defense, on the basis that Iraq was attempting to acquire weapons of mass destruction (WMD) and would allow them to be used against the U.S.

The attempt to promulgate a new theory of unilateral humanitarian intervention has at best a checkered history. It has not met with favor in the International Court of Justice nor among the published commentaries. As events unfolded, it became apparent that the WMD justification was based on faulty intelligence. The al Qaeda connection also proved to be highly unlikely.[41]

At a minimum, Iraq teaches the need for assessing the likely consequences of an action before it is taken. That would seem to be so elemental that the mere statement should be an insult to an adult, but it is clear that the invasion of Iraq was undertaken with no thought for the structure of the post-war society, the potential for increasing anti-western sentiment and thus fueling terrorist violence, or the impact of the entire situation on U.S. credibility in the world. A politician with an eye on values would not have failed to consider such consequences before acting. Values are the

---

[41] It is more likely that prior to the invasion, Osama bin Laden had some degree of hostility toward Saddam Hussein along with other "secular" Arab leaders. On the other hand, Iraq had harbored Abu Musab al-Zarqawi who had been sentenced to death by Jordan for various terrorist activities. Zarqawi may or may not have had links to bin Laden prior to the invasion, and intelligence sources differed on whether he was an associate of or a rival to bin Laden. After the invasion, elements of groups linked to al Qaeda, particularly Zarqawi and his associates, concentrated in Iraq and become principals in some of the insurgent resistance. Zarqawi subsequently declared himself to be in alliance with al Qaeda but he was killed by U.S.-led forces without shedding any further light on the degree of that interaction.

mechanism by which consequences are thoroughly vetted before a crisis arises so that an actor can rely on known values in the middle of a stressful situation.

Wisdom and Values in Military Action

Among the effects of the Iraq invasion have been a number of negative consequences for the U.S. and its foreign affairs. It has reduced the resources applied to the effort to apprehend Osama bin Laden, diverted resources that could have gone to support of emerging economies struggling with the effects of globalization, and diverted attention away from even more tragic issues such as human trafficking and organized crime. It is now widely acknowledged among political leaders and commentators that the invasion of Iraq has made the U.S. less safe than it was before.

The invasion of Iraq was a strategic blunder of catastrophic proportions – horrifically unwise in its inception. As a teaching moment, it demonstrates value choices that should be borne in mind in all future discussions of the role of military force. The principal driving value behind the decision was the very language of war itself. Once the Bush administration was able to sell the media on the "Global War on Terror" (GWOT), then the public was easy to sell on rhetorical flourishes such as "if you're not with us, you're against us," or "fight them there so we don't fight them at home." The language of war gives all the decision power to the Executive. For the reasons given in the *Prize Cases* discussed above, there is no second-guessing the President on how to conduct a war once it has been decided to go to war.

The experience with military detentions in the struggle with terrorism has been disheartening for the rule of law. On the other hand, the apparent inclination of military professionals to stand up for the rule of law is encouraging. The heart of military operations is an emphasis on status rather than behavior. If a person is an enemy, then one takes action. By contrast, the civilian justice system emphasizes behavior. If a person is alleged to have done something, then use a trial to find out and punish. The MCA and the rhetoric of the Bush administration have attempted to obliterate this distinction in a clash with fundamental norms and values of the western world. It is now time for the "Ship of State to right itself."[42]

Values involved with the use of military operations in the effort against terrorism include:

- impacts of military action on the domestic scene – human casualties and policies
- impacts of the language of war – dampening debate and eroding liberties
- justifications of violence
- confusion of paradigms

---

[42] *Cf.* Mark Tushnet, *Defending Korematsu?: Reflections on Civil Liberties in Wartime*, 2003 Wis. L. Rev. 273, 274.

A Value-Oriented Approach to Policy

A practical, hard-nosed politician may be disinclined initially to pay much attention to the thought of values as driving policy. Values seem too soft, fuzzy-headed, and academic to satisfy the hard demands of political life. The reality, however, is that only a value-driven approach can provide long-term solutions to a long-term problem, and the problem of violence against civilian targets is a very long-term problem.

Law enforcement agencies should interact extensively with the intelligence community. All seem to agree on this following the 9/11 Commission report. But in the process, there are limits that need to be observed. Gathering of intelligence data on U.S. persons is somewhat circumscribed under FISA. The reasons given for this are usually framed in terms of "privacy," a label with the potential for understating the importance of the interests involved. Western liberal political philosophy depends directly on citizen participation in the political process, and political freedom is directly threatened by the mere accumulation of information about a person's political activities.

The restrictions on the military option are important because of the scope of power involved and the lack of independent judicial oversight. At a broad theoretical level, there is the oft-repeated policy that the military must always be under civilian direction. The President's Commander-in-Chief power is important but so are Congress' multiple roles such as: "To define and punish Piracies ... and Offenses against the Law of Nations," "To declare War," "To raise and support Armies," "To make Rules for the Government and Regulation of the land and naval forces." The military is subject to multiple rules of law – domestic U.S. law, the UCMJ, international law, and the domestic law of any nation in which it may be operating. These are complex and overlapping legal regimes making the role of the military lawyer a central facet of military operations today. The legal officer has taken a permanent seat next to the battlefield commander, and the Center for Law and Military Operations produces critical guidance for those officers. But when push comes to shove, the decision to employ armed force is primarily a political decision. That decision will be better guided when the political decision makers (the decision elite) are cognizant of the legal restrictions.

With regard to the third leg of the tripod, the intelligence services, the rules become even more amorphous. Some of the limits are constitutional under the general heading of privacy. Most, however, are composed of structural limitations contained within Executive Orders or congressional reorganization bills. The creation of an "intelligence czar," in the form of the National Intelligence Director, begins rather than ends the debate over whether it is either possible or wise to consolidate all intelligence activities of the U.S. under a single hierarchy. The virtues of splitting domestic from foreign intelligence, as well as the arguable benefits of competition among agencies, will continue to be debated for some time.

In classic law school fashion, I'll try to compose one simple scenario that brings out all the issues in the agenda of this paper. Assume that a joint task force of CIA, FBI, and special forces operatives have pinpointed the location of a known ranking member of a terrorist organization in Damascus. Should they kill him or try to capture and spirit him out of the country? If the latter, where do they take him and what do they do with him?

It is incredibly difficult to have a clear-headed discussion of the options if policy has already been fore-shortened by the language of war. If the target were located on U.S. soil, then the only feasible answer would be recourse to the processes of civilian law enforcement (the attempts to do otherwise with Jose Padilla notwithstanding). A presumption in favor of civilian law enforcement processes is still appropriate when operating overseas, but the presumption weakens dramatically with the likelihood of meeting resistance in the other country's policies. In that instance, clandestine action may well become the only feasible option. But that doesn't necessarily mean assassination, which could well be illegal under U.S. law as well as the law of the host nation. And capture does not answer all questions with regard to what to do with the person. There is little in U.S. law on which to base an argument that detention and interrogation in another (friendly) nation would be illegal, but there are political risks that can be fully appreciated only with a full and complete understanding of the legal principles involved.

These are the kinds of discussions that need to take place in many places among many participants. With a more thorough understanding of the options will come a more thorough understanding of the interactions among the three principal legs on which public safety rests. There is no reason to pick one to the exclusion of the others. Each has its roles to play and none can be maximally effective without the others.

It is to be hoped that once the panic subsides, then pursuit of terrorists can be brought within the mainstream of American law. It is not easy to do so because domestic legal regimes have not been thoroughly integrated with international norms and expectations. Even with the examples of piracy and slavery behind us, there is no established legal analysis for dealing with transnational criminals of violence. That remains a challenge and bringing that problem within the mainstream of American law will not be easy.

This language of Lord Hoffman is worth special emphasis:

> Of course the government has a duty to protect the lives and property of its citizens. But that is a duty which it owes all the time and which it must discharge without destroying our constitutional freedoms. There may be some nations too fragile or fissiparous to withstand a serious act of violence. But that is not the case in the United Kingdom. When Milton urged the government of his day not to censor the press even in time of civil war, he said:
>
> > Lords and Commons of England, consider what nation it is whereof ye are, and whereof ye are the governours.
>
> This is a nation which has been tested in adversity, which has survived physical destruction and catastrophic loss of life. I do not underestimate the ability of fanatical groups of terrorists to kill and destroy, but they do not threaten the life of the nation. Whether we would survive Hitler hung in the balance, but there is no doubt that we shall survive Al-Qaeda. The Spanish people have not said that what happened in Madrid, hideous crime as it was, threatened the life of their nation. Their legendary pride would not allow it. Terrorist violence,

> serious as it is, does not threaten our institutions of government or our existence as a civil community.[43]

The language of war that was chosen after 9/11 reflected not an emergency but a form of panic. The administration chose to play on the fears of the American public rather than paying attention to the values of the American public. And in the long run we are paying an extraordinary price for that diversion.

In October 2001, the United States had the most credibility and power of any nation or empire in the history of the world. We had the opportunity to use our influence to reshape in fundamental ways the methods by which the nations of the world cooperated in combating violence. Because our political leaders played to short-term political whim rather than long-term political values, we have squandered that credibility and destroyed the hope of international cooperation in this arena for at least another generation. The next administration should begin rebuilding by embracing the universal values of fair trial and human dignity.

[43] A. v. Home Secretary ¶95 & 96, [2004] UKHL 56, [2004] All ER (D) 271.

Biographies of Authors

M. Cherif Bassiouni

M. Cherif Bassiouni is Distinguished Research Professor of Law at DePaul University College of Law and President of the International Human Rights Law Institute. He is also President of the International Institute of Higher Studies in Criminal Sciences in Siracusa, Italy and Honorary President of the International Association of Penal Law (President 1989–2004) based in Paris, France. An expert on international criminal law and human rights, he is the author of 27 books, the editor of 48 books and the author of 239 articles. His publications have been translated in several foreign languages. He is the recipient of four honorary degrees from France, Ireland, Italy and the U.S. and the recipient of the highest medals of Austria, Egypt, France, Germany and Italy. In 1999, he was nominated for the Nobel Peace Prize for his work on the establishment of the International Criminal Court. He has served in various capacities with the United Nations, among those Chairman of the Security Council Commission to investigate war crimes in the former Yugoslavia and Independent Expert on Human Rights in Afghanistan.

Akeel Bilgrami

Akeel Bilgrami is the Johnsonian Professor of Philosophy and the Director of The Heyman Center for the Humanities at Columbia University. He is also a member of Columbia's Committee on Global Thought. He got a first degree in English Literature from Bombay University and then studied Philosophy, Politics and Economics at Oxford, as a Rhodes Scholar. He got a Ph.D from the University of Chicago. He joined Columbia University in 1985 after spending two years as an Assistant Professor at the University of Michigan, Ann Arbor. His publications include the following books: *Belief and Meaning* (Blackwell 1992), *Self-Knowledge and Resentment* (Harvard University Press 2006). *Politics and The Moral Psychology of Identity* from Harvard University Press and *What is a Muslim?* from Princeton University Press, both due in 2008. He has published over 50 articles in Philosophy of Mind as well as in Political and Moral Psychology. Some of his articles in these latter subjects speak to issues of current politics in their relation to broader social and cultural issues.

Martha Crenshaw

Martha Crenshaw is a Senior Fellow in the Center for International Security and Cooperation at the Freeman Spogli Institute for International Studies and Professor of Political Science by courtesy at Stanford University. She taught at Wesleyan University in Connecticut from 1974 to 2007. She has written extensively on the issue of political terrorism. She serves on the Executive Board of Women in International Security and chairs the American Political Science Association Task Force on Political Violence and Terrorism.

Tom Farer

Tom Farer is Dean of the Graduate School of International Studies at the University of Denver, Honorary Professor of Peking University, and past President of the Association of Professional Schools of International Affairs (APSIA). He is former President of the Inter-American Commission on Human Rights and also of the University of New Mexico. He has previously taught at the law schools of Columbia, Harvard, Rutgers, Tulane, and American University and international relations at American University's School of International Service, Johns Hopkins School for Advanced International Studies and at Princeton's Woodrow Wilson School. His books include *Toward a Humanitarian Diplomacy*, *Warclouds on the Horn of Africa*, *The Grand Strategy of the United States in Latin America*, *Transnational Crime in the Americas*, *Ends and Means in Central America*, and *Beyond Sovereignty*. Dean Farer has served as special assistant to the General Counsel of the Department of Defense, special assistant to the Assistant Secretary of State for Inter-American Affairs, legal advisor to the UN Intervention Force in the Somali Republic (1993), Advisor on the Ugandan Constitution (1994) and legal advisor and self-defense instructor for the Police Force of The Somali Republic. He is a graduate of Princeton University (A.B. Magna cum Laude) and Harvard Law School (J.D. Magna cum Laude) where he was Notes Editor of the Harvard Law Review.

Marilyn Friedman

Marilyn Friedman is Professor of Philosophy at Washington University in St. Louis. She is also Research Professor of Social Justice at the Centre for Applied Philosophy and Public Ethics, Charles Sturt University and Australian National University. Her publications in political philosophy, feminist theory, and ethics have appeared in a number of journals, including *Journal of Philosophy and Ethics*, and numerous edited collections. Friedman's authored books include *What Are Friends For: Feminist Perspectives on Personal Relationships and Moral Theory* (Cornell), *Political Correctness: for and Against* (Rowman & Allenheld, co-authored), and most recently, *Autonomy, Gender, Politics* (Oxford). She has co-edited *Feminism and Community* (Temple), *Mind and Morals: Essays on Ethics and Cognitive Science* (MIT), and *Rights and Reason: Essays in Honor of Carl Wellman* (Kluwer). Her most recent edited collection is *Women and Citizenship* (Oxford). She is currently completing a project on female terrorists.

Amos Guiora

Amos N. Guiora is Professor of Law at the S. J. Quinney College of Law, University of Utah. Professor Guiora teaches Criminal Law, Global Perspectives on Counter-terrorism, Religion and Terrorism and National Security Law. At the S.J. Quinney College of Law, Guiora in collaboration with other leading experts at the S.J. Quinney College of Law, will help lead the school's efforts to provide cutting-edge research, innovative training, and public service initiatives in the prevention and mitigation of global conflict. His publications include the published casebook Global Perspectives on Counter-terrorism (Aspen 2007), as well as the forthcoming titles Constitutional Limits on Coercive Interrogation (Oxford 2008); Terrorism Primer (Aspen 2008); and, as general editor, Annual Review – Top Ten Global Security Law Review Articles, Vol. I (Oxford 2008). Professor Guiora writes and lectures extensively on issues such as legal aspects of counterterrorism, terror financing, international law and morality in armed conflict. From his twenty years of experience with the Israel Defense Force, Guiora continues to educate IDF commanders and soldiers in international law and morality of the use of force.

George F. Hepner

George F. Hepner is a Professor of Geography at the University of Utah in Salt Lake City, Utah. His major areas of research involve geographical analysis using remote sensing and geographic information systems (GIS), hazard response and mitigation, and international environmental assessment. He has been a research fellow and consultant to the Image Processing Laboratory, at the Jet Propulsion Laboratory, California Institute of Technology, and the Risk and Response Management Program at Lawrence Livermore National Laboratory. He is the Director of the University of Utah center of the Southwest Consortium for Environmental Research and Policy, supported by the USEPA to perform research in the U.S.-Mexico border region. He currently serves on Mapping Sciences Committee of the National Research Council (NAS) and the academic accreditation panel of the U.S. Geospatial Intelligence Foundation. He was an editor of the AGU environmental change journal, *Earth Interactions*, 1999–2003. In 2001–2002 he was elected as the national President of the American Society for Photogrammetry and Remote Sensing (ASPRS).

Bruce Hoffman

Bruce Hoffman is a tenured professor in the Security Studies Program at Georgetown University's Edmund A. Walsh School of Foreign Service, Washington, DC. Professor Hoffman previously held the Corporate Chair in Counterterrorism and Counterinsurgency at the RAND Corporation and was also Director of RAND's Washington, D.C. Office. From 2001 to 2004, he served as RAND's Vice President for External Affairs and in 2004 he also was Acting Director of RAND's Center for Middle East Public Policy. His publications include the highly influential *Inside Terrorism* (2nd ed. 2006).

Ken Jameson

Ken Jameson is Professor of Economics at the University of Utah, formerly at Notre Dame. The main focus of his research is the economic development of Latin America. He has worked in most countries of Latin America, most recently concentrating on Ecuador and Peru. He has published widely in academic journals and books. His recent work is on dollarization in Latin America, on institutionalism and development, on the role of indigenous movements in the Latin American political process, and on the Latin American presence in the United States. Recent articles have appeared in The Journal of Economic Issues, Applied Economics, International Journal of Political Economy, and Latin American Politics and Society. He was also a co-author of the February, 2006 monograph "The Economic Impact of the Mexico-Utah Relationship." He was an observer of the Venezuelan recall election with the Carter Center. He has consulted for U.S. and Latin American government agencies and non-profits, conducting field research in most of Latin America.

Benjamin Judkins

Benjamin Judkins first discovered international relations while an undergraduate at the University of Rochester. He went on to receive his PhD from Columbia University in 2004 and is currently an Assistant Professor of Political Science at the University of Utah. His training is in international relations and international political economy and his current research areas include economic statecraft and the intersection of religion and international politics. His prior publications include a study of left-right party alignment and trade policy, co-authored with Helen Milner, in *International Studies Quarterly*, and multiple papers on economic sanctions. Much of his current research focuses on religiously generated social capital as an important resource in addressing economic and political problems at both the domestic and international level.

Ibrahim A. Karawan

Ibrahim Karawan is Professor of Political Science at the University of Utah in Salt Lake City. Between 1995 and 1997 he was Senior Fellow for Middle East Studies and Directing Staff Member at the International Institute for Strategic Studies, IISS, in London. Professor Karawan is the author of *The Islamist Impasse* (Oxford University Press, 1997) and a frequent contributing analyst to the BBC World Service, CNN, *Al-Jazeera* satellite Television, and Radio Swiss International.

Wayne McCormack

Wayne McCormack is Professor of Law at the University of Utah. He is a graduate of Stanford and the University of Texas School of Law. He clerked on the Ninth Circuit, taught at the University of Georgia, served as Associate Director of the Association of American Law Schools, and joined the Utah faculty in 1978. In addition to three stints as Associate Dean for Academic Affairs, he coordinated the University of Utah's involvement with the 2002 Olympic Winter Games (1997–2002), in which role he became immersed in security planning and counter-terrorism. He is the author of numerous articles and books, including *Federal Courts* (Matthew Bender 1984), *Constitutional Law: Principles and Policies* (Michie, 1992, 1996; Lexis/Nexis 2002, 2007) (with Barron, Dienes, and Redish), *Legal Responses to Terrorism* (Lexis/Nexis 2005), and *Understanding the Law of Terrorism* (Lexis/Nexis 2007). Professor McCormack teaches constitutional law, law of terrorism, civil procedure, and judicial process.

Richard Medina

Richard Medina is currently a Ph.D. student in the Department of Geography at the University of Utah. He earned his Bachelor's and Master's degrees in Geography from California State University, Los Angeles. His research interests include: spatial analysis, complex systems in real and social spaces, and Geographic Information Systems (GIS).

Martha Nussbaum

Martha Nussbaum is Ernst Freund Distinguished Service Professor of Law and Ethics at the University of Chicago, with appointments in Philosophy, Law, and Divinity. She is an Associate Member of the departments of Classics and Political Science, a Member of the Committee on Southern Asian Studies, and a Board Member of the Human Rights Program. She also held appointments and taught at Brown University, Harvard, and Oxford. Professor Nussbaum has been a member of the Council of the American Academy of Arts and Sciences and a member of the Board of the American Council of Learned Societies. She was a research advisor at the World Institute for Development Economics Research, Helsinki, a part of the United Nations University, President of the Central Division of the American Philosophical Association (1999–2000), and President of the Human Development and Capability Association (2006–08). She has received honorary degrees from over thirty colleges and universities in the United States, Canada, Asia, and Europe. Among her awards are the Grawemeyer Prize in Education in 2002 and the Faculty Award for Excellence in Graduate Teaching at the University of Chicago in 2004. A major philosopher and public intellectual of our time, Professor Nussbaum is the author of over fifteen books, including *The Fragility of Goodness* (1986), *Cultivating Humanity* (1997), *Women and Human Development* (2000), *Upheavals of Thought: The Intelligence of Emotions* (2001), *Hiding from Humanity: Disgust, Shame and the Law* (2004), and *Frontiers of Justice* (2006). Her forthcoming books include *The Clash Within: Democracy, Religious Violence, and India's Future* (2007) and *Liberty of Conscience* (2008). She has also edited thirteen books, including *The Quality of Life*, with Amartya Sen (1993).

Monisha Pasupathi

Monisha Pasupathi is an Associate Professor of Developmental Psychology at the University of Utah. She received her Ph.D. in Psychology from Stanford University in 1997, and served as a post-doctoral fellow in the Center for Lifespan Psychology at the Max Planck Institute for Human Development, Berlin, Germany, from 1996–1999. She joined the University of Utah in 1999. She is interested in the relationship between memory, storytelling, and self development across the lifespan. Her past work, for which she received the Richard Kalish innovative publication award from the Gerontological Society of America, has examined listeners and storytelling in adulthood. Her current research centers on the development of moral and collective identity in childhood and adolescence, and how that development is reflected in, and furthered through, storytelling.

Stephen Reynolds

Stephen Reynolds is Professor of Economics, Interim Director of International Programs of the Institute of Public and International Affairs and Associate Dean of the College of Social and Behavioral Science, University of Utah. He received a doctoral degree (1970) in economics from the University of Wisconsin-Madison. He joined the faculty of the University of Utah in 1969. Reynolds' areas of specialization are international economics, economic development of Southeast Asia and multinational firms' trade and investment. His more recent scholarly papers have focused on the conditions preliminary to and the recovery from the Asian Crisis of 1997. He has professional experience in Asia, Africa, Europe and Latin America, has received support from the National Science Foundation, US Agency for International Development, US Department of Energy and US Department of Education.

Frank Salter

Frank Salter is a Senior Research Associate in the Max Planck Research Group for Human Ethology, in Andechs, Germany. He received his doctorate in 1990 from Griffith University, Brisbane, Australia, for a thesis that applied urban anthropological and ethological methods to field observations of command in various institutional settings. His areas of specialization are biosocial approaches to power, ethnicity, and nationalism. He has taught at universities in Central and Eastern Europe, London, and most recently at the University of Utah. Publications include two monographs, *Emotions in Command: Biology, Bureaucracy, and Cultural Evolution* (1995/2007) and *On Genetic Interests: Family, Ethnicity, and Humanity in an Age of Mass Migration* (2003/2006). He is presently researching fluctuations in ethnic mobilization and methods for comparing the influence of ethnic groups within states.

Amartya Sen

Amartya Sen is Lamont University Professor, and Professor of Economics and Philosophy, at Harvard University and was until recently the Master of Trinity College, Cambridge. He has served as President of the Econometric Society, the Indian Economic Association, the American Economic Association and the International Economic Association. He was formerly Honorary President of OXFAM and is now its Honorary Advisor. Born in Santiniketan, India, Amartya Sen studied at Presidency College in Calcutta, India, and at Trinity College, Cambridge. He is an Indian citizen. He was Lamont University Professor at Harvard also earlier, from 1988–1998, and previous to that he was the Drummond Professor of Political Economy at Oxford University, and a Fellow of All Souls College (he is now a Distinguished Fellow of All Souls). Prior to that he was Professor of Economics at Delhi University and at the London School of Economics. Amartya Sen's books have been translated into more than thirty languages, and include *Collective Choice and Social Welfare* (1970), *On Economic Inequality* (1973, 1997), *Poverty and Famines* (1981), *Choice, Welfare and Measurement* (1982), *Resources, Values and Development* (1984), *On Ethics and Economics* (1987), *The Standard of Living* (1987), *Inequality Reexamined* (1992), *Development as Freedom* (1999), *Rationality and Freedom* (2002), *The Argumentative Indian* (2005), and *Identity and Violence: The Illusion of Destiny* (2006), among others. Amartya Sen has received honorary doctorates from major universities in North America, Europe, Asia and Africa. He is a Fellow of the British Academy, Foreign Honorary Member of the American Academy of Arts and Sciences, and a member of the American Philosophical Society. Among the awards he has received are the "Bharat Ratna" (the highest honour awarded by the President of India); the Senator Giovanni Agnelli International Prize in Ethics; the Alan Shawn Feinstein World Hunger Award; the Edinburgh Medal; the Brazilian Ordem do Merito Cientifico (Grã-Cruz); the Presidency of the Italian Republic Medal; the Eisenhower Medal; Honorary Companion of Honour (U.K.); The George E. Marshall Award, and the Nobel Prize in Economics.

Cecilia Wainryb

Cecilia Wainryb is a Professor of Developmental Psychology at the University of Utah, and a Fellow of the American Psychological Association. She received her Ph.D. in Human Development from the University of California at Berkeley in 1989, and subsequently served as a post-doctoral fellow (1990–1992) in the Department of Psychology at the University of Haifa, Israel, where she conducted research on the social and moral development of Druze children and families. She joined the University of Utah in 1993. Her research interests center on how children and adolescents develop moral understandings through their everyday experiences, and how culture, power inequalities, and societal violence shape this developmental process. Her work has appeared in numerous journals including Child Development and Developmental Psychology. Most recently she published a research monograph, *Being Hurt and Hurting Others: Children's Narrative Accounts and Moral Judgments of their Own Interpersonal Conflicts* (2005, with Brehl and Matwin), and an edited book, *Social Development, Social Inequalities, and Social Justice* (2007, with Smetana and Turiel).

Polly Wiessner

Polly Wiessner received her Ph.D. in Anthropology and Archaeology from the University of Michigan in 1977. She worked as a researcher at the Max Planck Institute for Human Ethology in Germany for 15 years and is currently is a Professor of Anthropology at the University of Utah. She has carried out studies among the among the !Kung (Ju/'hoansi) Bushmen of the Kalahari Desert over the past 30 years on subsistence, sharing, reciprocity, and social security systems to reduce risk. For the past 20 years she has conducted ethnohistorical studies among the Enga of Highland New Guinea, tracing developments in warfare, ritual, and exchange that occurred from the time from the introduction of the sweet potato some three hundred years ago until present. She is currently looking at developments in Enga inter-clan warfare with the replacement of the bow and arrow with high-powered weapons. She has published numerous books and articles including: *Food and the Status Quest* (with W. Schiefenhoevel), *Historical Vines: Enga Networks of Exchange, Ritual and Warfare in Papua New Guinea* (with Akii Tumu) and *From Spears to M-16s: Testing the Imbalance of Power Hypothesis among the Enga.*

Index